FAITHFUL TO THE END

AN INTRODUCTION TO
HEBREWS THROUGH REVELATION

TERRY L. WILDER, J. DARYL CHARLES,
and KENDELL EASLEY

NASHVILLE, TENNESSEE

978–0–8054–2625–0

Published by B&H Publishing Group
Nashville, Tennessee

Dewey Decimal Classification: 227
Subject Heading: BIBLE. N.T. EPISTLES—STUDY
BIBLE. N.T. REVELATION—STUDY

1 2 3 4 5 6 7 8 9 10 • 14 13 12 11 10 09 08 07
SB

To William E. Bell Jr. and Chester Wood,
beloved professors who have had a tremendous impact
on countless students of the Word of God.

CONTENTS

PREFACE

In classroom and scholarly study the Gospels, Acts, and Pauline letters receive far more attention than does the so-called "end" of the New Testament: Hebrews, James, 1 and 2 Peter, 1, 2 and 3 John, Jude, and Revelation. We hope to assuage this neglect to some degree with this work written solely on the biblical books of Hebrews through Revelation. Each of us has addressed what we deemed important to treat in an introductory work of this nature. We have carefully placed the biblical letters in their respective contexts and considered traditional introductory items like authorship, destination and recipients, provenance, purpose, etc. We have also examined these books' major themes and surveyed their contents. Care was taken in this book to be uniform in content throughout but not so uniform as to stifle each contributor's writing style.

This book can be used as a reference work or textbook on the college or seminary level for introductory NT courses strictly on Hebrews to Revelation. It can also serve as a text in a semester's course on Acts through Revelation or Romans through Revelation. Teachers and students alike know well that in courses with the latter scope very few professors actually get through the entire NT. This book can help professors address quickly that which is lacking.

Finally, I would be remiss if I did not mention something about why this book was given the title *Faithful to the End*. Each of these biblical letters in some fashion contains a strong theme of being faithful and persevering in the faith. For example, the writer of Hebrews urges his readers to persevere in faithfulness and not to go back into Judaism and the Old Testament religious system. James the Lord's brother exhorts his letter's recipients to rejoice in trials for their faith and endure them until the Lord returns. In 1 Peter the apostle encourages his readers to stand firm in the faith despite being persecuted as temporary residents in a foreign land. Similarly in 2 Peter he encourages his recipients to keep living virtuous, godly lives despite false teachers in their midst who are denying the return of Christ and living immorally. Offsetting the impact of false teachers who have influenced the church, the apostle John provides assurance of salvation for professing believers who meet the criteria of being persistently faithful in obedience, loving their fellow Christians, and believing that Christ has indeed come in the flesh. Second John and 3 John encourage their readers to be faithful in not sustaining the ministry of false teachers and in showing hospitality to traveling Christian preachers, respectively. Jude urges his readers to contend earnestly for the faith against heretics. Lastly, in each of the seven letters to the churches of Asia in the book of Revelation, Jesus promises some special blessing to "those who overcome," that is, genuine believers who cannot be shaken from continued allegiance and faithfulness to Christ.

Our hope and prayer is that God might use this text to help its readers not only to learn about these NT books but also to appropriate the message contained in each. We serve a wonderfully holy, loving, and gracious God. May we be faithful to the end!

Terry L. Wilder, General Editor
Associate Professor of New Testament and Greek
Midwestern Baptist Theological Seminary
Kansas City, Missouri

One

HEBREWS

Persevere in Faithfulness

I n exploring the letter to the Hebrews, we are engaging simultaneously one of the most fascinating books in the entire Bible and one of the reputedly most difficult NT documents to understand. At the outset, then, we are both intrigued and intimidated. The reasons for this intimidation are multiple, arising from several obstacles:

- The letter requires a preliminary knowledge of OT writings, people, events, and institutions, not least of these being Israel's cultic sacrificial system, which is challenging even to *students* of the Bible. The combination of multiple citations from the Psalms, such as one finds in the first chapter, and a cursory knowledge of the OT sacrificial order, assumed in chapters 7–10, seems daunting, preventing the average reader from even attempting to wade through the whole epistle.
- Correspondingly, some contemporary readers would be relatively illiterate in terms of their knowledge of the Bible and the OT in particular. The average layperson more than likely has not read through the entire Bible and almost assuredly has not read through those books of the Bible from which the writer to the Hebrews draws most of his material (the Psalms excluded).
- The letter begins without any lead-up, in sharp contrast to the "letters" of the NT.[1]

don't be discouraged if you don't understand.

Unless otherwise indicated, all Scripture quotations in this chapter are from the New International Version (NIV).

[1] The obvious exception is 1 John.

1

- Moreover, Hebrews does not mirror the standard *form* of a letter. There is no identification of the writer, no introduction, no Christian greeting,[2] no salutation, and there are relatively few specific or personal references that might earmark the document as to author, recipients, destination, and surrounding circumstances.[3] We are correct to note that Hebrews takes on the character of a *sermon*, based on the writer's urging the readers to "bear with" his "word of exhortation" (13:22), even when the sermonic style was adopted in its final "letter" form.

- Nothing concrete is known of the recipients or the circumstances that produced the letter. Clues are present throughout, but one must dig in order to string these markers together in a coherent fashion. That there is *some* sort of crisis among the recipients is clear. The nature of this crisis and its extent, however, are not.

- Hebrews is very different in character from other documents of the NT. To illustrate, the Synoptic Gospels are a rendering of God's in-breaking into the world, through which the kingdom of God is made visible. The Gospel of John attempts a witness to God's definitive statement about divine revelation through Christ. In the Pauline epistles we find a strong emphasis on God's grace in Christ, which justifies us, freely and forensically, apart from any taint of works-righteousness. A counterpart to Paul is the emphasis in James on good works. Authentic Christian faith will demonstrate, i.e., give evidence of, its presence in our lives through our deeds. And the Revelation represents an attempt to depict hostility between

---

[2] For example, a typical greeting that one might expect to find in the epistles of the NT would be "grace and peace to you."

[3] On letter writing in the ancient world, see F. X. J. Exler, *The Form of the Ancient Greek Letter* (Washington, D.C.: Catholic University of America Press, 1923); W. G. Doty, *Letters in Primitive Christianity* (Philadelphia: Fortress, 1973); J. L. White, "Ancient Greek Letters," in *Greco-Roman Literature and the New Testament*, ed. D. E. Aune (SBLSBS 21; Atlanta: Scholars, 1988), 85–105; idem, *The Body of the Greek Letter* (SBLDS 2; Missoula: Scholars, 1972); idem, *Light from Ancient Letters* (Philadelphia: Fortress, 1986); S. K. Stowers, *Letter-Writing in Greco-Roman Antiquity* (LEC 5; Philadelphia: Fortress, 1986); and A. J. Malherbe, *Ancient Epistolary Theorists* (SBLSBS 19; Atlanta: Scholars, 1988). On the apostle Paul's letter writing, see as well J. L. White, "St. Paul and the Apostolic Letter Tradition," *CBQ* 45/3 (1983): 433–44; D. E. Aune, "Early Christian Letters and Homilies," in *The New Testament in Its Literary Environment*, ed. W. Meeks (LEC 8; Philadelphia: Westminster, 1987), 193–94; and more recently, J. Murphy-O'Connor, *Paul the Letter-Writer: His World, His Options, His Skills* (Collegeville: Liturgical, 1995).

the world and Christian faith. But the epistle to the Hebrews is quite different, engaging in a multifaceted presentation of Jesus' covenantal mediation of our access to God.

- The writer's method of argumentation strikes us as strange. In addition to the fact that no other NT letter commences without any personal greeting, Hebrews begins with a declaration of salvation history—not what one might expect in a personal letter to friends.

- A cast of strange, and at times cryptic, characters parades across the stage of the letter. While the wilderness generation (chaps. 3 and 4) is by no means unfamiliar to most Bible readers, the choice of Melchizedek, to whom a total of eight verses in the OT are devoted, as an illustration strikes us as bizarre. Furthermore, what book of the Bible—NT or OT—develops an argument around *angels*? To encounter such, and that barely five verses into the letter, is to enter abruptly a world with which the average reader is wholly unfamiliar.

- And what do we make of passages such as those found in Hebrews 6? Do these verses teach that Christians indeed can fall away from the faith? Remove themselves from divine grace? Lose their salvation?

- Finally, the contemporary reader is left perplexed when encountering very solemn and disconcerting admonitions such as those recorded in 6:4–8 and 10:26–31. What are we to make of these statements? Are these warnings or threats merely theoretical? Are they present merely for rhetorical effect? Or do they suggest that Christians indeed can actually fall away from grace?

Intrigue should not be eclipsed by intimidation, however, regardless of how daunting the challenges of Hebrews might seem. The richness of the letter, despite those features that perplex the contemporary reader, beckons us yet today. There awaits the hungry inquirer a treasure of insight and understanding into both the divine purpose, mediated by "the Son," and the human response to the divine purpose. For those who are willing to move beyond the letter's traditional neglect, or beyond "Christianity Lite," Hebrews offers life-changing perspectives on the nature of faith, perseverance, and witness, as well as on the exalted and unchanging object of that faith. The Christian community of any era cannot afford to neglect the message of Hebrews. Indeed, there may be no generation that has ever needed the message of Hebrews more than our own.

Setting, Audience Situation, Destination, and Date of Writing

To whom was this letter written and why? Answers do not come easily. Hebrews begins as if it were a sermon. We find no customary opening, designation, or greeting that characterize the epistles of the NT. Who were these people, and where were they located? Were they Christians or Jews or Jewish Christians or Gentile Christians familiar with the OT? And what was the nature of the "suffering" and "hardship" they were enduring that necessitated a letter like Hebrews? This anonymous epistle has engendered no little speculation as to the identity and location of its recipients.

The earliest appearance of the heading "To Hebrews" (*Pros Hebraious*)[4] dates to the late second century.[5] Clement of Alexandria, according to Eusebius,[6] was said to know of this title, as did Tertullian (early third century).[7] What is meant by "Hebrews" remains a mystery, although in its few occurrences it denotes language or descent. Are they Jews? Jewish Christians? The frequency of OT allusions in the letter is striking, whatever the role that it plays. Is the reference perhaps a metaphor, not unlike reference to the "twelve tribes" in Jas 1:1 and the diaspora in 1 Pet 1:1, directed at readers of a mixed—i.e., Jewish and Gentile—background?

Whoever these people were, they were known reasonably well by the writer. Whether or not these were "second-generation Christians," as many commentators assume from the inference in 2:1 and 2:3, the writer was well acquainted with their past and their present condition (2:1; 6:11–12; 10:32–34; 12:4–5), commended them for their generosity (6:10) and their sympathy toward those

---

[4] In the NT, the term *Hebraios* can refer to either descent (e.g., 2 Cor 11:22—"Are they Hebrews? So am I"—and Phil 3:5—"a Hebrew of Hebrews") or language (Acts 6:1: Grecian Jews alongside Hebraic Jews).

[5] The earliest manuscript is noted by B. M. Metzger, *A Textual Commentary on the New Testament* (Stuttgart: UBS, rev. 1975), and F. F. Bruce, *The Epistle to the Hebrews* (rev. ed.; Grand Rapids: Eerdmans, 1990), 3 (n. 4) to be p. 46.

[6] Eusebius, *Hist. eccl.* 6.14.3.

[7] Tertullian, *On Modesty* 20.

in prison (10:34), chided them for their immaturity (5:11–6:3),[8] questioned their relationship to leadership in the church (13:7,17), and hoped to visit them soon. Both author and recipients had a relationship with Timothy (13:23).

Wildly divergent commentary has been offered over the last century as to whom the letter was addressed. Explanations include, though by no means are confined to, the following:

- The letter was written to a group of Jews originally belonging to the Qumran community who were converted to Christianity but who maintained their former messianic beliefs (Y. Yadin, A. S. Woude, H. Kosmala).
- The letter mirrors a "Hellenized" or "progressive" Judaism, based on correspondences between Hebrews and Acts 7 and the model of Stephen (W. Manson).
- The letter was written by a Philonic convert to Christianity who came from the Alexandrian school of Judaism in which typological exegesis flourished (C. Spicq, S. Stowers).
- The letter represents Platonic-style dualist philosophy that emphasized the heavenly and spiritual while downplaying the earthly and the material (C. K. Barrett, J. W. Thompson).
- The author of the letter wrote from the standpoint of pre-Christian Gnosticism, which focused on the spiritual or heavenly rather than the material world (E. Käsemann).
- The letter is a Jewish-Hellenistic homily (H. Thyen).
- The letter was written to reconcile differences between Jewish and Samaritan forms of Christianity (E. A. Knox).
- The letter sets on display first-century Jewish Merkabah mysticism (H. M. Schenke, O. Hofius).[9]

In light of the heading "to Hebrews" and reliance on the OT and Jewish tradition material, much traditional interpretation has assumed that the letter represents a Judaizing tendency or dispute

---

[8] There is no reason to think, with W. Barclay (*The Letter to the Hebrews* [rev. ed.; Philadelphia: Westminster, 1957], xxi), that Hebrews is "a letter written to a little group of people who were training to be teachers in the Christian Church." The admonitions appear generic in character, i.e., to laypersons and not leadership. Otherwise, we might expect statements such as one finds in Jas 3:1.

[9] The number of explanations for the background to the epistle is legion and the literature itself is massive. See L. D. Hurst, *The Epistle to the Hebrews: Its Background of Thought* (SNTSMS 65; Cambridge: Cambridge University Press, 1990), which volume is devoted to an assessment of various theoretical constructions.

with Judaism or that it is written to dissuade Jewish converts to Christian faith from returning to Jewish religion. The "Jewish" interpretation of Hebrews, in varied forms, has been remarkably persistent and for good reason. Significant disagreement exists among commentators as to who the recipients of the epistle were. Were they practicing members of the Jewish faith? Perhaps Jews who converted to Christian faith and were considering a return to Jewish religion? Or were they Gentiles who were adequately rooted in both Jewish and Gentile thought worlds? How one views the background of the audience is intricately related to how one interprets the letter.

Upon closer inspection, we find that the letter does not allude to the temple, which one might initially expect, were its recipients living in or near Palestine. Nor does it reflect anti-Jewish tendencies or polemical features, which would be anticipated were the recipients considering a return to Jewish religion. Significantly, nothing in Hebrews parallels Paul's argument to the Galatians—no argument against law or legalism or works-righteousness, no mention of circumcision, no sustained emphasis on the cross.

Indeed, as the bulk of the writer's argument suggests, and as the material in the closing section of the letter (i.e., chaps. 11, 12, and 13) indicates, there are *deep sympathies* toward and a strong appreciation of the shadows, patterns, and types furnished in the old covenant. A shared base of theological knowledge and orientation exists between the writer and his readership. Whether this *requires* his readers to be former Jews is the subject of much debate;[10] the correspondence may also be explainable on the basis of extensive interpenetration of Jewish and Gentile cultures, especially in the Diaspora.[11]

Establishing any sort of social or historical context for Hebrews depends first and foremost on the profile that emerges from the letter. The epistle indeed mirrors a struggle, but this struggle is not with Judaizing elements in the church. What precisely is the character of the struggle, and what is the nature of the writer's burden? It is the struggle to endure, to be faithful, to persevere with joy (10:32,36,38; 12:1,2,3,7,27; 13:1). And it is a struggle that unites, rather than separates, the people of God in the old and the new. Hence, the compari-

---

[10] For example, elements found in Hebrews such as extended treatment of the sacrificial system, allusion to "dead works," and correlating "shedding of blood" with "forgiveness of sins" would certainly be highly relevant to readers with a Jewish heritage.

[11] So P. Ellingworth, *The Epistle to the Hebrews: A Commentary on the Greek Text* (NIGTC; Grand Rapids/Carlise: Eerdmans/Paternoster, 1993), 22–23.

son to the OT covenant community is meaningful. Wandering in the wilderness, priesthood, and sacrifice have their full explanation and fulfillment in the life and ministry of God's exalted Son; therefore, the new covenant is a "better" or "superior" one. Nevertheless, faith in a God who has spoken unites both covenant people.

The interpretive approach that Hebrews represents an allegorizing tendency that stems from the same school of Alexandrian Judaism as Philo[12] has much to commend it. This approach is certainly supported by compelling evidence, not least of which is the extensive use of type and antitype. Consider the vocabulary of the writer—*hupodeigma* (copy, pattern, outline) in 4:11 and 8:5; *tupos* (symbol, example) in 8:5,9 and 9:23; *skia* (shadow) in 8:5; *antitupos* (antitype) in 9:24—as well as the rampant use of typology throughout the letter—e.g., the tabernacle or tent, Melchizedek, the high priest, the wandering of God's people, the temple, the covenant. This line of thinking is difficult to eliminate, given the sheer weight of the evidence in its favor.

Whether the use of typology and the language of "shadows" (8:5) in the epistle reflect Hellenistic, and specifically Platonic, influence or Hebrew exegetical technique has been vigorously debated by some. The answer may lie somewhere in the middle.[13] The writer's relationship to his readers and the resultant literary strategy suggest a likely double background for both, Greek as well as Hebrew influence.[14]

The discoveries at Qumran in the mid-twentieth century resulted in reinterpretations of NT material. It should come as no surprise that Hebrews was center stage in the reevaluation. In its

---

[12] So, e.g., C. Spicq, *L'Epitre aux Hebreux* (2 vols.; Paris: Gabalda, 1952); H. W. Montefiore, *A Commentary on the Epistle to the Hebrews* (HNTC; New York: Harper & Row, 1964); and S. G. Sowers, *The Hermeneutics of Philo and Hebrews* (Richmond: John Knox, 1965).

[13] Thus argues G. E. Sterling, "Philo," in C. A. Evans and S. E. Porter, eds., *DLNT* (Downers Grove: InterVarsity, 2000), 792.

[14] One need not maintain the writer to be adopting the Platonic notion that reality exists only in the "heavenly" realm, of which the present world is a mere "copy" or "shadow." Hebrew/Jewish thinking did not advocate the Greek/Platonic belief that this world is not reality, for such a view in fact diminishes the material world. Based on a theology of creation, Judeo-Christian belief counters and dignifies—even when it prevents idolizing of—the material world. The argument in Hebrews is not that the material world is not real or that it is unimportant; rather, it is that events and institutions and people in the old economy are shadows or types of greater truths—truths that bridge *both* the seen and unseen world. As evidence of this important distinction, the present world—inclusive of our present bodies—is destined not for some cosmic *ash heap*, rather, for glorious *transformation* (whatever that may entail). Such is the firm teaching of the NT. Thus, the view of commentators like William Barclay (*The Letter to the Hebrews*, xiv–xv), needs some moderation.

essence the Qumran line of thinking on the origin of the book of Hebrews assumed that the recipients of the letter were former members of the Qumran sect who had embraced the Christian faith and were "carrying with them some of their precious beliefs."[15]

Principal points of contact, for advocates of this school, were several. Scholars who reinterpret Hebrews based on the Qumran discoveries point out several points of contact. First, like Heb 1:1, Qumran contrasts the prophets with the popular eschatological belief that a prophet like Moses would appear. Further allusions to Moses in the letter, in addition to the wilderness generation are seen by some as confirmation of this line of interpretation. Further rationale was thought to be the purported Qumran belief in two messianic figures, one a high priest (Aaronic) and the other a lay figure (Davidic), expected to emerge in the last days. Perhaps the most inviting feature in the letter to draw comparisons to Qumran is the role of angels not only in Qumran theology and eschatology but also in Hebrews.

[handwritten margin note: generation that wandered the wilderness for 40 years]

Given the obvious touchpoints between Qumran belief and Hebrews, how might these similarities bear on the epistle's destination? To what extent are we justified in interpreting Hebrews against the background of the Qumran community?

The question of whether the letter's opening salvo, namely, the declaration of Jesus' superiority to the "prophets," is to be understood in the light of—and as a correction to—Qumran belief is intriguing and in many respects compelling. Nevertheless, even for most Qumran scholars, the role of the eschatological "prophet"— i.e., the "prophet like Moses" (Deut 18:15)—who was to appear in the last days is not wholly clear; considerable disagreement exists as to the prophet's identity.[16] Moreover, reference in the epistle is made to "the prophets," not the singular "prophet" (1:1) and thus requires too much from the reader to qualify as a polemic against sectarian Jewish eschatological notions.[17] Correcting a particular eschatological notion is not the thrust of Heb 1:1–4. The context is

---

[15] Y. Yadin, "The Dead Sea Scrolls and the Epistle to the Hebrews," in *Aspects of the Dead Sea Scrolls*, eds. C. Rabin and Y. Yadin (ScrHier 4; Jerusalem: Magnes, 1958), 38.

[16] Compare, for example, the varied explanations of Y. Yadin, "The Dead Sea Scrolls and the Epistle to the Hebrews," ScrHier 4 (1958): 53–54; W. Brownlee, *The Dead Sea Manual of Discipline* (BASORSup 10–12; New Haven: Yale University Press, 1951), 35; and J. T. Milik, *Ten Years of Discovery in the Wilderness of Judea* (London: SPCK, 1959), 126, all of whom have devoted considerable study to Jewish sectarian belief.

[17] By contrast, John 1 is a transparent mirroring of contemporary Jewish eschatological ideas. For in that material no fewer than 11 more or less messianic titles appear, including

continuity in and fulfillment of the divine purpose; the same God who sent the prophets has now sent the Son. What's more, the function of 1:1–4 is introductory, not polemical. These verses serve a similar function as the prologue to the fourth Gospel. In addition, *prophetēs* occurs only twice in the epistle—in 1:1 and 11:32, hardly constituting a polemic of any sort against distorted eschatological notions.

A related factor that speaks against the Qumran line of interpretation [*place in Israel*] is that allusions to Moses in Hebrews do not fit the eschatological "prophet like Moses" of the Qumran sect. Rather, these allusions are better explained when we view them as part of an overall contrast, using typology, between the old and new covenants—a contrast that includes mediator, tabernacle, sacrifice, and high priest. Hebrews does single out Moses for attention; in the larger scheme of things, he is a minor character. Chapters 7–10 stress the nature of the better covenant and Christ's ability to mediate that better covenant. L. D. Hurst has summarized it well: "Rather than indicating any Moses *redivivus* theme, Moses in Hebrews falls into the category of traditional biblical typology. . . . There is no use of Deuteronomy 18 in Hebrews, nor is Moses anything other than a figure of the past who points forward to the 'better things' of Christ."[18]

The recipients of Hebrews, according to the Qumran line of interpretation, are further thought to have believed, based on the documents *Covenant of Damascus* (CD) and the *Manual of Discipline* (1 QS), that a Davidic *and* an Aaronic messiah would appear, the latter of which for the purposes of reinstituting Levitical sacrifice. Accordingly, the readers would have necessitated a polemic advocating the superiority of Jesus that simultaneously demonstrated Jesus' high priestly work and His uniting of the kingly and priestly offices.[19] But in Hebrews, significantly, there exists no trace of a Davidic messianic figure and, thus, no hint of Jesus establishing union between Aaronic and Davidic lines. This would surely be strange were the letter in fact a polemic that was aimed at correcting or countering sectarian Jewish eschatological notions. The

the Word, the Word made flesh, the Light, the Christ, Elijah, the Prophet, the Lamb of God, Rabbi, the One about whom Moses wrote, Son of God, and King of Israel.

[18] Hurst, *The Epistle to the Hebrews*, 52.

[19] F. C. Fensham wrote three decades ago that this manner of interpreting Hebrews is beyond dispute. See his essay "Hebrews and Qumran," *Neotestamentica* 5 (1971): 9–21.

primary emphasis in Hebrews is Jesus' supremacy and the fact that this supremacy lies at the heart of the new covenant.

There is a notable abruptness with which Jesus' high priest-hood is introduced in 4:14: "Therefore, since we have a great high priest." No discussion of the priesthood—or of messianic expecta-tions, for that matter—precedes this remarkably abrupt transition. Such a transition would be strange if a thoroughgoing polemic were needed to counter sectarian Jewish thinking. What's more, in Hebrews Jesus as high priest is never compared to any other escha-tological figure—an omission that would be most conspicuous in an argument directed at Qumran devotees or sympathizers. Finally and relatedly, the writer argues in extended fashion that the sacrifi-cial order of the old covenant is inadequate and has been replaced by a "better," eternal order—all in the person and work of the Son. That is, the argument is not for a *reappearance* of the eschatological prophet; it is that one greater than the prophets has *already* ap-peared in His priestly function—on earth and in heaven.

Before we leave the subject of Qumran and its relationship to Hebrews, several observations about the high profile of the angels in Hebrews remain. Without our denying possible connections be-tween motifs in the NT and sectarian Judaism, it would appear that the argument from angels in Hebrews 1 and 2, rather than being a polemic against those who are preoccupied with angelic beings, is simply one component in a multilayered strategy to show the superiority of Jesus. This case for superiority is accomplished through proof texts that collectively show a fundamental ontologi-cal distinction between the Son and angelic beings who are called "sons of God" in the OT. Angels are *part of creation*, while the Son is *the mediating agent of creation*. And whereas the angels are mes-sengers "sent forth" (*apostellō*) that "serve those who will inherit salvation" (1:14), Jesus is the "apostle" (*apostolos*) and high priest of the faith (3:1).

Having presented a case for the Son's divinity and His corre-sponding exaltation, the writer establishes another side of the Son, His full humanity, and this is done also in relation to the angels. In Hebrews 2 a portion of Psalm 8 is interpreted Christologically in order to comment on the paradox that finds the glorified, exalted Son taking on the form of "common man" for a brief season and made "a little lower than the angels." The Son establishes solidar-ity with human creatures; this solidarity is accomplished through suffering. Saints who are perfected are brought to God by the Son, who also was "perfected" through suffering. This establishes beyond any shadow of doubt both His worthiness and His full identification with humans. The Son and "sons of glory" are joined by the common experience of suffering—a message that is meaningful for those who due to suffering and hardship perhaps consider not persevering.[20]

Angels are described as covenant "messengers" (cp. 2:2) who, as already noted, are "sent out" (*apostellō*) to serve those who inherit salvation (1:14). Significantly, Jesus is *the* covenant "messenger" (*apostolos*, 3:1) insofar as he is high priest who leads people to God (2:10). While the angels are exalted, even "sons" of the Most High (see, e.g., Job 1:6 and Ps 89:6), they pale in comparison to "the Son." In Hebrews 1 and 2, the angels do not lack glory; rather, they possess an inherent glory due to their station. And yet that glory pales when held in contrast to that of the Son, who "is the radiance of [divine] glory" and the "exact representation of his being" (1:3).

The Son's superiority to the angels is predicated on His agency in creation (1:2), His preexistence and union with God, (1:3) as well as His purification of the sins of humankind (1:3). Significantly, it is the latter aspect that forms the heart of the epistle. The Son's purification of "many sons" resulted in His glorification (corresponding to His "ascension") and enthronement by God (1:4,13–14; 2:8 [implied in 1:8]). For this reason the writer announces that the Son inherited a name that is "superior to theirs [the angels']" (1:4). Jesus is superior as mediator of the new covenant, and this means that He is superior to those servants of the Almighty who, in other ways and in times past, mediated God's covenant with humankind (1:1,14; 2:2).

The point to be made is this: the purpose of the initial comparison to angels is not a humbling or lowering of the angels; it is, rather, an exalting of the Son. In support of this perspective, Jesus is said to have been "made a little lower than the angels" (2:9)—a statement that would be counterproductive in any argument designed for Qumran sectaries. In the end the angels constitute one of several building blocks in the writer's argument, each of which enhances *continuity and comparison*. Jesus is superior to the angels

[20] For an excellent overview of the role that angels play in the Christology of the NT, see S. F. Noll, "Angels, Heavenly Beings, Angel Christology," in *DLNT*, 44–48.

(chaps. 1 and 2), to Moses (chaps. 3 and 4), to the Levitical priesthood (chaps. 4 and 5), to the "high priesthood" of the enigmatic
Melchizedek (chap. 7),[21] and to the entire sacrificial order of the
old covenant (chaps. 8–10). This cumulative case for superiority
should evoke a response of faithfulness in the reader that is *commensurate with* Christ's superiority. The theological "architecture"
being employed in Hebrews 1 and 2 is not designed to inhibit people who are considering a return to Judaism.[22] Rather, it more plausibly mirrors an audience that fails to honor, or grasp, adequately
the Son's example.

To the present, various elements in the Qumran perspective on
Hebrews continue to maintain an attractiveness, engendering speculation among its proponents even decades after the discoveries at
Qumran. A helpful response to and partial refutation of this line of
thinking has come from the writings of F. F. Bruce.[23] Bruce readily
acknowledges touchpoints between theological categories and images employed at Qumran and those found in Hebrews. At the same
time he argues that the Qumran community was only one of multiple Jewish groups representing broader Judaism. For example,
Josephus speaks of other groups found in the Diaspora, away from
Judea, which practiced baptisms (cp. Heb 6:2) and ritual cleansing.[24] The implication is that such individuals were "Hellenists,"
perhaps a mixture of former Jews and Gentiles, whose knowledge
of the OT and Israel's traditions was substantial when not firsthand
(as it would have been in Jerusalem).[25]

Several additional factors inform our profile of the recipients,
and thus the epistle's destination. If the epistle was addressed only
to Jews or Jewish Christians, why were important Pauline concepts and watchwords such as fulfillment, justification, circumci-

---

[21] The purpose of the Melchizedek "midrash" in Hebrews 7 has more to do with underscoring *the basis of priesthood* than with emphasizing mysterious or divine qualities. Priesthood in
chapter 7 is perpetual and antecedent; but the focus remains the character and very nature of
"priesthood."

[22] Thus, against the view of W. J. Webb, "Suffering," in *DLNT*, 1139, and others.

[23] See esp. F. F. Bruce, *Second Thoughts on the Dead Sea Scrolls* (2nd ed.; London:
Paternoster, 1961); idem., "'To the Hebrews' or 'To the Essenes,'" *NTS* 9 (1963): 217–32;
idem., *The Epistle to the Hebrews* (rev. ed.; Grand Rapids: Eerdmans, 1990 [1964]), 7–9; and
idem., "The Kerygma of Hebrews," *Int* 23 (1969): 3–19.

[24] Josephus *Ant.* 18.19.

[25] In favor of an interpretation that Hebrews is addressed to a homogenous and not mixed
group is Eusebius' observation that, until AD 70, the church at Jerusalem was "fully composed of Hebrews" (*Hist. eccl.* 4.5).

sion, the cross and the gospel wholly absent from the epistle?[26] The central Pauline burden of works-righteousness and legalism does not enter into the argument of Hebrews, in sharp contrast to Romans and Galatians.[27] The unique literary character of the epistle (see below), with its polished Greek and notable rhetorical flourish, as well as the absence of any allusion to the temple (which we would expect to be included were Hebrews addressed to readers in Judea before AD 70) also bear in significant ways upon our interpretation.

And if in fact the recipients have learned about the OT on a secondhand basis (2:3), and if they represent a mixture of former Jews and Gentiles (given the absence of Jews-versus-Gentiles argumentation in the letter, as contrasted with Romans or Galatians), then a metropolitan setting away from Judea is quite possible. Some commentators have suggested Ephesus, Antioch, Alexandria, and Rome as likely destinations. The writer's allusion to "those from Italy" (13:24) and Clement of Rome's (late first century) acquaintance with the letter would certainly make Rome a plausible option, even when we are resigned to uncertainty.[28]

The statement in 2:3 that the gospel had been "confirmed" among the recipients by eyewitnesses of the Lord, i.e., apostles, is highly suggestive. Unlike the apostle Paul, the writer does not claim direct revelation from the Lord as an eyewitness, suggesting distance both in time and geography to Christian beginnings. Additionally, mention in 6:10 of the readers' assisting the needy might be interpreted as a hint that the readers were not from the Palestinian region, since in Acts the latter are depicted as poverty-stricken and recipients of aid from other churches (Acts 11:27–30; Rom 15:26; 1 Cor 8–9).[29]

---

[26] A sole reference to the cross in Hebrews 12:2 is the one exception, and here the emphasis is not atonement or propitiation but *endurance*. The Christian endures because Jesus the model endured.

[27] All references to the "law" in Hebrews are nonpolemical and occur in a context wholly different from Romans and Galatians.

[28] Acts 2:10 indicates that "both Jews and converts to Judaism" were in Rome. However, see n. 26. F. F. Bruce believes that the letter's profile points to Rome as the destination. He writes that "there is little doubt in my mind that the Epistle to the Hebrews was written to a Jewish-Christian group in Rome in the sixties of the first century." "The new evidence," according to Bruce, "confirms the impression already formed by a comparison of certain allusions in this epistle—e.g. the 'instruction about ablutions' in Hebrews 6:2—with indications that the Jewish substratum of early Roman Christianity had affinities with some of the 'baptist' movements of Palestinian Judaism" (*Second Thoughts on the Dead Sea Scrolls* [4th ed.; Grand Rapids: Eerdmans, 1972], 150–51).

[29] This observation has been made by T. D. Lea and David Alan Black, *The New Testament: Its Background and Message,* 2d. ed (Nashville: Broadman & Holman, 2003), 499.

Dating Hebrews is also informed by how we interpret references to "hardship," "suffering," and "persecution" in Hebrews (e.g., 10:32–33; 11:32–38; 12:7; 13:13). How should we understand the writer's statement that "you have not yet resisted to the point of shedding your blood" (12:4)? Is it to be taken literally, as most commentators do, or figuratively? If it is meant literally, then Jerusalem and Judea would be ruled out as a possible destination. Such would also place the letter before the persecution under Nero in the mid 60s, assuming in light of the reference to Timothy (13:23) an earlier (i.e., Neronian) rather than later (Domitian)[30] wave of persecution.[31] If one assumes an earlier wave (i.e., Neronian.), this would rule out Jerusalem and Judea.[32]

The closing allusion to "those from Italy" (13:24) suggests to numerous commentators that native Italians were sending greetings back home. This congregation may well have been a house church, given the language of "household" and "house" in the letter (3:3–6; 8:8,10; 10:21). Given the uncertainty and lack of precision surrounding the question of destination, establishing a date for the epistle is difficult. There are good reasons, however, for assuming that it was written before AD 70. An important internal marker is the allusion to Timothy (13:23), assuming that this "Timothy" is the ministry companion of Paul. A further consideration is the reference to and development of the tabernacle, not the temple, as a type. Were the temple not yet destroyed, it would be reasonable to expect references to it in the writer's description of ritual sacrifice and the priesthood.

Finally, the use of Hebrews by Clement of Rome, as already noted, requires a dating that is prior. Thus, any time between AD 60

---

[30] AD 81–96.

[31] W. L. Lane (*Call to Commitment: Responding to the Message of Hebrews* [Nashville: Thomas Nelson, 1985], 22) ventures the following as background to Hebrews: "The writer prepared his sermon for some of the Jewish Christians who had shared the expulsion from Rome with Aquila and Priscilla (Acts 18:1–2). They had firsthand experience of the cost of discipleship. . . . Now, however, it is about fifteen years later." G. H. Guthrie (*Hebrews*, NIVAC [Grand Rapids: Zondervan, 1998], 20) conjectures: "A potential danger to this community seems to lie in the temptation to reject Christianity and return to Judaism proper." What is not clear is why persecution would drive one to *Judaism*, unless, of course, Jewish religion retains a conspicuous "protected" status in the empire. The writer's complaint, moreover, that his readers should have been mature (5:12) does not speak to the issue of "a return to Jewish faith" or a Judaizing tendency. Guthrie rightly notes, however, that "the exact mix of Jews and Gentiles in this church must remain a mystery" (ibid.).

[32] If one assumes that genuine persecution is implied, then earlier ill treatment may have been a result of the Claudius edict that resulted in Jews (and Jewish Christians) being expelled from Rome (cp. Acts 18:2).

and 95 is plausible, assuming the date of AD 96 that is typically assigned *1 Clement*. Given the uncertainty and lack of precision surrounding the question of destination, establishing a date for the epistle remains imprecise and open to conjecture.

Important Themes and Subthemes

1. *Faith* (2:17; 3:2,5,6; 4:2,3,14; 6:1; 10:22,23,38; 11:1–39; 12:2; 13:7). In Hebrews faith possesses a distinctively ethical quality. Faith, to the writer, is a response of faithfully persevering through hardship. This persevering faith is rooted in hope and promise and, thus, in the trustworthiness of God's character. God's promises are guaranteed, but our response is not. The enduring and qualitative nature of faith, therefore, is important to grasp (chap. 11), notably, its verification, its certainty, its relationship to unseen reality, and its object. The qualitative nature of faith is so important to grasp that the extended catalog of the faithful is strategic to the letter's argument. All of the individuals commended had to struggle; all were faced with insurmountable obstacles. The "genealogy of belief" that is recorded in Hebrews 11 is a necessary and rhetorically effective counterpart to the genealogy of disbelief in 3:7–11.

The allusions to Abraham in the letter are fourfold and, therefore, highly illustrative. The name of Abraham first occurs in the context of identification. The Son demonstrates solidarity with "the children of Abraham" for the purpose of atonement. Why Abraham? Perhaps the second allusion serves to clarify. In 6:13–20 the idea of promise is central. God had promised "many descendents" (6:14; cp. Gen 12). Therefore, the "binding of Isaac" (cp. Gen 22) represented for Abraham a supreme test. But "after waiting patiently," Abraham "received what was promised" (6:15). The point of the example is patient endurance based on the trustworthiness of God's Word and God's character. God binds Himself by an "oath" (6:16–18); in the words of the psalmist, "He remembered his holy promise given to his servant Abraham" (Ps 105:42). Thus, Abraham represents a model of faithful perseverance. The readers should be encouraged that they will receive what God has in fact promised.

The third allusion to Abraham occurs in the wider argument of priesthood; Jesus' priesthood is superior to the Levitical shadow, a priesthood that has antecedent action in the figure of Melchizedek.

Because the Levitical priests tithed (Num 18:26–28; Neh 10:38–39; cp. also Josephus *Ant.* 20.9.2,8) and because Abraham represents the Levites through patriarchy, the writer of Hebrews observes that Levi actually tithed to Melchizedek, who, viewed in this light, becomes the greater.

The fourth allusion to Abraham occurs in the catalog of the faithful, recorded in chapter 11. Of all the paradigms listed, Abraham receives the most extensive treatment and, thus, is exemplary. He obeyed God's call "and went" (11:8), an action that certainly was not easy since he "did not know where he was going." He made this unknown realm his home like an "alien in a strange land" and "living in tents"—a description of "not belonging" with which the readers surely can identify. Nevertheless, he kept pressing toward an ultimate goal.

Moreover, Abraham trusted God for a son, even when, naturally speaking (being "as good as dead"), this seemed utterly impossible. The result? Descendants as numerous as the sand of the sea, and this from the one son whom Abraham was asked to offer back to God as a sacrifice (11:17–19). The tradition of the "binding of Isaac" fascinated Jewish imagination, as evidenced by Jewish extrabiblical literature, in which the tradition developed a life of its own.[33] Abraham is thus a paradigm of faithful obedience in wider Jewish tradition, and the presence of the Isaac tradition suggests that the writer of Hebrews was influenced by this tradition.[34]

Faith, then, in Hebrews, is *being faithful*, and faithfulness is demonstrated in the context of testing and adversity. Faith is active, world engaging, and at times world countering. It is, quite simply, a commitment to *please God* through what one does (10:38; 11:5,6; 13:21), a commitment that often will entail hostility from the world. The writer's concern for faithfulness on the part of his readers, emphasizing the *human response* rather than divine impartation, stands in notable contrast to the Pauline accent on faith as a divine gift, independent of human activity.[35]

---

[33] See, e.g., Sir 44:20; *Jub.* 17:15–18:19; 1 Macc. 2:52; *4 Macc.* 7:11–14; 13:12; 16:18–20; Philo, *Abr.* 167–297; Josephus, *Ant.* 1.13.1–4; 18.5; 23:8; 32:1–4; and 40:2–3.

[34] Thus, N. Calvert-Koyzis, "Abraham," in *DLNT*, 2–4. Calvert-Koyzis sees in the concluding admonition toward hospitality (13:1–2) a veiled allusion to Abraham, given the implicit grace of hospitality that he evidenced in the Genesis 18 narrative and the development of Abraham's hospitality as a theme in extrabiblical literature (e.g., *T. Abr.* 1:1–3; Phil, *Abr.* 107–10; and Josephus, *Ant.* 1.11.2).

[35] Hebrews stands closer to James in this regard. Faith cannot be divorced from works; it expresses itself in concrete ways.

2. **Witness** (1:3; 2:17; 3:5; 7:8,17; 10:2,4,11,15,28; 11:2,4 [2x],5,39; 12:1): the human part. To give witness to something is to *confess* (13:15) and *profess* (4:14) its ultimate reality. Confession and profession are verbal expressions of our highest priorities and commitments. To "confess his name" (13:15) will exact a price in this world. But with confidence, the believer confesses, "The Lord is my helper; I will not be afraid. What can man do to me?" (13:6). Verbal declaration is powerful and carries with it significant repercussions. Confession is important to the writer (3:1; 4:14; 10:23; 11:13; 13:15).

It is difficult to identify precisely the degree of suffering, insult, and persecution (2:18; 10:32–33; 12:2,7; 13:12,13) the recipients of the letter have endured. The writer does acknowledge that as of the present they have not yet struggled "to the point of shedding blood" (12:4)—a statement that might be taken literally in the sense of martyrdom or may be intended as hyperbole. The four allusions in the letter to prison or "chains" (10:34; 11:36 [2x]; 13:3) would seem to suggest that the ordeals associated with Christian faith are not life threatening but nevertheless serious. Moreover, the catalog of the faithful in chapter 11, i.e., those who died in the faith, prepares the reader for the *martus* (witness) notion in 12:1 (cp. 11:4,35,37). The persevering witness of those who have gone before them is intended to spur the readers on to faithfulness in their own witness, regardless of where that might lead.[36]

3. *Hope* (3:6; 6:11,18,19; 7:19; 10:23): what draws us on. Hope is rooted in a certain confidence regarding the future and God's ultimate salvation. "Confidence" or "confident" (used in 3:14; 4:16; 6:9; 10:19,35; 13:6) and "salvation" (1:14; 2:3,10; 6:9; 9:28; 10:39) are key words in Hebrews. The reason for confidence, of course, is a deeper awareness of particular promises (6:12,13,15; 10:23; 11:9[2x],11,13,17,33; 12:26),[37] coupled with an assurance of an "inheritance" (*klēronomia*: 1:14; 9:15; 11:7,8) and the giver's

---

[36] Lea and Black (*The New Testament: Its Background and Message,* 507) write, "The author of Hebrews was not dealing primarily with the question of the endurance of believers in their faith. He was dealing with the lifestyle of his readers. . . . If they turned from Christ, they would not find salvation anywhere else. He did not feel, however, that they would prove to be apostates." It is supremely difficult to draw the line between "lifestyle" and "endurance in the faith," as Lea attempts. Apostasy is a turning aside, a lapse, a decision not to persevere, and such is precisely what burdens the writer. On the other hand, what are the theological implications of apostasy represents a separate matter, one which Hebrews does not address.

[37] Appearing 14 times in noun form and 4 as a verb, "promise" is something of a catchword in Hebrews.

oath of integrity (3:11; 6:13,17; 7:21,22). Hope, then, is not wishful thinking; it issues out of, and is anchored in, the very nature of God Himself.

The eschatological element is strong in the letter, as evidenced by the emphasis laid on the believer's "inheritance," yet it has a distinctly ethical twist. On the one hand, entrance into a future kingdom (10:35–37) is guaranteed; at the same time, one must persevere (10:36). In Hebrews, Christ both fulfills the promise, salvifically, and guarantees its realization, eschatologically, over time. For this reason the writer of Hebrews develops the notions of swearing (3:11,18; 4:3; 6:13,16; 7:21) and oath confirmation (6:16–20; 7:18–28) as well as covenant in a manner without parallel in the NT.[38] The notion of covenant, *diathēkē*, is based on promise or guarantee and is to be understood as a "divine, legal arrangement."[39] Literally everything depends on the trustworthiness of this arrangement. Therefore, the "gospel" is more than divine goodwill or good intentions. It contains a guarantee; that is to say, it is statutory in nature.

4. **Sin and apostasy** (1:3; 2:17; 3:13; 5:1,3; 7:27; 8:12; 9:15,28; 10:4,6,8,11,12,17,18,26 [2x]; 11:25; 12:4; 13:11). Believers have been "cleansed once for all" from sin (10:2). The frequency of the expression "once for all" in Hebrews (6:4; 9:7,26,27,28; 10:2; 12:26,27) is deliberate and carries enormous implications for one's understanding of the finality of Christ's purging and purification of sin. Sin has attractive power (implied in 11:25 through the example of Moses, who resisted the "pleasures of sin for a short time"). Sin as expressed through not obeying or disobedience (*apeitheia*) and hardness of heart (the concern in 3:7–4:13; esp. 3:13,15; 4:7) must be taken seriously; hence, the firm, multiple warnings there and elsewhere in the letter. Just as true faith expresses itself in endurance and obedience (5:8), so unbelief expresses itself in not persevering (4:6), a chief concern of the writer.

The context in which sin is understood and portrayed in Hebrews is not its universality or pervasiveness or the "original" Adamic nature. Rather, the emphasis of the writer is that sin expresses volition; it is an act of human yielding, a decision. In Hebrews, sin

---

[38] Half of all allusions to *diathēkē*, "covenant," occur in Hebrews (7:22; 8:6,8,9 [2x],10; 9:4 [2x],15 [2x],16,17,20; 10:16,29; 12:24; 13:20).

[39] Ernst Käsemann, *The Wandering People of God: An Investigation of the Letter to the Hebrews* (Minneapolis: Augsburg, 1984), 30.

is first and foremost *apostasy*, for that is how the writer understands disobedience. Some in the early church believed the letter to address the problem of postbaptismal apostasy. Do the texts of Hebrews 6:4–6 and 10:26–31,35–39 teach the possibility of rejecting grace, of losing a salvation they had possessed? Is the warning theoretical or practical? Rhetorical or real? Any answer to this question turns in part on how we understand the writer's vocabulary: sin is depicted in the letter as yielding to "temptation" (3:7–9; 4:15; 12:4; cp. 2:18), "turning away" (3:12; 6:6), "falling" (4:11), "going astray" (5:2), "drifting away" (2:1), "hardening the heart" (3:7,12,13; 4:7), "rebelling" (3:16), "falling short" (4:1), "falling away" (6:6), "throwing away" (10:35), and "shrinking back" (10:38,39). All of these underscore for the readers the volitional aspect.[40]

To yield to temptation, to harden one's heart, to sin and disobey, and to turn away and depart is to be ashamed of Christ; thus, the strategic counter by the writer that neither Christ (2:11–12; 12:2), nor God Himself (11:16), nor people of faith (11:4–40) were "ashamed" of identification. Our example is He who was "tempted in every way, just as we are—yet was without sin" (4:15; cp. 2:18), for Christ bore our "disgrace" (13:13) by suffering (13:12) and enduring the cross (12:2). For this reason the writer of Hebrews sets forth a case for the incomparability of Christ.

What is then left for the readers? The writer admonishes his readers toward repentance (6:1,6), remembering earlier days (10:32), not "ignoring" their salvation (2:2), not hardening their hearts (3:7–4:11), encouraging one another daily (3:13), and holding fast their confession (3:1; 10:23; 13:15). Repentance on their part will entail remembering "those earlier days after you had received the light" (10:32) and throwing "off everything that hinders and the sin that so easily entangles" (12:1). All other admonitions in the letter—and they are many—are alternative ways of describing this about-face—e.g., paying "more careful attention" (2:1), fixing "your thoughts on Jesus" (3:1), encouraging "one another"

---

[40] A similar argument is presented in the brief yet rhetorically sophisticated Epistle of Jude. Therein the readers are warned to "contend for the faith" against those who would worm their way in and pervert "the grace of our God" and "deny our only master" (vv. 3,4). Numerous historical examples, stereotypical of apostasy in Jewish tradition, are presented to illustrate the seriousness of this perversion of the faith and denying the Master: unbelieving Israel, the fallen angels, Sodom and Gomorrah, Cain, Balaam, and Korah (vv. 5–7,11).

(3:13), entering into rest (4:11), holding to our profession of faith (4:14), and the cluster of admonitions recorded in 12:19–25.

A major factor in this turn-around in attitude is suggested by the writer of Hebrews: What will we actually *fear*? Will a person in the end be motivated by the *fear of man* (11:24–27) or the *fear of God*, a God who *requires* fear (3:10–11,16–18; 6:4–6; 10:26–31; 12:18–21,23,25–29)? The past models of faith clearly demonstrate the difference. With confidence the believer confesses, "The Lord is my helper; I will not be afraid. What can man do to me?" (13:6).

While the writer of Hebrews does not develop a "theology of apostasy," his warnings are somber in tone. If the readers do not repent, if they "deliberately keep on sinning after we have received the knowledge of the truth," then "no sacrifice for sins is left, but only a fearful expectation of judgment and of raging fire that will consume the enemies of God" (10:26–27). Indeed, Hebrews would seem to teach that a person may go so far in apostasy that God refuses him the opportunity of repentance.[41] Curiously, Esau is mentioned later in the epistle as the one who sold yet sought to re-possess his birthright. The writer notes that he was "rejected" and found no chance to repent, though he sought it with tears (12:16–17). A precedent for judgment is present. A warning against hard-heartedness follows (12:25–29).

The warning passages in the epistle (2:1–4; 6:4–8; 10:26–31; 12:25–29) at first glance seem to teach the possibility of apostasy in the Christian life,[42] but they actually warn believers to perse-vere in faithfulness. If the ones being addressed do not persevere, then they can expect judgment. They were merely professors of the faith and not possessors; for the mark of a believer is perseverance. Though some who profess Christ may choose not to persevere, the believer in Jesus really cannot help but do so. Not surprisingly, particular interpretations of these warning passages informed the early church's teaching regarding repentance, forgiveness, and res-toration for those who had left Christian fellowship.

---

[41] Thus I. H. Marshall, *Kept by the Power of God: A Study of Perseverance and Falling Away* (Minneapolis: Bethany Fellowship, 1969), 147.

[42] Along these lines, several factors would seem to militate against a "hypothetical" read-ing of these warning verses in Hebrews—among these: (1) the writer's warning of the readers several times throughout the epistle, and (2) the very language used—"restoring again to re-pentance," former "enlightenment," "tasting the heavenly gift," "tasting the goodness of the word of God and the powers of the age to come," "being partakers of the Holy Spirit," and "falling away."

Given the argument of "superiority" that unfolds throughout the epistle, the question arises as to how the "warning passages" fit within the broader argument. For the writer of Hebrews, perseverance and salvation are both past and future oriented. There exists simultaneously a finality about what God has said and done and the human need to persist in faithfulness. Pilgrims are never too comfortable in this world if indeed they are motivated by unseen realities. Each of the warnings is addressed to professing Christians. The implication is that one can choose not to obey and persevere. Lapse is a moral decision, a commitment of the will. Further, the tone of the writer suggests that lapse is not merely hypothetical; it is a possibility. A difficult question emerges: In the case of apostasy and willful disobedience, does God retain the prerogative not to grant repentance? Can a person's heart be hardened to the extent that repentance is foreclosed?

We may state, briefly, what is clear from Scripture and from Hebrews. Humans are volitional beings and possess the ability to disobey and reject truth. Indeed, the OT is filled with such examples. Judgment ultimately awaits such a disposition. Although the writer of Hebrews does not state *at what point* a person has removed himself from the truth, he is clear that the possibility is to be avoided. Significantly, the overarching trajectory of Hebrews is positive, not negative. The writer is at pains to build a case not for the judgment of God but the superiority of God's Son. The readers are simply called to live in that light.

There is no language or argument in Hebrews to the effect that people are predestined to sin or to faithfulness. It is a conscious decision that must be made and continually embraced. Temptation is an ever-present reality, but Christians have a pioneer and champion, who was tempted in all ways just as they are. As such, Jesus perfects faith. There is no legitimate reason people must fall away, even under hardship. God has provided richly for their salvation.[43] Their call is a call to persevere.[44]

5. *Endurance and perseverance* (3:13;4:11;10:23,24,32,36; 11:27; 12:1,2,3,7). The strong emphasis in the letter on sin and turning away produces the necessity of building a strong case for persevering.

---

[43] See the perspective of I. H. Marshall, *Kept by the Power of God: A Study of Perseverance and Falling Away* (Minneapolis: Bethany Fellowship, 1969), 137–57.

[44] The notions of election and predestination do not play any significant role in the argument of Hebrews. Rather, Christ's example in the midst of suffering and His glory are sufficient to motivate the readers. Jesus is pioneer and perfecter of our faith.

As in James, 1 Peter, and Revelation, in Hebrews the world is understood to be a place of testing, hardship, and temptation. The goal of such testing is to persevere, to endure, as any good soldier or athlete. Having passed the test of the present life, one looks to a final day of judgment (10:27; 12:25–29), at which time the faithful and the faithless receive their respective reward. To stress perseverance is to stress the human side of hope, to be goal oriented in a manner that alters our perspective of the present. It is an expression of hope and promise and reflects one's commitment to lay hold of the goal. Perseverance lays hold of the future reward already in the present.

In James, perseverance is a mark—a necessary mark—of maturity (Jas 1:2–12). A similar association can be detected in Hebrews, to the extent that the readers should have progressed further in their faith than they have (5:11–14). Unlike James, the writer of Hebrews seeks to call forth faithfulness by emphasizing the superiority of the author and perfecter of faith. Hardship can be endured because Jesus, the champion of faith, endured suffering—suffering to the point of death—on our behalf.

Authentic faith, the letter of Hebrews reminds its readers, expresses itself in the ability to endure and persevere. Perhaps weary of their sojourn as aliens and strangers (11:13), they are reminded of Christ's example, as well as numerous models of faithfulness from the past (11:4–40). The model of the Son's suffering and endurance for the sake of humanity is a linchpin in the writer's broader argument; hence, it is a recurring theme (2:5–18; 4:15–16; 5:7–9; 7:26–28; 9:15,26–28; 10:10). The Son traveled the same road as the weary pilgrims to whom the letter is addressed. Because he did not abandon it, they are not to abandon it as well. The Son's persistence in enduring His sojourn should spur the sons of creation to endure as well.

Given the place of perseverance in the letter, the writer's emphasis on entering into "rest" is noteworthy. Rest in chapters 3 and 4 has a past as well as a present and a future character. In contrast to Israel's failure to enter rest as a result of its wilderness wandering, Christians are admonished to enter a rest that is anticipated by the promised land of Canaan. One *struggles* to enter *rest*; clearly, the relationship is paradoxical. While there is a future aspect to this entrance, the warnings of the letter indicate that a vital part of rest lies in the present if only the readers will *choose* to possess it by persevering.

[margin handwritten note:] a mature Christian should be able to persevere

The ethics of Hebrews, self-described as a "word of exhortation" (13:22), is an ethics of perseverance. The problem is not knowledge; it is rather a matter of the will. Will the readers find the fortitude to do what is known to be right? Or will disobedience (2:1), spiritual dullness (5:11), immaturity (5:12–14), and weariness (12:4) prevail over conscience? Those to whom the letter is addressed are exhorted, "Do not forget to do good and to share with others, for with such sacrifices God is pleased" (13:16).

6. *Conflict, suffering, and death* (2:9,10,14,18 [2x]; 5:8; 6:1; 9:14,15,16,17,26,27; 10:32,33; 11:19,32–38; 12:4,7; 13:12,13): distinguishing faith from the world. Unlike other parts of the NT, there is no emphasis in Hebrews on Satan, spiritual warfare, demons, and the like in order to account for the struggle. Rather, this struggle is depicted in utterly human terms. To this end the writer uses the language and imagery of the *agōn*, the struggle ("the race" in 12:1): "Therefore . . . let us throw off everything that hinders and the sin that so easily entangles, and let us run with perseverance the race marked out for us." The position taken in this volume is that the suffering being addressed in Hebrews should be understood against the background of the recipients' willingness to stand and be a witness for Christ, not their "pain related to the departure from Judaism."[45] The hardship that the readers should endure is made bearable by two important elements in the writer's argument: (1) Jesus' willingness to suffer on our behalf and (2) the reality of the Son's glorification and enthronement, both of which are united in the exhortation found in 12:2.

7. *Wandering* (3:7–4:11). Israel's 40 years is a type or foreshadow of the experience of the Christian community. Indeed, the parallels between the old and new covenant communities pervade much of the epistle. And one of the features common to many of the heroes of faith (chap. 11) is that they were wandering, seeking another city, journeying forward by faith as pilgrims, whose vision transcended this world. As with Israel in the wilderness, so it is with the new covenant community as it journeys in the present life. Believers are "aliens and strangers" (11:13). Theirs is a pilgrimage fraught with promise and peril.

---

[45] *Contra* W. J. Webb, "Suffering," in *DLNT*, 1139. Furthermore, the language with which the writer calls his readers to endure suffering and hardship expresses itself in terms of *hupomenō* and not *hupopherō*, the latter term being a stronger term, often associated with deep suffering and grief (e.g., 1 Cor 10:13; 2 Tim 3:1; and 1 Pet 2:19).

Wandering is not the end of the story, however. The writer of Hebrews presents as an ultimate goal Zion, the holy city. But it is a Zion that is distinctly transformed (12:22). This heavenly city, whose "architect and builder is God" (11:10), is a city that "cannot be shaken" (12:28).

8. *Covenant* (7:22; 8:6,7,8,9,10,13; 9:1,4,15,18,20; 10:16; 12:24; 13:20). Covenant expresses itself in two ways in Hebrews: similarity (continuity) and difference (discontinuity). Similarity is evidenced, for example, in the writer's use of type and antitype between Israel and the church; both have been the chosen people of God (4:9; 11:25). Difference is demonstrated, for example, in the superiority of the new covenant that has been mediated by Jesus (implicitly and explicitly in chaps. 1, 8, 9, and 10). The new covenant is "better" because it is abiding; it lasts forever (5:6; 7:17,21,24,28; 9:12,14; 13:20). We should keep in mind the standard ratification of any binding covenant to the ancient mind, whether that covenant is human or divine: blood. In Hebrews blood is both purificatory and ratifying. ← *not sure what this means*

9. *Blood and cultic cleansing* (1:3; 2:14,17; 3:1; 5:1–10; 6:19–10:18; 12:24; 13:11–16,20). Absent from Hebrews is the standard theology of the cross that we find developed in the Pauline epistles. Here, rather, the reader encounters OT cultic and sacrificial language and imagery to highlight the work of Christ. The writer's statement, "Without the shedding of blood there is no forgiveness" (9:22), constitutes the basis of much of his argument. The blood of Christ is qualitatively different from that of animal sacrifices (9:12–14; 10:5–10); it is a once-for-all sacrifice that is eternally efficacious. It is also a sacrifice that purges the conscience (9:14; 10:11–14,22).

Significantly, mention of "purifications for sins" is almost immediate (1:3) in the letter while the notion of "purification" occurs elsewhere as well (9:23; 10:22). Christ as sin-bearer surfaces in 9:26,28; 10:4,11. Hebrews emphasizes not only the finished work of Christ on the cross but the *process* of purification as well. The cross, as one writer notes, "is the climax of a process of sacrifice that embraces the whole incarnation of the Son, through which he unites Himself to flesh and blood, so that he might then truly represent us as our high priest in offering Himself for us and entering the presence of God."[46]

10. *Sonship* (1:2,3,5,8; 2:6,10,13,14; 4:14; 5:5,8; 6:6; 7:3,28; 10:29; 11:24; 12:5,6,7,8). Sonship, the principal theme of chapter 1, is an important motif throughout the letter. Sonship bespeaks relationship and essential identity. God Himself bestows the title on Jesus, with the significance that the Son is the content or substance of the divine "inheritance." He has been "appointed heir of all things," and "through whom he made the universe." The Son is the "exact representation" of God. In sitting down at the right hand, the Son "inherited a name superior" to that of the angels; hence, the ascension gives Jesus His exalted rank and glory. But sonship as a title of honor is also predicated on His sacrifice. As a result of this, He became the *archēgos*,[47] i.e., the author or captain of our salvation (2:10), the "author and perfecter of our faith" (12:2), and thus, an eternal "high priest" (5:4–5) for all.[48] Such eulogy as we find in Hebrews agrees with Philippians 2:5–11—*kenōsis* leading to exaltation—and Revelation 5 (the Lamb-Lion's worthiness, based on sacrifice).

The emphasis in Hebrews 1 is not incarnation but enthronement based on sacrifice. Jesus' greatness and glory require comparison in order to be fathomed and appreciated. Of interest: angels are also described as sons. Assumed: their rank is high, yet in comparison they are inferior. The revelation of the Son occurs throughout. The Son is "now crowned with glory and honor." Why? "Because he suffered" and experienced death "for everyone" (2:9).

11. *Completion and perfection*. The term *teleioun*, found 23 times in the NT, occurs nine times in Hebrews (2:10; 5:9; 7:19,28; 9:9; 10:1,14; 11:40; 12:23),[49] suggesting an important emphasis. "Perfection" in Hebrews has both theological and ethical significance. How do we understand Jesus' completion? Not in an ethical sense of the Son of God but rather in the context of salvation history. Jesus is the mediator of salvation and thus "completes" or "fulfills" the purposes of God through His eternal sacrifice. As the "Son," He leads the way for many "sons," or in the words of Otto Michel, He establishes "the right relationship of humankind

---

[46] S. Motyer, "The Theology of the Cross," in *DLNT*, 261.

[47] The *archēgos*, in contemporary parlance, was the guardian of a city, and thus, the hero (Gerhard Delling, *archēgos*, *TDNT*, 1:487).

[48] Jesus is also our "apostle" and high priest (3:1).

[49] The noun form, *teleiotēs*, occurs in 6:1.

to God."[50] Moreover, Jesus' completion (5:9; 7:28) is in regard to His glorification, not His ethical development. Jesus' "perfecting," therefore, stands in relationship to His many "sons" who need to be perfected, many of which are resisting this process; hence, the purpose of the letter.

For this reason the author describes his readers as "slow to learn" (5:11) and infantile (5:13), in need of relearning elementary truths (5:12), which is to say, "milk, not solid food." Maturity is the stated goal (5:14), which, it is suggested, the readers have not attained. Perfection in Hebrews is an earthly process that has heavenly implications. Jesus, the captain of our salvation, is the model in this regard: He submitted Himself to suffering, shame, and disgrace, and as such was exalted at the right hand of God the Father. As mediator of salvation, Christ could achieve completion only through suffering, and only in this way did He become the captain of their salvation.

Both in essence and example Jesus is captain and leader; He is "captain" in both eschatological and ethical senses. Such would appear to be the rationale behind 2:10–11; the "Son" becomes the link to the "sons." The essence of sonship, after all, is *union*, and in the letter to the Hebrews, this means the realm of flesh and blood.[51] The Son, through His atoning sacrifice, leads many "sons" to glory (2:10) and is God's emphatic and abiding declaration that sin loses its power over the community (12:1–4; 13:8,11–14).

12. *Glory and majesty* (1:3 [2x]; 2:7,10; 3:3; 5:5; 8:1; 9:5). In 1:5–2:18 we find a sustained contrast between the Son and angels in which the Son's "superiority" and majesty and glory are proclaimed. The Son's glory is predicated upon His relational or ontological as well as functional superiority. The latter issues out of His incarnation (having been "made a little lower than the angels"), suffering (having "suffered death so that . . . he might taste death for everyone") and ascension/enthronement (God having "put everything under his feet"). Thus, the Son is "now crowned with glory and honor."

---

[50] O. Michel, *Der Brief an die Hebraeer* (KEK 13; Goettingen: Vandenhoeck & Ruprecht, 1936).

[51] It is not necessary to relegate this terminology to the gnostic dualism of spirit versus matter that was nascent in the first century and then flowered in the second, *contra* Käsemann, *The Wandering People of God,* (131–67) and others.

Why would the writer need to emphasize Christ's glory?[52] In Hebrews it serves the purpose of comparison. Jesus is presented as superior to all of creation, including the angels, who are exalted in their right. At the same time, as the glorious one who is "superior" fully identifies with humble creation, He is made "a little lower than the angels" as a result of condescension and suffering for our sake. It may well be that there are many in the community who have a deficient understanding of the Son—deficient in their comprehending the Son's preexistent and heavenly state (1:3,6,10,12; 7:3; 13:8) but deficient also in their estimation and appreciation of His high priestly work (1:3; 2:9–11; 3:1; 5:1–10; 7:1–10:18), and thus His role in mediating a "better" covenant (7:22; 8:6,7,8,9,10,13; 9:1,4,15,18,20; 10:16; 12:24; 13:20).

This deficiency is previewed in the letter's opening verses: the Son is the express likeness of being and glory, and the ascension bestows upon Jesus an exalted rank and glory, based on His high priestly work. In sitting down at the right hand, the Son "inherited a name superior" to that of the angels. Thus, the pastoral needs call for a literary-rhetorical strategy on the part of the writer that will emphasize the Son's essential glory as well as His functional glory—a glory that is consummated in His ascension, whereby Jesus' exalted rank and glory are confirmed.

While the atoning, priestly ministry of Christ is the primary focus of most study in Hebrews, and properly so, often overlooked is the place of the Son's ascension in the letter. And yet no other book of the NT develops the theological significance of Christ's ascension and enthronement at the right hand of the Father as this letter. Thematically, it appears as bookends in the letter, serving the important rhetorical purposes of inclusio at the outset (1:3) and the near-conclusion (12:2) of the writing. Exaltation and enthronement are the "completion" of the Son's saving work. At the right hand of God, the Son continually makes intercession for His own (7:26; 8:1; 10:12). By virtue of His priestly ministry as well as His enthronement, the Son is doubly worthy—an argument that has been masterfully and meticulously constructed by the writer through extensive use of the OT and Jewish tradition material.

The language of Christ's ascension and session in Hebrews is distinct from its Pauline counterpart (e.g., Eph 1:20–22; 4:8–10;

---

[52] Every reference to "glory" in Hebrews but one is linked to Jesus.

very interesting!

Phil 2:6–11; Col 3:1; 1 Tim 3:16). The Son's exaltation in Hebrews is foremost predicated on His atoning work on earth and His pioneering work on behalf of humanity. This work, moreover, is "completed" in the heavenly realm (4:14; 6:19–20; 9:1–28). In the unfolding of the writer's argument, Jesus' priestly office and the ascension are inextricably linked.[53] While it recedes somewhat, the ascension is nevertheless present throughout much of the high priestly argument. Although the Son transcends all of creation, yet He expresses full solidarity with that creation. Christ's saving work begins on earth and is completed in heaven (4:14). Jesus enters the holy place "by his own blood" and once-for-all, eternal sacrifice (9:12,24). His ascension "perfects" His redemptive work.

Clearly, given the amount of material in Hebrews devoted to Jesus' high priestly ministry, many in the community did not adequately grasp the significance of Jesus' death. His entrance into human history and His full identification with humanity, in all its suffering and disgrace, in the end refract back on Him a glory greater than even His preexistent exalted stature. Christ's session (1:3,13; 8:1; 10:12; 12:2) now facilitates perpetual intercession on behalf of those He redeemed (2:18; 4:15–16; 7:25). That all things are now subjugated to Christ (2:8; 10:13) and that He "sat down at the right hand of the throne of God" (12:2) should greatly encourage the readers. Just as He suffered, the Son was rewarded and glorified. As they persevere in their hardships, they, too, will receive their eternal reward.

13. *Divine speaking* (1:1–2,5,6,7,8,13; 2:3,4; 3:7,10,11,15; 4:3,4,5,7,8,12; 5:5,6,12; 6:13,17; 7:17,21,22; 8:8; 9:20; 10:5,8,9,15; 12:25,26; 13:5,7). A prominent theme in the epistle to the Hebrews is that God has spoken (and, on occasion, "testified" and "sworn"). The epistle begins, "In the past God spoke to our forefathers through the prophets." This prophetic speech, however, is quickly and authoritatively overshadowed by a greater revelation: "but in these last days he has spoken to us by his Son." Even in the chain of citations from the Psalms throughout chapter 1, emphasis is laid on what God "says"; on every occasion that Scripture is cited, God *speaks* or *testifies*. What God has said and what He says in the present are critically important. His word is alive, and the writer is emphatic about this point: "The word of God is living and active.

prophecy is overshadowed by Jesus' words

---

[53] This linkage has been aptly noted by W. J. Larkin Jr., "Ascension," in *DLNT*, 98–99.

Sharper than any double-edged sword, it penetrates even to dividing soul and spirit, joints and marrow; it judges the thoughts and
attitudes of the heart" (4:12).

If we learn anything from the letter, it is that *God speaks* and that
His speech is authoritative.[54] In Hebrews the apex of God's speaking
is the agent of His Son, who as the preexistent Son is also the medium of creation (1:2), the "firstborn" of God (1:6; 12:23)[55] who
leads many "sons to glory" (2:10), the antitype of Moses (3:1–6),
the great and eternal high priest (4:14–5:10; 7:1–10:18).

The implications of God's speaking are staggering yet reassur-
ing, anchoring us in times of hardship: God does not abandon His
people; His word is His pledge of abiding presence. For this reason
"God has said, 'Never will I leave you; never will I forsake you'"
(13:5).[56] Since God has spoken once for all, definitively through
the Son, to refuse the One who has spoken is to invite the wrath
of God (2:1–3; 3:7–19; 6:4–6; 10:26–31; 12:14–29). An important
element in the writer's "word of exhortation" (13:22) is *not to refuse
him who speaks* (12:25).

14. *Mediation.* God has mediated revelation of Himself in a variety of ways. Indeed, this is the opening pronouncement of the letter. God has mediated Himself through the prophets, through the
angels, through Moses, through the institution of the high priesthood, through Melchizedek (who antedates Israel, the priesthood,
and the sacrificial system), through the sacrificial system of the old
covenant, and once for all, through Jesus.

To the average contemporary reader, much in the epistle to the
Hebrews is striking. Perhaps foremost is the extended role that angels play in the writer's rhetorical strategy as well as the abundant
use of typology to demonstrate the extent to which Jesus was anticipated in the old covenant. As to the function of angels as mes-
sengers or servants, William Lane believes the implications to be
"startling": we are not left defenseless in the world, for without
them we could not maintain our commitment to the Son. Moreover,

---

[54] Hence, the placement of the multiple warnings against hardening of the heart (chaps. 3,
4, and 12).

[55] A significant amount of debate in recent years has been generated over a reputed "Logos
Christology" in Hebrews that is thought to draw on the language and imagery of wisdom.
As it applies to Hebrews, see J. Swetman, "Jesus as Logos in Heb 4:12–13," *Bib* 62 (1981):
214–24, and R. Williamson, "The Incarnation of the Logos in Hebrews," *ExpTim* 95 (1983):
4–8. For a useful summary, see P. A. Rainbow, "Logos Christology," in *DLNT*, 665–67.

[56] Here the writer is citing relevant parts of Deut 31:6,8.

angels protect and provide for the people of God, regardless of our awareness.[57] As to the use of typology in Hebrews, an earthly pattern or type in the form of the Levitical priesthood, the tabernacle, as well as the blood sacrifices, serves as a foreshadow of the finished work of Christ. With atonement provided by Christ, whose sacrifice is perfect, no need for sacrifice remains (8:12–13; 9:25–26; 10:17–18).

It is fitting that some have called Hebrews the epistle of priesthood, for the development of Christ's ministry in terms of priestly mediation is unique to the NT. The Levitical priesthood is but a prologue to—indeed, a foreshadow of—that which is once and for all fulfilled in Christ. In fact, Melchizedek, whose priesthood antedates and in some respects foreshadows the Levitical system, already is understood by the writer to point beyond himself and beyond Aaron's line to greater redemptive history. Through its abundant use of typology, Hebrews is emphatic about the association between shadow and reality, earthly and eternal. The temporal is "only a shadow of the good things that are coming" (10:1).

Literary Features

Hebrews has been uniformly depicted as a highly stylized midrashic homily or sermon that incorporates sophisticated rhetorical forms.[58] As a sermon it serves as a "response to a crisis of faith"[59] arising from trying circumstances in the life of the readership. The writer identifies his epistle as a "word of exhortation" (*logos tēs paraklēseos*, 13:22; implied in 12:5; cp. also Acts 13:15). Hebrews corresponds with the standard genre of the sermon as practiced in first-century Jewish and Christian contexts—the use of an authoritative text or exemplar that is followed by a subsequent conclusion and related exhortation drawn from it.[60] This repetitive or cyclical pattern in the sermon gives it a pronounced rhetorical effect.[61]

---

[57] *Call to Commitment*, 37.

[58] Representative is G. Zuntz, *The Text of the Epistles* (London: Black, 1953), 286.

[59] So Lane, *Call to Commitment*, 22, and idem, "Hebrews," in *DLNT*, 443.

[60] L. Wills, "The Form of the Sermon in Hellenistic Judaism and Early Christianity," *HTR* 77 (1984): 277–99. H. Attridge (*Hebrews* [Hermeneia; Philadelphia: Fortress, 1988]), refers to the second component as the "paraenetic interlude."

[61] One might readily identify three smaller sermons—3:1–4:16; 8:1–10:25; and 11:1–12:3—within the broader structure of Hebrews. J. L. Bailey and L. D. Vander Broek (*Literary Forms in the New Testament: A Handbook* [Louisville: Westminster/John Knox, 1992], 193)

While Hebrews, strictly speaking, does not closely conform to the epistolary genre, lacking any author identification, greeting, or prescript,[62] it does contain a postscript, closing personal greetings, and a benediction, in accordance with epistolary convention. Throughout the course of Hebrews, the document increasingly appears less as an essay or sermon and more like an epistle (e.g., 3:12; 4:1–2,14; 5:11–12; 6:9,13; 10:19–39; 12:1–13:25). These transitions indicate that Hebrews was addressed to a particular Christian community, to which the writer senses a strong pastoral commitment. However the composition of Hebrews took place, the writer's concluding remark, "I have written you only a short letter" (13:22), may be accepted at face value.

Even to the relatively unsophisticated reader, Hebrews demonstrates a style of prose that is striking. The rhythm or cadence, the rhetorical effect of alternating paradigm and paraenesis (exhortation), and creative use of language are worthy of note and indicative of an artist. In terms of their alliterative effect and style—consider 1:1 alone as a striking example: *Polumerōs . . . polutropōs palai . . . patrasin . . . prophētais*—the very opening verses of the epistle are thought by some to be virtually unparalleled in the NT.[63] In addition, the images used in Hebrews, fully apart from direct allusions to the OT (i.e., Israel's wilderness wandering, Melchizedek, the tabernacle, priesthood, the Day of Atonement, and the heroes of faith), are quite vivid and varied, derived from numerous sources. These include:

- freedom from slavery (2:15),
- stewardship of a house (3:1–6),
- the Word of God as a sword (4:12),
- fruitful and barren land (6:7–8),
- hope as an anchor that secures (6:19),
- freedom from slavery due to a ransom or purchase price (9:15),

observe that the "sermons" beginning in 3:1 and 8:1 both conclude with the words "Since then we have."

[62] First John is comparable in this respect, lacking epistolary elements and yet qualifying as an epistle.

[63] W. Barclay writes: "This [1:1–4] is the most sonorous piece of Greek in the whole New Testament. It is a passage that any classical Greek orator would have been proud to write. The writer . . . has brought to it every artifice of word and rhythm that the beautiful and flexible Greek language could provide" (*The Letter to the Hebrews*, 1).

- viewing the distant shore from sea (11:13),
- pilgrimage (11:13),
- the gymnasium[64] or marathon (12:1), and
- fatherhood and sonship (12:5–11).

The list of words from classical literature that are used in Hebrews but nowhere else in the NT is lengthy. B. F. Wescott identified fifty such terms.[65] Further, some 85 terms from the LXX are found in Hebrews but nowhere else in the NT.[66] Paronomasia and alliteration occur regularly enough throughout the letter to suggest a writer who is a wordsmith—for example:

- 1:1   *Polumerōs . . . polutropōs palai . . . patrasin . . . prophētais,*
- 2:10   *di' hon ta panta kai di' hou ta panta,*
- 5:8   *emathen aph' hōn epathen,*
- 10:34   *tēn harpagēn tōn huparchontōn humōn . . . prosedexasthe . . . exein . . . kreittona uparxin*
- 10:39   *esmen upostolēs eis apōleian . . . alla pisteōs eis peripoiēsin psuchēs.*

Such striking usage of language indicates a writer of considerable linguistic and rhetorical skill. At the same time it suggests a readership that is more than likely in a Greek-speaking environment (as opposed to Judea, for example).[67]

The writer's choice of citations gives the impression that he may have been aware of particular catechetical traditions with Christological significance that had been handed down.[68] Hebrews 1 alone, for example, which contains eight connections to the OT in a span of merely 14 verses (Pss 110:1; 2:7; 2 Sam 7:14; Deut

---

[64] To depict the need to persevere, in 12:1 the writer uses the word "struggle," *agōn*, which in the athletic context often refers to a wrestling match.

[65] B. F. Westcott, *The Epistle to the Hebrews* (London: Macmillan and Co., 1909), xlv.

[66] Ibid.

[67] This contrasts with the Epistle of Jude, which due to its language, imagery, and use of Jewish traditional material more than likely is addressed to Jewish Christians in or around Palestine. See J. D. Charles, *Literary Strategy in the Epistle of Jude* (Scranton/London/Toronto: University of Scranton Press/Associated University Presses, 1993), chapter 3 ("The Epistle of Jude in Its Palestinian Milieu").

[68] To make as strong a case as E. Käsemann, that the writer of Hebrews was aware of and using particular catechetical and liturgical traditions (*The Wandering People of God*, 168), is speculative and requires more than the text permits.

32:43; Ps 104:4; 45:5–7; 102:25–27; and again 110:1), allows for (but does not require) this association.

A precise quantifying of OT references in Hebrews eludes us since the writer combines direct citations and fragmentary citations with general allusions, reminiscences, familiar phraseology, and use of extrabiblical traditions. The bulk of the OT material cited by the writer comes from the Pentateuch and the Psalms. Significantly, the writer frequently frames his citations in terms of God speaking and not with the typical Pauline formula "it is written"; 23 of his citations have God as the speaker.[69]

Following the rather dramatic, when abrupt, opening declaration of the Son as God's definitive revelation, the writer builds a comparative case for the Son's superior glory by means of a catena or chain of OT citations and partial citations. This technique entails stringing together statements from Ps 2:7; 2 Sam 7:14; Deut 32:43; Ps 96:7 (LXX); Ps 103:4 (LXX); Ps 44:7–8 (LXX); and Ps 101:26–28 (LXX). What serves to unite these varied quotations is the use of particular catchwords—for example, "son," "angel," or "glory." This literary feature has the rhetorical effect of amplifying the comparison intended.[70]

An effective rhetorical device used in Hebrews is the ethical catalog. It is used in its normal, abbreviated form in 7:26 and in an expanded form in chapter 11, where moral paradigms are showcased for the reader's consideration.[71] The recording of ethical lists was a salient feature of moral-philosophical discourse in Hellenistic culture and later in Hellenistic-Jewish literature. Extending from the Homeric era, the ethical list comes into full bloom in the teaching of the Stoics. Rhetorically speaking, the ethical list has an epideictic function. That is, it is intended to instill praise or shame in the hearer or listener. Vice and virtue lists were an effective teaching

[handwritten margin note: what is the ethical catalog?]

---

[69] See the helpful overview by G. H. Guthrie, "The Old Testament in Hebrews," in *DLNT*, 841–50.

[70] G. H. Guthrie analyzes Hebrews on the basis of the relationship between linguistic elements in the letter and the contextual flow of the argument. See his volume *The Structure of Hebrews: A Text-Linguistic Analysis* (NovTSup 73; Leiden: Brill, 1994), as well as his essay "Discourse Analysis," in D. A. Black and D. S. Dockery, eds., *Interpreting the New Testament: Essays on Method and Issues* (Nashville: Broadman & Holman, 2001), 253–71.

[71] B. L. Mack (*Rhetoric in the New Testament* [Minneapolis: Fortress, 1990], 73–77) classifies Heb 11:1–12:3 as an encomium. Whether we view this material as an extended virtue catalog or an encomium, both literary genres belong to the same broader family; they are rhetorical devices aimed at instilling praise.

tool among Stoics,[72] and early Christian writers, understandably, found good reasons for incorporating the ethical list into their writings.[73] Because the ethical teachings of Stoicism and Christianity are shaped by the same moral-social conditions, touch points between Stoic discourse and the NT are numerous.[74] The cataloging of virtues and vices is an important feature of the Christian paraenetic or hortatory tradition, and most of the lists used in the NT show some debt to their pagan and Hellenistic-Jewish counterparts.[75]

While a shorter listing of moral paradigms is used in 2 Pet 2 (the fallen angels, Noah's generation, Sodom and Gomorrah, Lot, Balaam) and Jude (unbelieving Israel, the fallen angels, Sodom and Gomorrah, Cain, Balaam, Korah, Enoch), in Hebrews the list is expanded for the purpose of exhortation: "Therefore, since we are surrounded by such a great cloud of witnesses, let us . . ., let us . . . Let us . . . Consider him . . ." (12:1–3).[76]

Perhaps most conspicuous about Hebrews is the writer's strong reliance on extrabiblical Jewish tradition material. Four noteworthy examples are the wilderness motif (chaps. 3 and 4), the Abraham traditions (chaps. 2, 6, 7, and 11), the Melchizedek midrash (chap. 7), and the catalog of the faithful (chap. 11). The Melchizedek motif in Hebrews 7, so baffling to many a reader, mirrors an intriguing debt to later Jewish traditions and has peculiar affinities especially to rabbinic commentary on Melchizedek that

---

[72] For a fuller discussion of vice and virtue in Stoic discourse and the function of the ethical catalogue, see J. D. Charles, *Virtue Amidst Vice* (JSNTSup 150; Sheffield: Sheffield Academic Press, 1997), 99–127.

[73] On the use of the ethical catalog by Christian writers, see B. S. Easton, "New Testament Ethical Lists," *JBL* 51 (1932): 1–12; M. J. Suggs, "The Christian Two Way Tradition: Its Antiquity, Form, and Function," in *Studies in the New Testament and Early Christian Literature* (NovTSup 33; Leiden: Brill, 1972), 60–74; N. J. McEleney, "The Vice Lists of the Pastoral Epistles," *CBQ* 36 (1974): 2–3,19; and J. D. Charles, "Vice and Virtue Lists," in C. A. Evans and S. E. Porter, eds., *DNTB*, 1252–57.

[74] In the Pauline letters, for example, vice lists occur in Rom 1:29–31; 13:13, 1 Cor 5:10–11; 6:9–10; 2 Cor 12:20–21; Gal 5:19–21; Eph 4:31; 5:3–5; Col 3:5,8; 1 Tim 1:9–10; 2 Tim 3:2–5; Titus 3:3, while virtue lists occur in 2 Cor 6:6; Gal 5:22–23; Eph 4:23,32; 5:9; Php 4:8; Col 3:12; 1 Tim 4:12; 6:11; 2 Tim 2:22; 3:10. Elsewhere in the NT, ethical lists are found in Matt 15:19; Mark 7:21–22; Jas 3:15,17; 1 Pet 2:1; 3:8; 4:3,15; 2 Pet 1:5–7; Rev 9:21; 21:8; 22:15. The most extensive virtue catalog in the NT, recorded in 1 Pet 1:5–7, mirrors both Christian and pagan ethical lists. While faith and love are the "bookends" of ethical formation, the other six virtues are all found in comparable pagan lists and conveniently allow themselves to be incorporated into the writer's purpose.

[75] Ethical catalogs, for the most part, do not appear in the OT (apart from a text like Prov 6:16–19). They appear to be the fruit of Hellenistic cultural influence.

[76] Lists of moral paradigms occur in Jewish literature as well—for example, in Sir 16:5–15; *Jub.* 20:2–7; *3 Macc.* 2:3–7; *T. Naph.* 2:8–4:3; *CD* 2:14–3:12; and *m. Sanh.* 10:3.

are not found in Genesis 14 or Psalm 110. Moreover, the discovery in Qumran Cave 11 of a fragmentary Melchizedek text in 1965 generated an enormous amount of speculation regarding sectarian Jewish eschatological expectations and a possible connection to Hebrews 7. Resultant Melchizedek studies, which establish the plausibility of some exegetical link between the writer of Hebrews and sectarian Judaism, unfortunately have yielded exceedingly divergent interpretations and defy any sort of consensus.[77]

Various Moses traditions also interlock in Hebrews 11. Five elements are mentioned in the text of 11:23–28—the decision of Moses' parents to hide him following his birth, his refusal to assume the status of Egyptian royalty, his decision to identify with his suffering people, his decision to leave Egypt, and his commitment to keep the Passover. Several details in this brief narrative go beyond the actual text of the OT, at best intimated by the OT but stated explicitly, for example, by Philo[78] and Josephus.[79]

Evidence of further reliance on extrabiblical Jewish tradition material seems plausible in Hebrews. While they evade certainty, numerous extrabiblical parallels to Hebrews are worth noting and invite comparison. These include:

- Wis 7:26 (cp. Heb 1:3);
- Philo, *The Worse Attacks the Better* 40 (cp. Heb 4:12);
- Philo, *On Husbandry* 2 (cp. Heb 5:12–14); and
- *Martyrdom and Ascension of Isaiah* 5:13 (cp. Heb 11:37).

While not a parallel, the intriguing admonition in Hebrews to show hospitality to strangers (13:2) invites comparison with Sir 11:29–34, in which precisely the opposite advice is given: "Receive a stranger into your home and he will upset you with commotion . . . and . . . estrange you from your family" (cp. Heb 13:2). A chief element in the writer's extravagant use of Jewish tradition material is his extensive use of typology. Hebrews joins the General Epistles in sustained use of typological exegesis for the sake of illustration and/or comparison.[80] Typological interpreta-

---

[77] The literature on Melchizedek in Hebrews is massive, although a helpful overview of explanations is contained in Hurst, *The Epistle to the Hebrews*, 52–63.

[78] Philo, *Life of Moses* 1.149.

[79] Josephus, *Ant.* 4.3.2.

[80] In the General Epistles, typology is typically pressed into the service of exhortation (using moral paradigms) rather than Christology. See in this regard J. D. Charles, "Old Testament

tion grows out of the conviction that contained within Israel's history are principal forms of divine activity that point to the ultimate purposes of God.[81] From the standpoint of the NT writers, the theological center of this is the life, death, resurrection, and exaltation of the Son, Jesus Christ. OT characters, events, and institutions project themselves in ways that allow them to serve as paradigms in the Christian paraenetic (or hortatory) tradition. What is often baffling to the contemporary reader is the explicit link between OT texts and paradigms and their function in the NT. The manner in which they are used by individual writers is not at all straightforward.

No book of the NT is as richly laden with types as the epistle to the Hebrews. Typology is part of a technique in Hebrews to demonstrate the superiority of Jesus to the prophets, to the exalted angels,[82] to Moses, to the Levitical priesthood, to Melchizedek, to the sacrificial system itself, and finally to Zion and the city of God. The purpose of these illustrations is not so much to show *eschatological fulfillment* as it is to show *relationship and superiority*. The ethical and hortatory goal of the writer's extensive use of typology is that the readers, motivated by Jesus' sacrificial and moral example, will be able to endure opposition, not grow weary, and not lose heart (12:2–3). As a result, they will not be shaken (12:28).

Klyne Snodgrass identifies helpful guidelines for the reader in understanding how the NT appropriates OT material.[83] The reader must be aware of exegetical methods contemporary to the writer that would have governed how texts are being used. One should also look for "corporate solidarity" between the Old and the New, between Jesus and typological figures, between Israel and the church. Relatedly, eschatological fulfillment—whether through Christ or the Christian community—serves as a plumb line by which to interpret certain OT texts. Finally, our interpretation of

---

in the General Epistles," in *DLNT*, 834–41.

[81] The best resources on typology in the Bible remain L. Goppelt, *Typos: The Typological Interpretation of the Old Testament in the New* (trans. D. H. Madvig, Grand Rapids: Eerdmans, 1982), and G. W. H. Lampe and K. J. Woollcombe, *Essays on Typology* (Naperville: Allenson, 1957).

[82] Attridge's argument that comparison between Jesus and the angels merely serves as a "superficial rubric" (*The Epistle to the Hebrews*, 17–21) needs moderation. Each of the rhetorical building blocks in the writer's overall argument is calculated and decisive.

[83] Klyne Snodgrass, "The Use of the Old Testament in the New," in D. A. Black and D. S. Dockery, eds., *Interpreting the New Testament: Essays on Methods and Issues* (Nashville: Broadman & Holman, 2001), 209–29.

the OT is uniquely Christological. The NT writers wrote from a perspective that saw all things in the old covenant as pointing toward Christ, God's full and definitive expression of revelation. The NT's typological interpretation of the OT is a primary illustration of how these guiding assumptions are at work.

In seeking to understand NT writers' use of the OT, the reader must also be aware of specific Jewish methods of interpreting the Hebrew Scriptures. Several related practices were *midrash pesher* and the use of *testimonia*. Early Christian use of *testimonia*, i.e., a stringing together of various OT texts for liturgical or apologetic purposes that "testified" of Jesus' messiahship, mirrors a pre-Christian Jewish hermeneutical practice that was discovered at Qumran.[84] Earle Ellis distinguishes between these early Christian "testimonies" and "proof texts" in the narrower sense:

> The "testimonies" . . . presuppose a worked-out Christological understanding of the particular passages and are not simply proof texts randomly selected. The earliest Christians, like twentieth century Jews, could not, as we do, simply infer from traditional usage the "Christian" interpretation of a biblical word or passage. Proof texts standing alone, therefore, would have appeared to them quite arbitrary if not meaningless.[85]

Even when to Christian readers the NT's interpretation of the OT appears arbitrary, this is not the case. Rather, it stems from a salvific view of history, a postresurrection Christological perspective, and a typological understanding of the old covenant. Midrashic interpretation shows that "the prophets and teachers in the early church were not content merely to cite proof texts but were concerned to establish by exegetical procedures the Christian understanding of the Old Testament."[86] In Hebrews 1, assorted OT texts are linked together by the theme of sonship to demonstrate

---

[84] See J. A. Fitzmyer, "'4Q Testimonia' and the New Testament," *TS* 18 (1957): 513–37. A helpful overview is found in Snodgrass, "The Use of the Old Testament in the New," 218–22.

[85] E. E. Ellis, "How the New Testament Uses the Old," in *Prophecy and Hermeneutic in Early Christianity* (WUNT 18; Tübingen: Mohr, 1978), 150–51.

[86] Ibid., 162.

the Son's superiority to the angels.[87] The Son is qualitatively different from the angels.[88]

Midrash[89] may be understood as a kind of interpretive activity by which the writer attempts to apply insights from historical examples of the past to present realities.[90] Considerable study in recent years has shown the extent to which "midrashic" interpretation is used by the writers of the NT. Midrash entails two essential aspects: the citation of an authoritative text and commentary on that text. New problems and new situations must be addressed. Midrash comes into play to address, resolve, and affirm the religious community by way of traditions from the past. In linking OT traditions with the present, the midrashist might also help fill in those gaps which, almost teasingly, have been left out. For example, why did Cain kill Abel? What happened at Moses' death? Why did Abraham tithe to Melchizedek?

It would be misleading to assume that biblical scholars agree fully on what precisely constitutes "midrash." H. H. Brownlee[91] uses the term in a somewhat restricted sense, classifying a work as "midrashic" only if it exhibits a specific rabbinic mode of exegesis. R. Bloch,[92] on the other hand, argues for a broader definition. Midrash includes any reflection on a text that has as its aim a reinterpretation or "actualization" of that text for present circumstances. J. Doeve extends Bloch's position, viewing the Gospels themselves as Christian "midrashim." But regardless of how restrictive or inclusive one's definition of midrash is, its purpose is to make a text relevant by means

---

[87] It is significant that angels are frequently referred to as "spirits" in apocalyptic Jewish literature.

[88] It is plausible that the recipients of the letter in some manner were inclined to exalt angelic powers.

[89] The term *midrash* derives from the Hebrew verb that means "to inquire," "to investigate," and thus, "to interpret."

[90] Helpful resources on Jewish use of the midrashic exegetical method are A. Robert, "Les Genres litteraires," in A. Robert and A. Tricot, eds., *Initiation biblique* (3rd ed.; Paris: Duculot, 1954), 305–9; A. G. Wright, "The Literary Genre Midrash," *CBQ* 28 (1966): 118–38; E. Slomovic, "Toward an Understanding of the Exegesis in the Dead Sea Scrolls," *RQ* 7 (1969/70): 5–10; and G. G. Porton, "Defining Midrash," in *The Study of Ancient Judaism*, Vol. 1, ed. J. Neusner (Jersey City, N.J.: Ktav Publishing House, 1981), 55–92. On the NT writers' use of midrash, see J. Doeve, *Jewish Hermeneutics in the Synoptic Gospels and Acts* (Assen: Van Gorcum, 1954); E. E. Ellis, *Prophecy and Hermeneutic in Early Christianity* (Tübingen: Mohr, 1978); J. L. Bailey and L. D. Vander Broek, *Literary Forms in the New Testament* (Louisville: Westminster/John Knox, 1992), 42–49, 156–59.

[91] H. H. Brownlee, "Biblical Interpretation among the Sectaries of the Dead Sea Scrolls," *BA* 14 (1951): 76.

[92] R. Bloch, "Midrash," *DBSup* 5.1265–66.

of "creative historiography" or "creative philology."[93] Several notable examples of this "creative" interpretive technique in Hebrews are the comparison of Jesus to Moses and to Melchizedek.

The mystery that surrounds Melchizedek in the Genesis 14 narrative, coupled with the lack of explanation in Psalm 110, appears to have left plenty of room for speculation in Jewish tradition, whether in rabbinic exegesis, Josephus, or Qumran.[94] The most extensive development of the Melchizedek interpretation was a midrash found at Qumran, what is known as 11QMelchizedek. While it is certainly possible that the writer of Hebrews was indirectly adjusting mistaken messianic beliefs of the Dead Sea Scroll sect, the comparative argument using Jesus and Melchizedek could have been derived from the OT.[95]

Despite early witnesses that attributed Pauline authorship to Hebrews, what is altogether striking about the epistle is how the language and vocabulary differ from Paul's letters. Absent from Hebrews are numerous conspicuous features of Pauline literature—for example, the distinction between Jews and Gentiles, salvation going to the Gentiles, a forensic conceptualization of justification, the contrast between works, union with Christ (notably, use of the expression "in Christ"), the contrast of flesh and spirit, personal references to apostleship, ministry, and colleagues, problems related to liturgical practice, and a wide variety of divine names. Other elements that distinguish Hebrews from Paul's letters include anonymity, an appeal to eyewitness authority,[96] the sheer amount of attention devoted to the priesthood motif,[97] and the rather elegant style of language and rhetoric employed.[98]

---

[93] So Wright, "The Literary Genre Midrash," 129–30.

[94] See in particular F. L. Horton Jr., *The Melchizedek Tradition: A Critical Examination of the Sources to the Fifth Century AD and in the Epistle to the Hebrews* (SNTSMS 30; Cambridge: Cambridge University Press, 1976). The literature on Melchizedek in mainstream as well as sectarian Jewish tradition is massive. A helpful overview is W. M. Schniedewind, "Traditions of Melchizedek," in *DNTB*, 693–95.

[95] In addition to F. F. Bruce's evaluation of the Qumran interpretation of Hebrews (see n. 23), a balanced perspective is found in W. S. LaSor, "The Epistle to the Hebrews and the Qumran Writings," in *The Dead Sea Scrolls and the New Testament* (Grand Rapids: Eerdmans, 1972), 179–90.

[96] A statement of this sort by Paul would be unthinkable.

[97] Notable similarities between Hebrews and the Pauline Epistles are an understanding of salvation history that encompasses incarnation, cross, resurrection, and glorification, Christ's role in creation, use of OT typology (Abraham in particular), the new covenant, and allusion to Timothy.

[98] Much debate regarding the literary character of Hebrews has concerned the role that Philonic and Alexandrian exegesis plays in the writer's argument. Clearly, particular

The Old Testament in Hebrews

Understanding the relationship of the OT to the NT is central to a proper grasp of Christian theology. Thus, few issues are more important for the student of the Bible than NT writers' use of the OT. The OT Scriptures represent the theological environment in which early Christians were immersed and grew.[99] At the same time, everything they inherited from the Scriptures—whether as converts from Judaism or as Hellenists—was reinterpreted in the light of revelation of Christ's death, resurrection, and glorification. While virtually all of the material in Hebrews illustrates this, one particular citation is instructive. Psalm 110:1 occurs several times in the NT and is cited and reinterpreted by multiple sources—in Matt 22:44; Mark 12:36; Luke 20:42–43; Acts 2:34–35; 1 Cor 15:25–26—in addition to Heb 1:13. Texts such as Ps 110:1 likely achieved widespread usage in the church for confessional reasons (note the language of *homologeō/homologia* in 3:1; 4:14; 10:23; 11:13; 13:15).

What is perhaps most striking about Hebrews is the extent to which the OT, or traditions that derive from the OT, are marshaled by the writer for his own purposes. While most commentators identify 35 or 36 citations of the OT in the letter, this enumeration depends on how one "counts" citations. Are they full or fragmentary citations? In what cases is the author drawing from an extrabiblical source rather than the OT text? Do general allusions count as citations? For example, is Ps 105:42—"For he remembered his holy promise given to his servant Abraham"—being used in the writer's discussion of Abraham and promise in Heb 6:13–20?[100] Is Psalm 125, a Psalm of ascent, and 125:1 in particular ("Those who trust in the LORD are like Mount Zion, which cannot be shaken but endures forever"), the background to statements in Heb 12:22 and 26–28? And what shall we make of the Christological interpretation of Ps 40:6–8 found in Heb 10:5–10? Can

---

similarities cannot be denied. The position taken here is that similarities should not minimize the eschatological and theological differences between Hebrews and Alexandrian Judaism. The exalted and thoroughly developed Christology of the epistle causes us to read it alongside the other documents of the NT and not Hellenistic Judaism of Philo. The Christian writers adapt typological exegesis and usually not allegory from their Jewish counterparts, and this for historical as well as theological reasons. A balanced view of Alexandrian influence on Hebrews is found in J. M. Knight, "Alexandria, Alexandrian Christianity," in *DLNT*, 34–37.

[99] K. Snodgrass ("The Use of the Old Testament in the New," 209–11) summarizes quite effectively the theological environment of the early Christians.

[100] Few commentators adduce this as a citation or reference in Hebrews.

use of the keyword "sacrifice" and the allusion to a "body you prepared for me" be legitimately transferred to Christ?[101]

The density of citations or allusions to the OT in Hebrews is
unsurpassed.[102] Of all references in the epistle to OT material,[103]
14 are drawn from the Psalter and 13 from the Pentateuch, encom-
passing all five books. Midrash, chain quotations or testimonia,
analogy and contrast, an extended catalog, paraenesis and typology
are all skillfully employed by the writer, who is not concerned to
offer any sort of exposition of the OT text. He freely cites for his
own purposes,[104] working under the assumption that there is full
continuity between divine action in the old covenant and the new.
The church expresses continuity in the divine plan, not discontinuity. (This is true even when the contrast of superior to inferior is
regularly used throughout the letter.) It is clear that the writer has
a high view of the OT; it is divinely inspired and authoritative.

In the OT we find "shadows" or types of transcendent truth. The
thoroughgoing use of typological exegesis in Hebrews, already noted (see "Literary Features"), which facilitates his strategy of comparison, is cause for many commentators drawing parallels to the
Alexandrian school of exegesis with which Philo was associated.
While commonalities are not to be denied, Philonic interpretation
allegorizes in a manner not found in Hebrews. In Hebrews a definite
historical correspondence is necessary to show the Son's continuity
and organic unity with the OT, as well as to demonstrate that He is
"superior." Typology is not the same as allegory, for it is predicated
on an historical association.

---

[101] Despite W. C. Kaiser Jr.'s heroic attempt to discern "internal [Christological] clues in
Psalm 40" ("The Abolition of the Old Order and Establishment of the New: Psalm 40:6–8
and Hebrews 10:5–10," in *Tradition and Testament: Essays in Honor of Charles Lee Feinberg*
[Chicago: Moody Press, 1981], 19–37), I am less convinced. At the same time, I do share
Kaiser's conviction that Christological interpretation of the OT is not merely arbitrary.

[102] One might legitimately argue that, though much shorter in length, the same density of
citation or allusion to the OT is found in the epistles of James and Jude.

[103] Part of the difficulty in enumerating every specific use of OT material in Hebrews is that
the author does not use the customary introductory formula "It is written" that is often used
elsewhere in the NT. Many of these formulas are framed in such a way as to have God as the
speaker (G. H. Guthrie, "The Old Testament in Hebrews," *DLNT*, 842).

[104] *Contra* Ellingworth (*The Epistle to the Hebrews*, 41) it cannot be said that "the author
believes that Christ was active in OT history from the beginning." One may grant that the
Psalm citations mirror the writer's assumption that the New is revealed in the Old. But despite
the exalted view of the Son in Hebrews, the epistle does not present him as "active" in the OT
(even when he was the agent of creation [1:2])—only that forms of divine revelation in the
old covenant are types or shadows.

The catalog of the faithful, recorded in Hebrews 11, appears to blend OT characters and events with details that in time emerged in Jewish exegetical tradition. We have already noted (see "Literary Features") that the interlocking Moses traditions are recited in 11:23–28—his parents hiding him, identification with Israel rather than Pharaoh's daughter, embracing disgrace for Christ rather than Egypt's treasures, departure from Egypt without fear of the king, and his keeping of the Passover. Several of these elements extend the text of the OT itself, dependent upon both postbiblical sources[105] and a "Christianizing" of the story.

Theology and Christology of Hebrews

In contrast to the difficulty we encounter in establishing the destination of Hebrews and the precise identity of its recipients, there is little doubt about the letter's exalted theological perspective. It is a perspective that drinks deeply from the OT and Jewish tradition. At the same time it is a perspective that transcends Jewish theological thinking and one that is situated squarely within the mainstream of NT theology. As such, it interprets the OT through the lens of unfolding salvation history. It understands people, places, events, and institutions of the old covenant as types and foreshadows of greater realities.

Christology in Hebrews is built upon numerous strands; among these are royal Davidic inferences drawn from the Psalter, wisdom traditions that ascribe to the Son the agency of creation, isolated allusions to the prophets that anticipate the new covenant, comparison to Moses as a faithful covenant mediator, development of the "binding of Isaac" and the Melchizedek traditions that are part of Abrahamic promise, and most notably, in-depth typological interpretation of Israel's sacrificial system that is embedded in the Pentateuch. All of these strands underscore the exalted status of the Son, who is superior to any other expression of divine revelation that may have served as a foreshadow.

Theologically, several features in Hebrews are unique to the NT. One is the letter's introduction and development of Christ's transcendent priesthood in relation to that of Melchizedek.[106] Several

[handwritten margin note: Volume containing the Book of Psalms.]

[handwritten note: Very interesting]

---

[105] E.g., 4 Ezra 4:5; *Tg. Ps.-J.* on Deut 34:1; Philo, *Mos* 1.149; and Josephus, *Ant.* 4.3.2.

[106] It is plausible, as O. Cullmann (*The Christology of the New Testament*, (trans. S. C. Guthrie and C. A. M. Hall) Philadelphia: Westminster, 1959], 84–87, 90) argues, that at the

elements are important to the writer. Melchizedek antedates the Levitical system and thus serves to prefigure the priesthood of Christ. In contrast to the order of Aaronic priests, Jesus' priesthood is eternal (5:6; 7:11–28; 9:11–28; 10:1–18; 13:11–13). Also, Melchizedek is important because of how he stands in relation to Abraham, from whose seed the Messiah descended. The argument in Heb 7 rests on a typological interpretation of the OT and, as Oscar Cullmann has persuasively argued, more than likely used an already familiar Jewish tradition regarding Melchizedek.[107]

In addition, the exaltation and enthronement of the Son presented in Hebrews reflects the writer's indebtedness to the royal psalm tradition which comes to expression in Psalm 110, where enthronement and session unite David and Melchizedek. The Son's reign and authority are rooted in that of the eternal God, even when history awaits its consummation, when all enemies are made subject (1:13; 10:13; cp. 1 Cor 15:24–28).

A related feature distinguishes the Christology of Hebrews. It is the emphasis on Christ's "perfection" through suffering, by which the Son identifies fully in His humanity with creation and in its role in His exaltation and enthronement. Exaltation by way of suffering is the direction of the well-known hymn in Phil 2:6–11, although in Philippians this unit is abbreviated and serves the goal of illustrating what attitude is necessary to foster Christian unity. In Hebrews, it is part of the writer's greater argument for the Son's superiority, and specifically, for establishing Jesus' solidarity with Christians who suffer. That solidarity is exemplary and compelling; believers should be emboldened by their access to God, made possible by the "merciful high priest" who "perpetually lives to make intercession" for them. The writer's case for Jesus' humanity, unparalleled in the NT, is rich, nuanced, and pastorally sensitive.

While Christ's high priesthood is the chief Christology motif in Hebrews, it is by no means the sole one. The letter begins by extolling His sonship, of which there are three definable stages—preexistence, incarnation, and glorification/exaltation—distinguished in the writer's argument. The emphasis throughout Hebrews is the relationship between the latter two. Exaltation is predicated on the

time of Jesus there existed messianic interpretations of Ps 110 associated with Melchizedek. In fact, Jesus Himself quoted Ps 110 (Matt 22:41–46; Mark 12:35–37; Luke 12:41–44) in reference to his own person.

[107] Ibid., 84–90.

Son's earthly work, a work that is rooted in His willingness to suffer, and is "completed" in the heavenly realm.

The epistle begins with an unambiguous pronouncement of Jesus' preexistence, role in creation, and representation of divine glory. As the agent of creation,[108] the Son is portrayed in a manner that is reminiscent of Wisdom personified in Hellenistic Judaism. Jesus is also the *prōtotokos*, the "firstborn," who enters the world of humanity (1:6; 12:23), an emphasis found in Paul (cp. Rom 8:29; Col 1:15,18; Rev 1:5). This notion is related to the contrast in Hebrews between the Son's glory and His deep humiliation. Jesus' atoning death, the goal of His incarnation, leads to His majesty. Jesus participates in full humanity, yet He does so in sinless perfection. Jesus' preexistence is further intimated by a part of the chain quotation (from Ps 45:7–8), which declares the eternality of God's throne and implies the Son's precreational status. The Son's preexistence is further suggested late in the writer's argument by comparisons between earthly and heavenly sanctuary and earthly and heavenly priesthood (chap. 8).[109]

The eschatological perspective in Hebrews has been described as two dimensional. That is, a vertical or spiritual element appears alongside a horizontal or temporal. In terms of His earthly sojourn, Christ fulfills through His sacrifice what was anticipated in the old covenant. The spiritual dimension is represented through the heavenly temple, which is portrayed as both a present and eternal reality (chaps. 9 and 10).

Attestation and Authorship

The epistle to the Hebrews endured a fate not unlike that of the General Epistles and Revelation. The early church, broadly speaking, was uncertain about authorship, with eastern Christendom generally attributing the letter to Paul. The relationship of authorship to inclusion in the canon was particularly important in the case of Hebrews. Absent from earliest canonical listings, the epistle was nevertheless known and cited before the end of the first century, evidenced by Clement of Rome (AD 90s), who appears to cite freely from it.[110] Hermas (mid second

---

[108] In Pauline literature Jesus is both the agent and the goal of creation (Col 1:16–20).

[109] See D. B. Capes, "Preexistence," in *DLNT*, esp. 957–58.

[110] E.g., *1 Clem.* 36:1–5 (cp. Heb 1:3–4, 7; 2:18; 3:1); *1 Clem.* 9:3 (cp. Heb 11:5); *1 Clem.* 9:4 (cp. Heb 11:7); *1 Clem.*, 10:7 (cp. Heb 11:17); *1 Clem.* 17:1 (cp. 11:37); and *1 Clem.* 21:1 (cp. Heb 12:1).

century) showed notable affinities toward it, Justin Martyr may have used it,[111] Tertullian (early third century) was familiar with it under the title of "to Hebrews,"[112] and Clement of Alexandria, according to Eusebius,[113] referred to it as being written "for Hebrews."

The heretic Marcion, excommunicated by the church in Rome in AD 144, subsequently organized his own church and created a "canon" of Scripture that omitted Hebrews and the Pastoral Epistles. This is, of course, as we would expect, given his rejection of Judaism and the God of the OT. From the late second century Hebrews appeared to have quasicanonical status by some in the church due to its association by some in the church with Pauline writings, particularly in Eastern Christendom.

Eusebius appears to be divided in his judgment of the epistle. In one place he acknowledged that the letter, like Jude and 2 Peter, was disputed (*antilegomenon*)[114] by some over against the letters of Paul which are universally recognized: "The fourteen letters of Paul are obvious and plain, yet it is not right to ignore that some dispute the Epistle to the Hebrews, saying that it was rejected by the church of Rome as not being by Paul."[115] Elsewhere he wrote that Hebrews was "acknowledged" (*homologoumenon*), and part of his rationale for this acknowledgement was the letter's antiquity.[116] Evidence from patristic sources suggests that questions regarding the letter's authority arose due to its relationship to the Pauline corpus and to its perceived teaching on "postbaptismal" repentance (cp. 6:4–6 and 10:26–31). Despite its attribution to the apostle Paul[117] and comparison with the Pauline epistles in some quarters of the church, it did not achieve universal use and authority until the fourth century.

Notably absent from Hebrews are important Pauline concepts and watchwords such as fulfillment, justification, gospel, edification, and mystery. When we compare the language of "faith" in Paul and in Hebrews, notable differences stand out. In the Pauline epistles we find a strong emphasis placed on forensic justification, grace that op-

---

[111] So, e.g., Justin, *Dial.* 34 (cp. Heb 8:7); 13 (cp. Heb 9:13–14); and 67 (c p. Heb 12:18–19).

[112] This reference occurs in his early third-century work *On Modesty*.

[113] Eusebius, *Hist. eccl.* 6.14.3.

[114] Especially in Eastern Christendom, this would be understandable, due to the fairly widespread circulation of spurious documents (cp. 1 Thess 2:1–3)—Petrine pseudepigrapha as one notable example.

[115] Eusebius, *Hist. eccl.* 3.3.4–5.

[116] Ibid., 3.38.

[117] Origen hesitates to attribute it to Paul; for him, "God only knows" who wrote it. See ibid., 6.25.11.

poses works-righteousness, unmerited favor, our station "in Christ," spiritual liberty, a corresponding development of a theology of the cross, and the purpose of the law. These are strangely absent from Hebrews, however. By comparison, we find on multiple occasions the formula "purification for sins" (*katharizō; katharismos, katharos*: 1:3; 9:14,22–23; 10:22).[118] Virtually the entire argument set forth in the letter is bathed in the twin notions of sacrifice and mediation.

Moreover, faith in Hebrews is not foremost justification, as in Paul. Rather, it is responding to what is known and what has been revealed or done by God through the Son. The writer of Hebrews wished to emphasize the *ethical*, as opposed to legal or forensic, side of faith—an accent that is intended to make his readers "draw near." He was not attempting to join in Paul's struggle with legalism; his challenge was a group of Christians who were considering abandoning their faith. A closer resemblance to the language of Luke has caused some (for example, Clement of Alexandria, according to Eusebius)[119] to attribute Hebrews to the author of the Gospel and Acts.

Both in the early church and in the present, Hebrews has engendered no little speculation regarding possible authorship. Suggestions have ranged from Paul (Jerome, Augustine), Barnabas (Tertullian),[120] Luke or Clement of Rome (Thomas Aquinas, Calvin, Erasmus), Apollos (Luther),[121] to Priscilla (Adolf Harnack).[122] To the time of Clement of Alexandria, Luke and Clement of Rome joined the apostle Paul as the most likely candidates for authorship.[123] While we are left to speculate with Origen—as to the author's identity, "God only knows"[124]—the lack of certainty surrounding the matter of who wrote the letter, thankfully, does not

---

[118] In the Pauline Epistles, the notion of purification for sins occurs only once—in Titus 2:14.

[119] Eusebius, *Hist. eccl.* 6.14.

[120] Barnabas is called a son of encouragement or exhortation (*huios paraklēseos*, Acts 4:36); moreover, he was equally at home in both Jewish and Greek thought worlds.

[121] The attractiveness of Apollos as author of Hebrews becomes apparent from his depiction in the NT. He was a Jew born in Alexandria, and his eloquence and knowledge of the Scriptures are notable (Acts 18:24–28). The effectiveness of his ministry is in keeping with one who is a cultured Alexandrian Christian.

[122] Cp. Acts 18:26 and Romans 16:5. See A. Harnack, "Probabilia über die Addresse und den Verfasser des Hebräerbriefes," *ZNW* 1 (1900): 16–41. Undermining this view, however, is the self-referential masculine participle *diēgoumenon* used in Heb 11:32.

[123] Eusebius, *Hist. eccl.* 6.25.14.

[124] Ibid.

detract from the character and authority of the epistle.[125] In time Hebrews did achieve a canonical consensus within Christendom.

Whatever mystery surrounds the question of authorship, the writer was a skilled orator/rhetorician/writer/preacher who possessed an impressive knowledge of—and insight into—the OT as well as Jewish exegetical techniques. But he was more. He was a person of deep pastoral sensitivities, exuding great passion and compassion toward his readers—people with whom he had intimate acquaintance and for whom he had great concern.

Purpose

In an important volume that probes the message of Hebrews, esteemed German NT scholar Ernst Käsemann has argued forcefully that the motif of the wandering people of God, explicit in 3:7–4:13, is the principal motif of the letter.[126] Noting the writer's statement that "all these people" (recorded in Heb 11) who were "living by faith" were "aliens and strangers on earth" (11:13), Käsemann builds an impressive case for sojourning as the theme of the letter to the Hebrews. Indeed, the typology of pilgrimage is supremely applicable to the Christian community in significant ways. Wandering was the essence of Israel's existence, following her deliverance from bondage in Egypt and before her inheriting the promised land. Faith was requisite during those years of sojourn, a faith rooted in divine promise and what God had spoken. The danger for Israel was a hardening of the heart and the inclination toward disobedience. The potential for Israel's forsaking the promise was by no means inevitable; nevertheless, it was real and likewise can be applied to the Christian community as it finds itself an "alien and stranger" in the present world.

Wandering, therefore, is an "existential necessity" for the people of God.[127] In addition, the larger pattern of ancient Israel, that rest follows sojourning and toiling, is also applicable to the Christian community (4:1). This rest is founded on a proper

---

[125] Additional attempts in the modern period to identify the author have included Jude, Stephen (Acts 7), Philip the deacon (Acts 6), Epaphras (Col 1:7; 4:12; Phlm 23), and Mary the mother of Jesus.

[126] Ernst Käsemann, *The Wandering People of God: An Investigation of the Letter to the Hebrews,* (trans. R. A. Harrisville and I. L. Sandberg) Minneapolis: Augsburg, 1984).

[127] Ibid., 19.

understanding of and response to the gospel that has been declared by God Himself.

The concluding section of the epistle, beginning in 10:19, was thought by Käsemann to unfold the "wandering people of God" motif.[128] As evidence one might take note of the verbs of movement—e.g., in 10:22,33; 11:6; 12:18,22; 13:7,13. In addition, the *agōn* imagery, the language of struggle and enduring, would seem to strengthen Käsemann's argument (e.g., 10:32; 12:1,12).

Therefore, Käsemann argued, in addressing the "wandering people of God," the writer aimed at a "joyful enlistment in a cause already guaranteed by God." Because the future was "secured by God's present activity in the Word of promise," faith was requisite to ensure a "confident wandering."[129]

Käsemann's work in Hebrews is important for several reasons. It emerged at a time when the insights from discoveries of the Qumran community were already infusing NT studies, assisting us in better understanding the religious milieu of the NT world. Further, much of Käsemann's work in the NT was a much-needed reaction to the antisupernaturalistic assumptions of his teacher, theologian Rudolph Bultmann, and Protestant liberalism a generation prior to Käsemann. The response by Käsemann and others indeed represented a welcome turn in biblical studies and biblical theology. In addition, the combination of Käsemann's thoroughness and his sensitivity to religious currents both within as well as outside mainstream Judaism and Christianity make his work supremely useful and lend it enduring value, even when it requires particular adjustments and might strike some as dated.

Last, and most important, Käsemann has identified an element in Hebrews that is frequently neglected by commentators. For this reason, then, probing the epistle to the Hebrews through the lens of Käsemann's perspectives can assist us, sharpening our focus as we attempt to understand the letter's message.

In propounding the "wandering people of God" as the principal theme in Hebrews, Käsemann brought recognition to an important motif in the epistle that more often than not has received insufficient treatment even by students of the Bible. In order to ground his thesis, Käsemann isolated 3:7–4:13 as the key section of the entire epistle. In light of other interlocking subthemes in the letter (see below),

---

[128] Ibid., 22.
[129] Ibid., 43–44.

what is the support for Käsemann's thesis? Can his argument stand? Is the message of Hebrews that we are the wandering people of God? And would this theme be supported by the cumulative weight of innumerable ethical admonitions that are strewn throughout the letter (e.g., 2:1–3; 3:1,12,13; 4:1,14,16; 5:11–14; 6:1,4–6,11–12; 10:22,23,24,25,26–31,32–34,35–39; 12:1,2,3,4,5–6,12,15,25,28–29; 13:6,7,9,13,15,17,22)?

There is strong reason to question Käsemann's belief that pilgrimage is the central theme around which everything in the epistle is organized. Clearly faith as a pilgrimage is an important subtheme in Hebrews. It underscores important insights into the nature of faith and the challenges that life in this world present to faith. While wandering or pilgrimage is an effective and accurate metaphor for walking by faith, the pastoral dilemma being addressed would appear far deeper. Turning away, lapse from what is known to be true and revealed, failure to persevere, and not "wandering" per se, represent the burden of the writer.[130]

To be sure, pilgrimage is an important literary-rhetorical building block used by the writer in the overall architecture of the letter, and yet its linkage to material that both precedes and follows suggests that wandering is *one of several subthemes* rather than *the central motif* of Hebrews. Not merely pilgrimage, which is a relevant parallel between covenant communities, but lapse, turning aside, and failure to endure constitute the overarching burden of the writer. In support of this contention, consider the admonitions as well as the gentle—and at times not so gentle—warnings that lace the entire letter from beginning to end. Among these:

- "We must pay more careful attention, therefore, to what we have heard, so that we do not drift away. For if . . . , how shall we escape if we ignore such a great salvation. . . ?" (2:1–3).
- "Therefore . . . fix your thoughts on Jesus, the apostle and high priest whom we confess. He was faithful . . ." (3:1–2).
- "See to it, brothers, that none of you has a sinful, unbelieving heart that turns away from the living God. But encourage one another daily, as long as it is called Today, so that none of you may be hardened by sin's deceitfulness" (3:12–13).

---

[130] Hurst (*The Epistle to the Hebrews*, 70–71), has correctly identified the locus of thought in the epistle.

- "Therefore . . . let us be careful that none of you be found to have fallen short [of entering God's rest]" (4:1).
- "Therefore . . . let us hold firmly to the faith we profess" (4:14).
- "We have much to say about this, but it is hard to explain because you are slow to learn. In fact, though by this time you ought to be teachers, you need someone to teach you the elementary truths of God's word all over again . . ." (5:11–12).
- "Let us hold unswervingly to the hope we profess, for he who promised is faithful" (10:23).
- "If we deliberately keep on sinning after we have received the knowledge of the truth, no sacrifice for sins is left, but only a fearful expectation of judgment and of raging fire that will consume the enemies of God" (10:26–27).
- "Remember those earlier days after you had received the light, when you stood your ground in a great contest in the face of suffering" (10:32).
- "So do not throw away your confidence; it will be richly rewarded" (10:35).
- "Therefore . . . let us throw off everything that hinders and the sin that so easily entangles, and let us run with perseverance the race marked out for us" (12:1).
- "Consider him who endured such opposition from sinful men, so that you will not grow weary and lose heart" (12:3).
- "In your struggle against sin, you have not yet resisted to the point of shedding your blood" (12:4).
- "Therefore, strengthen your feeble arms and weak knees" (12:12).
- "See to it that you do not refuse him who speaks. If they did not escape when they refused him who warned them on earth, how much less will we, if we turn away from him who warns us from heaven" (12:25)?
- "Jesus also suffered outside the city gate to make the people holy through His own blood. Let us, then, go to Him outside the camp, bearing the disgrace he bore" (13:12–13).

Taken together, these are not the words of one who is merely encouraging Christians in general terms on their pilgrimage of faith (however trying that pilgrimage can be). There is something more at work here. There exists a crisis—an existential and *circumstantial* crisis of faith—that has afflicted those for whom this epistle is intended. As a result of this crisis, they have been tempted to leave their confession of faith and turn away from the Lord who purchased their redemption.

In his fine commentary *Call to Commitment: Responding to the Message of Hebrews,* William Lane has speculated, quite plausibly, that the Christians addressed in Hebrews were in Rome or southern Italy and that the description of the "sufferings," "insults," "persecution," and "prison" found in 10:32–34 corresponds to the hardships borne by Jewish Christians who were expelled by the emperor Claudius in AD 49 (cp. Acts 18:1–2). Lane's attempt at reconstruction is certainly compelling.

> Now, however, it is about fifteen years later. These Christians are fifteen years older. When a new crisis emerges, confronting them with the threat of a fresh experience of suffering, they are compelled to face the cost of discipleship all over again. The situation now facing the community appears more serious than the earlier one under Claudius. The pastor's declaration that "in your struggle against sin you have not yet resisted to the point of shedding your blood" (12:4) suggests that martyrdom may become a fact of Christian experience in the immediate future.[131]

— interesting thoughts

This speculative view is indeed plausible, consistent with references in the letter to suffering and persecution. At the same time it remains just that—speculation. That suffering and persecution are implied is clear from 10:32–34; the question, however, is to what degree. Undermining the belief of Lane and others that intense persecution is present, or around the corner, is the catalog of the faithful in chapter 11. Being faithful to divine revelation *and acting on that knowledge* is the thrust of the paradigms in Hebrews 11, not persecution per se or faithfulness in witness (even to the point of death). It is true that "by faith" Moses "chooses mistreatment" with his own people over "the treasures of Egypt" (11:24–28), although this does not bespeak persecution

---

[131] Lane, *Call to Commitment*, 22–23.

in the strictest sense on his part. It may be further granted that
the conclusion of the catalog (vv. 32–38) does indeed contain the
element of persecution leading to death, but this is illustrative
of a broader concern in chapter 11, namely, *how authentic faith
expresses itself* in a variety of life situations.[132]

Furthermore, the language used by the writer to exhort his readers toward perseverance in the face of hardship is generic language:
he consistently uses *hupomenō* and not *hupopherō*, of which the
latter is the stronger term, often associated with deep suffering and
grief (e.g., 1 Cor 10:13; 2 Tim 3:1; and 1 Pet 2:19).

Significantly, the letter's conclusion contains no allusion to wandering or sojourning. In chapter 12, following the rehearsal of men
and women of faith who *endured*, the emphasis is perseverance, not
being entangled by sin, and the necessity of discipline. "See to it,"
the writer admonishes, "that you do not refuse Him who speaks"
(12:25). This exhortation is immediately followed by a somber
warning regarding those of the past who *did* "refuse" Him. The readers are consequently admonished to go to Jesus "outside the camp,
bearing the disgrace he bore" (13:13). Such admonition doubtless
is linked with the difficulty for some among the readers to "confess
his name" (13:15).

Thus, the letter of Hebrews is addressed to a group of Christians
who were experiencing "a crisis of faith and a failure of nerve." It is
a "word of exhortation" (13:22), sermonic and epistolary in form,
that aims to address those whose confession has been shaken by
trying circumstances of life and who should have already attained
a certain measure of maturity. It is a "word" that "throbs with an
awareness of the privilege and the cost of Christian discipleship"
and "proves to be a sensitive, yet impassioned, pastoral response
to the sagging faith of . . . weary individuals who were in danger of
abandoning their Christian commitments."[133]

The strategy of the writer is to mount a case for the supremacy
of the Son. His argument consists of several building blocks, each

---

[132] The purpose of my distinction here is not to downplay or belittle the reality of persecution or martyrdom. It is rather to see persecution and/or martyrdom as a partial expression of
authentic faith and not the inevitability for *all*. That the recipients are called immature and
only capable of drinking milk (5:11–14) and the object of repeated and at times impassioned
admonitions does not necessarily point to a situation in which *martyrdom*—the end of faithful confession—is the issue; rather, these individuals are wrestling with *the most basic* deci-
sions in order to embrace what is normative for all Christian disciples—hardship, disgrace,
dishonor, and temptation.

[133] W. L. Lane, "Hebrews," in *DLNT*, 443.

of which serves the purpose of *comparison*. Jesus is superior to the angels (chaps. 1 and 2), which establishes His superiority as *the* "covenant messenger." He is superior to Moses (chaps. 3 and 4), by which the writer prepares his readers for the argument that the priesthood of Christ is superior to the Levitical order. He is superior to the Levitical priesthood (chaps. 4 and 5), to the "high priesthood" of the mysterious Melchizedek that was antecedent to the Levitical system (chap. 7),[134] indeed to the entire sacrificial order of the old covenant (chaps. 8–10). This cumulative and well-calculated case for superiority should evoke a response of gratitude and faithfulness that is commensurate with Christ's superiority.

The goal of the writer is to admonish and motivate his readers, through Jesus' sacrificial *as well as* moral example, so that, stated positively, they might endure opposition and hardship as a result of the faith, and negatively, they might not grow weary and lose heart (12:2–3).[135] Jesus is their pioneer and their champion. He has identified with them in all manner of human suffering and, thus, is worthy of their unconditional trust. Armed with this conviction, they will not be shaken (12:28).[136] The closing appeal for the readers to heed the writer's "word of exhortation" (13:22) confirms the primary reason for writing: they are to obey by persevering in faithfulness.

[handwritten: Good to remember]

---

[134] The purpose of the Melchizedek "midrash" in Hebrews 7 has more to do with underscoring *the basis of priesthood* than with emphasizing mysterious or divine qualities. Priesthood in chapter 7 is perpetual and antecedent; but the focus remains the character and nature of priesthood.

[135] Hence the letter should not be understood first and foremost as a warning to Christian converts from Judaism who are contemplating a return to Jewish religion. This argument can stand even when it is true that many of the Christians came to faith out of a Jewish background. To be sure, contrast is important to the writer's literary-rhetorical strategy, particularly in the material of 8:1–10:16. But the positive nature of Israel's covenant should not be denied or underestimated. Contrast *within continuity*, not full discontinuity that mirrors an anti-Jewish polemic, is the emphasis of the epistle.

[136] The perspective being adopted in this volume for discerning the message, and thus purpose, of Hebrews proceeds on the assumption and demonstration of a coherent theme that unfolds in consistent ways throughout the entire letter. For this reason the approach suggested by Paul Ellingworth (*The Epistle to the Hebrews: A Commentary on the Greek Text* [NIGTC; Grand Rapids/Carlisle: Eerdmans/Paternoster, 1993], 80) that "a coherent view of the whole situation can perhaps best be reached by beginning with the severe passages and working outwards to those which raise fewer problems" is to be rejected in favor of an approach that is in fact more "coherent." Part of the problem with historical interpretation of Hebrews is that it has adopted the approach recommended by Ellingworth. By contrast we would argue for the reverse: the "severe" passages in the letter are best accounted for by a coherent and unified account of the letter that does *not* begin with them but rather understands them *in context*.

Outline and Structure of Hebrews

The progression of thought in the letter, which moves from comparison to comparison, is relatively easy to discern.[137] Yet the multifaceted nature of the writer's argument, coupled with the dialectical movement back and forth between example and exhortation, raises some questions about the precise placement of divisions.[138] Depending on where the division lines are drawn, the writer has arranged his argument in roughly six, with "paraenetic or hortatory interludes" following each unit.[139] This pattern of argument in Hebrews, moving back and forth between paradigm or type and application, is a method similar to that found in Jude.

I. The Superiority of Christianity (1:1–10:18)
    A. Superiority to the Old Revelation (1:1–3)
    B. Superiority to Angels (1:4–2:18)
    C. Superiority to Moses (3:1–19)
    D. Superiority to Joshua (4:1–13)
    E. Superiority of Christ's Priesthood (4:14–7:28)
    F. Superiority of Christ's Priestly Work (8:1–10:18)

II. Subsequent Exhortations (10:19–13:17)
    A. Implications of Christ's Superiority for Perseverance (10:19–25)
    B. The Dangers of Apostasy (10:26–31)
    C. Exhortation to Recall the Past (10:32–39)
    D. Paradigms of Endurance from the Past (11:1–40)
    E. Jesus' Example of Perseverance (12:1–13)
    F. Related Moral Exhortations (12:14–17)

[137] We must modify E. F. Scott's contention that Hebrews represents "the riddle of the New Testament" (*The Epistle to the Hebrews: Its Doctrine and Significance* [Edinburgh: T. & T. Clark, 1922]). Regarding authorship, recipients, destination, and dating, textual indicators do not paint a perfectly clear picture. These questions, however, do not obscure the epistle's message.

[138] G. H. Guthrie (*Hebrews*, 27–30) has correctly observed in the structure of Hebrews this dialectic between exposition and exhortation. Such is the nature of midrash as a literary technique. The basic structure of midrash is twofold: citation of an authoritative text and related commentary on the text. L. Wills, ("The Form of the Sermon," 277–99) (see n. 60), has shown a three-part pattern characteristic of the first-century sermon as a genre: (1) scriptural or theological example, (2) conclusion drawn from the example, and (3) exhortation. This form, of course, we would recognize today in standard teaching and preaching on any given Sunday morning.

[139] The division suggested by D. Guthrie (*New Testament Introduction* [4th ed.; Leicester/ Downers Grove: InterVarsity, 1990],) with some modifications most accurately reflects the development of the writer's argument.

G. Restatement of the New Covenant's Superiority
    (12:18–29)
H. Epilogue (13:1–17)
III. Conclusion (13:18–25)

Selected Bibliography

Commentaries Based on the Greek Text

Ellingworth, P. *The Epistle to the Hebrews: A Commentary on the Greek Text*. NIGTC. Grand Rapids/Carlisle: Eerdmans/Paternoster, 1993.
Lane, W. L. *Hebrews 1–8*. WBC 47A. Waco: Word, 1991.
_____. *Hebrews 9–13*. WBC 47B. Waco: Word, 1991.
Moffatt, J. *A Critical and Exegetical Commentary on the Epistle to the Hebrews*. ICC. Rev. ed. Edinburgh: T. & T. Clark, 1948.

Commentaries Based on the English Text

Attridge, H. W. *The Epistle to the Hebrews*. Hermeneia. Philadelphia: Fortress, 1989.
Barclay, W. *Hebrews*. DSB. Edinburgh: Westminster, 1974.
Bruce, F. F. *The Epistle to the Hebrews*. NICNT. Rev. ed. Grand Rapids: Eerdmans, 1990.
Buchanan, G. W. *To the Hebrews*. AB 36. Garden City: Doubleday, 1972.
Casey, J. *Hebrews*. NTM 18. Wilmington: Michael Glazier, 1980.
Davies, J. H. *A Letter to Hebrews*. CBC. Cambridge: Cambridge University Press, 1967.
Guthrie, D. *The Letter to the Hebrews*. TNTC 16. Leicester/Grand Rapids: InterVarsity/Eerdmans, 1983.
Guthrie, G. H. *Hebrews*. NIVAC. Grand Rapids: Zondervan, 1998.
Hagner, D. A. *Hebrews*. GNC. San Francisco: Harper, 1983.
_____. *Hebrews*. NIBC. Peabody: Hendrickson, 1990.
Hering, J. *The Epistle to the Hebrews*. London: Epworth, 1970.
Hughes, P. E. *A Commentary on the Epistle to the Hebrews*. Grand Rapids: Eerdmans, 1977.
Jewett, R. *Letter to Pilgrims. A Commentary on the Epistle to the Hebrews*. New York: Doubleday, 1981.

Kistemaker, S. J. *Exposition of the Epistle to the Hebrews*. NTC. Grand Rapids: Baker, 1984.

Montefiore, H. W. *A Commentary on the Epistle to the Hebrews*. HNTC. New York: Harper & Row, 1964.

Morris, L. *Hebrews*. BSC. Grand Rapids: Eerdmans, 1983.

Nairne, A. *The Epistle to the Hebrews*. Cambridge: Cambridge University Press, 1921.

Smith, R. H. *Hebrews*. Minneapolis: Fortress, 1984.

Westcott, B. F. *The Epistle to the Hebrews*. London: Macmillan, 1909.

Wilson, R. M. *Hebrews*. NCB. Grand Rapids: Eerdmans, 1987.

Foreign Language Commentaries

Michel, Otto. *Der Brief an die Hebräer*. KKNT 13. Göttingen: Vandenhoeck & Ruprecht, 1936.

Spicq, C. *L'Épitre aux Hebreux*. 2 vols. Paris: Gabalda, 1952.

Studies

Guthrie, G. H. "The Old Testament in Hebrews." In *DLNT* 841–50.

_____. *The Structure of Hebrews: A Text-Linguistic Analysis*. NovTSup 73. Leiden: Brill, 1994.

Lane, W. L. *Call to Commitment: Responding to the Message of Hebrews*. Nashville: Thomas Nelson, 1985.

_____. "Hebrews." In *DLNT*, 443–58.

Lindars, B. *The Theology of the Letter to the Hebrews*. Cambridge: Cambridge University Press, 1991.

Two

JAMES

Tested Faith

When readers of the NT think of books whose writers speak straight and do not mince their words, they think of the letter of James. Though neglected by NT scholars, the epistle is a perennial favorite of many in the pew.[1] The latter fact is not difficult to understand because James contains much in the way of practical teaching. The letter instructs and helps believers in many ways with their everyday living, in speech and in conduct. And yet the content of this epistle also thunders forth with an OT-like prophetic voice, pricking the conscience, convicting the soul, and demanding that we change the way we live. James gets in the face of those who have the courage to read his letter, and he bluntly challenges them with the view that *people practice what they truly believe.*

[handwritten: main theme?]

Who was James? When did he write? To whom did he write and why? The answers to these kinds of questions in a study that highlights the letter will help those believers who love it to do so even more.

Author

The author of this letter identifies himself as "James, a slave of God and of the Lord Jesus Christ" (1:1). The writer surely was

Unless otherwise indicated, all Scripture quotations in this chapter are from the Holman Christian Standard Bible (HCSB).

[1] I am indebted to my former professor, William E. Bell Jr., now retired but formerly senior professor of religion at Dallas Baptist University, who instilled in me a deeper love of Scripture. Much of this article greatly reflects and is based on his excellent teaching and notes I gathered from him on James. Any errors, however, should be counted as mine. I wish also to thank my friend and NT colleague, Alan Tomlinson, for the many fruitful discussions on passages in James that I have had with him. I have used several of those ideas in this chapter.

a well-known yet humble leader to designate himself as such. Of the four men whose name "James" appears in the NT, the traditional view that the letter's author is James the half brother of Jesus (Matt 13:55) and leader of the Jerusalem church (Acts 15:12–21; Gal 1:19) is the most likely.[2] Support for the latter conclusion is found in the fact that James, the father of Judas, not Iscariot (Luke 6:16; Acts 1:13) is a somewhat obscure person, while James, the son of Alphaeus (Matt 10:3; Mark 3:18; likely also known as James the younger, Mark 15:40), though an apostle, is rather insignificant among the Twelve. Further, James, a prominent apostle, the brother of John and the son of Zebedee (Matt 4:21; Mark 1:19; 5:37; 9:2; 10:35; Acts 12:2), can be ruled out as the author because he was martyred about AD 44 (cp. Acts 12:2), long before this letter was written. James the Lord's brother is the best candidate for the author of the letter.

Several features within the letter itself are consistent with authorship by James the Lord's brother. First, James is replete with allusions to the teaching of Jesus, especially from the Sermon on the Mount (e.g., cp. Jas 4:11 with Matt 7:1–2; Jas 1:22 with Matt 7:24–27). James does not quote Jesus exactly, but his language strongly suggests he recalled the oral teachings of Christ. Second, the book's several direct quotations from the OT (2:8; 4:6) and indirect references to the OT (5:11,17) point to an author from a Jewish background. Third, clear similarities exist between the Greek of the letter and James' speech in Acts 15:13–21.[3]

Though not unanimous, the early church generally favored James the Lord's brother as the letter's writer. Origen identified James the apostle as the author (*Comm. Jo.*, frag. 126), but Rufinus's Latin translation of Origen mentions James the Lord's brother. Eusebius, the early church historian, placed the letter among his disputed books (*ta antilegomena*) but generally attributes its authorship to James the Lord's brother (*Hist. eccl.* 2.23.25; 3.25.3).

Some scholars, however, argue that the name *James* is a pseudonym. That is to say, they do not think that James the Lord's brother wrote this letter, but rather an unknown author did so using his name. Their arguments are threefold. First, they contend that

---

[2] For a full discussion of authorship and related issues, see Douglas J. Moo, *The Letter of James* (PNTC; Grand Rapids: Eerdmans, 2000), 9–22.

[3] For a full listing of linguistic similarities, see Donald Guthrie, *New Testament Introduction*, 4th ed. (Downer's Grove, IL: InterVarsity, 1990).

James surely would not have written this epistle without referring to his relationship with Jesus. However, many scholars believe that the lack of a reference reflects his humility. Further, James usually does not identify himself as the brother of Jesus; rather, somebody else does (cp. Matt 13:55; Mark 6:3; Gal 1:19).

Second, they argue that the discussion of faith and works in Jas 2:14–26 represents a misunderstanding of Paul's view of the relationship between faith and works. But Paul and James address different aspects of this relationship. Paul writes to say that salvation (i.e., justification) is not by works but by faith alone (cp. Rom 3:28). James writes in opposition to a view that emphasizes salvation by faith but minimizes the importance of works; he contends that faith must produce authenticating deeds. Some have explained James' and Paul's distinctive points of doctrine with the theory that James could have written his letter at a time during which Paul's teaching was only beginning to have an impact on the church yet before these two men had actually met.

Third, supporters of pseudonymity contend that a Galilean like James could not have written the high-quality, literary style of Greek found in the letter. But some scholars have argued that the well-polished style of Greek is exaggerated and that nothing in the letter indicates an acquaintance with the higher styles of Greek literature. Moreover, Greek was a language widely used in Palestine, and someone like James would have had ample opportunity to become fluent in the language. The degree to which Jews in Palestine were conversant in Greek should not be underestimated. *I never realized that!*

Finally, and decisively in this author's opinion, the extant documentary evidence indicates that the early church did not accept pseudonymity.[4] When discovered, it was soundly rejected. In the light of the above, no good reason exists to resort to a hypothesis of pseudonymous authorship for the letter of James.

The best candidate for the author of the letter is James the Lord's brother. He was a younger half brother of Christ. He and other brothers and sisters were born to Mary and Joseph after the birth of Jesus. James was not a believer during the public ministry

---

[4] See Terry L. Wilder, "Pseudonymity and the New Testament," in *Interpreting the New Testament* (Nashville: Broadman & Holman, 2001), 296–335; and idem, *Pseudonymity, the New Testament and Deception* (Lanham, Md.: University Press of America, 2004).

of Jesus (cp. John 7:5), but he saw the risen Christ and became a follower (cp. 1 Cor 15:7).

Roman Catholic scholars who argue for the perpetual virginity of Mary believe that James the Lord's half brother is either Joseph's son by a previous marriage or Jesus' cousin. This view, however, has no scriptural support whatsoever. Joseph and Mary no doubt had children, but they did so *after* the virgin birth of Jesus, and no evidence exists to indicate that Joseph was formerly married. Further, the Greek word *adelphos* plainly means "brother" and not "cousin."

Date and Place of Writing

According to Josephus, James was martyred because of events that occurred in AD 62.[5] The letter, therefore, must be dated before this time. As is well-known, several other factors also indicate an early date.

First, James describes in his letter some economic disparities between the rich and poor (cp. 5:1–6) that no longer existed after the war between the Jews and the Romans (c. AD 66). Thus, the letter had to be written before that time.

Second, James describes leaders in the church as "teachers" and "elders" (3:1; 5:14) rather than as bishops and deacons. This points to a relatively simple and early church organization.

Third, he uses the term "synagogue" (*sunagōgē*) to describe the place where Christians meet (2:2). This factor would suggest an early date in that Jews who had become Christians may not yet have separated from the synagogue communities in which they lived and worshipped with unbelieving Jews. Indeed, the letter has a heavily Jewish flavor and a scarcity of distinctively Christian concepts, which garners further support along these lines.

Fourth, James does not mention in his letter doctrinal truths found in later NT letters—e.g., "the Church as the body of Christ, the oneness of believing Jews and Gentiles, and the apostasy."[6]

Fifth, the Judaizer controversy over the so-called necessity of circumcision for believers had apparently not yet taken place (c. AD 47–48; cp. Acts 15:1). All of these factors when taken together point to a relatively early date of writing—likely in the early

---

[5] Josephus, *Ant.* 20.9.1.
[6] As summarized by Robert G. Gromacki, *New Testament Survey* (Des Plaines, IL: Regular Baptist Press, 1979), 339.

to mid-40s; we would venture to say c. AD 45. If this date is correct, then James was the first NT book to be written. Though several places have been suggested—e.g., Alexandria, Antioch, Jerusalem, Rome,[7] etc.—the place of the letter's origin is unknown. If, however, we are correct in saying that James the Lord's half brother wrote the epistle, then he likely did so from Jerusalem during his tenure as leader of the church there. This choice is the most logical possibility because in the NT James is always located in that city after he becomes a believer in Jesus[8] (e.g., Gal 1:19; 2:9; Acts 15:13; etc.).

Wow!

Recipients, Occasion, Purpose

James wrote "to the 12 tribes in the Dispersion" (1:1). Some scholars think this designation refers to non-Christian Jews in the dispersion. However, the letter's many imperatives can only be directed toward believers in Christ. Others believe that James wrote to all Christians, both Jew and Gentile, in which case the term "twelve tribes" is viewed in the sense of "spiritual Israel." The most plausible view, however, is that James wrote to Jewish Christians living outside of Palestine. These Jewish believers in Jesus were scattered outside of their homeland likely due to early persecutions that had arisen in Jerusalem (cp. Acts 8:1–4; 11:19). Further support that the letter's readers were Jewish Christians is found in the fact that James never brings up issues like the assimilation of Gentiles into the church.

Finding a unifying genre, theme, or purpose for the book of James is difficult (see "Literary Style and Genre"). The latter fact has led some to say that the letter is simply a loose collection of homilies and messages dealing with various subjects.[9] The latter description would certainly explain the apparent lack of literary coherence in James, but it is one with which we are not entirely comfortable. Why? Because the authors of letters, like most documents, usually

---

[7] For example, Sophie Laws (*A Commentary on the Epistle of James* [HNTC; New York: Harper & Row, 1980], 25–26), finding similarities between James and various works of Roman origin (e.g., 1 Pet, *1 Clement, Hermas*), believes that James may have written his epistle from Rome.

[8] Gromacki, *NT Survey*, 339.

[9] Thomas D. Lea and David Alan Black, *The New Testament: Its Background and Message*, 2d ed. (Nashville: Broadman & Holman, 2003), 516–17. So also D. A. Carson and Douglas J. Moo, *An Introduction to the New Testament* (2d ed.; Grand Rapids: Zondervan, 2005), 630.

wrote—though not always—with a discernible unity[10] and flow of thought. Though more general and not as situational as most letters, perhaps James is more situational than we realize. One thing seems certain: "Testing . . . while perhaps not the topic of the letter, is nevertheless . . . the context in which it must be read."[11]

Arguably, James wrote this letter to Jewish Christians driven out of Jerusalem by persecution who were now facing trials within *diaspora* synagogue communities scattered outside of Palestine to which they belonged. At the time of the letter's writing, these Jewish Christians likely would not yet have separated their worship, etc., from other Jews in the synagogue communities who did not believe in Jesus as Messiah. Consequently, if the latter scenario is correct, then such a situation and difference in worldviews would inevitably cause problems to arise. James exhorted his readers to consistent Christian living and addressed trials that had arisen within these synagogue communities. He gave pastoral advice to *diaspora* Jewish believers who were retreating from the faith because of persecution.

Literary Style and Genre

James begins with the typical introduction found in most epistles (1:1): "from A (sender) to B (recipient)"; however, it does not end with the conclusion usually seen in letters. Instead, James concludes somewhat abruptly with advice on rescuing erring believers who stray from the truth (5:19–20). Further, the letter is not addressed to a specific church; it does not contain any greetings, personal references, travel plans, or prayer requests. Such traits have led some to maintain that James should be viewed as a "literary letter."[12] Literary letters take basically the same form as nonliterary letters but are more general in content and meant for a widely general readership. James may have meant for his letter to be read by believers who were scattered yet now settled in several communities, which may explain why his epistle seems so impersonal.

[10] E.g., see J. B. Adamson (*The Epistle of James* [NICNT; Grand Rapids: Eerdmans, 1954, 1976, 1995], 20) who claimed that James displays a "sustained unity." For a fuller discussion on the efforts of scholars to determine James's structure and theme, see Moo, *James*, 43–46.

[11] Moo, *James*, 44.

[12] Carson and Moo, *Introduction*, 629; P. H. Davids, "The Epistle of James in Modern Discussion," *ANRW* 2.25.5 (1988): 3628–29.

What kind of a letter is James? Scholarly opinion is varied. Some identify the letter as *paraenesis*.[13] S. K. Stowers notes that in paraenetic letters "the recipient's friend or moral superior . . . recommends habits of behavior and actions that conform to a certain model of character and attempts to turn the recipient away from contrasting negative models of character."[14] Most scholars categorize James as *wisdom* literature,[15] which typically consists of a proverbial style and a general moral tone. Unquestionably, elements of both paraenesis and wisdom are present in the letter of James, to one degree or another. Suffice it to say that James rebuked and exhorted his readers to encourage certain behavior (e.g., 2:1–4; 3:9–12; 4:1–6, etc.). He was keen on correcting their moral conduct regarding matters such as trials, hearing and doing God's word, showing favoritism, faith and works, matters of speech, and divisiveness.

Theological Themes

James discusses a variety of theological themes in his letter, a sampling of which is listed below.[16]

1. **God** (1:5; 2:11,19; 3:9; 4:5,6,10,11,15; 5:4,7,8,9,10,11,15). Moo rightly notes that James "frequently grounds his exhortations about appropriate Christian conduct in the nature of God," and that three characteristics of God's nature are especially important in the letter: "his oneness, his jealousy, and his grace."[17] James is clearly monotheistic. For example, the Jewish creed that "God is one" is considered by him an example of correct belief (2:19). He also mentions God's oneness as the reason all of the commandments that God has issued must be obeyed (2:11). Referring to God, James lets his readers know in no uncertain terms that "there is one lawgiver and judge" (4:12). In a debated verse (4:5), God's jealousy is highlighted as motivation for believers to abandon any

[13] Martin Dibelius (*A Commentary on the Epistle of James* [Hermeneia; Philadelphia: Fortress, 1976], 5–11) is the most well-known advocate of this viewpoint.

[14] S. K. Stowers, *Letter Writing in Greco-Roman Antiquity* (Philadelphia: Westminster, 1986), 96.

[15] E.g., W. R. Baker, *Personal Speech-Ethics in the Epistle of James* (WUNT 68; Tübingen: Mohr-Siebeck, 1995), 7–12; Ben Witherington III, *Jesus the Sage: The Pilgrimage of Wisdom* (Minneapolis: Fortress, 1994), 238–47.

[16] This list of theological themes was compiled from those found in the commentaries of P. H. Davids, *The Epistle of James* (NIGTC; Grand Rapids: Eerdmans, 1982), 34–57; and Moo, *James*, 27–43. For a fuller discussion, please see their respective works.

[17] Moo, *James*, 28.

worldly competition for their devotion to God; for He is a jealous God who will brook no rivals. And this God who places such high and pervasive demands upon the lives of believers "gives a greater grace" and "gives grace to the humble" (4:6) out of His grace.[18]

2. *Suffering and Trials* (1:2–4,12; 2:1–13,14–26; 4:1–10,17; 5:7,19–20). This major theme underlies much of James. We would go so far as to say that it is the thread which ties together the entire epistle. The communities that James addressed faced suffering for their faith (1:2–4). He encouraged them to endure these trials patiently so that they might come through them perfected, i.e., tried-and-true (*dokimos*, 1:12). Some believers in these communities no doubt found the testing difficult and were tempted to blame God for their situation. They were warned by James not to put God to the test (1:13). Some of the trials that the believers were experiencing were economic (5:1–6), and other areas of their lives in the community were also being impacted by trials and the temptation to do evil (cp. 2:1–13; 4:1–11). The proper response to these trials was to endure them patiently (5:7–20), as they emulated others who exercised patience and endurance in trying times: the farmer, Job, and the OT prophets.[19]

3. *Eschatology* (1:10–11,12; 2:5,12–13; 3:1; 4:10, 5:1–6,9,12,20). Eschatology also plays a major part in the letter. James frequently warns his readers of the Lord's coming and the judgment that accompanies it so that he might provoke them to embrace proper attitudes and behavior (1:10–11; 2:12–13; 3:1; 5:1–6,9,12). For James, the coming of the Lord is imminent; it is near (5:8); indeed, "the judge stands at the door" (5:9). And James reminds his readers of the reward they will receive when the Judge comes, if their lives are obedient and pleasing to him (1:12; 2:5; 4:10; 5:20).[20]

4. *Poverty and Wealth* (2:5; 5:1–6). In the letter of James, God clearly has a concern for the poor, the outcast, and the downtrodden. Such concern is consistent with the tenor of Scripture (cp. Ps 68:5; Deut 10:18). James asks, "Didn't God choose the poor in this world to be rich in faith and heirs of the kingdom that He has promised to those who love Him?" (2:5). In other words, God's choice of poor people for inclusion in His kingdom gives evidence

---

[18] This summary was derived from information found in ibid., 28–29.

[19] This summary was gleaned from the discussion in Peter H. Davids, *James*, NIBC (Peabody, MA: Hendrickson, 1993), 35–38.

[20] This summary was taken from information found in Moo, *James*, 29–30.

of His great concern for them. With James' statements on poverty and wealth, we need to understand that he is not embracing a liberation theology, but he does denounce the rich with their wealth and possessions when others are deprived of life's basic necessities.[21]

5. *Faith, Works, and Justification* (2:14–26). This theme is the one for which James is best known. He does not advocate justification in the sense of salvation by works. Rather he clearly teaches that *doing demonstrates belief.* To be "justified" (*dikaioō*) by works in this passage means that one's faith is "authenticated" or "confirmed" by his deeds, i.e., proven to be real by what he does. In other words, faith produces authenticating deeds.

6. *Wisdom* (1:5; 3:13–18). Wisdom is an important theme in the letter of James but is specifically referred to only twice. Believers need wisdom when they are dealing with trials for their faith (cp. 1:2–4), and are encouraged to ask God for it if they lack it (1:5). Here wisdom is not "Christian wisdom" per se but rather "insight into God's purposes and ways" which leads to spiritual maturity.[22] In 3:13–18, wisdom is also at the center of James' contrast between "earthly, sensual, demonic" wisdom (3:15) and "the wisdom from above," i.e., from heaven (3:17). Wisdom in 3:13–18 is tied to one's behavior (3:13). On the one hand, persons who possess earthly wisdom, which is characterized by jealousy and selfish ambition, are involved in chaos and evil practices (3:16); on the other hand, people who possess the wisdom from heaven (3:17) are humble, perform good deeds (3:13), and bear the fruit of righteousness in peace (3:18).[23]

7. *Prayer* (1:5,6–8,17; 4:3; 5:15,17–18). James describes God as one who answers the prayers of believers with a singularity of devotion and lack of reproach (1:5). He reminds his readers that a condition for having their requests granted is praying in faith without any double-minded doubting (1:6–8; 5:15). He describes God as one who bestows good gifts upon His people (1:17), presumably in response to their prayers. He further points out that self-gratification renders prayer to God ineffective (4:3). He also provides for his readers the example of Elijah, a persecuted, righteous man, as one who experienced great power in prayer (5:17–18).[24]

---

[21] This summary was gathered from the discussion in Moo, *James*, 35–36.

[22] Ibid., 34.

[23] The summary in this paragraph was derived from ibid., 33–34.

[24] Some of the summary in this paragraph was garnered from the discussion in ibid., 37.

Canonical Recognition

→means it's not known for being a book of rules

James was slow in being recognized as canonical.[25] The letter was disputed in the early church down until the early fourth century primarily because of its Jewish flavor. The book contains little in the way of distinctive Christian doctrine.

Eusebius, the early church historian, cited James frequently and recognized the book as canonical, but he classified it among the "disputed books" (*ta antilegomena*), thus indicating that not everyone accepted its authenticity (*Hist. eccl.* 3.25.3). Fathers in the Eastern part of the early church accepted the book before those in the Western church, which had its hesitations. It was not until Jerome fully accepted James that the Western church did as well. Carson and Moo ask whether such hesitations in the early church concerning James's canonical status should also give us pause about its canonicity. They reply, "No. They were probably the product of a combination of uncertainty about the identity of the author (which James?) and the relative neglect of the book. Being practical and Jewish in its flavor, James was not the sort of book that would have been widely used in the doctrinal controversies of the early church."[26]

As is well-known, the most famous opponent of James was Martin Luther. He called the book a "right strawy epistle." The great problem that Luther saw was that James presented a seeming discrepancy with Paul's doctrine of justification by faith alone apart from works of law (e.g., cp. Rom 3:28). Jas 2:24 says that "a man is justified by works and not by faith alone." However, this problem, though to some degree difficult to interpret, does not mean that James should be counted as noncanonical.

James speaks of "works" to refer to something a little different from what Paul does. Paul argues that the works of the Mosaic law, a Jewish legal righteousness, is neither required nor contributes to one's salvation. James contends that a genuine faith will produce fruit, i.e., certain righteous acts; if not, then one's salvation can be questioned as to its authenticity. Thus, no contradiction exists between James and Paul. They are simply speaking on two different aspects of the same thing. Even Martin Luther later came to

[25] For fuller discussions of NT canonicity see Bruce M. Metzger, *The Canon of the New Testament* (Oxford: Clarendon, 1987), and F. F. Bruce, *The Canon of Scripture* (Downer's Grove, IL: InterVarsity, 1988).

[26] Carson and Moo, *Introduction*, 631.

moderate his views on James. His criticisms of the letter developed from the perspectives created by the polemical situation in which he found himself.

Highlights of James

Introduction (1:1–21)

Greeting (1:1). The sender of this letter is James, who describes himself as a "slave" (1:1a). The recipients of this letter are the 12 tribes in the *diaspora* (1:1b). The *diaspora* is a "scattering" caused by opposition and persecution.

God uses trials and persecutions for our faith in Christ to make us complete; they do not mean that we lack God's blessing (1:2–15). The message of 1:2–4 is that believers are to welcome various "trials" as from the Lord, which actually help to bring us to Christian maturity (cp. Rom 5:3–5; Heb 12:3–15). The term *trials* refers to testing and pressures for one's faith in Christ and does not likely mean trials in general (1:2). The word "patience" found in some translations, means "endurance" or "steadfastness."

The word "mature" does not mean sinlessly perfect (1:3). James ironically admonishes his readers to take joyful and special note of the benefit of persecutions and trials in their lives. When you pass through them, you recognize their value in producing endurance, i.e., "staying power" (1:2–3). Endurance is an essential quality that characterizes those who are "lacking nothing," i.e., those who are blessed by God (1:4). According to Jewish thought, God rewards the righteous and punishes the wicked. The latter idea can be found throughout the OT and especially in the book of Job. Thus, to go through trials and to be "lacking" indicates God's rejection and His refusal to bless.

Worldly wisdom and human ingenuity are inadequate for bearing up under trials of one's faith. The believer needs *divine* wisdom, i.e., spiritual insight (cp. Phil 1:9–10) into God's ways and purposes, which is abundantly available from God (primarily through his Word, cp. Jas 1:22–25) to those who ask in full assurance and believe that he will gladly and unhesitatingly answer. That is to say, if Christians lack wisdom to understand that God uses trials and persecutions to make them "complete," he will grant such understanding to those who ask for it (1:5–11). God generously grants such insight to believers who lack wisdom in the midst of their trials so that they may recognize that bearing up under trials brings them to completion (1:5).

This wisdom, however, does not come to the "unstable" (1:6–8). Those who are "unstable" (*akatastatos*) believe that trials in their lives indicate that God has rejected them and consequently refuses to bless. Such persons doubt God; their prayers are ineffective, and they are "doubting" or "double-minded" (*dipsuchos*) in their thinking (1:6–8).

James elucidates "wisdom" in a biting, ironic contrast. "Wisdom" entails knowing one's ultimate spiritual position (1:9–10a). On the one hand, the "humiliated brother" (*ho adelphos ho tapeinos*) is to take great confidence in his future exaltation; i.e., the persecuted believer is to rejoice in the eternal riches which are his because of his position "in Christ." The rich opponent, on the other hand, can only expect humiliation (1:9–10) and judgment (cp. 5:1–6).[27] James illustrates the fleeting position of the rich opponent and compares it to "flowering grass." In other words, the rich opponent's future destiny is like a withered, lifeless plant whose flower, separated from its root or source, "withers" (1:10b–11a; cp. 5:1–6). He will wither away also in his pursuit of earthly riches which are fleeting and deceptive (cp. Mark 4:19; 1 Pet 1:24).

Those who bear up under trials, however, are "blessed" (*makarios*); they receive God's approval and are highly favored. They will receive the blessing of God, viz., the "crown" which is (eternal) life (1:12). The latter belief militates against a common Jewish misconception that those whom God has blessed with wealth are "blessed" and have received divine favor (cp. Mark 10:23–26). James says that God ultimately blesses those who endure trials (1:12). However, it should be noted that while the Lord allows His people to be tested, He never tempts them to sin (1:13–15). When one succumbs and commits evil (as he might be tempted to do in

---

[27] The identity of the poor and the rich in James is considered a *crux interpretum* for the letter (esp. 1:9–11). Half of NT scholars believe that the poor and the rich are believers and unbelievers, respectively, while the other half holds that they are poor and rich Christians. It is not absolutely necessary here to decide who these groups are because the rich oppressors in this context are clearly persecuting the poor. Though the grammar of 1:9–11 at first look seems to favor the poor-and-rich-Christian view, the present writer, due to the overall context of the letter, holds that the poor and rich in James seem to be believers and unbelievers, respectively. The latter interpretation requires translating *tapeinos* as "humiliated" rather than "humble" or "poor."

retaliation for trials on account of his faith) he must realize that God did not desire that reaction—neither is He the cause of it. Rather, such sin arises from our own inward Adamic natures, and ultimately, without forgiveness, leads to death.

Exhortations introducing the letter body (1:16–21). James first introduces the body of his letter with an exhortation to his readers that they not be led astray, i.e., deceived, by yielding to trials and persecution (1:16). God does not intend evil toward us. He is the Creator and Sustainer of the heavenly bodies which give varying shades of light, unlike God who never changes (1:17). And God by His good will not only regularly bestows upon believers that which is good ("every generous act and every perfect gift is from above"), but He also brought them to new life through the message of truth, the gospel (cp. Eph 1:13; 1 Pet 1:23). The believers of James' day were the first of a long line of such believers (1:16–18).

James' second exhortation to his readers in this section is that they "be quick to hear, slow to speak, and slow to anger" (1:19). These commands introduce the key themes and content of the letter body. James reasons that man's anger does not accomplish the righteousness of God (1:20), i.e., it does not bring about "the righteous life that God desires" (NIV), and thus they are to receive the word in humility, ridding themselves of moral filth and excess (1:21).

Be Quick to Hear, Slow to Speak, and Slow to Anger (1:22–4:17)

James exhorts his readers, who were brought forth by the word of truth (1:18) and have received the word ("implanted word," *emphutos logos*) in humility (1:21), to be quick to hear, slow to speak, and slow to anger (1:22–4:12).

Be quick to hear (1:22–2:26). James first urges his readers to be quick to "hear" the word, i.e., to "do" the word (1:22–2:26). Truly "hearing" the word means that one "practices" the word (1:22–27) and does not show favoritism (2:1–13). To be sure, for James "doing" demonstrates "believing" (2:14–26). What one *believes* is what he *does*. And God is pleased by obedience to His word; mere lip service simply will not please Him.

1. Practice the word (1:22–27). James exhorts his readers to practice the word (1:22). The "word" is the "law of freedom," which is probably the specific command to "love your neighbor" (cp. 2:12–13). James provides a negative example of one who does not remember to practice the word (1:23–24). Then he gives a positive example of one who has the liberty to become an effectual "doer" of the word with respect to loving his neighbor (1:25). James next makes an application of the "perfect law" (1:26–27). "Pure religion" is practiced by one who bridles the tongue against a neighbor (1:26). "Pure and undefiled religion" shows concern for neighbors, especially orphans and widows (1:27).

2. *Do not show favoritism (2:1–13).* James also exhorts his readers not to show favoritism (2:1–13). The primary admonition he issues here is for them not to judge others on the basis of perceived blessings bestowed, as do the Jewish legalists (2:1). To illustrate, James provides a hypothetical example of discriminatory behavior (2:2–4). This illustration of discrimination seems to take place in the judicial setting (*beth-din*) of the "synagogue."[28] The term "meeting" or "assembly," found in many translations, is probably better translated from the Greek as "synagogue" (*sunagōgē*, 2:2). James explains what the appropriate verdict with God is concerning their display of distinctions and favoritism toward the rich. He says (2:4) that they thus become judges with evil thoughts, i.e., this is sinful.

He next explains why showing favoritism is wrong (2:5–13). First, showing favoritism contradicts God's own attitude demonstrated in His gracious election (2:5–6a). Second, showing favoritism does not make sense because the rich and religious opposition use their wealth to secure favorable judgments against Jewish Christians (2:6b–7). Indeed, they blaspheme "the noble name that you bear" (i.e., the Lord Jesus Christ; cp. 2:1). Third, showing favoritism violates the law of love (2:8–13). When you violate the law of love, it identifies you as breaking the command to "love your neighbor as yourself" (2:8–9; cp. Lev 19:18). Leviticus 19:18 admonished Israelites to love their neighbors as themselves (2:8) regardless of "status." And James reminds his readers that this commandment is as important as any other, and the breach of only one commandment brings one under divine judgment as though he had broken them all (2:10–11; cp. Gal 3:10; Deut 27:26).

James demonstrates that people who show favoritism are lawbreakers because they break the whole block of laws (2:10–11).

---

[28] E.g., see R. B. Ward, "Partiality in the Assembly: James 2:2–4," *HTR* 62 (1969): 87–97.

The law is an indivisible unity (2:11): God, who gave one law, indeed gave them all. James then urges his readers to show mercy in their dealings with others as those who will be vindicated at God's court with respect to the "law of freedom" (2:12–13; cp. Matt 5:7). If they show no mercy, they in turn will receive no mercy.

The "perfect law of freedom" (1:25; 2:12), and the "royal law" (2:8) do not refer to the Mosaic law (as though Christians were under that law today, cp. Rom 7:6; Gal 3:17–4:7). Rather, the principle of impartial love for fellow believers, while found in the law (Lev 19:18), was amplified and expanded by Jesus (cp. Luke 10:29–37, the "good" Samaritan), and is thus called the "royal law" because it was given by the King himself. In a real sense this Torah command finds its fulfillment in Christ.

The basic and obvious thrust of this passage is that there is absolutely no place in the church of Jesus Christ for discrimination. This teaching includes all types of discrimination: racial, economic, political, etc.

3. Doing demonstrates belief (2:14–26). James further makes clear that "doing" demonstrates "believing" (2:14–26). He explains that faith without works cannot save (2:14). He asks, "What good is it, my brothers, if someone says he has faith, but does not have works? Can his faith save him?" The answer is, "No." In other words, a genuine, saving faith is a faith that will produce good works—but *after* salvation. To illustrate the necessity of deeds, James provides a hypothetical example of a fellow believer who is in need of food and clothing and yet is offered only pious words by someone who is in a position to help (2:15–16). He concludes the latter illustration with the statement that faith without works is dead (2:17).

James next anticipates an objector who maintains that faith and works can be separated (2:18a). He responds that faith can only be shown by authenticating actions (2:18b–19), and he points out that even demons "believe," but they do not display the validating deeds (2:19). Verse 19 especially reminds us that assent simply to a theological proposition does not save. Demons believe that there is only one true God[29] and that Jesus Christ is His Son (cp. Luke 4:41), but they obviously are not saved. Rather, they "shudder" at the prospect of divine judgment.

---

[29] This statement likely could be a reference to the *shema* in Deut 6:4.

James again addresses the anticipated objector (2:20–26). He calls for him to recognize that "faith without works is useless" (2:20). To illustrate this principle, he points to the examples of Abraham and Rahab. He makes clear that Abraham was considered righteous, but he was confirmed by works (2:21). His willingness to sacrifice Isaac demonstrated the validity of the faith which saved him. James further explains Abraham's faith and his accompanying deeds (2:22–23) and emphasizes that justification requires faith demonstrated by works (2:24). James points out that Rahab was also considered righteous, but she too was confirmed by her deeds (2:25). Her willingness to risk her life (and that of her family) to protect Israel's scouts in Jericho (cp. Josh 2) demonstrated the validity of the faith which saved her. James then reiterates the principle that "faith without works is dead" (2:26).

In the light of the above, this passage clearly does not teach salvation by works, as some have contended, thus contradicting Paul in Romans 3:28. Paul and James address two different aspects of salvation. Paul, on the one hand, teaches in Romans that works do not contribute to salvation; i.e., they play no part in declaring one righteous before God. James, on the other hand, teaches that a saving faith must produce authenticating works. The latter emphasis by James is not so unlike Paul elsewhere where he teaches that works are the *result* of salvation (cp. Eph 2:10).

Be slow to speak (3:1–12). James next exhorts his readers, as those who have humbly received the word (cp. 1:21), to be slow to speak (3:1–12). He specifically reminds prospective teachers about the peculiar difficulty of not controlling the tongue; they will incur a stricter judgment (3:1).

Control of speech is a quality especially required in teachers (3:1–12). James gives the reason his readers should not rush to be teachers (3:2): "For we all stumble in many ways" (3:2a), and mistakes of the tongue are the most difficult to control. Only a "mature" person can control his tongue and thus his whole body (3:2b,c). Therefore, only mature Christians should attempt to teach.

James then provides three examples of small instruments which have great power, all of which illustrate the tongue's power (3:3–5)—first, a bit in a horse's mouth (3:3); second, a "rudder" of a ship (3:4); third, a small fire (e.g., a small abandoned campfire in a forest area) which can quickly start a large forest fire (3:5c). The application of these illustrations is that the tongue, though small, affects the entire body (3:5a–b,6). Indeed, when under the control of our sinful nature and empowered by satanic influence, it not only can control our whole body but also influence our entire human existence (3:6).

James issues another reminder to his readers that the tongue is impossible to bring completely under control (3:7–8). Though man has tamed virtually every kind of animal (3:7), he has not succeeded in taming his own poisonous tongue (3:8). James next provides an illustration concerning the tongue's inconsistency, viz., its "double–tonguedness." What an anomaly! The tongue praises God but curses men made in the image of God (3:9–10a). James reminds his readers that they ought not to be double tongued (3:10b), and he provides them with three illustrations which show that a pure heart is incompatible with inconsistent, double-tongued speech—a pure fountain, fig/fruit trees, and salt water (3:11–12). Nature itself is more consistent than double-tongued speech. Why? Because sweet and bitter water do not flow from the same spring (3:11); fig trees do not bear olives; vines do not bear figs (3:12); a salt water spring does not yield fresh water (3:12).

Be slow to anger (3:13–4:17). James now exhorts his readers (primarily still to potential teachers [3:1] and to those who have received the word in humility [cp. 1:21]) to be slow to anger (3:13–5:6).

1. True wisdom (3:13–18). As he instructs them to do so, James advises his readers of the "wisdom from above" which brings peace as contrasted with the "wisdom from the earth" which brings chaos and discord (3:13–18). The teacher (described in this passage as a "wise man," endued with "expert knowledge" Gk. *epistēmōn*) has access to two differing kinds of wisdom. He invites those who think that they are wise to demonstrate wisdom by deeds done in humility (3:13). He warns people who have jealousy and selfish ambition not to boast about wisdom (3:14). He then concedes to those he has warned that they have wisdom but that it is the earthly kind and not from above (3:15–16). James describes characteristics of the wisdom from above which produces a unifying peace (3:17–18). Hopefully, his readers will appropriate the "wisdom from above" (3:17), i.e., God's wisdom, which is "pure" (free from defilement), "peace-loving" (promotes peace between men), "gentle" (considerate), "easy to be entreated" ("open to reason," RSV), "full of mercy and good fruits" (exhibiting good works toward the needy and suffering), "without favoritism" (unbiased, cp. 2:4), and "without hypocrisy" (genuine, no facade).

The alternative wisdom, which produces bitter envy and strife (3:14), is not from above (3:15) but is "earthly" (arising from earth bound motives and instincts), "sensual" (unspiritual, cp. Jude 19), and "demonic" (demon-like, rather than Godlike). James summarizes this section in verse 18. In his Sermon on the Mount Jesus said, "By their fruits you shall know them" (Matt 7:20 NKJV). James says that the "harvest" or "fruit" of righteousness "is sown in peace by those who make peace," i.e., the teacher (primarily, but others by secondary application) who teaches divine wisdom will promote peace and well-being—not confusion and dissension. This, however, does not mean "peace" at any price (cp. Gal 1:6–9; 2:11; 5:12; Titus 1:13; 2 John 9–11; etc.).

2. *Human passions (4:1–10).* James then provides an overview of the havoc caused when worldly wisdom and its self-gratification dominates the corporate body of Christ (4:1–10). First, he says that self-gratification is the cause of wars and fighting (4:1–2). Second, he states that self-gratification hinders prayer (4:3). Third, he declares that self-gratification is abhorrent to God (4:4–6). Fourth, as a remedy, he says that self-gratification demands repentance (4:7–10). "Wars and the fights" (4:1) are in contrast to the peace of 3:18. Verses 1–12 deal primarily with the great problem of fighting and divisions among Christians, thus endangering the testimony and the existence of a local church. Christians today face no greater problem. But what is the cause of this problem? James says that it arises from our basic Adamic drive for self-gratification. "Pleasures" (4:1,3) is from the Greek word *hēdonē*, from which we derive the philosophical term "hedonism," meaning the view which regards pleasure as the chief goal of life. Thus, it is pure selfishness, seeking to satisfy one's own desires to the exclusion of others' interests, which produces conflicts and divisions.

Verse 2 probably should be rendered, "You desire and do not have; so you kill. And you covet and cannot obtain; so you fight and wage war." Hostility against fellow Christians arises from our inability to get our own way. Unfortunately, most believers can document church situations they have experienced along these lines. How do believers go about getting what they want legitimately? Verses 2b–3 provide the answer. Much of our lack stems from our failure to ask God for it. As believers look back on their lives from

[handwritten margin note: I've never thought of it that way!]

eternity, they will be astonished at what God would have done—if they had simply asked Him to do it (e.g., Matt 21:22). However, asking does not guarantee an answer (4:3) unless it is in God's will (cp. 1 John 5:14–15; John 15:7).

"Covet" in verse 2 is not the same word that is found in verse 1. Here the word is *epithumeō*, simply meaning "desire." "Adulterers" (4:4) does not occur in some of the oldest manuscripts of the NT and is thus of doubtful validity. "Adulteress," however, is sufficient to include males and females, arising from OT references to Israel as the wife of Jehovah (cp. Isa 54:5; Jer 3:20; Ezk 16:23; Hos 9:1, etc.). "World" (*kosmos*) is the evil world system (cp. 1 John 2:15–17). Those who love the "world" thus become guilty of spiritual "adultery," having betrayed their relationship to God. Verses 5–10 remind us that the indwelling Holy Spirit is jealous (cp. Exod 20:5, the second commandment) of any conflicting allegiance which believers exhibit (cp. also Exod 34:14; Deut 32:16; Zech 3:2). It is difficult to live a godly life in a wicked world, but God's continuing grace (4:6) is available to those who humbly (4:6b,9–10) submit themselves to God (4:7), resist the devil (4:7), and confess and forsake their sins (4:8).

3. *Evil speaking (4:11–12).* Finally, James gives a prohibition against slanderous, judgmental speech directed against a brother (4:11–12). Verses 11 and 12 seem to deal with the same problem that Paul addressed in Romans 14 (cp. esp. vv. 10 and 13), and which Jesus dealt with in Matt 7:1–5, i.e., hypocritically criticizing a brother for not measuring up to our standard (not God's). God is our Judge, and we are not to usurp his role. Such legalism breeds only criticism and divisions in the church.

4. *Arrogant planning which ignores God (4:13–17).* Unfortunately, those who continue to gratify self for material profit do so without considering the will of God (4:13–17).[30] James says, "Come now."[31] The teaching in this passage is obvious and self-explanatory. It is not wrong to plan ahead. It is wrong, however, for someone to be presumptuous, ignoring (1) his very limited knowledge, especially of future events, and (2) his finiteness, i.e., the extreme brevity of life. Thus, all future plans must be, "If the Lord wills." Anything

---

[30] R. W. Wall, "James," in *DLNT*, 559.

[31] Some question exists here as to whether this text should go with 4:1–12 and thus addressing those who gratify themselves without considering the will of God, or if it should be viewed with 5:1–6, addressing rich wicked businessmen who are outside of the believers' fellowship and do not include God in their plans.

else is sheer arrogance, and such arrogance is sin, especially for the Christian, who should know better.

A Prophetic Warning to the Wicked Rich in View of the Judge's Coming (5:1–6)

James issues a prophetic warning to the rich opposition in view of the Judge's coming (5:1–6). He introduces this warning in the manner of the OT prophets (5:1). The rich men in this passage are not pictured as Christians. They are like the "rich fool" of Luke 12:16–21. The warnings, however, are applicable to all who have wealth. The Bible does not condemn the rich because they are rich but rather because they have failed in their stewardship of the resources which God has allowed them to accumulate. They are not represented here as repentant but as suffering at the time of God's judgment.

James then conveys that abundant testimony will bring legal denunciations against the rich opposition in the future age (5:2–6). The first accusation is that the rich have used wealth for their own selfish purposes, believing that God has blessed them (5:2–3). "Moth-eaten" (5:2) and "corroded" (5:3) are all in the perfect tense in Greek, indicating past action with results continuing to the present. Thus they graphically describe the worthlessness of wealth in the eternal scheme of things. Wealth is to be used for good—not hoarded for selfish purposes. James says that the wealth of the rich will act as witnesses and testify against them (5:2–3b). He next issues an ironic statement of judgment in which he says that with their hoarding of wealth they are storing up judgment in respect to the last days (5:3c).

The second accusation against the rich is that they have cheated workers and lived wantonly (5:4–5a). The cries of their workers act as witnesses against them (5:4). The fraudulent treatment of the laboring man (5:4, cp. Deut 24:14–15), the extravagant, profligate lifestyle of the godless rich (5:5), and the ungodly manipulation of the judicial system to bring about false convictions of the poor who cannot adequately defend themselves (5:6) are particularly objectionable to the "Lord of Hosts (armies)."

The third and climactic accusation against the rich opposition is that they have done violence to "the righteous man" (5:6). In other words, the wicked rich have apparently even killed believers.

Concluding Exhortations (5:7-20)

Believers should persevere under trial until Christ the Judge returns (5:7–18). In the previous verses (5:1–6), James warns the wicked rich who were mistreating and persecuting the poor. He next calls for believers to persevere under trial in view of the Judge's coming (5:7–18).[32] He summarily exhorts them to be patient until the coming of the Lord (5:7a), who is called the judge (cp. 5:9). When Christ returns, all that is wrong and inequitable will be made right. As an example of patience, James points to the Palestinian farmer who is entirely dependent upon the early (October-November) and latter (April-May) rain (5:7); he patiently waits in hard times until the consummation of the harvest (5:7b–c).

James then reiterates his exhortation for believers to endure patiently because the Lord is near (5:8). He specifically exhorts these Christians not to turn on one another while enduring times of hardship, for the Judge is near (5:9). Grumbling and sniping at one another is likely to occur when under pressure and facing persecution. James then points to the Old Testament prophets as another example of patience; they patiently endured affliction and persecution (5:10, cp. Matt 5:11–12).

After stating earlier that those who persevere under trials are considered blessed (5:11a), James also cites the example of Job, who endured difficult circumstances and proved that no link exists between spirituality and prosperity (5:11b–c). The "outcome from the Lord" (5:11) means "the end of the matter which God brought about," i.e., Job's ultimate vindication. Further, James solemnly warns believers not to use oaths as a means to escape suffering for the faith so that they will not fall under condemnation (5:12). This verse does not prohibit the modern customary "swearing-in" sequence in court but rather using oaths flippantly to guarantee the truth of their statements.[33]

---

[32] See Terry L. Wilder, "A Call to Endure Persecution Patiently: A Fresh Look at James 5:7–20 in Context," *MJT* 1.1–2 (Spring 2003): 64–70.

[33] James's use of the phrase "above all" (*pro pantōn*) in verse 12 is somewhat problematic if the explanation not to use oaths flippantly to guarantee the truth of their statements is left without further clarification. Unless one interprets *pro pantōn* as hyperbole or some other sort of literary device, as many do, then James would appear to be saying that, above everything else in the Christian life, believers are to watch taking oaths. This understanding cannot be the correct one. Keeping in mind the letter's context at this point, we need to ask, "Why does James prohibit the taking of oaths?" *Answer:* When asked whether they are Christians by those who would persecute them, James's readers are instructed not to swear to God, to heaven, or to earth, using oaths frivolously to support the truth of their claims—presumably, negative ones

In the next six verses James advocates prayer as the remedy in suffering and trials (5:13–18). If believers are suffering affliction or misfortune because of the gospel, then they should pray (5:13a–b). If they are cheerful (i.e., have peace of mind in the midst of trouble), then those persons should respond by singing praises because they are not undergoing trials and persecution for their faith (5:13c). Believers who are feeble and sick because of trials for their faith are encouraged to call for prayer by the elders (5:14–15).

The major difficulty, of course, with the latter passage involves the anointing with oil and the promise of healing (5:14–16). Several interpretations are suggested: (1) the promise is a *carte blanche* one to sick Christians; (2) the promise is made to those Christians whose sickness is the specific result of sin; (3) the promise suggests that believers pray for the sick and get them the best medical help available (the oil); (4) this promise applies only to those sick Christians "whom God lays upon our hearts specifically" (the prayer of faith); (5) the promise involves the apostolic gift of healing, arguably no longer extant. Given the letter's context, however, this passage seems rather to refer specifically to prayer by the elders of the church for those who are "weak, without strength, or disabled, due to persecution" by the wicked rich.[34] Anointing with oil symbolizes the "setting apart" of the weak for God's care. The prayer for healing must be "if God wills," but when He does so will, nothing is impossible (5:16b–18).

James also instructs the corporate body of believers to engage in mutual prayer and to confess their sins in the midst of trials.[35]

---

like, "No, I am not a believer in Christ." Rather, when interrogated about their faith, they are simply and sincerely to say "yes" or "no" in response (5:12). The latter understanding, which then acts as a climax to James's statement on endurance in verse 11, then makes good sense of the problematic phrase "above all" that he uses as an initial phrase in verse 12.

[34] This nuance is certainly conceivable because the word is used that way elsewhere in the NT. For example, Paul uses the stative verb *astheneō* and its cognate noun *astheneia* metaphorically when he speaks of his persecution as an apostle (2 Cor 11:21,29–30; cp. Heb 4:15; Judg 6:6,15—LXX). Though the latter terms do often refer to physical sickness in the Gospels (e.g. Matt 8:17; 25:39; Mark 6:56; Luke 4:40; 5:15; John 4:46; 5:5; etc.), Paul uses them in 2 Cor 11 to refer to the physical and mental discomfort he has endured while preaching the gospel. For the apostle, weakness is physical discomfort due to persecution, imprisonments, beatings, stonings, dangerous travels, robberies, encounters with natural disasters, life without physical necessities, and distress over concern for the churches (2 Cor 11:23–29).

[35] To what kind of sins might James be referring? Interestingly, the reference to "sins" (*harmatia*) in verse 15 has a lexical connection to the "sinner" (*harmartōlos*) mentioned in verse 20. James seems to have in mind in verse 15 the sin of "straying away from the truth" that he addresses later in verses 19 and 20. If so, James would be saying in 5:15c that if the person has strayed from the truth while getting hammered for the faith, then those sins can be forgiven by God, provided he repents and returns. James issues the promise in 5:15 that the "prayer of

Indeed, the prayers of the persecuted "righteous" accomplish much (5:16). James then provides the example of Elijah, who experienced a similarity in feelings as well as in circumstances (5:17–18); that is to say, like James's readers, Elijah was a persecuted, righteous man who experienced power in prayer.[36]

Believers should rescue others who depart from the faith (5:19–20). James encourages believers to act as instruments in keeping straying persons from eternal death (5:19–20). That is to say, if a Christian brother strays from the truth, those who have not defected should attempt to bring the erring brother back. If a community member departs from the faith (in an attempt to escape persecution) and is brought back by a fellow believer (5:19), then the sinner will procure forgiveness, and his soul will be saved from death (5:20).

 Study Outline of James

I. Introduction (1:1–21)
- A. Greeting (1:1)
- B. God Uses Trials and Persecutions for Our Faith to Make Us Complete (1:2–15)
- C. Exhortations Introducing the Letter Body (1:16–21)

II. Letter Body: Be Quick to Hear, Slow to Speak, and Slow to Anger (1:22–4:17)
- A. Be Quick to Hear (1:22–2:26)
  1. Practice the Word (1:22–27)
  2. Do not show favoritism (2:1–13)
  3. Doing demonstrates belief (2:14–26)
- B. Be Slow to Speak (3:1–12)
  1. Control of speech: especially required in teachers (3:1–12)

---

faith" (cp. 1:6) by the elders will deliver or restore (*sōzō*) the person who is wasting away or fatigued (*kamnō*); further, the Lord will raise up the weak person. That is to say, God uses the prayer offered by faith to bring results: the person who is weak due to persecution is delivered from his quagmire and God restores him; he is able to stand again (cp. Ps 23, esp. vv. 4–6).

[36] Elijah is just one example of the "persecuted righteous." This is an extremely important term. Cp. the persecuted righteous in Matthew's Gospel (e.g., Matt 5:45; 23:35). Matthew 23 (v. 35) especially demonstrates the point. In that passage Jesus denounces the hypocrisy of the scribes and the Pharisees, pronounces woes on them, and says that they have disregarded and indeed will kill God's true messengers, with the result that the blood of the "righteous" will be upon them. I am grateful to Alan Tomlinson, my NT colleague, for pointing out this nuance of the term to me.

C. Be Slow to Anger (3:13–4:17)
   1. True wisdom (3:13–18)
   2. Human passions (4:1–10)
   3. Evil speaking (4:11–12)
   4. Arrogant planning that ignores God (4:13–17)
III. A Prophetic Warning to the Wicked Rich in View of the Judge's Coming (5:1–6)
IV. Concluding Exhortations (5:7–20)
   A. Believers Should Persevere Under Trial until Christ the Judge Returns (5:7–18)
   B. Believers Should Rescue Others Who Depart from the Faith (5:19–20)

Selected Bibliography

Commentaries Based on the Greek Text

Davids, Peter H. *The Epistle of James.* NIGTC. Grand Rapids: Eerdmans, 1982.

Martin, R. P. *James.* WBC. Waco, TX: Word, 1988.

Ropes, James Hardy. *A Critical and Exegetical Commentary on the Epistle of St. James.* ICC. Edinburgh: T. & T. Clark, 1916.

Commentaries Based on the English Text

Adamson, J. B. *The Epistle of James.* NICNT. Grand Rapids: Eerdmans, 1954, 1976, 1995.

Bray, Gerald Lewis, and Thomas C. Oden, eds. *James, 1–2 Peter, 1–3 John, Jude.* ACCS. Downer's Grove, IL: InterVarsity, 2000.

Davids, Peter H. *James.* NIBC. Peabody, MA: Hendrickson, 1993.

Dibelius, Martin. *A Commentary on the Epistle of James.* Hermeneia. Rev. H. Greeven. Philadelphia: Fortress, 1976.

Johnson, Luke Timothy. *The Letter of James.* AB. Garden City, NY: Doubleday, 1995.

_____. *The Letter of James.* NIB. Nashville: Abingdon Press, 2000.

Kistemaker, Simon. *Exposition of the Epistle of James and the Epistles of John.* NTC. Grand Rapids: Baker, 1986.

Laws, Sophie. *A Commentary on the Epistle of James*. HNTC/BNTC. New York: Harper & Row, 1980; Peabody, MA: Hendrickson, 1993.

Moo, D. J. *James*. TNTC. Grand Rapids: Eerdmans, 1987.

_____. *The Letter of James*. PNTC. Grand Rapids: Eerdmans, 2000.

Motyer, J. A. *The Message of James: The Tests of Faith*. BST. Downers Grove, IL: InterVarsity, 1988.

Nystrom, David. *James*. NIVAC. Grand Rapids: Zondervan, 1997.

Perkins, Pheme. *1 and 2 Peter, James and Jude*. IBC. Louisville: Westminster, 1995.

Reicke, Bo. *The Epistles of James, Peter, and Jude*. AB. Garden City, NY: Doubleday, 1964.

Richardson, Kurt. *James*. NAC. Nashville: Broadman & Holman, 1997.

Sleeper, C. Freeman, *James*. ANTC. Nashville: Abingdon Press, 1998.

Stulac, G. M. *James*. IVPNTC. Downers Grove, IL: InterVarsity, 1993.

Townsend, Michael. *The Epistle of James*. EC. London: Epworth, 1997.

Wall, R. W. *The Community of the Wise: The Book of James*. NTC. Harrisburg, PA: Trinity, 1997.

Foreign Language Commentaries

Burchard, Christoph. *Der Jakobusbrief*. HNT 15/1. Tübingen: Mohr-Siebeck, 2000.

Frankenmöller, *Der Brief des Jakobus*. Gütersloh: Gütersloher, 1994.

Mussner, Franz. *Der Jakobusbrief*. HTKNT. Freiburg: Herder, 1981.

Studies

Baker, W. R. *Personal Speech-Ethics in the Epistle of James*. WUNT 68. Tübingen: Mohr-Siebeck, 1995.

Bauckham, Richard. *James: Wisdom of James, Disciple of Jesus the Sage*. London: Routledge, 1999.

Chester, A. and R. P. Martin. *The Theology of the Letters of James, Peter, and Jude*. NTT. Cambridge: Cambridge University Press, 1994.

Edgar, David Hutchinson. *Has God Not Chosen the Poor? The Social Setting of the Epistle of James.* JSNTSup 206. Sheffield: Sheffield Academic Press, 2001.

Penner, Todd C. *The Epistle of James and Eschatology: Re-Reading an Ancient Christian Letter.* Sheffield: Sheffield Academic Press, 1996.

Wachob, Wesley Hiram. *The Voice of Jesus in the Social Rhetoric of James.* Cambridge: Cambridge University Press, 2000.

Wall, R. W. "James, Letter of." In *DLNT*, 545–61.

Three

FIRST PETER

Temporary Residents in This World

F ew documents of the NT challenge the reader to integrate faith in all of life as does 1 Peter. Here we find Christian proclamation and *paraenesis* (moral exhortation), theology and ethics, as wholly unified. The significance of 1 Peter, as one writer observes, is indeed disproportionate to its size.[1] First Peter is a message of hope and consolation that is contextualized within social and cultural challenges. It is addressed to Christians who must live faithfully and responsibly in a pagan cultural climate; fleeing the world is not a Christian option. For this reason 1 Peter retains abiding relevance for the Christian community of any age.

Three major areas of inquiry have characterized critical study of 1 Peter over the last 50 years—authorship, purpose, and literary form. More recent Petrine scholarship has concerned itself both with literary structure and sociological perspectives. A significant amount of this work has questioned, when not outright rejected, the literary integrity of the epistle. Notwithstanding the assessments of critical scholars such as Stephen Neill and John H. Elliott—1 Peter represents the "storm center" and "exegetical stepchild" of NT studies[2]—might seem somewhat extreme, the sheer

---

Unless otherwise indicated, all Scripture quotations in this chapter are from the Holman Christian Standard Bible (HCSB).

[1] E. Waltner (with J. D. Charles), *1–2 Peter, Jude* (BCBC; Scottdale/ Waterloo: Herald, 1999), 17.

[2] S. Neill, *The Interpretation of the New Testament 1861–1961* (London: Oxford University Press, 1964), 343, and J.H. Elliott, "The Rehabilitation of an Exegetical Step-Child: 1 Peter in Recent Research," *JBL* 5 (1976): 243–54.

volume of recent commentary on 1 Peter has presented us with fresh perspectives on the letter that are most welcome.[3]

At the very least, much of the recent work in 1 Peter has heightened our appreciation for the deft use of tradition material by the writer that informs his literary-rhetorical strategy and the epistle's literary unity.[4] The fact that wildly divergent methods have been applied to the letter by NT scholarship in a quest to discern a hermeneutical key, leading some to conclude that the study of 1 Peter is at a crossroads, is not to relegate the letter to the status of an enigma.[5]

Petrine scholarship over the last 50 years has been characterized by its questioning of the letter's authenticity based on several factors: the writer's linguistic sophistication, the role of "Silvanus," the matter of dating relative to the degree of persecution on display in the letter, and the apostle's assumed relationship with churches in Asia Minor. The broader assumption that 1 Peter is pseudonymous (see also "Authorship") requires our consideration. Several theories on authorship are to be identified.

[3] For a bibliography of 1 Peter scholarship up to c. 1982, see D. Sylva, "A 1 Peter Bibliography," *JETS* (1982): 75–89, reproduced under the title "A Critical Exploration of 1 Peter," in C. H. Talbert, *Perspectives on First Peter* (NABPRSS 9; Macon: Mercer University Press, 1986), 17–36. On more recent developments, see R. L. Webb, "The Petrine Epistles: Recent Developments and Trends," in S. McKnight and G. R. Osborne, eds., *The Face of New Testament Studies* (Grand Rapids: Baker, 2004), 373–90. Three detailed bibliographies of ancient, medieval, early modern, and modern sources on the epistle can be found in T. W. Martin, *Metaphor and Composition in 1 Peter* (SBLDS 131; Atlanta: Scholars, 1992), 89–338; L. Goppelt, *A Commentary on 1 Peter*, (ed. F. Hahn; trans. J. E. Alsup) Grand Rapids: Eerdmans, 1993), xxi–xlii; and J. H. Elliott, *1 Peter: A New Translation with Introduction and Commentary* (AB; New York: Doubleday, 2000), 155–227. Waltner, *1–2 Peter, Jude,* 18, has made the interesting observation that already in 1978, based on the bibliography of Goppelt, *1 Peter,* 148 of 326 scholarly items on 1 Peter were commentaries—rather remarkable in and of itself. W. L. Schutter, *Hermeneutic and Composition in 1 Peter* (WUNT 2/30; Tübingen: Mohr/Siebeck, 1989), 1–2, also identifies the growing stream of scholarly interest in 1 Peter since 1976. A considerable number of fine commentaries on 1 Peter have been written since 1978, and particularly since 1990. Especially noteworthy are those of Davids (1990), Marshall (1991), the translation into English of Goppelt (1993), Achtemeier (1996), and more recently, Elliott (2000), Schreiner (2003) and Jobes (2005). The commentary by Waltner (1999) is geared primarily toward pastoral usage. Important recent monographs on 1 Peter include those of T. Martin (1992), Miller (1993), Thuren (1995), Tite (1997), Campbell (1998), and Pearson (2001).

[4] See especially the work of Martin (ibid.), Schutter (ibid.), and Lauri Thuren, *Argument and Theology of 1 Peter: The Origins of Christian Paraenesis* (JSNTSup 114; Sheffield: Sheffield Academic Press, 1995).

[5] So, e.g., J. D. McCaughey, "On Rereading 1 Peter," *AThR* 10 (1983): 41, and S. C. Pearson, *The Christological and Rhetorical Properties of 1 Peter* (SBEC 45; Lewiston/Queenston/ Lampeter: Edwin Mellen, 2001), 2.

One interpretive approach seeks to locate in the epistle evidence of "pseudepigraphal machinery."[6] Accordingly, invented devices such as "Peter, an apostle" (1:1) or references to "Silvanus" (5:12) and "Mark, my son" (5:13) are construed as attempts to engender authority on the part of a writer. Another interpretive approach, perhaps uncomfortable with the ethical implications that attend pseudonymity theory, opts to speak of a "Petrine school" or "Petrine community."[7] In the words of Chester and Martin, the early church thereby "was affirming the leader's abiding presence and valuing the legacy of his continuing influence" and "appealing to what the apostle might have said if he had survived to a later decade."[8] As we shall observe, however, relatively strong support for the letter's apostolicity exists in the church's history. Any questions or challenges to Petrine authorship from critical scholarship are not without serious problems. Whether from the text itself or church tradition, no incontrovertible obstacles present themselves. To the contrary, the references in the letter to "Peter" are remarkably restrained—the very opposite tendency of pseudepigraphal writings.

It has been the inclination of NT scholars to affiliate 1 Peter, in part or in whole, with a baptismal homily or liturgy (see "Literary Features") in order to account for the letter's message and overall unity.[9] There is much to commend in this approach, given the variations on the baptismal theme adduced by wider NT scholarship. One's assessment of 1 Peter along these lines, of course, will hinge on whether baptism is thought to be a primary or a secondary motif. Any comprehensive analysis of 1 Peter's composition will of necessity need to reconcile baptism with the other primary motifs in the letter (see "Important Themes/Sub-Themes"). What is the writer's literary-

---

[6] So D. Guthrie, *New Testament Introduction* (4th ed.; Leicester/Downers Grove: InterVarsity, 1990), 778. Representative of this position is German NT scholar Norbert Brox. See, e.g., his essays "Zur pseudepigraphischen Rahmung des ersten Petrusbriefes," *BZ* 19 (1975): 78–96, and "Tendenz und Pseudepigraphie im ersten Petrusbrief," *Kairos* 20 (1978): 110–20. Brox carries over these assumptions in his commentary *Der erste Petrusbrief* (EKKNT 21; 3rd ed.; Zürich: Benziger, 1990).

[7] So, e.g., E. Best, *1 Peter* (NCBC; London: Oliphants, 1971), 63; M. L. Soards, "The Letter of 1 Peter: An Account of Research," in *ANRW* 2.25.5, 3827–49; and P. J. Achtemeier, "Newborn Babes and Living Stones: Literal and Figurative in 1 Peter," in M. P. Horgan and P. J. Kobelski, eds., *To Touch the Text: Festschrift for J. A. Fitzmyer* (New York: Crossroad, 1989), 207–36.

[8] So A. Chester and R. P. Martin, *The Theology of the Letters of James, Peter, and Jude* (NTT; Cambridge: Cambridge University Press, 1994), 91.

[9] T. G. C. Thornton has raised much-needed criticisms in light of the variously proposed baptismal liturgy theory. See his "1 Peter: A Paschal Liturgy?" *JTS* 12 NS (1961): 14–26.

rhetorical strategy that seems to emerge?[10] This we shall explore, but our initial task, however, lies elsewhere. What might we glean from the epistle about the author himself and about his audience?

Authorship

In contrast to 1 Peter's clarity of thought and profound theological message, its acceptance and influence in the church's interpretive history might appear somewhat uneven. In fairness, however, this "unevenness" is more a product of modern scholarship than it is the consensual witness of historic interpretation (see "Attestation"). Evidence indicates that 1 Peter was viewed widely and recognized as apostolic from the time of Eusebius (late third and early fourth centuries).

Let us consider the markings. To begin, the author's self-references are compelling and not easily explained away: "Peter an apostle of Jesus Christ" (1:1), "fellow elder" (5:1), and "witness of the sufferings of Christ" (5:1). The argument for apostolic authorship moreover is buttressed by intriguing personal references—one to "Silvanus" (5:12; cp. Acts 15:22; 2 Cor 1:19; 1 Thess 1:1; and 2 Thess 1:1), one to "Mark, my son" (5:13; cp. Acts 12:12),[11] and an allusion to "this second epistle" in 2 Pet 3:1. Not surprisingly, among the church fathers, this latter reference lent support for the conviction that Peter had commissioned the second Gospel narrative.[12] Furthermore, the author's conspicuously personal and intimate identification with both his readers and the sufferings of Christ has the effect of lending authority. Altogether, the letter's emphasis on suffering, its strong Christological trajectory, its hortatory character, and its fatherly tone are striking. They are in harmony with what we might expect from a

[10] Elsewhere I discuss the following issues relative to 1 Peter: literary features (286–90), themes (292–93), authorship (277–82), and attestation (277–82) in commentary on 1 Peter in the revised edition of the Expositors Bible Commentary (vol. 13; Grand Rapids, Zondervan, 2006).

[11] A plausible explanation of 2 Pet 1:15 is that it is a reference to the Gospel of Mark.

[12] Irenaeus (late second century) ascribes the letter to the apostle Peter (*Haer.* 3.1.1; 4.9.2; 5.7.2; and 4:16.5). J. R. Michaels, *1 Peter* (WBC 49; Waco: Word, 1988), xxxiii, adroitly observes the importance of geography: "The testimony of Irenaeus is significant because Irenaeus was active not only in Asia Minor but also in the West (i.e., Lyons in Gaul)." Eusebius acknowledges that the letter is one of the undisputed books (*Hist. eccl.* 3.25.2). Consider, in addition, further illuminating comments on 1 Peter by Eusebius (*Hist. eccl.* 2.15 and 6.25.8), Oecumenius, in his commentary on 1 Peter (PG 119:576), and Andreas (*CEC* 82–83), each of whom is cited, with English translation, in Bray, *James, 1–2 Peter, 1–3 John, Jude,* 126–27, and each of whom attests to the letter's authenticity.

If never would have guessed that!

disciple of Jesus who had denied his master but eventually had been entrusted with shepherding the flock of God (John 21:15–19). Much of the material in 1 Peter, given the plausibility of the author as an eye-witness to Jesus' earthly ministry, readily accords with material in the Gospel narratives—for example,

- salvation through Christ being prophesied (1:10–12)
- salvation as ransom through the blood of Christ (1:18–19)
- the command to love one another (1:22)
- being born again (1:23)
- good works that glorify God (2:12)
- the admonition to respect and render to the authorities (2:13–15)
- the admonition not to retaliate (3:9)
- blessing that issues from persecution and identification with Christ's name (3:13–17)
- allusion to the days of Noah (3:20)
- pastoral admonitions not to lord it over others (5:3)
- caution against succumbing to anxiety (5:7).[13]

As already noted, a major impediment for some who question the authenticity of 1 Peter is the letter's stylistic polish.[14] Beyond vocabulary and syntax, the letter's use of metaphors and rhetorical devices and acquaintance with the LXX suggest an author unlike the apostle described in Acts 4:13. Therein Luke depicts Peter and John as *anthrōpoi agrammatoi kai idiotai*, illiterate and unlearned.[15] The implication would seem patent: the chief apostles are not capable of a literary product that accords with 1 Peter. Some have responded to this obstacle that, given enough time following his

---

[13] Investigating the theological and linguistic parallels between 1 Peter and the Gospel tradition is the thrust of R. H. Gundry's two essays, "'Verba Christi' in 1 Peter: Their Implications Concerning the Authorship of 1 Peter and the Authenticity of the Gospel Tradition," NTS 13 (1966/67): 336–50, and "Further Verba on Verba Christi in 1 Peter," Bib 55 (1974): 211–32. E. Best, "1 Peter and the Gospel Tradition," NTS 16 (1970): 95–113, has done the same, although he adopts a different approach than Gundry. While Gundry assumes authenticity of the Gospel passages, Best ascribes any similarities to the early church's catechetical material. N. Hillyer (1 and 2 Peter, Jude [NIBC; Peabody: Hendrickson, 1992], 1–2) has also helpfully noted material and themes common to 1 Peter and the Gospels as well as to Acts, while Michaels (1 Peter, xl–xlii) considers the writer's use of the OT and the Gospel tradition.

[14] So, e.g., F. W. Beare, The First Epistle of Peter (3rd ed.; Oxford: Basil Blackwell, 1970), 28–30, and F. B. Craddock, First and Second Peter and Jude (WBC; Louisville: Westminster/John Knox, 1995), 12.

[15] Guthrie, New Testament Introduction, 763–64, maintains that the more likely meaning of agrammatos is "not formally trained" rather than "illiterate."

conversion, Peter would progress as an effective communicator.[16] This response, however, begs too many questions, not the least of which is presented by Matthew (Matt 26:73). The more plausible explanation, it seems, can be found in the text of 1 Peter itself: "Through Silvanus . . . I have written briefly" (5:12).[17]

As we look more closely at the role that Silvanus plays, and by keeping in mind the role of amanuenses, professional scribes or secretaries, in antiquity, the "problem" of authorship recedes significantly. The Silvanus mentioned in 5:12 is with reasonable certainty the "Silvanus" of Paul's letters (1 Thess 1:1 and 2 Thess 1:1) and the "Silas" of the book of Acts (15:37–40; 16:16–40; 17:10–15; 18:5–17). The significance of this figure in the emergent apostolic church is easily lost on the modern reader. Not only was he a ministry companion to Paul, he also possessed Roman citizenship (Acts 16:37). We may infer from this that he was a well-educated and cultured individual when contrasted with the apostle Peter.[18]

In the literature of antiquity we find abundant examples of professionally trained scribes or secretaries (Latin: *amanuenses*) being employed. In the Greco-Roman context, scribes trained for the purposes of dictation routinely served the relatively illiterate as well as those of the upper class and public officials, assisting by providing documentation, maintaining records and writing letters.[19] The role of the amanuensis would be especially pronounced in the provincial and cosmopolitan settings of Asia Minor.

The practice of Paul is a case in point, since the apostle composed letters both independently and in collaboration with others. For example, his Epistle to the Romans is dictated to and written by Tertius (Rom 16:22). Other instances in Paul' letters seem to suggest the presence of a co-sender or secretary (e.g., 1 Cor 16:21; Gal 6:11; Col 4:18; 2 Thess 3:17; and Phlm 19).[20] In the end, the problem of eloquence in 1 Peter is no real problem at all.

---

[16] So Hillyer, *1 and 2 Peter, Jude*, 2, and W. Grudem, *The First Epistle of Peter* (TNTC; Leicester/Grand Rapids: InterVarsity/Eerdmans, 1988), 27–31.

[17] As one commentator has remarked, these words indicate that "he [Silvanus] was more than merely Peter's stenographer." So W. Barclay, *The Letters of James and Peter* (DSB; 2nd ed.; Edinburgh: Saint Andrew, 1958), 43.

[18] On the peculiarities and distinctiveness of vocabulary and style in 1 Peter, see Elliott, *1 Peter*, 41–68.

[19] See the quite helpful background discussion in J. Murphy-O'Connor, *Paul the Letter-Writer: His World, His Options, His Skills* (GNS 41; Collegeville: Liturgical, 1995).

[20] Hereon see John B. Polhill, *Paul and His Letters* (Nashville: Broadman and Holman, 1999), 120–33.

We need not, then, view the language of 1 Peter as "problematic" or construe Silvanus as merely a bearer of the letter—as in the case of Tychicus in Col 4:7—as opposed to a secretary.[21] Rather, the reference to Silvanus in 5:12 most naturally suggests secretarial assistance, contra J.R. Michaels, who doubts Silvanus' role in writing, otherwise "his name would have been linked with Peter's at the outset,"[22] despite the fact that in Paul's case, Tertius as secretary appears not at the beginning but at the end (Rom 16:22). For that reason, the remarkable statement by F. W. Danker, that "Silvanus' role as midwife [is] largely irrelevant, and pseudonymous authorship [is] beyond the need of further demonstration,"[23] needs moderation. While the thought belongs to Peter, the writing in all probability belongs to Silvanus.

In marked contrast to 2 Peter, the first epistle bearing the apostle's name receives strong attestation in church tradition as genuine. Challenges to authenticity tend to be more recent and generally are rooted in literary and stylistic arguments. In what follows, literary and thematic considerations in 1 Peter require examination. However, before we analyze the literary texture of the letter, what can we know about its recipients?

Setting, Audience, Destination

First Peter combines features of private correspondence—e.g., terms of endearment (1:14; 2:11; 4:12), personal instructions (5:1–4), personal greetings (5:12–14), and a personal understanding of the readers' plight (1:6; 3:13–15)—with those of a public encyclical, which is to circulate among various Christian communities in a wider geographical area. The writer's appropriation of OT language and concepts, which are both direct and indirect, may or may not inform us more about the theological orientation of the writer than the actual recipients themselves.

The manner of the letter's address bears similarity to that of James (cf. Jas 1:1). In 1 Peter the recipients are addressed as "chosen exiles of the diaspora" who are scattered throughout the provinces of "Pontus, Galatia, Cappadocia, Asia, and Bithynia" (1:1), a

---

[21] Thus, e.g., Beare, First Epistle, 28, and P. J. Achtemeier, 1 Peter, Hermeneia (Minneapolis: Fortress, 1996), 8.

[22] Michaels, 1 Peter, 307.

[23] F. W. Danker, "1 Peter 1,24–2,17: A Consolatory Pericope," ZNW 58 (1967): 102.

combined region comprising northern Asia Minor.[24] Whether these people are new believers or not is unclear, despite the suggestive contrast of "before" and "after" that surfaces on occasion in the epistle (1:14–15,18,22; 4:1–5). In light of the governing metaphor of diaspora and "sojourning" (1:1,17; 2:11),[25] we may presuppose a racially mixed, Gentile social location on the part of the recipients, although the Jewish population of Asia Minor, and Galatia in particular (Acts 16:1–5), was considerable. What is more, they seem to be of diverse socio-economic standing, as evidenced by the relational duties that inhere in the household code (2:13–3:12). Already in the 50s, the gospel had penetrated Asia Minor, as indicated by Paul's letters. In addition, Paul's comments as recorded in Col 4:12–16 are richly suggestive that the door to Pontus and Bithynia would be open in the decade to come. The order in which the provinces are listed in the epistolary greeting is an indication to some scholars of a postal route traveled by a messenger in the delivery of this circular or encyclical letter.[26]

Locating the audience in 1 Peter is closely tied not only to the question of authorship but also to the nature of "suffering" or persecution on display in the letter. What is the precise nature of the persecution to which the recipients are subjected? And what might we gather concerning the sufferings that are mentioned in 1 Peter?

A close reading of the epistle suggests that their suffering probably has more to do with *discrimination* than with persecution per se and thus is generic in character.[27] What markers might point in this direction? The readers are said to "suffer for righteousness" (*paschoite dia dikaiosunēn*, 3:14) and be "ridiculed for the name of Christ" (*oneidizesthe en onomati Christou*, 4:14). Moreover, they endure "various trials" (*poikilois peirasmois*, 1:6) and "sufferings for Christ" (*eis Christon pathēmata*, 1:11). If their suffering

---

[24] Excepted is the province of Galatia, which extends southward.

[25] *Contra* Elliott, *A Home for the Homeless: A Sociological Exegesis of 1 Peter, Its Situation and Strategy* (Philadelphia: Fortress, 1981), 142–43, whose position is maintained in his recent commentary (*1 Peter*, 94–97, 476–83); we take the "diaspora" allusion in 1:1 to be metaphorical and not literal.

[26] So, e.g., F. J. A. Hort, *The First Epistle of St. Peter*, ed. B. F. Dunelm (London: Macmillan, 1989), 157–84, and C. J. Hemer, "Address of 1 Peter," *ExpT* 89 (1977/78): 239–43, while J. N. D. Kelly (*A Commentary on the Epistles of Peter and Jude* [London: Adam and Charles Black, 1969], 42) adduces Josephus, *Ant.* 16.21–23, as evidence of such an ordered route. K. Jobes offers a rather interesting conjecture regarding the audience: these were converts from elsewhere–"probably Rome"–and then displaced to Asia Minor (*1 Peter* [BECNT; Grand Rapids: Baker Academic, 2005], xi).

[27] Goppelt, *1 Peter*, 36–45, has perhaps best summarized the social setting facing the readers.

is more generic, then the admonition "Conduct yourselves honorably among the Gentiles, so that" they may see "your good works" (2:12) accords naturally with their social situation. The nature of this imperative has an enduring quality, particularly in the context of misunderstanding, alienation, and slander that are directed at them. These are, after all, realities that attend the normal Christian life and that are partially mirrored in the household code (2:18–25), which addresses everyday social obligations.[28] Consider the tone of the letter's opening admonition (1:13–16):

> For this reason, in girding up your minds and being sober set your hope fully on the grace that is yours in the revelation of Jesus Christ. As obedient children, do not be conformed to the passions that characterized the ignorance of your former life . . . but be holy in all your conduct.[29]

But there is more that shapes the contours of "suffering" in 1 Peter. The "suffering in the flesh" to which the readers are exposed is described in the context of "ceasing from sin" (*pepautai hamartias*, 4:1). No longer are they living "according to the flesh" (*en sarki*) as the Gentiles live (4:2–3); they are to be qualitatively different. For this reason, then, the Gentiles are "surprised that you don't plunge with them" in the same carnal excesses (4:4). A picture of the recipients begins to emerge: amidst a pagan cultural context, they are to live as Christian disciples. And in this sense, the "purification" that the readers are enduring (*hagnizō*, 1:22) is a process for which *they themselves* are responsible, not the Lord.

Doubtless a chief reason causing some interpreters to presuppose in 1 Peter a fiercer, concentrated, state-induced form of persecution is the allusion in 4:12 to the "fiery ordeal" that is testing the flock of God. Yet it is instructive to note that the verb "don't be surprised" (*mē xenizesthe*) appears previously in 4:4 to describe unbelievers' wonderment at why the Christians do not indulge in excesses. The sense of the Petrine admonition in 4:2 plausibly conveys moderate wonder rather than catastrophic paralysis—"Don't

---

[28] That public hostility and resentment—i.e., the normal reaction to Christian presence in the world—is argued more broadly by J. L. DeVilliers, "Joy in Suffering in 1 Peter," *Neotestamentica* 9 (1975): 64–86, and J.R. Slaughter, "The Importance of Literary Argument for Understanding 1 Peter, *BibSac* 152 (January-March 1995): 72–91.

[29] My translation.

even consider the possibility" rather than "Be faithful unto death." Were the readers facing political terror or likely death, one might expect stronger or more impassioned language.

Any attempts to appraise the degree of supposed imperial persecution being directed toward Christians remains speculative and entails a nuanced assessment, since provinces differed considerably and tensions varied throughout the Empire. To illustrate, the imperial cult seems to have had a far stronger presence in Ephesus, Pergamum, and Smyrna, as is faintly suggested in Rev 2:8–17:

> Do not fear any of the things that you will suffer. Indeed, the devil will throw some of you in prison, in order that you might be tested, and you will experience tribulation for ten days. Be faithful to the point of death, and I will give you the crown of life (Rev 2:10).[30]

This, however, was not the case universally, and the degree of immanent or impending persecution remains uncertain.

A further though related point to consider: to "honor the emperor" in the midst of Nero's mid-64 campaign against Christians strikes the reader as perverse. First Peter 2:13–15 is written in the same spirit as Rom 13:1–10. Only in the NT Revelation is the emperor demonized. At the other extreme, to honor the emperor in the face of second-century persecution, if some presuppose a late date for the letter, also leaves the reader incredulous. It is precisely this language—the language of respect toward political authorities—that is more suggestive of an earlier dating of 1 Peter.[31]

Several factors, then, require our consideration. We are already assuming a more generic variety of persecution being mirrored in the letter, one that is suggestive of the social norm for most Christians. If we take into account the relative restraint and positive disposition of the writer with regard to the governing authorities—quite remarkable in itself, especially over against the portrait of the powers in the NT Apocalypse—and if we view Christians' status, alongside Judaism, as broadly tolerated throughout the Empire, the social scenario that we are positing is not implausible. An interpretation of 1 Peter that assumes or requires a backdrop

---

[30] My translation.
[31] J. H. L. Dijkman, "1 Peter: A Later Pastoral Stratum?" *NTS* 33 (1987): 265–71.

of imperial or state-induced persecution may need moderation,[32] even when Christian persecution may be found in the reign of any emperor from the mid-first century onward. This, of course, does not take into account local outbreaks of persecution, which would vary greatly throughout the Empire.[33]

To assume the letter to be genuinely Petrine is to place it in the early to mid 60s. Traditional scholarship, locating 1 Peter in the 60s, has assumed the letter either to precede Neronic persecution or to correspond with its earliest stages. If, however, we are to presuppose that Neronic persecution is advanced, then we must reckon with the seeming absurdity of the reference in 2:13–15 to the political authorities, and particularly, the rhetorical question posed in 3:13.[34] And if we opt to assign to 1 Peter a later date,[35] concurrent with Domitian[36] (late first century) or Trajan (early second century) persecutions, we are still left with the same dilemma. Why the scandalously temperate admonitions to "respect" and "submit to every human institution . . . whether the Emperor . . . or the governors as those sent out by him to punish those who do evil and praise those who do good" (2:13–15)?

A further hint that bears upon the question of dating, even when it is secondary to the issues of authorship and persecution, is ecclesiastical in nature. Significantly, there is only mention in 1 Peter of elders: "For this reason I exhort the elders among you as a fellow elder and witness of Christ's sufferings" (5:1).[37] We find in

[32] D. Warden, "Imperial Persecution and the Dating of 1 Peter and Revelation," *JETS* 34/2 (1991): 203–12.

[33] Against the supposition that 1 Peter reflects the period of Domitian or Trajan, it should be kept in mind that Eusebius wrote that Peter was succeeded as bishop of the church in Rome in the year 66 (*Hist. eccl.* 2.25.2–5).

[34] Church tradition regarding Peter's martyrdom largely rests on the statements of Eusebius and 1 Clement that Peter was in Rome at the end of his life and that he died a martyr's death. Precisely where and when remain speculation.

[35] Beare, *First Epistle,* 41–43, is representative.

[36] Reicke, (*The Epistles of James, Peter, and Jude,* AB [Garden City: Doubleday, 1964], 72) 72, asks where the writer's instructions on confronting sacrifices to the emperor are, if 1 Peter is mirroring Domitian persecution. W. H. C. Frend downplays the level of persecution during Domitian's reign. "In Rome," he writes, "the persecution of Domitian does not appear to have amounted to very much" (*Martyrdom and Persecution in the Early Church* [New York: New York University, 1965], 217).

[37] Selwyn, *First Epistle,* 56–63; U. Holmer, *Die Briefe des Petrus und der Brief des Judas* (Wuppertal: Brockhaus, 1976), 14–15; Barclay, *Letters,* 165; and E. Schweizer, *Der erste Petrusbrief* (3rd ed.; Zürich: Theologischer Verlag, 1973), 11, all point to an early date based simply on church organization, since there is no mention in 1 Peter of a bishop or deacons. Elliott ("Rehabilitation," 254) holds a middle-of-the-road position, i.e., between AD 70

the letter no allusion to the office of bishop (*episkopos*) or to the deacon (*diakonos*), which, according to the "early Catholic" rubric, is precisely what one would expect in the late first century or early second.

What might we conclude? The most likely scenario, derived from both internal and external evidence, is that 1 Peter was written from Rome, with persecution imminent or building in the mid-60s. Conversely, to assume 1 Peter to be pseudonymous generally requires that it be situated in the persecutions under Domitian or Trajan. And while it is impossible to be conclusive about Peter's death, the warning by one NT scholar against "linking the question of the authorship of 1 Peter too closely to the question of date"[38] dodges issues that require specificity, since the questions of authorship and dating cannot be disengaged from one another, notwithstanding our imprecision in dating Peter's death, is perhaps overstated.

In addition to markers in 1 Peter that would seem to suggest generic discrimination, persecution or suffering, we have also argued that the recipients' social setting mirrors a diverse socio-economic standing that is strongly Gentile in flavor ("Conduct yourselves honorably among the Gentiles . . . so that they may see your good works," 2:12). This view is bolstered by multiple references to their pre-conversion life (e.g., 1:14,18; 2:9; 4:3–4), the relational duties expressed through the household code (2:13–3:12), and the pronounced exhortation toward civic duty and respect for the ruling authorities (2:13–17).

What about previous apostolic work in Asia Minor? No evidence indicates that either Peter or the apostle Paul had worked in these provinces (cp. Acts 16:6–7), although Luke tells us that people from "Cappadocia, Pontus and Asia" were present on the day of Pentecost (Acts 2:9). Were we, however, to assume that Paul is no longer alive, words of encouragement from the senior living apostle would be entirely appropriate.[39] In light of the senior apostle's burden to "feed my sheep" (John 21:15–19), an encyclical directed to churches in northern Asia Minor provinces via a postal

and 90, based on certain form-critical considerations (viz., the "re-working" of material in Christian circles).

[38] Michaels, *1 Peter,* lxi. Michaels goes to great lengths to relativize supposed allusions to Peter's martyrdom, whether from the Fourth Gospel (e.g., John 21) or from pseudepigraphal sources (e.g., *Epistle of Clement to James*).

[39] So Guthrie, *New Testament Introduction,* 773.

route would be altogether natural, especially if he sensed that time was drawing short (cp. 2 Pet 1:14–15). Hence, he could identify with believers whose suffering is said to be "worldwide" (5:9).

Important Themes and Subthemes

1. *Suffering*. Although it is painful (4:12), multifaceted (1:6), unjust (2:19), and very intimidating (3:14), suffering in 1 Peter is understood to have redemptive value (1:7). Therein one's faith is shown to be authentic. More importantly, as it affects the sufferer, it is for praise and *not* shame (4:16). This central theme surfaces at the outset in the letter (1:6–7) and is to be understood as predicated on one's identification with Christ. But Christ Himself also suffered, and this vicariously for us (1:11; 3:18). Consequently, Christians are left with Christ as their model to follow (2:8,21–25; 5:1). They do not return insult for insult or evil for evil (3:9–12); rather, they are to be encouraged that "the eyes of the Lord are on the righteous" (3:12) and entrust themselves to the one who judges justly (2:23).

The implications of Christ's example, moreover, extend not merely to one's predisposition or mental framework; that is to say, we suffer not merely because we are "called" to suffer or because it is good for the character. There is more to the story. Just as "the tables were turned," and the divine sufferer was exalted above his enemies to enthronement (3:18–22), so it will be with those who are presently mistreated for the name of Christ. The powers that animate evil in the present life will be wholly subjected to the one who sits enthroned at the right hand of God. To suffer, in 1 Peter, is to receive glory (1:11), and Christ's own suffering becomes paradigmatic for believers; they too will be glorified, even as their Lord (3:21–22). For the present, however, the faithful will be "protected by God's power" (1:5), a great source of comfort. The image of Christ as shepherd (2:25; 5:4) is consoling, because it implies care, compassion, empathy, and intimacy (cp. 5:7).

Peter, of course, is older and wiser now; he knows what it means to suffer as well, and this should further motivate his readers. Finally, great encouragement comes from knowing that "the same sufferings are being experienced by your brothers in the world" (5:9). The recipients of this letter, then, are not alone.

→ Dispersion of Jews beyond Israel

2. *Diaspora.* This theme makes its appearance immediately in the letter. First Peter is addressed to those who are "temporary residents of the Dispersion" (1:1). Troy Martin calls attention to the role played in 1 Peter by "the overarching and controlling metaphor of the Diaspora." From the opening verse to the letter's end,

> images and concepts from the Jewish Diaspora dominate the material. The Diaspora provides the author with an image contributor that allows him to describe his readers' ontological status as well as the morality ensuing from that status. The Diaspora provides general images that pervade the entire letter and specific images that are limited to the individual sections of 1 Peter and give rise to the metaphor clusters. It also provides the unifying link among the three metaphor clusters in the letter-body of 1 Peter. Thus, the Diaspora is the thematic motif of 1 Peter.[40]

Although we need not necessarily agree that "diaspora" constitutes the primary motif of 1 Peter, a strong case indeed might be made. "Diaspora" may be understood to have two purposes. First, it is intended to encourage the readers to engage the course of life in terms of a journey or sojourn. Second, it admonishes them not to grow faint in heart when they encounter trials, opposition to the faith, even grief—all of which arise in the context of their pagan social location. In light of this dual function of the "diaspora" metaphor, baptism may be understood to ground the saints once for all in those realities they have confessed—Christ's atonement and salvation, resurrection, ascension, and rule by session. In this sense, then, baptism "saves" (3:21), because in the context of suffering the saints are promised rescue by God, just as the water saved Noah. Christian discipleship, thus viewed, is a journey, a pilgrimage, a life as a "resident alien" (1:1; 2:11), wherein one is motivated by "a living hope" (1:3) that anticipates full consummation of God's victory.

3. *Glory and Victory over the Powers.* The hope of the Christian is necessarily anchored in Christ's resurrection (1:3; 3:21), by which He exposed and vanquished the powers of evil (3:22; cp. 1 Cor 15:20–27 and Col 2:15). The reminder that these powers are

---

[40] Martin, *Metaphor and Composition*, 273–74.

positioned at the feet of Christ in submission (3:22) is a rhetorically powerful strategy on the part of the writer, particularly when one is suffering abuse (2:15,18–25; 3:8–17; 4:4,12–16). In 1 Peter, an important theological and ethical reality is underscored: to suffer is to receive "glory" (1:7,11; 5:1; implied in 1:4). Glory is to be revealed (4:13; 5:1), resulting in an "unfading crown of glory" (5:4). The saints, according to 1 Peter, are *called* to glory (5:10).

4. *Hope*. The substance of the saints' "living hope" is not merely a future "reward in heaven," though it does entail that; rather, it entails more. Hope has present consequences insofar as in the saints' conflict with the world they are "protected by God's power" (1:5). At the same time it has important future consequences in that their suffering will lead to glorification and ultimate conquest over their enemies. Psychologically and pastorally, these perspectives on suffering are very important. The future reward, however one conceives it, is stated to be on reserve in heaven for the saints (1:4).

The language of salvation and the language of hope in 1 Peter are virtually synonymous. Salvation, while a theological reality, has, more importantly, ethical implications for the recipients of the letter. In addition, it is both present and future in scope. Their salvation consists in their being presently protected by God (1:5); it is further manifest in these last times (1:20); it finds confirmation in baptism, which is analogous to Noah and his generation (3:21); and it is a salvation whose implications are not yet fully revealed (1:9).

5. *Holiness* (see "Ethics in 1 Peter").

6. *Respect and Ordered Relationships*. First Peter is notable in the language that is used to describe relationships and authority. The reader encounters in the letter multiple references to "submission" (*hupotassō* or *hupotaggō*, 2:13,18; 3:1,22; 5:5) and "respect" or "honor" (*timaō*, 2:17–18; 3:7,15), as well as a generic predisposition toward authority of any sort on the part of the writer. This can be seen, for example, in various levels of social relationships (2:13–3:7), hence the significance of the "household code" in the letter. And it is much more explicit in how one views various levels of political authority that are ever-present realities (2:13–14,17). God and "Caesar," in 1 Peter, clearly are *separate but not mutually exclusive* domains.

7. *Election*. A further related subtheme in the epistle is election. Peter's ethical admonitions are laced with the language of "calling,"

a theological reality that has very important ethical ramifications. Knowing that Christian believers constitute God's elect (1:1); knowing that they have been "chosen according to the foreknowledge of God the Father" (1:2); knowing that the sufferings of Christ were divinely predicted (1:10); knowing that God has "called" believers to be holy (1:15); knowing that the cornerstone that was rejected by men was "chosen" and precious, having become the capstone (2:6–7), so that even those rejecting the truth somehow fit into the redemptive purposes of God (2:8); knowing that believers are "called" to follow Christ, since He is our example (2:21); knowing that Christians are "called" for blessing in order that we may inherit a blessing (3:9); knowing that they are "called" to "eternal glory in Christ" after they "have suffered a little" (5:10)—knowing all this, the saints can be encouraged to persevere in the midst of their difficulties.[41]

Literary Features

First Peter accords with the standard form of the Greek personal letter, with its introduction, greeting, body proper, and conclusion,[42] and it falls somewhere between public and private correspondence.[43] That is, 1 Peter is "public" to the extent that it is to be read in Christian communities extending throughout several provinces of Asia Minor, and it is "private" insofar as it addresses a specific readership on a specific issue. The letter of antiquity commonly opens with identification of the sender, the address to the receiver, followed by a greeting that is generic, although the sender's identity may be expanded and that of the recipient may be amplified. A modified greeting, "grace and peace," which is standard in most Pauline epistles, is employed in 1 Peter. Insofar as its recipients are geographically "dispersed" (hence the diaspora motif), the epistle might well be understood akin to an "encyclical."[44]

---

[41] Given the writer's burden, we might stop short of T. R. Schreiner's suggestion that Christians are foreordained to stumble (*1,2 Peter, Jude,* 112).

[42] On epistolary content and structure, see S. K. Stowers, *Letter Writing in Greco-Roman Antiquity* (LEC; Philadelphia: Westminster, 1986), and W. G. Doty, *Letters in Primitive Christianity* (Philadelphia: Fortress, 1973).

[43] Thus Craddock, *First and Second Peter and Jude,* 12.

[44] So Hort, *First Epistle,* 157–84; W. M. Ramsay, *The Church in the Roman Empire before AD 70* (5th ed.; London: Hodder and Stoughton, 1897), 279–95; idem, *The Letters to the Seven Churches* (London: Hodder and Stoughton, 1904), 183–96; Hemer, "Address," 239–43; Kelly, *A Commentary,* 3; Goppelt, who describes 1 Peter in terms of a *Rundbrief (Der erste*

As a literary form, the epistle, in the words of Klaus Berger, is "not only an external transmission form of written communication, but it is also essentially a major genre with constitutive characteristics."[45] Not only does the epistle constitute its own genre, it also serves as a "framing" mechanism for other genres. In 1 Peter, the epistolary form serves to "frame" the writer's word of exhortation (5:12). The letter is first and foremost paraenetic and hortatory, as evidenced by the inordinate number of imperatives scattered between 1:13 and 5:12.[46] Admonitions and prescriptives are the language of paraenesis, i.e., hortatory literature, and while paraenesis (the *logos parainētikos*; cp. Acts 27:9,22 and Heb 13:22), or moral exhortation, is found in some form in virtually every epistle of the NT, the Christian paraenetic tradition is perhaps most richly on display in the General Epistles.[47] Upon cursory examination we find that, in these letters, ethics and "pastoral theology," not theological propositions per se, are accentuated. Paraenesis concerns itself foremost with ethics (see "Ethics in 1 Peter" below), and it is the ethical that lies at the heart of 1 Peter;[48] hence, the appearance of rules of conduct, ethical proscriptions, warnings, and catalogs of virtue and/or vice that are so typical of paraenetic literature.[49]

A particular feature that is peculiar to paraenetic literature is the use of moral typology. Historical or legendary models that belong

---

Petrusbrief [KEK 11; 8th ed.; ed. F. Hahn; Göttingen: Vandenhoeck & Ruprecht, 1978], 44–45); Michaels, *1 Peter,* 9; and Chester and Martin, *Theology,* 98.

[45] K. Berger, "Hellenistische Gattungen im Neuen Testament," in *ANRW* 2.25.2, 1338 (my translation).

[46] Martin, *Metaphor and Composition,* 85, cites in this regard J. H. Moulton, who counts 28 imperatives in this portion of 1 Peter (*A Grammar of New Testament Greek* [Edinburgh: T. & T. Clark, 1906], 174).

[47] Both L. G. Perdue ("Paraenesis and the Epistle of James," *ZNW* 72 [1981]: 241–56) and R. W. Wall ("James as Apocalyptic Paraenesis," *ResQ* 32 [1990]: 11–22) have called attention to the role of paraenesis in James; I have noted elsewhere the paraenetic character of Jude and 2 Peter (J. D. Charles, *Literary Strategy in the Epistle of Jude* [London/Toronto/ Scranton: Associated University Presses/ University of Scranton Press, 1993], 72, and idem., *Virtue Amidst Vice: The Catalog of Virtues in 2 Peter 1* [JSNTSup 150; Sheffield: Sheffield Academic Press, 1997], 37–43 [implicit in 84–98]); while Thuren (*Argument and Theology of 1 Peter,*) and Martin (*Metaphor and Composition,* 85–121) argue for its guiding presence in 1 Peter.

[48] Those who proceed from the assumption that 1 Peter is paraenesis include Selwyn, *First Epistle;* D. L. Balch, *Let Wives Be Submissive: The Domestic Code in 1 Peter* (SBLMS 26; Chico: Scholars, 1981); D. Hill, "'To Offer Spiritual Sacrifices' (1 Peter 2:5): Liturgical Formulations and Christian Paraenesis in 1 Peter," *NTS* 16 (1982): 37–59; and Martin, *Metaphor and Composition,* 85–134.

[49] On the paraenetic tradition in general, see Berger, "Gattungen," 1075–77, and A. J. Malherbe, *Moral Exhortation: A Greco-Roman Sourcebook* (LEC; Philadelphia: Westminster, 1986), 124–29.

to popular tradition serve to warn or prod the readers toward a particular ethical standard. Thus, for example, in 1 Peter Christ (2:21–28; 3:18–22; and 4:1–2) and Sarah (3:1–6), as well as the author himself (5:1–5), serve as models for the audience. Similarly, in the epistle of James we find Abraham, Rahab, Job and Elijah as ethical paradigms, while in 2 Peter and Jude a whole spate of characters fulfill this role—among them, unbelieving Israel, the fallen angels, Noah and his contemporaries, Sodom and Gomorrah, Lot, Balaam and his ass, Cain and Korah.[50] These paradigms reflect the writer's use of both the OT and extrabiblical Jewish tradition material (see "Old Testament").

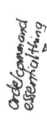

That 1 Peter qualifies as paraenesis is supported and defined by several conspicuous lexical phenomena—notably, the abundance of imperatives. Throughout the letter the readers are repeatedly admonished toward particular behavior in innumerable ways—for example: "gird up the loins of the mind [and] be sober" (1:13 NKJV); "be holy in all your conduct" (1:15 NKJV); "love one another fervently with a pure heart" (1:22 NKJV); "rid yourselves of all malice and all deceit" (2:1 NIV); "crave pure spiritual milk" (2:2 NIV); "abstain from fleshly lusts" (2:11 NKJV); "submit yourselves to every ordinance" (2:13 NKJV); "honor all people" (2:17 NKJV); "love the brotherhood" (2:17 NKJV); "fear God" (2:17 NKJV); "honor the king" (2:17 NKJV); "arm yourselves also with the same mind" (4:1 NKJV); "be serious" (4:7 NKJV); "do not be surprised at the painful trial . . . but rejoice" (4:12–13 NIV); "let none of you suffer" (4:15 NKJV); "let him not be ashamed" (4:16 NKJV); "submit yourselves to your elders" (5:5 NKJV); "humble yourselves" (5:6 NKJV); "be sober, be vigilant" (5:8 NKJV).

In keeping with the hortatory purpose of the letter are literary-rhetorical features that are typical of paraenetic literature. In 1 Peter, these include ethical catalogs (i.e., vice and virtue lists), the household or station, and antithesis. Both in literature and in oral tradition, the ethical catalog is a principal teaching device in Stoic ethical discourse, and for this reason lends itself well to the writers of the NT. Virtue lists and vice lists, because of their ability to stereotype and typecast desirable or undesirable behavior, are commonly employed by the NT writers; 13 virtue lists and 23 vice

---

[50] Elsewhere I have explored the hermeneutical tendencies and use of moral typology in the General Epistles in "Interpreting," 433–56.

lists occur.[51] Four such lists are employed in 1 Peter—two vice lists (2:1 and 4:3) and two virtue lists (1:13–15 and 3:8–9).

Paraenesis also exploits antithesis or contrast in its use of the moral paradigm. This feature functions in similar fashion to the ethical list through its contradistinguishing of positive and negative behavior and figures prominently in 1 Peter: the believers' former and present life (1:14–15 and 2:1–2); believers versus unbelievers (2:7–9 and 4:4–5); proper versus improper conduct (2:20); a woman's inner disposition versus her outward appearance (3:3–4); reviling versus blessing (3:9); just versus unjust suffering (4:15–16); and proper versus improper ways of leading (5:1–3).

To say that 1 Peter interpretation has exhibited diverse exegetical approaches is something of an understatement. Perhaps the chief factor contributing to this diversity is the epistle's literary character. Consider, for example, W. L. Schutter's important study of the composition of 1 Peter. Schutter identified six variations of hermeneutical method: (1) telescoping an OT text; (2) uniting a catena of texts through a single idea; (3) conflating multiple texts; (4) using a "text-plot"; (5) associating a text with a known exegetical tradition; and (6) using florilegia (i.e., numerous texts strung together).[52] A similar diversity is on display in Troy Martin's near-exhaustive examination of the last century of 1 Peter scholarship.[53] Among the interpretive options presented for 1 Peter are the following:

- a combination of two different letters[54]
- a baptismal homily in its entirety
- a letter with a baptismal sermon spliced therein[55]

[51] See J. D. Charles, "Vice and Virtue Lists," in C. A. Evans and S. E. Porter, eds., DNTB (Downers Grove/Leicester: InterVarsity, 2000): 1255; see also B. S. Easton, "New Testament Ethical Lists," JBL 51 (1932): 1–12.

[52] Schutter, Hermeneutic and Composition, 43.

[53] Martin, Metaphor and Composition. Martin's volume is devoted to an analysis of the letter's structural integrity. In his survey of scholarship, Martin identifies six general explanations for the composition of 1 Peter. And more recently, S. C. Pearson (The Christological and Rhetorical Properties of 1 Peter [SBEC 45; Lewiston: Mellon, 2001]) identifies five: (1) epistle, (2) baptismal homily, (3) baptismal liturgy, (4) apologetic tract, and (5) homiletic midrash.

[54] Thus, for example, Hort, First Epistle, 3; J. W. C. Wand, The General Epistles of St. Peter and St. Jude (WC; London: Methuen, 1934), 1–2; and C. F. D. Moule, "The Nature and Purpose of 1 Peter," NTS 3 (1956/57): 1–11.

[55] E.g., H. Gunkel, Der erste Brief des Petrus (SNT 2; Göttingen: Vandenhoeck & Ruprecht, 1906), 530; Reicke, The Epistles, 74; O. S. Brooks, "1 Peter 3:21—The Clue to the Literary Structure of the Epistle," NovT 16 (1974): 290–305; and more recently, Schutter, Hermeneutic and Composition, 35–43.

- a sermon with a letter appended thereto[56]
- a letter containing two baptismal homilies[57]
- a paschal liturgy[58]

Structurally, some see in 1 Peter no rhyme or reason, but rather only a less-than-coherent series of exhortations[59] or unrelated themes.[60]

But if we assume with most commentators some sort of variation on the baptismal theme as an organizing motif in the letter, our attempts to read a baptismal or liturgical context into 1 Peter are not without problems, since we encounter only one reference to baptism in the entire epistle. Such leaves room for ample hermeneutical speculation.

One interpretive approach that has resisted the baptismal rubric is J. H. Elliott's *A Home for the Homeless*.[61] For Elliott, the chief organizing element in 1 Peter is that of "temporary residents" (1:1; cp. 2:11). But in Elliott's view this is no metaphor; rather, the reader is to understand it in a literal, socio-political sense, signifying people who are marginalized and socially disenfranchised. Troy Martin's thorough critique of Elliott has pointed to the inadequacies of Elliott's position,[62] even when the pilgrim theme is indeed important to the letter's interpretation. As with James' usage of the same image (1:1), diaspora in 1 Peter suggests itself metaphorically, and it functions as a counterpart, non-literally, to the image of "Babylon" (5:13) at the end of the epistle.

How we construe this image governs our overall exegetical trajectory. The depiction of the readers as "diaspora," as Kelly properly observes, is in keeping with how the early church understood

---

[56] E.g., A. von Harnack, *Geschichte der altchristlichen Litteratur bis Eusebius,* vol. 1 (Leipzig: Hinrich, 1897), 451; R. Perdelwitz, *Die Mysterienreligion and das Problem des I. Petrusbriefes* (Giessen: Töpelmann, 1911), 12–15; W. Bornemann, "Der erste Petrusbrief: Eine Taufrede des Silvanus?" *ZNW* 19 (1920): 161; H. Windisch, *Die katholischen Briefe* (HNT 4/2; 2nd ed.; Tübingen: Mohr/Siebeck, 1930), 46–47; Beare, *First Epistle,* 8; and A. R. C. Leaney, *The Letters of Peter and Jude* (CBC; Cambridge: Cambridge University Press, 1967), 8.

[57] R. P. Martin, "The Composition of 1 Peter in Recent Study," in *Vox Evangelica: Biblical and Historical Essays* (London: Epworth, 1962), 40.

[58] F. L. Cross, *1 Peter, A Paschal Liturgy* (2nd ed.; London: Mowbray, 1957), 20. The position of R. P. Martin "1 Peter," 40, resembles to a certain degree that of Cross: 1 Peter is an epistle that incorporates catechetical and liturgical material.

[59] E.g., C. E. B. Cranfield, *1 and 2 Peter and Jude* (TBC; London: SCM, 1960), 122; W. C. van Unnik, "First Letter of Peter," *IDB* 3:759; and W. Schrage (with H. Balz), *Die "katholischen" Briefe* (NTD 10; Göttingen: Vandenhoeck & Ruprecht, 1973), 64–65.

[60] E.g., Goppelt, *1 Peter,* 8–12; Elliott, *A Home,* 284; and Balch, *Let Wives,* 124.

[61] Elliott has incorporated this approach into his important 2000 AB commentary.

[62] Martin, *Metaphor and Composition,* 144–46.

itself by maintaining the habit of "transferring to itself, as the new Israel, the language appropriate to the experience of the old."[63] To understand "diaspora" metaphorically in 1 Peter is not to deny that believers are "marginalized" in the world. It is, however, to see the image alongside other metaphors that occur throughout the letter—among these, a holy people, a chosen people, the household/temple of God (all of which appear in 1:14–2:10), sojourning, and righteous suffering (2:11–3:12 and 3:13–5:12).[64]

Consider another corollary: the "household servants" (2:18–25), who are a part of the household imagery. As Carol Osiek and David Balch point out, the household image is important because it "provides an anchor of identity in a sea of strangerhood,"[65] particularly since the saints are *paroikoi* (1:17; 2:11) and *parepidēmoi* (1:1; 2:11). In the end, the theme of diaspora with its corollaries lends a unity and coherence to our interpretation of the letter in a way that baptismal motif does not.

Another literary-rhetorical feature of 1 Peter, to which much attention is devoted in the literature, is the so-called household or "station" code.[66] In antiquity, household codes recapitulate the duties and obligations that reflect the wider family circle. Accordingly, to illustrate, husbands and wives are to display reciprocal love and respect while children are to demonstrate obedience and household servants are to be respectfully submissive. In 1 Peter, four of these categories are present—servants and masters (2:18–20), wives (3:1–6), and husbands (3:7); a fifth, children, is absent. A sixth category, "everyone" (3:8–9; 5:5), suggests itself, given the letter's emphasis on respect and subordination, which mirrors the function of the generic household code.[67]

It is the nature of paraenesis that lying behind the social situation of the audience is more often than not a relationship to the

---

[63] Kelly, *A Commentary*, 4.

[64] See the extensive commentary on this cluster of associated images in Martin, *Metaphor and Composition*, 161–267, as well as the very helpful overview of the language and thought world of 1 Peter found in Achtemeier, *1 Peter*, 3–23.

[65] Carol Osiek and David Balch, *Families in the New Testament World* (Louisville: Westminster John Knox, 1997), 190.

[66] Two helpful examinations of the household code and related literature are D. C. Verner, *The Household of God* (SBLDS 71; Chico: Scholars Press, 1983), and D. L. Balch, "Household Codes," in D. E. Aune, ed., *Greco-Roman Literature and the New Testament* (SBLSBS 21; Atlanta: Scholars Press, 1988), 25–50. On the use of the household or "station" code in 1 Peter, very thorough and helpful discussions are found in Martin, *Metaphor and Composition*, 124–30, and Goppelt, *1 Peter*, 162–228.

[67] So Martin, *Metaphor and Composition*, 126.

author that approximates that of a mentor to his disciples or a fa-
ther-figure, an association that lends moral authority to his instruction and exhortation.[68] In 1 Peter, this is accomplished in several
ways. The author gently reminds them of models to follow (3:18–
22; 3:13–14), he empathizes with his readers (1:1; 5:1–5), and he
utilizes terms of endearment (4:12). Together these elements have
the effect of fostering a moral compulsion in the direction of proper
conduct.

Finally, an analysis of the literary character of 1 Peter requires
comment on its comparison to 2 Peter. In placing the two epistles
side by side, NT scholars are generally agreed, based on linguistic,
historical and theological considerations, that they do not derive
from the same author. Unlike 2 Peter, which typically is thought
to be chiefly eschatological in its outlook but bereft of theological
affirmation,[69] 1 Peter is uniformly praised for its rich Christology.[70]
The difference in theological orientation between the two letters,
however, may well be explained by pastoral and editorial concerns
that are specific to each audience (fully aside from the issue of secretarial assistance). It is generally acknowledged that while both
letters contain an elevated use of the Greek, their distinctions out-
weigh their commonalities so as to make a common authorship
problematic. Furthermore, as I argue elsewhere,[71] their appropriation of biblical and extrabiblical Jewish tradition material would
seem to differ in methodogy. For example, 2 Peter does not use any
direct citations, whereas 1 Peter makes use of Jewish sources directly and indirectly. At the same time, both letters make paraenetic
use of their sources, creatively marshaling typology and metaphor
for moral exhortation. Moreover, both address an audience that is
located in a pervasively Gentile cultural context, even when the
specific needs of each readership are unique.

Upon closer inspection, 1 and 2 Peter exhibit numerous points
of resemblance—lexical, theological and rhetorical in their consti-

that's crazy!

---

[68] So Berger, "Gattungen," 1076.

[69] Against this view, see the section in this book on "Theology of 2 Peter."

[70] Thus Chester and Martin, who are representative: "Probably no document in the New Testament is so theologically oriented as 1 Peter, if the description is taken in the strict sense of teaching about God. The epistle is theocentric through and through, and its author has a robust faith in God which he seeks to impart to the readers. The author's mind is filled with the centrality of the divine plan and purpose in both human and cosmic affairs, from the opening exultation . . . to the closing affirmation and appeal" (*Theology*, 104).

[71] Charles, "1 Peter," *EBC* 13, 288–89.

tution[72]—that are striking and of note[73]: (1) Christ's second coming is a major focus of both letters (1:7,13; 4:13; 5:4 // 1:16; 3:12). (2) Correlatively, the theme of judgment surfaces in both (1:17; 2:21; 4:5–6,17 // 2:3–4,9,11; 3:6–7). (3) Much of the material in both is devoted to the presentation of a distinctive Christian social ethic (1:13–17,22; 2:1,11–20; 3:1–17; 4:1–19; 5:1–11 // 1:5–15; 2:4–22; 3:1–7,11–18). (4) Divine "foreknowledge" (*epignōsis*) in both letters establishes the basis upon which the saints can interpret the dealings of God (1:2 // 1:2–3,8; 2:20). (5) An important subtheme in both letters is divine election, the cornerstone of the ethical life (1:1,15; 2:4,6,9,21; 3:6,9; 5:10,13 [*suneklektos*] // 1:3,10 [*eklogō*]).

(6) Correlatively, the language of "reservation" or "keeping" (*tēreō*) is employed in both letters (1:4 // 2:4,9,17; 3:7). (7) In both letters, grace and peace are "multiplied" to the readers (1:2 // 1:2). (8) Divine glory (*doxa*) and the glory of Christ feature prominently in both letters (1:7,11,21,24; 4:11,13–14; 5:1,4,10–11 // 1:3,17; 2:10; 3:18). (9) Being holy (*hagios*) is an important subtheme in both letters (1:12,15–16; 2:5,9; 3:5 // 1:18,21; 2:21; 3:2,11). (10) Correlatively, the saints as "righteous" (*dikaios*) and "righteousness" (*dikaiosunē*) are prominent in both letters (2:24; 3:12,14,18; 4:18 // 1:1,13; 2:5,7–8,21; 3:13).

(11) Being "without blemish" (*amōmos, aspilos*), whether denoting Christ or the saints, is important to both letters (1:19 // 3:14). (12) One's manner of "conduct" (*anastrophē*) is of utmost importance in both letters (1:15,18; 2:12; 3:1–2,16 // 2:7). (13) The triune God—the Father, Christ the Son, and the Spirit—is presented in both letters (1:2–3,11–13,17,19; 2:5,21; 3:4,15–16,18–19,21; 4:1,6,11,13–14; 5:1,10,14 // 1:1,8,11,14,16–17,21; 2:20; 3:4,18). (14) Prophets, prophesying, and/or prophecy occur in both letters (1:10 // 1:21; 2:1,16,19; 3:2). (15) Correlatively, the "word(s) of the Lord"/"prophets" (1:23,25; 2:8; 3:1 // 1:19; 3:2,5,7) figure(s) prominently in both.

(16) Both letters conclude with an exhortation to grow or stand fast in the grace of God (5:12 // 3:18), which is an important

Similarities of the letters

---

[72] See also ibid., 289–90.

[73] *Contra* W. Marxsen (*Introduction to the New Testament*, trans. (G. Buswell) Philadelphia: Fortress, 1970), 236, who asserts that "the contents do not reveal a 'Petrine character' in any way," thus making it "unlikely for a number of reasons that Peter was the author of this work." These numbered points are taken from J. Daryl Charles, "1 Peter," in *Hebrews—Revelation*, ed. Tremper Longman III and David E. Garland, EBC vol. 13 (Grand Rapids: Zondervan, 2006), 289–90.

concept for both writers (1:2,10,13; 2:19–20; 3:7; 4:10; 5:5,10,12 // 1:2; 3:18). (17) Both letters use moral paradigms to promote Christian ethics (2:21–25; 3:5–6,18–20; 5:1 // 2:4–10,15–16). (18) Noah appears in both letters as a model of faithfulness (3:20 // 2:5). (19) The fallen angels are depicted as imprisoned in both letters (3:19 // 2:4). (20) The flood is mentioned in both letters (3:20 // 2:5; 3:5–6).

(21) Correlatively, the disobedient are described as "unjust" (3:18 // 2:9,13,15). (22) "Salvation" (*sōtēria*) from the Lord appears in both letters (1:5,9–10 // 3:15). (23) Virtue, i.e., "moral excellence" (*aretē*), appears in the Petrine letters three of the four times it is found in the NT (2:9 // 1:3,5). (24) "Brotherly affection" (*philadelphia*) is commended in both letters (1:22; 3:8 // 1:7). (25) God "supplies in abundance" (*epichorēgeō, chorēgeō*) for the saints as described in both letters (4:1 // 1:5,11).

(26) The writer of both letters addresses his readers as "dear friends" (2:11; 4:12 // 3:14). (27) Both letters use the metaphor of redemption drawn from the slave market (1:18 // 2:1), (28) thereby reminding readers of their spiritual freedom (*eleutheria*) (2:16 // 2:19). (29) Both letters appeal to the longsuffering (*makrothumia*) of God (3:20 // 3:9,15). (30) Correlatively, this knowledge spawns greater endurance (*hupomonē*) in both letters (2:20 // 1:6).

(31) Both letters condemn the licentiousness (*aselgeia*) of surrounding, pagan culture (4:3 // 2:2). (32) Both letters warn the readers to abstain from fleshly lusts (*epithumia*) (1:14; 2:11; 4:2–3 // 1:4; 2:10,18; 3:3). (33) Both letters appropriate an eschatological perspective that links present living with future promise (1:5,7,20–21; 4:13 // 2:3–4,9,11; 3:3,6–7). (34) In both letters the world "perishes" (*apollumi*) (1:7 // 3:6,9). (35) The only occurrence of the rare word "eyewitness" in the NT is in the Petrine letters, in its verb form (*epopteuō*) and noun form (*epoptēs*) respectively (2:12; 3:2 // 1:16).

(36) The intended result of both letters is that the saints be "established" (*stērizō*) in their faith (5:10 // 1:12). (37) Moreover, this being "established" stands in direct relation to the saints' "knowing" (*eidotes, eidotas*) (5:9 // 1:12). (38) The reality of the angelic realm, both in facilitating and resisting the divine purpose, is mirrored in both letters (1:12; 3:19,22; 5:8 // 2:4). (39) In both letters the writer's self-designation is "an apostle of Jesus Christ" (1:1 // 1:1). (40) Personal apostolic reminiscences are used in both letters

(5:1 // 1:14,16–18). (41) And both letters contain similar doxological praise ("To him belong the glory . . . forever") (4:11c // 3:18b).

Old Testament and Noncanonical Tradition Material in 1 Peter

First Peter is unsurpassed in both its theological texture and its dependence on the OT. Even a cursory reading of the letter reveals an intimate acquaintance with OT concepts and imagery on the part of the writer. This comes to expression both in direct citation and indirectly through his use of language, imagery, and theological orientation.[74] Such familiarity has led Chester and Martin to contend that with the possible exception of Romans and Hebrews, "no NT book . . . is so permeated with OT hints and ideas" as 1 Peter.[75] Whether or not 1 Peter might eclipse Romans and Hebrews—or James, for that matter—allusion to the OT is as dense in 1 Peter as in any document in the NT.

Following, then, is a listing of direct and indirect dependence on Old Testament tradition material—a listing that is meant to be illustrative and not exhaustive: (1) use of the "sojourning"/diaspora metaphor (1:1,17; 2:11); (2) the designation of the readers as "chosen" (1:1; 2:4; 5:13); (3) the foreknowledge of God (1:2); (4) allusion to the sprinkling of blood (1:2); (5) reflections of Mal 3:3 (1:7); (6) allusion to the prophets of old (1:10–12); (7) admonition to be holy as the Lord is holy (1:16); (8) reflections of Exod 12:5; Lev 22:19–21; and Deut 17:1 (1:19); (9) citation of Isa 40:6–8 (1:24–25); (10) citation of Ps 34:8 (2:3); (11) reminiscences of Ps 118:22 (2:4); (12) reflections of Isa 56:7 (2:5); (13) reflections of Exod 19:5–6 (2:4,5,9); (14) allusion to the offering of sacrifices (2:5); (15) citation of Isa 28:16 (2:6); (16) citation of Ps 118:22 and reflections of Isa 8:14 (2:7–8); (17) allusion to a chosen race

---

[74] See, in this regard, E. G. Selwyn, "Eschatology in 1 Peter," in W. D. Davies and D. Daube, eds., *The Background of the New Testament and Its Eschatology* (Cambridge: Cambridge University Press, 1956), 394–401. W. M. Swartley, "Intertextuality in Early Christian Literature," in R. P. Martin and P. H. Davids, eds., *DLNT* (Downers Grove: InterVarsity, 1997), 538, identifies 19 citations in 1 Peter. Schutter, *Hermeneutic and Composition*, 5–43, believes that half of the epistle consists of OT material. Two attempts to illuminate the hermeneutic used in 1 Peter are D. E. Johnson, "Fire in God's House: Imagery from Malachi 3 in Peter's Theology of Suffering (1 Pet 4:12–19)," *JETS* 29/3 (1986): 285–94, and W. L. Schutter, "1 Peter 4:17, Ezekiel 9:6 and Apocalyptic Hermeneutics," in K. H. Richards, ed., *SBLSP* 26 (Atlanta: Scholars, 1987), 276–84.

[75] Chester and Martin, *Theology,* 88.

(2:9); (18) allusion to a holy nation (2:9); (19) allusion to a people for God's own possession (2:9); (20) reflections of Isa 42:16 (2:9); (21) allusion to Hos 1:6,9–10; 2:23 (2:10); (22) allusion to the day of visitation (2:12); (23) reflections of Isa 53:4–5,7,9,11 (2:22–24); (24) use of the sheep-shepherd metaphor (2:25; 5:2,4); (25) allusion to Sarah and Abraham (3:2,5–6); (26) citation of Ps 34:12–16 (3:10); (27) allusion to Noah (3:20); (28) reflections of Ps 110:1–2 (3:22); (29) allusion to grumbling (4:9); (30) allusion to judgment (4:17); (31) reminiscences of Prov 11:31 (4:17–18); (32) reflections of Ps 31:5 (4:19); (33) use of the Babylon metaphor (5:13).[76]

What is striking to the reader is the writer's ability to take OT concepts and images and intertwine them with important themes. An example of this, already noted, is his creative use of the "stone" passages, a feature unique to 1 Peter, and the people/priesthood/ nation passages, designed to emphasize solidarity. Conspicuous in the letter is a strong undercurrent of sacrifice (1:2,19; 2:5,9,22,24– 25; 3:18; 5:2–4); rooted in the system of atonement in the OT, it weaves its way throughout the letter and is subordinated to the greater theme of suffering.[77]

Not only is the writer directly dependent on the OT, he also appears to be conversant with—and borrowing for the sake of illustration—noncanonical traditional material. One trace of such is found in 1:12, where the angels are depicted as yearning to peer into the substance of human salvation. No explanation or direct parallel to this phenomenon is found in the OT. A Jewish apocalyptic reference to angelic activity and a targumic expansion of "Jacob's ladder," however, are suggestive. In the text of *1 Enoch* 9:1, the angels are said to observe carefully the events on earth. The verb used to describe the angels' activity, *parakuptō*, is the same verb used in 1 Peter 1:12. In *Targum Neofiti* (Gen 28:12) one finds angels ascending and descending to observe Jacob. According to the text, they too "earnestly desire" to behold this man of God. It

[76] See also Charles, "1 Peter," *EBC* 13, 283–84. P. H. Davids (*The First Epistle of Peter* [NICNT; Grand Rapids: Eerdmans, 1990], 211 has listed not only direct citations but also perceived allusions to the OT, some of which I have noted, others of which are more difficult to assess, though likely. On the matter of varying hermeneutical approaches toward Jewish tradition material and the degree to which such material is "borrowed," particularly as it is on display in the General Epistles, see Charles, "Noncanonical Writings," 814–19, and "The Old Testament," 834–41.

[77] Elsewhere I investigate 1 Peter's use of the OT more fully in Charles, "Old Testament," 834–41.

is well possible that 1 Peter makes use of imagery and language associated with a Jewish midrashic tradition in order to depict divine mystery.

One instance of Jewish midrashic tradition to which considerable literature is devoted is 1 Pet 2:4–17, the Christologized stone metaphor. Here the writer would appear to combine OT references with contemporary notions of God's people. While a visible link to Isa 28:16; 44:28 and Ps 118:22 is evident, its reinterpretation applied to the Christian community bears some resemblance to Qumran exegesis (e.g., 1 QS 5:5–6; 8:5; 1 QH 6:25–26). Whereas the stone in the OT is the king, in later Jewish tradition it is the actual people of God. The image in 1 Peter is in keeping with this theological development.[78]

First Peter 3:6, part of a paraenesis on proper relationships, would appear to be an allusion to Genesis 18. However, Sarah's obedience to Abraham is not at all a prominent feature of the OT narrative. It does, however, appear with some frequency in the pseudepigraphical *Testament of Abraham* (first century), which makes abundant use of the title "my lord Abraham" (5:12; 6:2,5,8; 15:4). In 1 Peter the writer is less concerned to recite the Genesis narrative than to establish a point of correspondence between Sarah and Christian women.

One further example of possible extrabiblical tradition material in 1 Peter is worthy of comment. In one of the more enigmatic texts of the NT, 3:18–22, we find a cryptic expansion of the suffering theme. Christ, afterward suffering for sins, "made a proclamation to the spirits in prison who in the past were disobedient." In apocalyptic literature, prison is not the location of human souls but of angelic punishment (e.g., Rev 18:2; 20:7). In Jewish apocalyptic literature, the role of these "imprisoned spirits" is prominent. *First Enoch* is exemplary. Christ's "descent," it is worth noting, is not unlike that depicted in *1 Enoch* 12, where Enoch is commissioned to go preach to the fallen angels. While the amount of scholarly literature on this difficult text of 1 Peter is enormous, and while exegetical conclusions vary wildly, 1 Peter uses angelic typology for the purpose of addressing pastoral needs. Given the attention to fallen angels in first-century apocalyptic literature, 1 Peter may

---

[78] See N. Hillyer, "Rock-Stone Imagery in 1 Peter," *TynB* 21 (1970): 39–70, and P. Minear, "The House of Living Stones: A Study of 1 Peter 2:4–12," *Ecumenical Review* 34 (1982): 238–48.

well be portraying Christ as an "end-time Enoch" who proclaims judgment to the fallen principalities and powers (cp. Col 2:15).

Theology and Christology of 1 Peter

The theological texture of this epistle is remarkable in its richness. The Christology of 1 Peter is rooted in the twin notions of lordship and suffering. Much like the NT Apocalypse, in which Jesus is both Lion and Lamb, Ruler-Judge, and atoning Sacrifice, 1 Peter masterfully combines both theological poles and holds them in proper tension. And indeed an understanding of both is essential for Christian witness in a pagan world. To emphasize conquest over the powers, as the writer does, apart from identification with Christ's death is to run the risk of a Christian triumphalism and an inability to empathize with fellow humans. To emphasize only sacrificial suffering, however, without a glimpse or preview of the victory consummated, is to withhold a key ingredient in motivating the Christian disciple.

Conquest and suffering are united in 1 Peter in what can be viewed as a theology of suffering leading to glorification (1:4,7,11; 3:18–22; 4:13; 5:4; see "Themes"). Sacrifice is both vicarious and exemplary. And it has both present and future implications. Similarly, the reality of Christ's resurrection entails both present and future ramifications. To lose sight of the one or the other distorts Christian theology and hamstrings the Christian disciple and its vibrant social ethic.

First Peter portrays God in multifaceted ways and accentuates His essential attributes. He is a "faithful Creator" (4:19), a "Father" (1:2,3,17) to whom those who suffer should commit themselves; He is the One who judges justly (2:23); a shepherd (5:2) to whom shepherds in the church should look for wisdom; a God whose Spirit of glory rests on us (4:14); and the "God of all grace" (5:10,12). Moreover, He

- elects and chooses (1:1; 2:4,9 [twice]; 5:10),
- has foreknowledge (1:2),
- has given us "a new birth into a living hope" (1:3),
- has reserved the believer's future inheritance (1:4),
- judges impartially (1:17),
- has raised Jesus from the dead and glorified Him (1:21),

- speaks living words (1:23),
- has a will, a purpose (2:15; 4:2,19),
- waits "patiently" (3:20),
- is enthroned with all authority (3:22),
- dispenses grace (4:10),
- provides strength (4:11),
- opposes the proud (5:5),
- lifts up the humble with His mighty hand (5:6),
- shepherds His flock (5:2),
- restores and strengthens those who suffer (5:10), and
- possesses all power (5:11).

In the NT, theology and ethics are indivisible. And in 1 Peter this wedding is abundantly on display.

Ethics in 1 Peter

Through abundant and creative use of OT imagery, citations, and moral types, 1 Peter establishes a strong basis for acting ethically. The writer's chief burden is this: "Live virtuous lives among the pagans so that . . . they may see your good works and glorify God on the day of visitation" (2:12[79]; cp. Matt 5:16). First Peter 1:16, a citation of Lev 11:44, represents the standard both for Israel as a covenant people and for the church. The ethical basis of Christian living remains the same: holiness rooted in the divine nature. Consider the vocabulary of holiness in the letter: living as a free person, not using freedom as a cover-up for evil (2:16); sanctification through the Spirit (1:2); purification (1:22); the Spirit as holy (1:12); the priesthood as holy (2:5); and a nation as holy (2:9).

Hence, the writer calls his readers to a plan of living that is distinct. Thereby they remain unspotted by the world—a world to which they are called. There is no fleeing the world, no isolation, no withdrawal. First Peter is proactive, not reactive. Christians are to emulate Christ, not claim victimhood, and they are to commit to God the Creator (4:19) the justness of their cause when they are mistreated. The point of emphasis in 1 Peter is *what believers can do*, not how unjust their abuse or their surroundings might seem. And what precisely are they admonished to do?

---

[79] My translation.

- Resist the enemy (5:9).
- Be self-controlled and alert (2:13; 5:8).
- Stand firm (5:9).
- Take accountability seriously (5:1–6).
- Be submissive and respectful (2:13–3:7; 5:5).
- Do not retaliate (3:9).
- Abstain from fleshly lusts (2:11).
- Live virtuous lives (2:12).
- Rejoice at what God is doing (1:7).
- Prepare the mind for action (2:13).
- Rid oneself of worldly attitudes (2:1).
- Entrust oneself to Him who judges justly (2:23).

For this, on the day of divine visitation, pagans will acknowledge believers' good works (2:12). Such should undergird the Christian's social ethic in a morally corrupt environment.

Attestation, Early Sources

C. A. Bigg has written: "There is no book in the New Testament which has earlier, or better, or stronger attestation."[80] What is impressive is the relative absence of any credible voices in the early church that challenge the epistle as authentically Petrine. The Fathers, with few exceptions, held 1 Peter to be genuine. These witnesses include Irenaeus,[81] Clement of Alexandria,[82] Eusebius,[83] Didymus,[84] Augustine,[85] Oecumenius,[86] and possibly *1 Clement*[87] as well as Papias.[88] Clement is said by Eusebius (in *Hist. eccl.* 6.25.8) to have offered commentary on all the "catholic epistles." In support of apostolic authorship, several commentators find fairly

---

[80] C. A. Brigg, *A Critical and Exegetical Commentary on the Epistles of St. Peter and St. Jude* (ICC; Edinburgh: T. & T. Clark, 1901), 7.

[81] Irenaeus, *Haer.* 4.9.2; 5.7.2; and 4.16.5.

[82] Clement, *Paed.* 3.11–12 and 4.18–20.

[83] Eusebius, *Hist. eccl.* 3.3.

[84] Didymus, PG 39:1755.

[85] Augustine, *Doct. Christ.* 2.12.

[86] Oecumanius, PG 119:513.

[87] Bigg, *Epistles,* 9, attempts to identify close parallels between *1 Clement* (late first century) and 1 Peter. J. B. Mayor (*The Epistle of St. Jude and the Second Epistle of St. Peter* [New York: Macmillan, 1907], cxx) and Wand (*The General Epistles,* 9) believe that Clement's use of 1 Peter is notable. Kelly (*A Commentary,* 12) also finds numerous correspondences between *1 Clement* and 1 Peter.

[88] We learn of Papias through Eusebius (*Hist. eccl.* 3.39.17), who writes that Papias had cited 1 Peter.

transparent evidence of acquaintance with 1 Peter in Polycarp's letter to the believers in Philippi (early second century).[89] First Peter was not considered by Eusebius to be one of the *antilegomena*, the disputed books, unlike 2 Peter.[90] Some patristic witnesses such as Didymus the Blind and Oecumenius acknowledge in 1 Peter rather close affinities to the Epistle of James, noting that the authors of both letters were apostles.[91]

Attestation for 1 Peter's authenticity, in the final analysis, would appear as strong as that of any NT document. For this reason, J. H. Elliott's breathtaking foreclosure—i.e., that it is "virtually certain that 1 Peter is a pseudonymous letter" (*1 Peter*, 124)—requires moderation. Correlatively, R. P. Martin's assertion that "the question of authorship remains unresolved"[92] may be somewhat overstated, just as his remark that "the traditional view which accepts the claims of the epistle to be apostolic is more reasonable than any alternative hypothesis" is somewhat understated. And while F. B. Craddock's statement—"Arguing for or against Petrine authorship has lost its importance for most students of this letter"[93]—may describe the current mindset among historical-critical scholars, his rationale for scholarly "indifference"—"This letter represents the teaching and preaching of Simon Peter and extends that ministry into Asia Minor, whether or not Simon penned it, dictated it, or was the source of the content used by a follower of his"—will be unsatisfactory for many. Clearly, the evidence is overwhelming that the early church did not share this view of authorship.

Purpose

In his commentary on 1 Peter, Erland Waltner observes that the letter's "potential significance for contemporary church life and

---

[89] E.g., Kelly, *A Commentary*, 2; Michaels, *1 Peter*, xxxii; and Guthrie, *New Testament Introduction*, 760.

[90] Eusebius, *Hist. eccl.* 3.3 and 6.25. At the same time, Eusebius draws attention to several "spurious" and "questioned" Petrine works—among these the *Gospel of Peter*, the *Acts of Peter*, the *Apocalypse of Peter*, and the *Doctrine of Peter*.

[91] A patristic consensus is outlined in G. Bray, ed., *James, 1–2 Peter, 1–3 John, Jude* (ACCS 11; Downers Grove: InterVarsity, 2000), 65. Didymus the Blind writes: "Why does Peter, an apostle to the Jews, write to those who are scattered in the dispersion, when most of them were still living in Judea at the time? To understand his meaning, we have to compare what he says with texts like 'I am a pilgrim and stranger on earth, as were all my forefathers'" (PG 39:1755, the English translation of which appears in Bray, *James, 1–2 Peter, 1-3 John, Jude*, 65–66).

[92] Chester and Martin, *Theology*, 92.

[93] Craddock, *First and Second Peter and Jude*, 13.

ethics" is "larger than the brevity of the letter suggests."[94] Indeed, it is. Interpreters who are generations—indeed, centuries—removed sing its praises as "one of the most significant and convicting works of the New Testament"[95] and "one of the easiest letters in the New Testament to read, for it has never lost its winsome appeal to the human heart."[96] And this is as it should be, given its themes of suffering, hope, promise, and divine care.

As noted already in our examination of important themes, attention to the author's vocabulary assists the reader in illuminating the author's purpose for writing. The language of "suffering" is pervasive. This suffering, moreover, has two sides: both the saints and Christ "suffer"[97] innocently; indeed, the saints share in the "sufferings"[98] and "testing"[99] (*pathēma*) of Christ. And, because this suffering is universal, the writer stresses the human element—Christians' responsibility—in responding properly. Given the attention devoted to suffering, it is not incidental that, initially, the saints are depicted as "called" or "chosen"/ "elect" and that this language surfaces multiple times throughout the epistle.[100] In fact, the language of "calling" forms something of an inclusio in the letter's opening and closing (1:1; 5:10).[101]

While all commentary acknowledges the theme of suffering in 1 Peter, there exists great diversity of opinion, mirrored in various form-critical considerations already noted, regarding the degree and character of suffering present. For this reason, then, a con-

---

[94] Waltner, *1–2 Peter, Jude,* 17.

[95] So Luther; see *Luther's Works,* 12.260, Bertram translation.

[96] So Barclay, *Letters,* 138.

[97] The verb *paschō* occurs 12 times (2:19–21,23; 3:14,17–18; 4:1[twice],15,19; 5:10), with the verb *hupomenō* appearing twice in 2:20. The link between the saints who suffer (*paschō*) and Christ, the paschal lamb who suffered, is immediate: in the epistolary opening the readers are linked to "the sprinkling of the blood of Jesus Christ" (1:2; cp. also the reference to Christ as "a lamb without defect or blemish," 1:19).

[98] First Peter 1:11; 4:13; and 5:1,9. Significantly, the generic word for "affliction," *thlipsis,* does not occur in the letter. "Suffering" is conceived of in 1 Peter primarily in terms of *pathēma* and *paschō.*

[99] The "testing" or "temptation" (*perasmos*) that they encounter (1:6; 4:12) is reminiscent of that which Christ endured. "Trial," *dokimos,* occurs once—in 1:7.

[100] The verb *kaleō* occurs six times (1:15; 2:9,21; 3:6,9, 5:10) in the letter, while the designation "chosen"/"elect" is used four times (1:1; 2:4,6,9).

[101] Significantly, the language of calling is buttressed by the "stone" passages in 1 Peter (2:4–8), which borrow the stone metaphor from Is 28:16 (the selected, precious cornerstone), Ps 118:22 (the stone that the builders rejected), and Is 8:14 (the stone of stumbling). This strong emphasis of divine purpose—revealed in part to the prophets of old and fully realized in the crucified, risen, and ascended Lord who now sits in power ruling over the cosmos—is important for the readers in light of a second dominant theme.

cise rehearsal of representative views is fitting.[102] Elliott[103] sees in 1 Peter "resident aliens," people who are sociologically marginalized. Schutter[104] believes 1 Peter is a homily on righteous suffering, and specifically, a suffering that leads to glory. Michaels[105] likewise sees the theme of humiliation leading to exaltation as a prominent motif in 1 Peter, with a basis in the OT, in the Gospel narratives, and in other Christian literature. Hillyer[106] maintains that the emphasis of 1 Peter is hope, given the grace of God that enables the readers to overcome trial and tribulation. For Clowney,[107] as well, bearing witness to the grace of God is the letter's burden.

Goppelt[108] identifies the letter's central theme as living in a non-Christian society and overcoming hardship. Similarly, Krodel[109] understands the epistle to communicate encouragement and consolation on the basis of divine grace to believers under duress. Mounce[110] believes the letter is intended to extend hope to those enduring hardships as a result of their Christian commitment, while Donelson[111] sees 1 Peter as a reflection of alienation due to the Christians' moral rigor.[112] And Waltner[113] holds that the burden of the letter is aimed at *how* the readers respond to their experience of suffering, with Christ as their model.

From the strong theological affirmations that are lodged within the letter's greeting, the structure of 1 Peter unfolds—a structure that is carefully crafted. The saints are simultaneously "chosen according to the foreknowledge of God the Father" and "temporary residents of the Dispersion" (1:1–2), although the order of these two is critically important insofar as one's ability to "sojourn" is secured by the knowledge of one's identity. Consequently, the

---

[102] See also Charles, "1 Peter," *EBC* 13, 293.

[103] Elliott, *A Home,* 48 and 129.

[104] Schutter, *Hermeneutic and Composition,* 108.

[105] Michaels, *1 Peter,* 295.

[106] Hillyer, *1 and 2 Peter, Jude,* 104.

[107] E. P. Clowney, *The Message of 1 Peter: The Way of the Cross* (BST; Downers Grove/Leicester: InterVarsity, 1988), 24.

[108] Goppelt, *A Commentary,* 19.

[109] Krodel, "1 Peter," 42.

[110] R. H. Mounce, *Born Anew to a Living Hope: A Commentary on 1 and 2 Peter* (Grand Rapids: Eerdmans, 1982), 5.

[111] From Donelson, *Hebrews to Revelation: A Theological Introduction* (Louisville: Westminster John Knox, 2001), 71.

[112] Donelson's reflections on suffering in 1 Peter, in *From Hebrews to Revelation,* 69–86, constitute one of the most thoughtful and nuanced discussions that can be found. See also Davids's excursus "Suffering in 1 Peter and the New Testament" in *First Epistle,* 30–44.

[113] Waltner, *1–2 Peter, Jude,* 18.

major blocks of material in 1 Peter, thus, are devoted to—and issue from—these themes: the readers are (a) a called and holy people (1:13–2:10), (b) strangers and sojourners in this world (2:11–3:12), and (c) sufferers whose righteous suffering, ultimately, will be vindicated (3:13–5:11). The message of 1 Peter has been aptly summarized by Chester and Martin—"1 Peter is designed to inculcate that our lives are not at the mercy of ruthless forces outside [our] control, and that the beneficent power called God has entered our human experience of suffering and distress—and triumphed"[114]—and by Waltner—"The word of Peter is that these Christian believers, though aliens and strangers, are indeed the people of God, chosen by God, graced by God, given dignity, strength, and destiny, and born anew to a living hope."[115]

Outline and Structure of 1 Peter

I. Opening (1:1–2)
II. Body of the Letter (1:3–5:11)
   A. Theological Prolegomena on Christian Hope (1:3–12)
     1. The Basis for Hope (1:3–5)
     2. The Benefits of Hope (1:6–9)
     3. The Privilege of Hope (1:10–12)
   B. Christian Identity as the New Diaspora Community (1:13–2:10)

     1. The new community's lifestyle (1:13–2:3)
       a. The lifestyle of holiness (1:13–16)
       b. The lifestyle of reverence (1:17–21)
       c. The lifestyle of love (1:22–25)
       d. The lifestyle of transformation (2:1–3)
     2. The new community's identity (2:4–10)
       a. The paradox of election and rejection (2:4–8)
       b. God's people as God's elect (2:9–10)
   C. Christian Witness as a Diaspora Community (2:11–3:12)
     1. The necessity of good deeds (2:11–12)
     2. The necessity of ordered relationships (2:13–3:12)
       a. A Christian view of authority (2:13–17)

---

[114] Chester and Martin, *Theology,* 114.
[115] Waltner, *1–2 Peter, Jude,* 21.

Selected Bibliography

Commentaries Based on the Greek Text

Arichea, D. C., and E. A. Nida. *The Translator's Handbook on the First Letter from Peter.* New York: United Bible Societies, 1980.

Bigg, C. A *Critical and Exegetical Commentary on the Epistles of St. Peter and St. Jude.* ICC. Edinburgh: T. & T. Clark, 1901.

Michaels, J. R. *1 Peter.* WBC 49. Waco: Word, 1988.

Selwyn, E. G. *The First Epistle of St. Peter.* London: Macmillan, 1946.

Commentaries Based on the English Text

Achtemeier, P. J. *1 Peter.* Hermeneia. Minneapolis: Fortress, 1996.

Barclay, W. *The Letters of James and Peter.* DSB. 2nd ed. Edinburgh: Saint Andrew Press, 1958.

Beare, F. W. *The First Epistle of Peter.* 3rd ed. Oxford: Basil Blackwell, 1970.

Beasley-Murray, G. R. *The General Epistles: James, 1 Peter, Jude and 2 Peter.* BG 21. London/New York/Nashville: Lutterworth/Abingdon, 1965.

Best, E. *1 Peter.* NCBC. London: Oliphants, 1971.

Boring, M. Eugene. *1 Peter.* ACNT. Nashville: Abingdon, 1999.

Bray, G., ed. James, *1–2 Peter, 1–3 John, Jude.* ACCS 11. Downers Grove: InterVarsity, 2000.

Calvin, J. *Commentaries on the Catholic Epistles: The Epistle of Jude; The First Epistle of Peter; The Second Epistle of Peter.* Edited and translated by J. Owen. Grand Rapids: Eerdmans, 1948.

Charles, J. D. "1 Peter." EBC 13. Rev ed. Grand Rapids: Zondervan, 2006.

Clowney, E. P. *The Message of 1 Peter: The Way of the Cross.* BST. Downers Grove/Leicester: InterVarsity, 1988.

Craddock, F. B. *First and Second Peter and Jude.* WBC. Louisville: Westminster/John Knox, 1995.

Cranfield, C. E. B. *1 and 2 Peter and Jude.* TBC. London: SCM, 1960.

Davids, P. H. *The First Epistle of Peter.* NICNT. Grand Rapids: Eerdmans, 1990.

Elliott, J. H. *1 Peter: A New Translation with Introduction and Commentary.* AB37B. New York: Doubleday, 2000.

Goppelt, L. *A Commentary on 1 Peter.* Edited by F. Hahn. Translated by J. E. Alsup. Grand Rapids: Eerdmans, 1993.

Grudem, W. *The First Epistle of Peter.* TNTC. Leicester/Grand Rapids: InterVarsity/Eerdmans, 1988.

Hillyer, N. *1 and 2 Peter, Jude.* NIBC. Peabody: Hendrickson, 1992.

Hort, F. J. A. *The First Epistle of St. Peter.* Edited by B. F. Dunelm. London: Macmillan, 1989.

Jobes, K. H. *1 Peter.* BECNT. Grand Rapids: Baker Academic, 2005.

Kelly, J. N. D. *A Commentary on the Epistles of Peter and Jude.* London: Adam & Charles Black, 1969.

Kistemaker, S. J. *Exposition of the Epistles of Peter and of the Epistle of Jude.* NTC. Grand Rapids: Baker, 1987.

Leaney, A. R. C. *The Letters of Peter and Jude.* CBC. Cambridge: Cambridge University Press, 1967.

Marshall, I. H. *1 Peter.* IVPNTC. Leicester/Downers Grove: InterVarsity, 1991.

McKnight, S. *1 Peter.* NIVAC. Grand Rapids: Zondervan, 1996.

Miller, D. G. *On This Rock: A Commentary on First Peter.* Allison Park: Pickwick, 1993.

Moffatt, J. *The General Epistles: James, Peter and Judas.* MNTC. London: Hodder & Stoughton, 1928.

Mounce, R. H. *Born Anew to a Living Hope: A Commentary on 1 and 2 Peter.* Grand Rapids: Eerdmans, 1982.

Perkins, Pheme. *First and Second Peter, James, and Jude.* IBC. Louisville: John Knox, 1995.

Plumptre, E. H. *The General Epistles of St. Peter and St. Jude.* CBSC. Cambridge: Cambridge University Press, 1892.

Reicke, B. *The Epistles of James, Peter, and Jude.* AB. Garden City: Doubleday, 1964.

Richard, E. J. *Reading 1 Peter, Jude, and 2 Peter: A Literary and Theological Commentary.* Macon, GA: Smyth & Helwys, 2000.

Schreiner, T. R. *1,2 Peter, Jude.* NAC 37. Nashville: Broadman and Holman, 2003.

Senior, D. *1 & 2 Peter.* NTM 20. Wilmington: M. Glazier, 1980.

_____. *1 Peter, Jude and 2 Peter.* Sacra Pagina. Wilmington: Michael Glazier, 2002.

Stibbs, A. M., and A. F. Walls. *The First Epistle General of Peter.* TNTC. Grand Rapids: Eerdmans, 1959.

Vaughan, C., and T. D. Lea. *1, 2 Peter, Jude.* BSC. Grand Rapids: Zondervan, 1988.

Waltner, E., and J. D. Charles. *1–2 Peter, Jude.* BCBC. Scottdale/Waterloo: Herald, 1999.

Wand, J. W. C. *The General Epistles of St. Peter and St. Jude.* WC. London: Methuen, 1934.

Foreign Language Commentaries

Balz, H., and W. Schrage. *Die katholischen Brief: Die Briefe des Jakobus, Petrus, Johannes und Judas.* NTD 10. Göttingen: Vandenhoeck & Ruprecht, 1973.

Brox, N. *Der erste Petrusbrief.* EKK 21.

Chain, J. *Les Épitres catholiques: La seconde ép_tre de saint Pi_rre, les ép_tres de saint Jean, l'ép_tre de saint Jude.* 2nd ed. *EBib.* Paris: Gabalda, 1939.

Knoch, O. *Der erste und zweite Petrusbrief. Der Judasbrief.* RNT. Regensburg 1990.

Michl, J. *Die katholischen Briefe.* RNT 8. 2nd ed. Regensburg: Pustet, 1968.

Schelkle, K.-H. *Die Petrusbriefe. Der Judasbrief.* HTKNT 13/2. 5th ed. Freiburg/Basel/Wien: Herder, 1980.

Spicq, C. *Les Ép_tres de Saint Pi_rre.* SB. Paris: Gabalda, 1966.

Windisch, H. *Die katholischen Briefe.* 2nd ed. Tübingen: Mohr, 1930.

Wohlenberg, G. *Der erste und zweite Petrusbrief und der Judasbrief.* KNT 15. Leipzig: Deichert, 1915.

Studies

Bauckham, R. J. "James, 1 and 2 Peter, Jude." In D. A. Carson and H. G. M. Williamson, eds., *It Is Written: Scripture Citing Scripture. Essays in Honour of B. Lindars.* Cambridge: Cambridge University Press, 1988, 303–17.

Bechter, S. R. *Following in His Steps: Suffering, Community, and Christology in 1 Peter.* Atlanta: Scholars, 1998.

Chester, A., and R. P. Martin. *The Theology of the Letters of James, Peter, and Jude.* NTT. Cambridge: Cambridge University Press, 1994.

Elliott, J. H. "First Epistle of Peter." In ABD 5 (New York: Doubleday, 1992): 169–278.

_____. *A Home for the Homeless: A Sociological Exegesis of 1 Peter: Its Situation and Strategy.* Philadelphia: Fortress, 1981.

Martin, T. W. *Metaphor and Composition in 1 Peter.* SBLDS 131. Atlanta: Scholars Press, 1992.

Schutter, W. L. Hermeneutic and Composition in 1 Peter. WUNT 2/30. Tübingen: Mohr-Siebeck, 1989.

Thuren, Lauri. Argument and Theology of 1 Peter: The Origins of Christian Paraenesis. JSNTSS 114. Sheffield: Sheffield Academic Press, 1995.

Four

2 PETER

A Call to Virtue Amidst Vice

Along with the epistle of Jude, 2 Peter may have the dubious distinction of being consistently overlooked; it never seems to get the attention and respect that it deserves. While relative inattention seems to be the fate of the General Epistles as a whole, this is particularly the case with 2 Peter.[1] Beyond the matter of neglect, however, one might legitimately argue that 2 Peter has suffered more misunderstanding than any other NT document, including the Epistle of Jude. Any reader wishing to enter into serious study of 2 Peter will almost immediately encounter supreme challenges. Unhappily, both neglect and misunderstanding have attended 2 Peter at both the scholarly and the lay level. It is only inevitable that the latter should follow the former, since the guild serves as a resource for the pastor-teacher and the layperson.

But it must be emphasized that this relative inattention has not occurred in a vacuum. In no small measure it is a reflection of prevailing attitudes of NT scholarship—attitudes rooted in an almost universally accepted "early Catholic" interpretation of the letter (see "Authorship" and "Setting" below). "Early Catholicism" is so named because of its fundamental conviction that 2 Peter mirrors second-century developments in the life of the Christian church and thus precludes the possibility that the letter is genuinely Petrine. And because "early Catholic" assumptions about the

[handwritten margin note: Interesting]

Unless otherwise indicated, all Scripture quotations in this chapter are from the New International Version (NIV).

[1] On which, see J. D. Charles, "Interpreting the General Epistles," in D. A. Black and D. S. Dockery, eds., *Interpreting the New Testament: Essays on Methods and Issues* (Nashville: Broadman & Holman, 2001), 433–56.

epistle continue to color much commentary, they shall require a thoroughgoing critique.

However, we begin by acknowledging salutary developments in the study of 2 Peter in recent decades. One impetus came from Tord Fornberg's important volume *An Early Church in a Pluralistic Society: A Study of 2 Peter*, published in 1977. *An Early Church* was significant insofar as it challenged the exegetical starting-point of standard commentary on 2 Peter. Fornberg saw the need to probe—and reconstruct—the social location of the audience based on markers supplied by the text itself, arguing that the readers were immersed in a pervasively pagan social environment—perhaps in Asia Minor, Syria, or even Rome. Because it focused on textual indicators rather than proceeding from theological presuppositions external to the text, one important consequence of Fornberg's study was to challenge the near-universal "early Catholic" assumption that 2 Peter was mirroring the church's battle with second-century Gnosticism.

Several studies subsequent to Fornberg's also served to challenge the operating assumptions of "early Catholic" thinking. In his provocative essay "The Form and Background of the Polemic in 2 Peter,"[2] Jerome Neyrey responded to Ernst Käsemann's criticisms that parts of 2 Peter were disconnected, "embarrassing" and "dubious."[3] Because Käsemann's analysis "did not attempt to understand 2 Peter in its proper historical context,"[4] Neyrey contended that these criticisms were misplaced. Neyrey buttressed his argument by making comparisons between 2 Peter and Plutarch's *De Sera Numinis Vindicta*, an Epicurean polemic against divine providence with its denial of afterlife and divine judgment.

Whether or not one is convinced by the parallels to Plutarch and broader themes of Epicurean moral detachment, by presenting fresh comparative materials dating roughly contemporary with emergent Christianity Neyrey, in a creative way, contributed toward the furnishing of a new starting point by which to reassess 2 Peter. Neyrey's fine Anchor Bible commentary (1993) further explores first-century comparative material.[5]

[2] Jerome H. Neyrey, "The Form and Background of the Polemic in 2 Peter," *JBL* 99 (1980): 407–31.

[3] Ernest Käsemann, "An Apologia for Primitive Christian Eschatology," in *Essays on New Testament Themes* (London: SCM, 1964), 135–57.

[4] Neyrey, "The Form and Background of the Polemic in 2 Peter," *JBL* 99 (1980): 407.

[5] Jerome Neyrey, *2 Peter, Jude: A New Translation with Introduction and Commentary* (AB 37C; Garden City: Doubleday, 1993).

In addition to the work of Neyrey, several other essays that were published about the same time deserve mention—two in particular because they move the discussion of ethics and eschatology in 2 Peter in a helpful direction by calling attention to similar apologetic parallels from pagan literature. Rainer Riesner compares the description in 2 Peter 3 of cosmic conflagration with its counterpart (*ekpurēsis*) in the Stoic teaching whereby he underscores the fundamental difference in the two worldviews. There exists a radical discontinuity between Judeo-Christian understanding of the cosmos and its Stoic parallel, even when 2 Peter is borrowing Stoic categories.[6] C. P. Thiede, utilizing a similar interpretive approach, provides further evidence from both pagan literature and the early church fathers to suggest that 2 Peter is mirroring contemporary pagan-Christian philosophical debates over cosmology and cosmic conflagration.[7]

Without question, the greatest impetus to renewed interest in 2 Peter came from Richard Bauckham's highly acclaimed commentary on 2 Peter and Jude (1983) and Duane Watson's rhetorical criticism of the same two epistles (1988). Both volumes brought welcome attention to the two neglected NT books. Challenging the adequacy of the "early Catholic" rubric imposed on 2 Peter, Bauckham correctly noted the absence in Jude and 2 Peter of early Catholicism's primary distinguishing features—e.g., a fading of the parousia hope, the increasing institutionalization of the early church, and a crystallizing of faith into set forms or formulas.[8]

Since the early 1990s there has been a steady stream of commentaries that mirror a debt to Bauckham's and Watson's work. These

---

[6] Rainer Riesner, "Der zweite Petrus-brief und die Eschatologie," in G. Maier, ed., *Zukuenftserwartung in biblischer Sicht: Beitraege zur Eschatologie* (Wuppertal: Brockhaus, 1984), 124–43. Significantly, Riesner suggests a dating for 2 Peter that might possibly fall within the apostle Peter's lifetime.

[7] C. P. Thiede, "A Pagan Reader of 2 Peter: Cosmic Conflagration in 2 Peter 3 and the OCTAVIUS of Minucius Felix," *JSNT* 26 (1986): 79–96. See also E. Lövestam, "Eschatologie und Tradition im 2. Petrusbrief," in W. C. Weinrich, ed., *The New Testament Age: Essays in Honor of B. Reicke* (2 vols.; Macon: Mercer University Press, 1984), 2:287–300. Lövestam also concerns himself with the eschatological question in 2 Peter. The focus of Lövestam's study is the Jewish model of flood typology as an apologetic response, with consideration given to parallels from intertestamental literature, rabbinic literature, the Synoptics, and Jude. What is absent, in my view, from Lövestam's otherwise helpful treatment of eschatology and ethics is a discussion of the literary, social, and theological distinctives that set 2 Peter apart from Jude.

[8] To Bauckham's argument can also be added a further cardinal assumption made by early Catholic exegesis: presumption that the Spirit's charismatic work resides in an office. Both 2 Peter and Jude mirror quite the opposite: in 2 Peter the Spirit inspires prophetic utterance (1:21); in Jude the Spirit inspires persons (v. 19) and prayer (v. 20), distinguishing authentic from inauthentic believers (v. 19).

include Neyrey (1993), Perkins (1995), Lucas and Green (1995), Knight (1995), Craddock (1995), Moo (1996), Charles (1999), Watson (2000), Richard (2000), Kraftchick (2002), Knoch (2002), Harrington (2002) and Schreiner (2003). While monographs on 2 Peter remain few and far between, two volumes, both of which build on and expand the work of Bauckham, Watson, Fornberg and Neyrey, require some comment. It was particularly Fornberg's *An Early Church* that served as inspiration for *Virtue Amidst Vice* (1997), in which I attempted to extend the trajectory of Fornberg's thinking about the social setting markers in 2 Peter. My concern was to identify the writer's literary-rhetorical strategy in address-ing his readers, who seemed to be located in a pervasively Gentile location. In this volume the reader will sense my priority to assess critically the reigning assumptions of "early Catholic" while at the same time identifying a literary strategy at work in the epistle that sets 2 Peter apart from Jude. It is the thesis of *Virtue* that 2 Peter offers a window into the moral world and philosophical discourse of Greco-Roman paganism—a world in which moral skepticism, consummating in a denial of moral accountability, is on display.

At the heart of 2 Peter's hortatory strategy, I attempt to argue, is the application of Christian paraenesis by borrowing contemporary Hellenistic moral ideals and categories. The challenge set before the Christian community is to validate its profession with virtuous liv-ing in the context of a cultural climate that can only encourage vice. Thus it is argued in *Virtue* that the burden of the writer of 2 Peter is less theological and eschatological doctrine—presupposed by the "early Catholic" hypothesis—than *ethics and virtuous living.*[9]

The most important study in 2 Peter since the publication of Duane Watson's 1988 monograph unhappily has received limited attention due to its Swedish publisher. In my estimation, its exposure is inversely proportionate to its value. *Sharers in Divine Nature: 2 Peter 1:4 in Its Hellenistic Context*, by James M. Starr, is a veritable treasure of back-

---

[9] I advance this argument as well in two essays: J. Daryl Charles, "The Language and Logic of Virtue in 2 Peter 1:5–7," *Bulletin of Biblical Research* 8 (1998): 55–73, and idem., "On Angels and Asses: The Moral Paradigm in 2 Peter 2," *Proceedings of the Eastern Great Lakes and Midwest Biblical Society* 21 (2001): 1–12. See also my commentary on 2 Peter, which is part of the revised edition of the Expositor's Bible Commentary (vol. 13; Grand Rapids: Zondervan, 2006), wherein broader issues relative to 2 Peter are examined: history of inter-pretation and composition (359–63), canonical considerations (363–65), authorship, pseud-onymity and destination (365–71), literary relation to Jude (371–73), recent Petrine schol-arship (373–76), and themes (376–79). For a more pastoral orientation toward 2 Peter, see Erland Waltner and J. Daryl Charles, *1–2 Peter, Jude* (BCBC; Scottdale: Herald Press, 1999).

ground information in its exploration of linguistic and philosophical concepts that surface in 2 Peter. For this very reason the title of Starr's volume is somewhat misleading, since its investigation extends well beyond the limits of one verse. *Sharers* is perhaps the best resource available for placing 2 Peter in its Hellenistic milieu. Starr demonstrates remarkable dexterity in weaving together theological, historical and cultural threads that converge in the letter and thus distinguishes his work from much commentary on 2 Peter. A salient feature of *Sharers* is that while it is in constant conversation with critical scholarship and diverse methodologies, it is not subservient to methodological constraints or historical-critical presuppositions about 2 Peter that originate outside the text. *Sharers* succinctly captures the purpose of the letter: 2 Peter is concerned to "shape the events of the present in view of the inevitable future judgment of the individual's character" while calling to the reader's attention the "ever-present danger in the narrative structure of 2 Peter . . . the possibility of moral collapse."[10] Starr's book represents the best in its synthesis of 2 Peter scholarship to date.

Authorship

The writer of 2 Peter introduces himself as "Simon Peter, a servant and apostle of Jesus Christ" (1:1) and proffers eyewitness testimony from the mount of transfiguration (1:16–18). In addition he notes that this is the "second epistle" he has written to them (3:1), and he predicts his own imminent death (1:13–15). Nevertheless, critical scholarship, with its "early Catholic" reading and assumed post-apostolic dating of the epistle, is virtually unanimous that Peter himself was not the author. Thus, J. N. D. Kelly in his commentary can write, "Scarcely anyone nowadays doubts that 2 Peter is pseudonymous,"[11] giving the impression that anyone who challenges the scholarly consensus of the guild must be a virtual flat-earther. NT scholar Willi Marxsen is even more insistent: "The author cannot possibly be Peter."[12] And even Richard Bauckham, despite challenging some of early Catholicism's assumptions, holds 2 Peter nonetheless to be "fiction" of an "entirely transparent" kind

---

[10] James M. Starr, *Sharers in Divine Nature: 2 Peter 1:4 in Its Hellenistic Context* (ConBNT 33; Stockholm: Almquist & Wiksell, 2000), 50.

[11] J. N. D. Kelley, *A Commentary on the Epistles of Peter and Jude* (BNTC; London: Adam & Charles Black, 1969), 235.

[12] Willi Marxsen, *Introduction to the New Testament: An Approach to Its Problems*, trans. G. Buswell (Philadelphia: Fortress, 1970), 244.

that derives from a Petrine "circle." This verdict, that the letter is not authentic, is for Bauckham "decisively reinforced" by two bits of evidence: literary genre and dating.[13]

With this kind of certitude on the part of NT scholarship, one seriously wonders why 2 Peter still, at the cusp of the twenty-first century, remains in the NT canon and why, for example, *1 Clement* or the *Shepherd of Hermas* hasn't taken its place. But is the case for 2 Peter's pseudonymity "entirely conclusive," as critical scholarship asserts? And what is the evidence? We shall need to probe the argument for pseudonymity. This argument rests on several planks, each of which will need to be scrutinized. Chief among these are dating, which is the by-product of an "early Catholic" reading of the letter, linguistic or stylistic considerations, and the writer's choice to cast some of his thought in the literary form of a "farewell address" or "testament." While these factors figure in our discussion of the readers' social situation (see "Setting") and the author's literary-rhetorical strategy (see "Literary Features") below, they bear also significantly on the question of authorship.

First, to the issue of the "farewell address" or "testament." Because the testament was a known literary genre, of which the pseudepigraphal *Testaments of the Twelve Patriarchs* is the best-known example,[14] and because the author of 2 Peter is thought to utilize this device (1:12–15), the letter is assumed to be fiction. By means of the testamental genre it is broadly assumed that the name and influence of significant leaders in the church were perpetuated by their circle of disciples. A posthumously published "farewell address," according to this explanation, represents an appropriate way of transmitting the apostle's vision. Significantly, to pose as a leader and to write in the name of a leader are thought to create "no ethical problem for the ancients, and especially in farewell addresses"[15] nor raise theological questions. Thus, based on the accepted use of the testamental genre in antiquity and the noble intentions of the unknown writer, we may conclude that 2 Peter was "transparent" fiction to its initial readers and to the contemporary reader. Michael Green, one of the few NT scholars over the last fifty years to buck the consensus of the

[13] Richard Bauckham, *Jude, 2 Peter* (WBC 50; Waco: Word, 1983), 134–35.

[14] Other examples include the *Testament of Job*, the *Testament of Moses*, and the *Testament of Adam*.

[15] F. B. Craddock, *First and Second Peter and Jude* (WBC; Louisville: Westminster John Knox, 1995), 92.

scholarly guild, has conveniently summarized this widely accepted stance regarding 2 Peter, which is thought to be:

> both a letter and also an example of the type of work we meet in the Testaments of the Twelve Patriarchs. . . . The author's aim was to defend apostolic Christianity in a subapostolic situation, and this he does, not by having recourse to his own authority, but by faithfully mirroring apostolic teaching which he adapts and interprets for his own day. "Peter's testament" formed the ideal literary vehicle for his plans. . . . Nobody ever imagined it came from Peter himself. The literary convention of the Testament was too well known. Such is the theory.[16]

Green finds this view perplexing. Perplexing because if indeed 2 Peter was transparently a pseudepigraphon (to its readers), it is surely strange that no question of morality would arise.[17]

Because "the testamental function of the farewell speech in no way proceeds from the [apostolic] witness and guarantor of [apostolic] tradition himself,"[18] the genre of the farewell speech or testament[19] is seen as an attempt by later generations to "guarantee" the apostolic tradition faithfully.[20] Standard testamental or "valedictory" address is thought to contain notice of one's imminent death, paraenesis or moral exhortation, eschatological predictions mediated through dreams or visions, an historical overview, a transfer of authority, and blessings or curses.[21] Examples of farewell speeches recorded in Scripture—notably Deut 34:1–4; Luke 22:24–30; John 13–17, and Acts 20:17–37—upon examination would seem to borrow from but not be confined to this pattern. Being broadly assumed by critical scholarship is that the authors

[16] Michael Green, *2 Peter and Jude* (TNTC 18, rev. ed.; Leicester/Grand Rapids: InterVarsity /Eerdmans, 1989), 34–35.

[17] Ibid., 34.

[18] Thus O. Knoch, *Die "Testamente" des Petrus und Paulus: Die Sicherung der apostolischen Überlieferung in der spätapostolischen Zeit* (SBB 62; Stuttgart: KBW, 1973), 28 (my translation).

[19] On the genre of the testament in the NT, see W. S. Kurz, *Farewell Addresses in the New Testament* (Collegeville: Liturgical Press, 1990).

[20] Bo Reicke (*The Epistles of James, Peter, and Jude* [AB 37; New York: Doubleday, 1964], 146–47) appears to have been the first to posit the testamental hypothesis for 2 Peter. Commentary since has assumed this starting point; thus, e.g., Bauckham, *Jude, 2 Peter*, 131–35; Watson, "The Second Letter of Peter," in NIB, vol. 12 (Nashville: Abingdon, 1998), 323–61; and more recently, S. J. Kraftchick, *Jude, 2 Peter* (ANTC; Nashville: Abingdon, 2002), 73–76.

[21] See Kurz, *Farewell Addresses*, 48–52, and Knoch, *Die "Testamente,"* 28–31.

of pseudepigraphal testaments, who are chronologically removed from the apostles, nevertheless take a necessary (when secondary) place alongside the apostles and prophets (cp. Eph 2:20) in guarding and transmitting the apostolic tradition to the subapostolic church. That use of the testamental genre raises no ethical questions is seen in the explanation of Frederick Danker: "In most cases there was no attempt to deceive the public, but to say, 'If N. N. were living, this is what N. N. would say to us.'"[22]

But Green will have none of it, believing that pseudonymity theory requires too much of us, and therefore, is open to serious challenge. Green's basis for objection is this:

> It was into a church exercising this sort of [lack of]
> discrimination that we are asked to believe 2 Peter was
> surreptitiously inserted. I find it very hard to believe.
> It was not as though we were plentifully supplied with
> examples of orthodox pseudepigrapha which were
> cheerfully accepted by the second-century church and
> later generations.[23]

With Green, we might ask: How can it be so confidently asserted, as mainstream scholarship has done, that 2 Peter was "intended to be entirely *transparent* fiction"? Can later generations in fact be "guaranteeing" the apostolic tradition in this manner?

To assess pseudonymity theory, with its problems, forthrightly, as Michael Green has done, is to point out what is painfully obvious yet conveniently side-stepped: proponents of pseudepigraphy in 2 Peter—and specifically, the testamental hypothesis—attempt to adduce evidence for a phenomenon in Christian literature that *has never been shown to have existed.*[24] While the amount of literature devoted to the question of Christian pseudepigraphy is massive,[25]

---

[22] "2 Peter," in G. Krodel, ed., *The General Letters* (Minneapolis: Augsburg, 1995), 84.

[23] Green, *2 Peter and Jude*, 34.

[24] Green's argument is developed in both *2 Peter Reconsidered* (London: Tyndale, 1961) and *2 Peter and Jude*. Green's argument reinforces that of D. Guthrie in "The Development of the Idea of Canonical Pseudepigrapha in New Testament Criticism," in R. P. Martin, ed., *VE* 1 (London: Tyndale, 1962), 43–59.

[25] A comprehensive bibliography of literature up to 1965 is found in W. Speyer, "Fälschung, literarische," *RAC* 7:271–78. A more recent survey of the literature is found in J. D. Charles, *Literary Strategy in the Epistle of Jude* (Scranton/Toronto/London: University of Scranton/ Associated University Presses, 1993), 81–90. For a more recent attempt to justify the use of pseudepigraphy in the NT, see D. G. Meade, *Pseudonymity and Canon: An Investigation into the Relationship of Authorship and Authority in Jewish and Earliest Christian Tradition* (WUNT

discussion frequently falls short of satisfying answers to questions such as those posed by Bruce Metzger:

> From an ethical point of view, is a pseudepigraphon compatible with honesty and candor, whether by ancient or modern moral standards? From a psychological point of view, how should one estimate an author who impersonates an ancient worthy . . . ? Should we take him seriously, and, if we do, how does this bear on the question of his sanity? From a theological point of view, should a work that involves a fraud, whether pious or not, be regarded as incompatible with the character of a message from God?[26]

Good question → (handwritten annotation)

To pose these questions is eminently reasonable, as Metzger has done, at the ethical, psychological and theological levels. Yet another question is not so easily dispelled—one that is methodological, namely, how to reconcile the "fictive" and the real occasion in pseudepigraphal literature in general. In order to make sense of epistolary writing, both the identity of the author and the social location of the audience must be reconciled to the text of the epistle itself.[27] To what extent is the testamental hypothesis imposed upon, as opposed to *leading from*, the text?

Does 2 Peter in fact conform to the pattern of testamental literature? In what ways? Does it deviate? In what ways? It should be emphasized that 2 Peter is free of legendary and apocryphal elements

---

39; Tübingen: Mohr, 1986). A helpful response to Meade's position can be found in E. E. Ellis, "Pseudonymity and Canonicity of New Testament Documents," in W. J. Wilkins and T. Paige, eds., *Worship, Theology and Ministry in the Early Church* (JSNTSup 87; Sheffield: JSOT Press, 1992), 212–24; T. D. Lea, "Pseudonymity and the New Testament," in D. A. Black and D. S. Dockery, eds., *New Testament Criticism and Interpretation* (Grand Rapids: Zondervan, 1991), 535–59; T. L. Wilder, "Pseudonymity and the New Testament," in D. A. Black and D. S. Dockery, eds., *Interpreting the New Testament: Essays on Methods and Issues* (Nashville: Broadman & Holman, 2001), 296–335. In addition, see the aforementioned arguments set forth by Green and Guthrie.

[26] B. Metzger, "Literary Forgeries and Canonical Pseudepigrapha," in *New Testament Studies—Philological, Versional and Patristic* (Leiden: Brill, 1980), 1, 22. See also Terry L. Wilder, *Pseudonymity, the New Testament, and Deception* (Lanham, MD.: University Press of America, 2004), whose recent monograph on pseudonymity and the NT provides answers to some of the type of questions that Metzger asks.

[27] Here we must dissent from Fornberg's explanation (*An Early Church*, 10–11), which is insufficiently free of "early Catholic" restraints on the text. He writes that 2 Peter was written "when the church became aware of the distance to the first Christian generation, and therefore wished to hold fast to the leading personalities of the first generation in order to solve problems of her own time."

that tend to characterize spurious documents, of which both second- and first-century BC Jewish apocalyptic testaments as well as Petrine pseudepigrapha of the second century are notorious examples.[28] Equally telling is the wholesale absence from 2 Peter of apocalyptic dreams or visions and the element of blessings or curses, which are salient features of the standard testamental genre. By contrast, the stamp of the epistle is *decidedly and explicitly prophetic*—"and we have the word of the prophets made more certain" (1:19a)—rather than apocalyptic. Also absent from 2 Peter is the characteristic transfer of authority, which William Kurz views as the "primary function" of the biblical farewell address to "describe and promote transition from original religious leaders . . . to their successors."[29]

Significantly, rather than transfer authority, 2 Peter contains testimony to the author's own authority, an authority that needs application in light of the exigencies at hand among his readers. The writer's presence on the mountain of transfiguration is not some "cleverly invented story" for the purpose of deceiving others[30]; rather, it serves as an apostolic imprint that is left behind for the sake of the church: "We were eyewitnesses of his majesty . . . we ourselves heard this voice" (1:16–18). The reminiscence of the transfiguration account, frequently thought by commentators to render the epistle inauthentic due to its differing from the synoptic version, serves two purposes. First, it establishes a thematic link to the parousia in chapter 3. It is a foreshadow not only for the apostles but for all believers of "the power and coming of our Lord Jesus" (1:16; cp. 3:4,8–10). Second, and more immediately, it testifies to the writer's own authority.

Further complicating the case for pseudonymity is that fact that 2 Peter, moreover, begins with substantial didactic material, which tends *not* to be a part of pseudepigraphal farewell speeches. Lastly, and not insignificantly, the allusion in 2 Peter to the writer's death (1:14) is not immediate, neither is it prominent; rather, it is injected only parenthetically *after* the substantial paraenetic and didactic portions of the letter—and this only in a veiled manner. The spe-

---

[28] Precisely this was the chief reason for 2 Peter's difficulty in achieving canonical recognition among the early church fathers.

[29] Kurz, *Farewell Addresses*, 50.

[30] Consider the apostle Paul's own words in this regard, as if attune to the possibility of apostolic imitation, that his readers are "not to become easily unsettled or alarmed by some prophecy, report or letter supposed to have come from us, saying that the day of the Lord has already come. Don't let anyone deceive you in any way" (2 Thess 2:2–3a).

cial appeal of the farewell address, it should be emphasized, is the relationship of the audience to the one standing before death, as is understood by the passion and drama of the John 13–17 narrative.

The argument advanced by both Guthrie and Green, that no evidence in Christian literature of an orthodox pseudepigra- phon exists, plus the lack of parallels between known testaments and 2 Peter, places the testamental hypothesis on shaky ground. Furthermore, as Earle Ellis has emphasized, early Christian writ- ers knew how to transmit the teachings of an authority figure without engaging in pseudipipraphal literary devices.[31] If the epistle is a pseudepigraphon, then the degree to which the writer is attempting deception is breathtaking: "We did not follow clev- erly invented stories . . . ; we were eyewitnesses . . ." (1:16); "we ourselves heard this voice . . . when we were with him" (1:18); "Dear friends, this is now my second letter to you" (3:1). In the end, why is it *not* possible, or permissible, that Peter the apostle may have cast his exhortation in the form of a letter that *incorpo- rates in a selective manner* "testamental" features?[32] After all, Paul's "valedictory" speech to the elders of the church at Ephesus (Acts 20:17–37) may serve to illustrate that a farewell speech may adopt characteristics of a "last will" or "testament" without being re- stricted to pseudepigraphal genre.

Surely the impressive commitment of critical scholarship to pseudonymity theory must be taken seriously. At the same time, statements such as that of Bauckham, that "Second Peter bears so many marks of the testamental genre . . . that readers familiar with the genre must have expected it to be fictional,"[33] require some moderation. For as James Starr, in his exhaustive study of the lan- guage of 2 Peter, remarks, "2 Peter is often described as belonging to the tradition of Jewish 'testaments,' but these at best exhibit only a tenuous similarity of genre to 2 Peter."[34]

The implication of apostolicity as it relates to the possibility of pseudonymity in the NT is this: "apostolic pseudepigrapha," strictly speaking, is a contradiction in terms, since not even well-intended literary motives, expressed under the name of an

---

[31] Ellis, "Pseudonymity," 220.

[32] While Green acknowledges this possibility (*2 Peter and Jude*, 35–36), Bauckham says no (*Jude, 2 Peter*, 134–35).

[33] Thus Bauckham, *Jude, 2 Peter*, 134.

[34] Starr, *Divine Sharers*, 4.

apostle, warrant apostolic authority.[35] Given the apostles' role in
the church's foundation (Eph 2:20; 3:5), the ethical dilemma of
why the church would sanction the use of pseudepigraphy in the
service of advancing Christian orthodoxy does not evaporate as
readily as critical scholarship might contend. The function of the
apostolate was *authoritative and binding* in nature. For this reason, "friends of the apostle," subsequent-generation disciples, and
Pauline or Petrine "circles" were not accorded apostolic authority
by the early church, even when critical scholarship today might.
Apostolic witness is not merely personal testimony that broadly
agrees with what the apostle himself would have said. It is, rather
"infallibly authoritative, legally binding deposition, the kind that
stands up in a law court. Accordingly, that witness embodies a
canonical principle; it provides the matrix for a new canon, the
emergence of a new body of revelation to stand alongside the covenantal revelation of the Old Testament."[36] Correctly, Earle Ellis
has argued that "scholars can not have it both ways. They cannot
identify apostolic letters as pseudepigrapha and at the same time
declare them to be innocent products with a right to a place in the
canon."[37]

There exists, however, one further element that needs exploring. If, with the consensus of critical scholarship, we refuse to
permit 2 Peter to be the work of the apostle himself, can we categorically rule out the possibility that he obtained secretarial assistance? That is to say, the fact *that* an epistle such as 2 Peter
might issue from the apostle in the historical setting, illuminated
from within the text, is not to say *how* it might issue from him. At
some point we must be willing to ask whether 2 Peter even allows
for the remote possibility of some sort of scribal help via an amanuensis. E. I. Robson, for one, invites the modern reader to make
allowances for dictation in the NT, for "when an ancient writer

---

[35] A postbiblical source no less than Tertullian informs us that the writer of the pseudepigraphal work *The Acts of Paul and Thecla*, regardless of the best of intentions in seeking to pass
off his work under the name of the apostle Paul, was punished as a forger by being defrocked
as a presbyter (*Bapt.* 17).

[36] Thus R. B. Gaffin, Jr., "The New Testament as Canon," in H. M. Conn, ed., *Inerrancy and
Hermeneutic: A Tradition, a Challenge, a Debate* (Grand Rapids: Baker, 1988), 176.

[37] Ellis, "Pseudonymity," 224. It is reasonable to conclude with Donald Guthrie regarding
2 Peter: "It did not require much foresight for an old man to suggest that his end was not
far away. Moreover, a pseudepigraphist writing this would not appear to add anything to
the information contained in the canonical sources, in spite of writing after the event" (*New
Testament Introduction* [4th ed., Leicester/Downers Grove: Intervarsity, 1990], 821).

wanted to write, his one anxiety seems to have been how he could best avoid writing; and the convenience of the slave-amanuensis enabled him so to avoid it, by allowing him to declaim, talk, even babble garrulously, at will, hardly feeling that he was making any special literary effort."[38]

We have already explored in 1 Peter the dimensions that secretarial assistance adds to our interpretation. This neglected perspective, which would account for significant differences in the language and style of 1 and 2 Peter, is amplified by G. J. Bahr:

> The influence of the secretary would be even greater if he were left to compose the letter himself along general lines laid down by the author. The result would be that the letter might represent the basic thought of the author, but not necessarily his terminology or style. . . . It may be that the discrepancy between what Paul wrote and what he spoke was due to the abilities of a secretary who was expert in the composition of letters.[39]

The differences in vocabulary and style between 1 and 2 Peter render entirely plausible the use of different secretaries.[40]

We must draw our discussion of pseudonymous authorship to a close. An underlying assumption of all pseudonymity theory is that because a work ultimately found acceptance by the church as canonical, pseudonymity as a literary device in the end is acceptable. And any authority the writer possesses—whether he is

---

[38] "Composition and Dictation in New Testament Books," *JTS* 18 (1917): 296.

[39] G. J. Bahr, "Paul and Letter Writing in the First Century," *CBQ* 28 (1966): 475–76.

[40] In the view of Bauckham, the language alone "makes it improbable that the apostle could have written 2 Peter" (*Jude, 2 Peter*, 158). By contrast, for Jerome the difference in style and expression between 1 and 2 Peter could be accounted for on the basis of different amanuenses (*De vir. Ill.* 1). Antedating the Pauline Epistles by a century, Cicero frequently at the end of his letters—and occasionally in the middle—offered explanations for writing with his own hand or dictating (e.g., *Fam.* 3.6; *Ad Att.* 2.23; 7:138.12; 13.9; 14.21; 16.15). Similarly, the apostle Paul shows evidence of both practices in his letter writing: his epistles are stated to have been written with his own hand as well as dictated: "I, Paul, write this greeting in my own hand" (1 Cor 16:21); "see what large letters I use as I write to you with my own hand" (Gal 6:11); "I, Paul, write this greeting with my own hand" (Col 4:18); "I, Paul, write this greeting in my own hand, which is the distinguishing mark in all my letters. This is how I write" (2 Thess 3:17); "Only Luke is with me. Get Mark and bring him with you, because he is helpful to me in my ministry" (2 Tim 4:11); "I, Paul, am writing this with my own hand" (Phlm 19); "with the help of Silas, whom I regard as a faithful brother, I have written to you briefly" (1 Pet 5:12).

a member of a "Petrine school," a "Petrine agent," or some individual several generations removed from the apostle—inheres in
the fact that he is "faithfully interpreting" the apostolic tradition.
Accordingly, we are asked to believe that because the writer's motives were noble and because a work, relatively speaking, was "orthodox," the church in time was accepting of it. But this appraisal
requires too much of us, asking us to suspend judgments that both
the text of the NT and church tradition impose upon us. Roger
Beckwith, in his evaluation of Jewish and Hellenistic attitudes
toward literary pseudepigraphy, reminds us that, in Hellenistic
Jewish circles, the only category of pseudonymity that *does* seem to
have been acknowledged was that which involved no pretense or
deception, that is, where no secrecy was made of a work's pseudepigraphal character (such as the book of *Wisdom*, "written by the
friends of Solomon in his honor"). At the same time, Beckwith
gently chides biblical scholarship for advancing hypotheses that
avoid drawing the conclusion that Jews and Christians did not
in fact reckon pseudepigraphy as an acceptable literary device.[41]
Precisely this undiscerning attitude is what prompted J. A. T.
Robinson, no theological conservative (!), to quip that "there is
an appetite for pseudonymity [among critical scholars] that grows
by what it feeds on."[42] Robinson is doubtless on to something. It
is precisely the concern for pseudonymity that would appear to
underlie Paul's exhortation to the Thessalonians not to be shaken
by a "letter supposed to have come from us" (2 Thess 2:2). The
implication here is patent: others were not averse to using his apostolic pedigree. Paul, of course, penned this statement not many
years before 2 Peter would have been written.

What remains inexplicable, particularly in 2 Peter 1, is the accent on the writer's own moral authority. If it is assumed from the
outset that the letter is from an individual other than the apostle, 2 Peter is then read with a view of ferreting out evidence that
would support the notion of pseudepigraphy. The result is, among
others, that the self-referential allusions such as one finds in 1:1
("Simon Peter, an apostle") and 1:16–18 (eyewitness testimony of
the transfiguration event) are to be viewed as literary hubris at best
and forgery at worst. In the end, one is left, with the majority of NT

[41] Roger Beckwith, *The Old Testament Canon of the New Testament Church* (Grand Rapids: Eerdmans, 1985), 274–433.

[42] J. A. T. Robinson, *Redating the New Testament* (London: SCM, 1976), 186.

scholars, to hypothesize about postapostolic scenarios and make inferences about a theologically inferior document of the NT.

If, on the other hand, the writer is defending himself as well as the integrity of the Christian gospel (as Paul was forced to do on occasion),[43] his own authority rests on nothing less than his historical relationship to Jesus. That (a) the writer seems not dependent on synoptic accounts of the transfiguration and (b) the pseudepigraphal *Apocalypse of Peter* makes use of 2 Peter together have been interpreted as casting doubt on 2 Peter's authenticity. Despite the overwhelming consensus of biblical scholarship in rejecting Petrine authorship, satisfactory explanations of the "eyewitness" language in these verses have yet to be offered. Michael Green calls attention to "the apostolic 'we'" in "we were eyewitnesses"—indeed, a necessary accent *if* Christian truth is being undermined (cp. 1 Cor 15:3–8,12–34; 1 John 4:1–3).[44] It is supremely difficult to envision moral authority resting in the literary product of one who, even though well intentioned, must resort to specious statements such as "we were there with him on the holy mountain." Such requires too much from the reader.

While it is true, as Andrew Chester and Ralph Martin write, that the status of 2 Peter "as part of the New Testament canon with normative value is both an ancient and a modern challenge,"[45] this challenge should not be overstated. One unfortunate by-product of contemporary scholarly thinking about 2 Peter is that the epistle has been marginalized in mainstream biblical studies, thus joining Jude's "most neglected" status. J. Ramsey Michaels is correct to state that the case against authenticity in 2 Peter has been overstated; and he is correct in his observation that "most of its content is perfectly credible as early tradition, oriented primarily to the apostle's own lifetime."[46] When all is said and done, the pseudepigraphal hypothesis, when scrutinized, asks far too much of us. Indeed, the pseudepigraphal hypothesis seems to have contributed significantly toward 2 Peter's marginalization—a marginalization from which the guild and the laity are still recovering.

---

[43] First Corinthians 4 is one such striking example.

[44] Green, *2 Peter and Jude*, 93.

[45] Andrew Chester and Ralph Martin, *The Theology of the Letters of James, Peter, and Jude* (NTT; Cambridge: Cambridge University Press, 1994), 47.

[46] J. Ramsey Michaels, "Second Peter and Jude—Royal Promises," in G. W. Barker et al., eds., *The New Testament Speaks* (New York: Harper & Row, 1969), 351.

Setting, Audience Situation, Destination, Date of Writing

In sharp contrast to 1 Peter, the absence of names and places in 2 Peter renders it difficult to arrive at any conclusions regarding the identity of the recipients of the letter and their social situation. Notwithstanding the lack of certainty as to the provenance and destination of the letter, the letter does contain textual indicators pointing to a particular social location in which the readers find themselves, as Fornberg's important study attempted to argue. It is well possible that the letter is addressed to Christians in Greece or Asia Minor, where Paul's letters had already circulated (3:15–16).[47] Despite similarities to Jude, which reflects a distinct Palestinian Jewish-Christian milieu,[48] 2 Peter suggests an audience in pagan Gentile surroundings.

What indicators do we have? Among such are:

- the allusion to equality (1:1), an important political virtue to the Hellenistic mind
- the mystical-philosophical language of partaking in the "divine nature" (1:4)
- use of a catalog of virtues (1:5–7), a common rhetorical device among Stoic moral philosophers
- strongly worded paraenesis (moral exhortation) in the face of apparent ethical lapse (e.g., 1:12–15)
- use of the term "eyewitness" (1:16), a technical term in classical Greek used to describe those who had achieved the highest degree of Eleusian mystery-religion experience
- a reference to Tartarus (2:4), the subterranean abyss and place of punishment in Greek mythology
- the allusion to Noah's generation (2:5)
- comparison to Lot's predicament in Sodom (2:6)
- use of Balaam typology (2:15–16), which suggests apostasy and moral decay
- use of common and pagan proverbial images to depict apostasy (2:20–22)
- a moral apologetic against radical relativists (3:3–7)

---

[47] If one assumes 2 Peter to be authentic, it is likely to have been written from Rome shortly before the apostle's death (1:15).

[48] Most commentary acknowledges the Jewish-Palestinian milieu of Jude, which I develop at length in Charles, *Literary Strategy*.

- multiple allusions to the Hellenistic virtue of piety (1:3,6,7; 3:11)

Traditional commentary on 2 Peter tends to be highly derivative in character, unified in the conviction, as we have observed at some length already, that the letter is not authentically Petrine. From the modern perspective, several factors might be cited as contributing to 2 Peter's questionable status. One is the letter's struggle to achieve canonical status in the early church. Another is the obvious literary relationship to Jude. A further factor is the letter's relationship to 1 Peter and our difficulty in reconciling the language and style of 2 Peter with the NT portrait of the apostle. Yet another obstacle is the predominance of an "early Catholic" reading of the epistle, with its governing historical-theological assumptions. These assumptions we will need to probe.

For roughly a century and a half the governing presupposition of NT scholarship has been that 2 Peter is mirroring a second-century church at war with the forces of Gnosticism. Few have stated the *sine qua non* of critical scholarship as clearly and resolutely as Willi Marxsen, in his *Introduction to the New Testament*:

> So long as we assume the traditional idea of canonicity and accept as permanently normative only what derives from the apostles or the disciples of the apostles, as did the early Church, "not genuine" is a serious charge to make. . . . But if we admit its pseudonymity we are far more likely to place the letter in its particular historical context and to be able to understand it. Whether we draw the line [of composition] at the beginning of the second century or earlier is simply a matter of choice. If we make the cut at the beginning of the second century, we are faced with a relatively compact body of literature. We could perhaps exchange 2 Peter for the Didache and Jude for 1 Clement, but this is of no significance as far as basic [interpretive] principles are concerned, and we should therefore not make it a problem.[49]

These words were published in 1970. Already in 1958 Marxsen had published his seminal work, *Der 'Frühkatholizismus' im Neuen*

---

[49] Willi Marxsen, *Introduction to the New Testament* (Philadelphia: Fortress, 1970), 12–13.

Testament ("Early Catholicism in the New Testament"), at a time when Marxsen joined other influential NT scholars such as Ernst Käsemann in training an emerging generation of theologians and exegetes who would influence NT interpretation up to the present day. While that next generation of scholars has all but disappeared from the academy, the effects of Marxsen's generation still linger, regardless of the extent to which postmodernism informs present-day theory. The point to be made is simply this: biblical studies inherits a starting-point that has been assumed by prior generations of biblical scholars, and in the case of 2 Peter this starting-point is the assumption that the letter is *not* apostolic.

In describing the *Sitz im Leben* or life setting of 2 Peter, Marxsen had this to say:

> This document gives us a glimpse of the situation of the Church at a relatively late period. The eschatology which looks to an imminent End has fallen into the background, and one has to adjust oneself to living in the world (cp. esp. the Pastorals). The Church is in the process of becoming an institution. . . . In the post-Pauline period—long after Paul, in fact, for he has already become a "literary entity" belonging to the past—the futurist eschatology of the Church is attacked by the Gnostics. "Where is the promise of his coming? For from the day that the fathers fell asleep, all things continue as they were from the beginning of the creation" (iii.4). Though far removed from the beginnings of the Church, the author is seeking to remain in continuity with these beginnings and sets out an "apologia for the primitive Christian eschatology" in its apocalyptic form.[50]

It goes without saying that an "early Catholic" reading of the NT is by no means confined to 2 Peter or Jude. What does need emphasis is that here it is applied in its most concentrated and radicalized form. Critical scholarship, with very few exceptions, uniformly assumes the epistle to be the latest of the NT writings,[51]

---

[50] W. Marxsen, *Der 'Frühkatholizismus' im Neuen Testament* (BIBS 21; Neukirchen: Neukirchener Verlag, 1958), 244.

[51] Biblical scholarship in the main tends to favor a dating of the epistle that ranges from the late first or early second century (e.g., Bauckham, *Jude, 2 Peter*, 157–62), and thus roughly a generation removed from the apostles, to the late second century (e.g., A. Vögtle, "Die

mirroring second-century developments in the life of the church. While Käsemann and Marxsen develop the wider theological implications of "early Catholicism" for NT study, Ferdinand Hahn summarizes the implications of "early Catholic" thinking for interpreting 2 Peter: "Even though the implications might not yet be clearly seen, there is a practical awareness that the apostolic era is surely closed and that the immediate postapostolic period is soon ending. Hence, now the present tradition material must be preserved in its basic meaning and form."[52] And if Hahn's position appears unequivocal, K.-H. Schelkle's verdict is to announce foreclosure: "The letters [2 Peter and Jude] say themselves that the generations of the church are past. . . . The Apostolic era is closed and lies behind."[53]

"Early Catholic" thought proceeds on the basis of certain historical and theological assumptions about the biblical text. Documents that are "early Catholic" are post-apostolic, as viewed from the earlier, purer, "Pauline" perspective.[54] The term "early Catholicism" (German: *Frühkatholizismus*) is understood to represent the period of transition from earliest Christianity to the postapostolic church—a transition completed with the disappearance of the imminent expectation of the parousia or Second Advent, a growing institutionalization of the church, and need for a teaching office (which replaces the charismatic work of the Spirit), an increasing dichotomy of priests and laity with a correlative emphasis on canonical authority to safeguard the church's teaching, and the codification of beliefs into creedal confessions for the purposes of defending the faith against Gnostic heresy.

For our purposes, 2 Peter, in the words of James D. G. Dunn, is said to be "a reaction to the repeated disappointment of apocalyptic hopes [in Christ's return]," it "is a prime example of early

Schriftwerdung der apostolischen Paradosis nach 2. Petr 1,12–15," in *Neues Testament und Geschichte: O. Cullmann zum 70. Geburtstag* [Zürich/Tübingen: Theologischer Verlag/Mohr-Siebeck, 1972], 297–305), during which time the NT canon was taking shape. Notable exceptions to this include Green, *2 Peter Reconsidered* and *2 Peter and Jude*; Guthrie, *New Testament Introduction*, 811–42 (originally published in 1962 as *Hebrews to Revelation*, 137–85); N. Hillyer, *1 and 2 Peter, Jude* (NIBC; Peabody: Hendrickson, 1992), 9–12; and Charles, *Vice Amidst Virtue*, 11–75.

[52] F. Hahn, "Randbemerkungen zum Judasbrief," *TZ* 37 (1981), 209–10 (my translation).

[53] K.-H. Schelkle, "Spätapostolische Briefe als frühkatholisches Zeugnis," in J. Blinzer *et al.*, eds., *Neutestamentliche Aufsätze für J. Schmid* (Regensburg: Pustet, 1963), 225 (my translation).

[54] See in this regard Ernst Käsemann, "Paul and Early Catholicism," in *New Testament Questions Today* (Philadelphia: Fortress, 1969), 236–51.

Catholicism."[55] The presence of "early Catholic" phenomena, therefore, undermines the notion that 2 Peter can be authentically Petrine. Hence, Ernst Käsemann can describe the epistle as "dubious" and displaying irreconcilable theological contradictions,[56] while Gunter Klein believes it inconceivable that 2 Peter is authentic and in the same league as the epistles of Paul:

> This writer could not have dreamt that his own letter would join—and in fact follow—in the same canonical collection the letters of Paul, whose writings he held to be suspect. . . . For this reason, the clearly inescapable question puts our assurance of faith to the test, namely, whether we can ultimately consider the epistle of 2 Peter, with its conceptualization of canon, to be canonical.[57]

In fairness, we should respond by noting that there is partial truth in the "early Catholic" interpretation. There is indeed a denial of the Second Advent, but it is on the part of *the deniers*, not the author. And we can grant, with proponents of early Catholicism, that there are new theological developments in the early church. But this is already apparent in the mid 50s, as evidenced by the hints of nascent Gnosticism already in the Christian community at Corinth.

Unhappily, the upshot of an "early Catholic" reading of NT documents is that it creates a "canon within the canon," i.e., it views certain writings of the NT as authentic reflections of the early church's identity and thus of highest theological import—closely resembling the Gospels or Pauline teaching on justification—while relegating other NT documents to the perimeter of the canon. In this light, then, pronouncements by critical scholars, however unflattering, are hardly atypical. Thus, Wolgang Schrage views 2 Peter as "lacking," although he concedes that it is not "worthless,"[58] and Gunter Klein is challenged to find anything of redemptive value in the letter:

---

[55] J. D. G. Dunn, *Unity and Diversity in the New Testament: An Inquiry into the Earliest Character of Christianity* (Philadelphia: Westminster, 1977), 351.

[56] Käsemann, "An Apologia," 156–57.

[57] G. Klein, "Der zweite Petrusbrief und der neutestamentliche Kanon," in *Ärgernisse: Konfrontationen mit dem Neuen Testament* (Munich: Chr. Kaiser Verlag, 1970), 112 (my translation).

[58] H. Balz and W. Schrage, *Die katholischen Briefe: Die Briefe des Jakobus, Petrus, Johannes und Judas* (NTD 10; Göttingen: Vandenhoeck & Ruprecht, 1973), 123 (my translation).

> The author . . . wants to restore the fragile doctrine
> of last things to a new credibility, but he is only able
> to destroy it yet further. In spite of how vigorously he
> asserts himself, he is basically helpless. . . . The de-
> fender of Christian hope has had his feet pulled out
> from under him. . . . The dubious manner with which
> he treats his subject is a clear reflection of the writer's
> own lack of self-assurance.[59]

It will not do, however, merely to point out, with F. B. Craddock,
that "arguing for or against Petrine authorship has lost its importance for most scholars."[60] That Petrine pseudepigraphs were circulating in the second century was not unimportant to the early
fathers. For this reason, they agonized over the difference between the spurious and the genuine. What we *can* say, rather, is
that because of the conspicuously negative assessment of the letter,
2 Peter (and with it, Jude) has labored under a heavy load. Hence,
a reconstruction of the setting is the first order of business, requir-
ing a critical assessment of "early Catholicism" and its purported
second-century ecclesiastical phenomena.

It needs reiteration that the problem with "early Catholicism"
is not in its observation of second-century developments, nor that
documents of the NT foreshadow "early Catholic" theological tendencies that mature in the second and third centuries. The problem,
rather, lies with its starting point, namely, "early Catholicisms"'
foundational assumption that apostolic authorship presents an
"obstacle" to NT exegesis.[61] It is thus automatically presupposed
that the writer is far removed from the beginnings of the church
and that pseudonymity, via the literary device of a "testament," allows us to penetrate the full meaning of the letter. Therefore, we
can say with J. D. G. Dunn, "I would want to insist that in not a few
compositions Martin Luther and John Wesley, for example, were as,
if not more inspired, than the author of II Peter."[62] *First Clement*

---

[59] Klein, "Der zweite Petrusbrief," 111–12 (my translation).

[60] Craddock, *First and Second Peter and Jude*, 13.

[61] Alignment with the church's historical consensus constitutes a major stumbling block
for many historical-critical scholars. For evangelicals it is a necessary precommitment in the
exegetical task and something that they are prepared to do. To defer to the church's consensual exegesis historically is not to be obscurantist; rather, it is to acknowledge the limitations
of both the interpretive community and the exegete.

[62] Dunn, *Unity and Diversity*, 374–86.

or *Barnabas*, therefore, can be substituted for 2 Peter or Jude, and without any theological significance.

Previously, we noted the salient features of the "early Catholic" rubric. Chief among these is that the church has abandoned the hope of the parousia. As it turns out in 2 Peter, quite the opposite is on display. With great earnestness the readers are admonished that the eschatological day of reckoning is *certain*. The fact that a morally earnest and pastorally sensitive explanation for the "delay" is offered (3:8–13) cannot itself be construed to mean that the parousia hope is fading. The reason for this is not a fading hope but divine longsuffering: "The Lord is not slow in keeping his promise, as some understand slowness. He is patient with you, not wanting anyone to perish, but everyone to come to repentance" (3:9). Notice as well the effect of the parousia on its audience: to the believer it serves as hope and encouragement, but to the false prophet and the moral skeptic, it is a *threat*.[63] The primary issue, from the standpoint of the writer, is not *timing* but the *fact* of a day of reckoning. Those who would ascribe to 2 Peter a late date due to a "fading Parousia hope" fail to note that the earliest NT letters we possess, 1 and 2 Thessalonians, address this issue. Both early and later NT documents mirror the same eschatological tension.[64]

Let us, however, take "early Catholic" claims at their own merit. Käsemann writes: "We have to state clearly and without evasion that this hope proved to be a delusion and that with it there collapsed at the same time the whole theological framework of apocalyptic."[65] Franz Mussner concurs: "The detachment [from the apostolic period] represents a vacuum in the church's history that almost gives the impression of a 'fracture' . . . One must imagine oneself in that situation, with the burning question that confronted them: The apostles are dead. What now?"[66] If, as Käsemann and Mussner contend, the NT does give evidence of an "early Catholic" church evacuating an imminent parousia hope, then the church of any age faces a serious dilemma: How does the church resist the temptation

---

[63] Thus, Green, *2 Peter and Jude*, 27.

[64] E.g., Heb 10:36–39; James 5:8; 1 Pet 4:7; 2 Pet 3:1–10; and Rev 22:20. Even in subapostolic writings this is still the case—e.g., *Did.* 10:6; *1 Clem.* 23:5; *2 Clem.* 12:1,6; *Barn.* 4:3; and *Herm. Vis.* 3:8,9.

[65] Ernest Käsemann, "The Beginnings of Christian Theology," in *New Testament Questions for Today* (Philadelphia: Fortress, 1969), 106.

[66] Franz Mussner, "Die Ablösung des Apostolischen durch das nachapostolische Zeitalter und ihre Konsequenzen," in *Wort Gottes in der Zeit* (Festschrift K.-H. Schelkle; Düsseldorf: Patmos, 1967), 169–70 (translation mine, emphasis his).

to abandon its allegiance to Him after the "cardinal error" of a false hope, given Jesus' assertions about a possible imminent return, has been exposed? His teaching surely leads to quite delusory—and pastorally deleterious—results. Wittingly or unwittingly, the "early Catholic" scenario reconstructed by critical scholarship creates the impression of succeeding generations of early Christians who are dull and spiritually undiscerning.

Jaroslav Pelikan and I. Howard Marshall have cautioned against imbibing wholesale an "early Catholic" backdrop to NT studies. Both contend that while the imminence of the Second Advent was indeed part of Jesus' teaching, it is not what "early Catholic" proponents have made it out to be.[67] Pelikan prefers to speak of a *shift within the polarity* of the "already-not yet" tension inherent in the Christian message. This "shift" issues out of a renewed appreciation for ethical imperatives that define the church's relationship to the world. And indeed every generation of Christians struggles with this tension, not only the early church.

Our reconsideration of the NT's eschatological perspective leads us to rethink basic "early Catholic" assumptions. Does "early Catholicism"—with its supposed "delay" in the parousia hope and second-century reconstruction—imply *a priori* a wrong exegetical or theological starting point? Is it an interpretation *imposed upon* rather than *drawn from* the text?

One further aspect of "early Catholic" thought requires comment. In 2 Peter there is no reference to church office holders, which is requisite if the letter is a mirror of second-century developments. Rather, what we do discover is that the onus for spiritual discernment is placed on the individual believers themselves; the flock is admonished to guard itself. Consider the epistle's paraenetic language: the readers are exhorted to "make every effort" to strengthen the ethical underpinnings of their faith (1:5). Much in the Pauline mode of exhortation, 2 Peter is a call for members of the Christian community to be on guard themselves and live virtuous lives.

There is, relatedly, no ecclesiastical control over doctrine that manifests itself in 2 Peter in the way that "early Catholic" exegesis requires. What is utterly conspicuous, in fact, is the silence of the

---

[67] I. H. Marshall, "Is Apocalyptic the Mother of Christian Theology?" in G. F. Hawthorne and O. Betz, eds., *Tradition and Interpretation in the New Testament* (Grand Rapids/Tuebingen: Eerdmans/Mohr-Siebeck, 1987), 333–42, and J. Pelikan, *The Emergence of the Catholic Tradition (100–600),* vol. 1, *The Emergence of the Catholic Tradition* (Chicago: University of Chicago Press, 1971), 123–24, 130–31.

ecclesiastical voice in the letter. Not an institution, not an office, but the inspiration of the Holy Spirit is at work in the people of God (1:21b).[68]

Finally, to presuppose a late date for 2 Peter, with mainstream scholarship, is consequently to assume that all of Peter's letters would have long been accessible—to both the author and the readers. But this creates a dislocation in the mind of the reader, as Green has pointed out. The statement in 3:15–16 makes less sense if penned by a pseudepigrapher. To "Peter," Paul is a "beloved brother"; to Polycarp, several generations removed, he is "the blessed and glorious Paul." In the second century, given the maturity of heretical teachings, one may have been inclined to view Paul either as an arch-villain or as the apostle *par excellence*. But it is rather dubious that Paul would have been referred to as a "dear brother" by later generations.[69]

The "early Catholic" reading of 2 Peter, as we have observed, presumes a second-century setting for the epistle. Part of the agenda, then, is to adjust the church's eschatological expectations, given the assumption that the imminent expectation of the parousia has disappeared and that false doctrine is the need of the hour. If on the other hand, not doctrine per se but *moral corruption* threatens the community (which, of course, always seeks and expresses itself in doctrinal justification), then we would expect an argument from the writer of 2 Peter that simultaneously emphasizes the necessity of virtuous living among the faithful and condemnation of the morally depraved. And this is precisely what is on display in the letter. The burden of the writer is primarily ethical, not doctrinal—a reading of the letter that finds confirmation in the paradigms, each of which emphasizes moral debauchery, as well as the character of the opponents, who are said to

---

[68] Rightly understood, 2 Peter 1:20–21 has nothing to do with scriptural interpretation, the church's official teaching office, or a primitive type of church magisterium. The issue at hand, supported by the letter's contextual flow, is *prophetic and authoritative speech*. The author, who is claiming to be an eyewitness of the transfiguration (12:16–18), is vigorous in his assertion: "And we have the word of the prophets made more certain" (1:19), for which a better translation might be: "Thus we have the prophetic message attested." It is the inspiration of the Spirit that is said to convey authority. This interpretation is confirmed when we consider the basic motifs and solutions to the church's threat mounted by Ignatius, Clement, or Hermas in the postapostolic period: e.g., calling the bishop, through whom Christ's authority is necessarily channeled; securing the church's authority by doing everything according to the proper order; and proclaiming penance and rationed forms of grace.

[69] Green, *2 Peter and Jude*, 158–59.

"deny" (*arneomai*, 2:1) Christ. "Denial" is the language of apostasy. Our argument that 2 Peter is foremost concerned with ethics rather than doctrine will be buttressed—or undermined—by prominent themes that emerge from the letter, to which we shall now turn.

Important Themes and Subthemes

1. *Virtue and godly character* (1:3,5 [2x],6–7; 2:9; 3:11). Three prominent motifs in the epistle surface in 2 Peter 1.[70] The first of these relates to a godly lifestyle and virtuous character (1:3–11). The author, by way of introduction, places notable emphasis on divine resources available to the Christian for living a godly life. Divine power and promises have been provided so that the readers might escape moral corruption in the world around them. This demarcation, the writer takes great pains to point out, depends not merely on the promises themselves (great as they are), but on the ethical response of the Christian. To this end, the author uses a Stoic rhetorical device, a catalog of virtues, to exhort his readers to a higher ethical plane.[71] Verses 3–7 have been said to constitute a page from "current pagan textbook morality."[72]

The net effect of the catalog, which suggests moral progress, should not be lost on the reader: human cooperation with God, while it does not *cause* righteousness, nevertheless "confirms" or validates the believer's "call and election" (1:10). Piety or godliness, another important catchword in 2 Peter (1:3,6–7; 2:9), expresses generic reverence and occurs in both religious and nonreligious contexts. The NT term seems to carry both Christian and broader Hellenistic connotations: it serves to accent a particular way of life and behavior that is worthy of praise. The soul of religion, after all, is its practice. In 2 Peter, piety stands in direct and conspicuous opposition to "moral corruption" (1:4; 2:12 [2x],19) and "evil desires" (1:4; 2:10,18; 3:3).

2. *Knowledge* (1:2–3,5–6,8,12,14,16,20; 2:9,20–21 [2x]; 3:3,17,18). A second theme surfacing almost immediately in the epistle is that of "knowledge," which both as a noun and in its related

---

[70] See also Charles, "2 Peter," *EBC* 13, 376–79, where these three are developed more fully.
[71] Charles, *Virtue Amidst Vice*, 99–111.
[72] Kelly, *A Commentary on the Epistles of Peter and Jude*, 306.

verb forms functions in 2 Peter as something of a catchword.[73] For this reason, the writer intends "to keep on reiterating these things," even though the readers "already *know* them and are established in the truth that formerly had come" to them.[74] He deems it necessary to "refresh the memory" of his audience and seeks to "make every effort" in admonishing them "to recall these things." Knowledge—both the generic variety and of God (1:2–3; 3:18)—is exceedingly important to the writer. Not insignificantly, knowledge and grace both open (1:2) and close (3:18) the epistle, forming something of an inclusio for rhetorical effect.[75] The burden of 2 Peter is not "knowing" in the doctrinal or theological sense so much as remembering, and thus living, what one knows to be true.

In addition, Balaam typology, abbreviated in Jude, is expanded in 2 Peter to illustrate the moral accountability that accompanies "abandoning" the knowledge of God (2:15–16). To abandon knowledge of the truth, i.e., apostasy, is not foremost a doctrinal issue; rather it is ethical.[76] The knowledge motif is reiterated once more in 2 Peter 2 by means of two proverbial images—the dog returning to its vomit and the pig returning to the mud. To have had knowledge of the truth and then to deny that truth is depicted in rather severe terms (2:20–22).

3. *Apostasy* (2:1–3,14–15,20–22; 3:17). The paradigms of 2 Peter 2—the fallen angels, Noah's generation, Sodom and Gomorrah, and Balaam—together point toward a state of moral decay and moral compromise that portend irrevocable judgment. Moreover, all function to remind the audience of pagan socio-cultural forces that inundate the believer. Nevertheless, while those forces are formidable and intimidating, they are not overwhelming. Perhaps most disturbing are the allusions to disenfranchised angels and to Balaam. Both remind the reader that it is precisely because the angels did in fact rebel and Balaam was in fact seduced for the purposes of leading Israel astray that apostasy is a real possibility for those who "profess" Christ. Thus, the warning proffered in 2 Peter cannot

---

[73] "Knowledge" and "knowing" receive particular emphasis in 2 Peter 1 (vv. 2–3,5,6,8,16,20), not because of a purported second-century gnostic threat—*contra* J. Moffatt, *The General Epistles: James, Peter and Judas* (MNTC; London: Hodder and Stoughton, 1928), 361–63, and others—but because of the grace the Christian believer has already received (1:1–4).

[74] Emphasis mine.

[75] Accompanying this is a second set of subthemes, life and godliness (1:3 and 3:11), which enhances the rhetorical and hortatory effect of this inclusio in the letter.

[76] Here we wish to distinguish between "apostasy," by which we refer to the departure from or leaving what one knows to be true, and "heresy," which is false, errant or radically "sectarian" teaching that breeds doctrinal distortions.

be construed as "hypothetical." Rather, the author is countering a painfully real situation. Of all the characters in the OT and in Jewish tradition, it is Balaam who embodies apostasy, something which genuine believers cannot commit.

The writer's use of moral typology climaxes in his rather striking use of two graphic images—the dog returning to its vomit and the pig returning to the mud. The accompanying observation is this: it would be better not to have been born than to know the truth and renounce it (vv. 20–22). The moral types and the imagery being used agree with the description of those who threaten the community: they "deny" the Master Himself, Jesus Christ (2:1). That is, they *depart* (2:14) from what they know to be true.[77] The radical nature of denying is what results in the moral skepticism being mirrored in 2 Peter 3; moral skeptics, in the end, are left to deny the possibility of any sort of moral accountability.

4. *Judgment* (2:3–4,9,11; 3:7), *destruction* (2:1 [2x]–3; 3:7,16), *and salvation/Savior* (1:1,11; 2:20; 3:2,18,15). Whereas the use of moral typology in Jude is designed to underscore categorical judgment alone, in 2 Peter 2 it has a dual function—to underscore both judgment *and* salvation. In Jude, by contrast, God is Judge, and judgment is categorical; in 2 Peter, however, God is both Judge and Savior.[78] Both epistles, to be sure, express the reality of coming judgment in terms and imagery that strike the reader as fierce and unrelenting. In 2 Peter 2 the judgment theme initially appears as a condemnation of the opponents. It is then substantiated in the author's reciting of historical types. But whereas in Jude moral typology functions to announce only judgment, in 2 Peter it also reminds the readers of the reality of divine mercy. Hence, Noah and Lot—not mentioned in Jude—are depicted as righteous amidst their contemporaries (2:5–9a).

Significantly, in 2 Peter 3 the motifs of virtue, judgment, and the knowledge of God are united in the writer's apocalyptic exhortation to the moral skeptic (3:3–7) and in the concluding admonitions to the readers toward perseverance and virtuous living (3:8–18).

---

[77] On Balaam typology in Jewish traditional material, see G. Vermes, "The Story of Balaam," in *Scripture and Tradition in Judaism: Haggadic Studies* (SPB 4; Leiden: Brill, 1973), 127–77; M. S. Moore, *The Balaam Traditions: Their Character and Development* (SBLDS 113; Atlanta: Scholars, 1990); and J. T. Greene, *Balaam and His Interpreters: A Hermeneutical History of the Balaam Tradition* (Atlanta: Scholars, 1992).

[78] Apocalyptic eschatology is used in both Jude and 2 Peter, although in the latter it functions as part of a moral apologetic directed at the radical moral skeptic whose worldview is pagan.

Insofar as the ethical life has been the burden of the writer, thus shaping his literary-rhetorical strategy on display in 1:3–2:22, it remains for the writer to expose and critique those individuals who by reason of moral license and moral skepticism actually call into question the very existence of a created moral order.

Ancillary to the judgment-versus-salvation contrast is the wickedness-versus-righteousness dualism that is central to apocalyptic literature in general. In biblical literature this contrast is not designed to be predictive[79] or revelatory; rather, it is used to call the readers or listeners to a decision, to elicit a response. It is first and foremost ethical. The at-times strongly apocalyptic character of 2 Peter, notably in chapters 2 and 3, reflects the wicked-righteous contrast, pointing to judgment and deliverance/salvation respectively.[80]

Literary Features

The focus of most critical study of 2 Peter tends to be twofold: the question of authenticity and the literary relationship to Jude. Because of the numerous and unmistakable instances of literary dependence, J. M. Starr observes, "Scholarly research on 2 Peter has more than anything else been an investigation of parallels."[81] Indeed it has. And not without reason, for of the 25 verses in Jude, parts or all of 19 verses are found in 2 Peter. Four options account for literary dependence: (1) Jude borrows from 2 Peter[82]; (2) 2 Peter borrows from Jude[83]; (3) both 2 Peter and Jude borrow

[79] Herein the NT Apocalypse and portions of Hebrews, 1 Peter, 2 Peter, and Jude distinguish themselves from Jewish apocalyptic literature, in which the predictive and revelatory elements are chiefly on display.

[80] The amount of literature on the wicked-versus-righteous dualism is enormous. A helpful survey can be found in L. J. Kreitzer, "Apocalyptic, Apocalypticism," in R. P. Martin and P. H. Davids, eds., *Dictionary of the Later New Testament and Its Developments* (Downers Grove, IL: InterVarsity, 1997), 55–68.

[81] Starr, *Sharers in Divine Nature*, 7.

[82] Thus E. H. Plumptre, *The General Epistles of St. Peter and St. Jude* (Cambridge: Cambridge University Press, 1926), 268; C. Bigg, *A Critical and Exegetical Commentary on the Epistles of St. Peter and St. Jude* (ICC; Edinburgh: T. & T. Clark, 1902), 216–23; and T. Zahn, *Introduction to the New Testament* (3 vols.; Edinburgh: T. & T. Clark, 1909), 2:250–51.

[83] Thus F. H. Chase, "Peter, Second Epistle of," HDB 3:799–809; F. Maier, "Ein Beitrag zur Priorität des Judasbriefes," *TQ* 87 (1905): 547–80; J. B. Mayor, *The Epistle of St. Jude and the Second Epistle of St. Peter* (New York/London: Macmillan, 1907), i–xxv; J. Chaine, *Les Épîtres catholiques: La seconde Épître de saint Pierre, les Épîtres de saint Jean, l'Épître de saint Jude* (EBib; Paris: Gabalda, 2nd ed., 1939), 18–24; K.-H. Schelkle, *Die Petrusbriefe. Der Judasbrief* (HTKNT 13.2; Freiburg: Herder, 1961), 138–39; E. M. Sidebottom, *James, Jude and*

from a common third source[84]; or (4) 2 Peter and Jude stem from one and the same author.[85] The question of literary dependence involves arguments that are both external to the text and internal. External factors—e.g, the "early Catholic" hypothesis—arise from attempts by scholars to identify the historical and theological scenario behind 2 Peter. Internal factors would include indicators such as borrowed tradition material, vocabulary, rhetorical technique, or prevailing verb tense.

In the end, it is impossible to be conclusive about the question of literary dependence, regardless of which of the four alternative positions seems most compelling. What may be said with some degree of confidence is that redactive interests differ in 2 Peter and Jude, resulting in two differing literary-rhetorical strategies that are constructed according to the needs of each audience. And it is well possible that the differences, more than the similarities, in the end serve as our most useful interpretive clue.

But who drew from whom, or what common third treatise might have been used by both, does not undercut the authority of either. Again, Green puts the matter in proper perspective:

> If Paul was not averse to adapting to his own purposes the writings of heathen poets, lists of Stoic virtues, fragments of hymns, or the dubious war-cries of his opponents . . . is there any reason to suppose that Peter would be unwilling to draw from the work of a brother of his Master, should it prove to be the case that the Epistle of Jude was written first?[86]

Indeed, the parallels between the two epistles, both in vocabulary and in concept and imagery, are striking, leaving no doubt of some manner of literary relationship between them: (1) both authors describe themselves as "servants" of Jesus Christ (2 Pet 1:1; cp. Jude 1); (2) grace and peace are to be multiplied to the readers (1:2; Jude 2); (3) the readers have a received faith (2:1; cp. Jude 3); (4) both

2 Peter (NCB; London: Thomas Nelson, 1967), 95; T. Fornberg, *An Early Church* (chap. 3); Bauckham, *Jude, 2 Peter,* 142; Neyrey, *2 Peter, Jude,* 122; Chester and Martin, *Theology,* 139; and Kraftchick, *Jude, 2 Peter,* 80.

[84] Thus E. I. Robson, *Studies in the Second Epistle of St. Peter* (Cambridge: Cambridge University Press, 1915); Reicke, *Epistles,* 189–90; C. Spicq, *Les Épîtres de Saint Pièrre* (SB; Paris: Gabalda, 1966), 197; and Hillyer, *1 and 2 Peter, Jude,* 13.

[85] Thus Robinson, *Redating,* 192–95.

[86] Green, *2 Peter and Jude,* 24.

epistles understand Christian faith in terms of a divine "call" (1:3,10; cp. Jude 1); (5) opponents deny Christ's lordship (2:1; cp. Jude 4); (6) destructive heresies have been secretly brought in (2:1; cp. Jude 4); (7) the opponents are licentious in their ways (2:2; cp. Jude 4); (8) the opponents' judgment has been declared long ago (2:3; cp. Jude 4); (9) the fallen angels serve as a moral paradigm (2:4; cp. Jude 6); (10) the fallen angels are reserved in darkness for judgment (2:4; cp. Jude 6); (11) Sodom and Gomorrah serve as a moral paradigm (2:6; cp. Jude 7); (12) the opponents walk according to the flesh, indulge in their lusts and do not hesitate to despise authority (2:1; cp. Jude 8,18); (13) God's angels exhibit restraint in contrast to the opponents (2:11; cp. Jude 9); (14) the opponents are compared to brute beasts, irrational by nature (2:12; Jude 10); (15) Balaam serves as a moral type (2:15–16; Jude 11); (16) the opponents are portrayed as spots or blemishes (2:13; Jude 12); (17) the opponents have erred, forsaking the right way (2:15; cp. Jude 11); (18) the opponents are compared to clouds (2:17; Jude 12); (19) deepest darkness has been reserved for the opponents (2:17; cp. Jude 13); (20) the opponents are boastful, lustful and seductive (2:18; cp. Jude 16); (21) the apostasy of the opponents has been predicted (3:2; cp. Jude 17); (22) scoffers in the last days are predicted (3:3; cp. Jude 18); (23) Jewish-Christian eschatological thinking is present (3:5–10; cp. Jude 14–15); (24) the readers are admonished to be without spot or blemish (3:14; cp. Jude 24); (25) the readers are admonished toward stability (3:17; cp. Jude 24); (26) for the readers to fail to persevere is described in terms of "stumbling" or "falling" (1:10; cp. Jude 24); (27) God is understood as "savior" (2:7,9; cp. Jude 25); (28) doxological praise is ascribed to Jesus Christ as both Lord and Savior, now and forever (3:18; cp. Jude 25).[87]

The amount of verbal and graphic parallels is impressive. Nevertheless, paying attention to the unique redactive interests of each writer reveals a unique literary-rhetorical strategy at work in each letter. For this reason it is helpful to observe the ways in which the two epistles differ: For example, (1) the author of 2 Peter claims apostleship, whereas Jude identifies himself as a being a brother of James; (2) Jude's language and imagery reflect a Palestinian Jewish-Christian milieu, whereas 2 Peter mirrors a more

---

[87] See also Charles, "2 Peter," *EBC* 13, 372.

pervasively Gentile social environment; (3) Jude exhibits a rampant use of triplets, a pattern not conspicuous in 2 Peter; (4) whereas Jude plunges immediately into theological controversy, in 2 Peter the controversy is reserved for later in the epistle; (5) 2 Peter uses the moral paradigms to emphasize both deliverance and judgment, whereas in Jude the paradigms categorically announce judgment; (6) paradigms and tradition material are used in Jude that would be meaningful to readers with a Jewish background (e.g., Michael the archangel, the *Assumption of Moses*, *1 Enoch*, Cain, and Korah), whereas tradition material used in 2 Peter is more meaningful for an audience surrounded by Gentiles; (7) in 2 Peter the fallen angels are said to have been cast into Tartarus, whereas Jude speaks of the fallen angels as being reserved in chains in Hades; (8) the fallen angels in 2 Peter, moreover, are said generically to have "sinned," whereas Jude describes them specifically as those "who did not keep their positions of authority but abandoned their dwelling"; (9) Jude cites verbatim an extrabiblical text (*1 Enoch* 1:9), whereas no direct citations are used in 2 Peter; (10) 2 Peter is a tract consisting primarily of exhortations toward virtuous living, spelling out the contours of Christian ethics; Jude is a tract announcing condemnation; (11) the reference to Sodom and Gomorrah in Jude is unqualified, whereas in 2 Peter the emphasis is on Lot's struggle with surrounding wickedness; (12) 2 Peter shows evidences of both a personal relationship to the readers and challenges to the author's authority; (13) 2 Peter contains an expanded Balaam typology; (14) 2 Peter suggests future developments among the apostate, whereas Jude suggests that these developments are present and matured; (15) "knowledge" and "piety" or "godliness" are important catchwords in 2 Peter; (16) 2 Peter mirrors possible circulating arguments that deny moral accountability and thus proffers a moral "apologetic" by incorporating eschatological typology; and (17) the author of 2 Peter gives the impression of personal relationship to the apostle Paul, reflecting on Pauline Epistles that have been circulating.[88]

Despite the unmistakable literary dependence between the two epistles, it is significant that there is virtually no *identical* verbal correspondence between the two, since one would naturally expect precisely the opposite. What might this suggest? Unique editorial

---

[88] See also Charles, "2 Peter," *EBC* 13, 372–73. The first three chapters in Mayor (*The Epistle*) provide a near-exhaustive discussion of literary convergence and divergence in the two epistles.

concerns that emanate from two differing social settings. The writers choose and structure their material as literary "brick and mortar" in order to address specific needs in the community.

Our probing and accentuating a literary-rhetorical strategy on display in 2 Peter that is distinct from Jude sharpens our focus in a way that allows us to press beyond verbal similarities between the two letters. Why the use of language, image, and concepts that would appeal to a more Gentile audience? Why the sustained use of paraenetic language and ethical categories, particularly in the early part of the letter? And precisely what is it that should be so urgently "recalled" by the readers (1:12–15)?

The literary-rhetorical strategy of the writer can be detected in the development of the letter's argument. Following the epistolary greeting, a Stoic rhetorical device for inducing moral progress, a catalog of virtues (1:5–7) is employed to outline the contours of Christian "life and godliness." This contains standard features of Stoic ethical lists— e.g., virtue, knowledge, self-control, reverence endurance, brotherly affection.[89] To manifest a virtuous life is to prevent an ineffective and unfruitful life (1:8–9). Conversely, to lack the virtuous life is analogous to blindness resulting from neglecting truth. The opening call in 2 Peter, therefore, is a call to moral self-responsibility.

That 2 Peter is a call to moral progress is clarified by the strong language of paraenesis,[90] or moral exhortation, throughout 2 Peter 1. Such language, pastorally speaking, is intended to spur the readers on to virtuous living. Authentic faith will not fail to validate itself in the moral life. A distinctly Christian ethic will resist the tide of surrounding culture and produce a moral excellence. Tragically, in the view of the author, some have disregarded the divine "promises" (1:4; implied in 1:9,12 and 15) and as a result of their intercourse with society have "forgotten" their "cleansing from past sins" (1:9). Worse yet, some are even entertaining the notion, if not aggressively propagating it, that there is *no moral authority* before which they ultimately must account (2:1; 3:3–5); hence, the function of moral typology in the material to follow.

A detailed sketch of the opponents figures prominently in 2 Peter 2. Standard commentary on the allusion to "false prophets"

---

[89] For a fuller discussion of the contrast between Christian and Stoic ethics, see Charles, *Virtue Amidst Vice*, 99–111.

[90] On the language of paraenesis as a literary genre, see K. Berger, "Hellenistische Gattungen im Neuen Testament," in W. Haase, ed., *ANRW* 2.25.2, 1075–77, and A. J. Malherbe, *Moral Exhortation: A Greco-Roman Sourcebook* (Philadelphia: Westminster, 1986), 124–29.

and "false teachers" in connection with "heresies" in 2:1–3 formly assumes that 2 Peter was written for the purpose of combating false doctrine, and specifically, Gnostic heresy. But does this interpretation fit the textual markers? The writer's extensive ethical vocabulary on display throughout 2 Peter 1 and 2 indicates the precise nature of the pastoral problem at hand. This vocabulary strongly suggests that the problem is first and foremost ethical and not doctrinal[91]: "pleasure," "licentiousness," "depravity," "lusts of the flesh," "covetousness," "defilement," "lawless," "vanity," "irrational beasts," "morally corrupt," "adulterous," "returning to one's own vomit," and "wallowing in mud." The dilemma is not that the Christian community has wrong theological beliefs; it is, rather, that they are not living up to the knowledge of the truth that they already possess, hence the function of the moral paradigm.

Four types or paradigms (2:4–9) illustrate for the writer a dual emphasis of judgment and salvation—judgment for the wicked but salvation for those who persevere (see "Old Testament" below). The fallen angels encounter categorical judgment because of their decision to depart from the knowledge they possessed, as did Noah's contemporaries and Sodom and Gomorrah. By contrast, Noah and Lot are spared due to their "righteousness."[92] Strengthening the writer's argument is the Balaam tradition, at the center of which stands a figure in Jewish interpretive history who was considered notorious as an example of apostasy, i.e., denying the truth.

Finally, the literary character of 2 Peter also raises important questions of genre. And here we only recapitulate: because "the testamental function of the farewell speech in no way proceeds from the [apostolic] witness and guarantor of [apostolic] tradition himself,"[93] one is left to conclude, based on scholarly consensus, that 2 Peter is not authentically Petrine. Yet, the presupposition that well-intended pseudonymous "functionaries," several generations removed, are the ones guaranteeing transmission of the apostolic tradition, is a peculiarly modern assumption that finds no support among the church fathers.

At issue is not the possibility that the writer could have borrowed elements of a conventional literary genre. Indeed, much of biblical

---

[91] The priority of ethics over doctrine in 2 Peter does not minimize the relationship between belief and practice, which is one of organic unity. It is rather a question of emphasis.

[92] Lot's "righteousness" is comparative, not absolute, as the Genesis 19 narrative makes abundantly clear.

[93] Knoch, Die "Testamente," 28.

literature does precisely this. The presence of the farewell address or testament elsewhere in the NT (e.g., Luke 22:24–30; John 13–17; Acts 20:17–35) would suggest that the genre can be—and is—adapted by the writers of the NT and that pseudepigraphy need not be presumed.

In the end, what must be called into question is the insistence of exegetes that 2 Peter is "fictional," and "transparently" so, as critical scholarship requires. Claims made in the epistle itself must be judged on their own merits. The writer of 2 Peter makes conspicuously bold and authoritative claims—claims to authorship, to apostolic authority, and to privileged, apostolic eyewitness testimony. These are claims that do not permit themselves to be so readily dismissed.[94]

NT scholar Terry L. Wilder has compared NT pseudonymity as advanced by mainstream biblical scholarship with Samuel Clemens' use of a pseudonym to write popular novels such as *Huckleberry Finn* and *The Adventures of Tom Sawyer*. Clemens' use of "Mark Twain," observes Wilder, was acceptable and legitimate for two reasons. First, there was no historical figure named "Mark Twain" with whom the reader would confuse the actual author of these books. Second, Clemens did not use his pseudonym for the purpose of securing recognition or authority—precisely the reason for its usage in antiquity. On the contrary, Clemens made use of an *unremarkable* literary convention of the day. In this way, Wilder is quite correct to note that the very reasons for its practice in antiquity—to deceive and garner moral authority—disqualifies it as a literary vehicle by which NT documents were written.

Old Testament and Jewish Tradition Material in 2 Peter

The General Epistles reflect a conspicuous debt to the OT and the Jewish exegetical tradition. They are rich in their appropriation of characters, events, and imagery associated with Israel's history. In the main, it is the literary tendency of the General Epistles to display their relationship to and dependence on the OT—as well as extrabiblical Jewish tradition—literature through indirect allusions rather than direct citations. This is frequently found in the context of moral and hortatory instruction by the writer, and such is decidedly the case with 2 Peter.

---

[94] A fuller discussion of the testamental hypothesis is found in Charles, *Virtue Amidst Vice*, chapter 2.

Although the use of the OT in 2 Peter is not as dense as in Jude, it is noteworthy and pervasive nonetheless. Several partial citations (2:22 // Prov 26:11; 3:8 // Ps 90:4; 3:13 // Isa 65:17) combine with the writer's use of prophetic typology applied to the Christian community for the purposes of condemning the apostate and exhorting the faithful. The letter incorporates imagery and motifs that are part and parcel of Jewish apocalyptic, even when they are mixed with conspicuously Gentile features in the letter—e.g., use of a catalog of virtues resembling popular Stoic philosophizing, a reference to "Tartarus," Lot's depiction as a "righteous" sufferer amidst pagan debauchery, Balaam as a spiritual prostitute, the use of two common proverbs, and flood-fire typology couched in Stoic terms that is directed against moral relativists—to suggest that the audience location is pagan-Gentile and not Palestinian-Jewish.

While cryptic allusions to the fallen angels, Noah and his contemporaries, Lot and Sodom and Gomorrah, and Balaam remain tantalizingly unqualified to the modern reader, they were readily understood by the recipients of 2 Peter and serve as poignant reminders. In Jewish tradition the example of the disenfranchised angels appears frequently alongside hard-hearted Israel, Sodom and Gomorrah, and Noah and the flood as types of apostasy and rebellion upon whom divine judgment fell; hence, they constitute something of a "hall of fate" or "hall of shame"[95] in Jewish history.

Several features differentiate the angelology of the intertestamental period from that of the OT. In the former, their depiction becomes far more elaborate and systematic, with a number of figures having their names and functions expressly stated. Jewish apocalyptic literature knows between four and nine echelons of angelic authorities. The chief angels in heaven's multitiered hierarchy develop strategies, superintend nations, reveal secrets, intercede for the saints, and filter prayers of the righteous.[96]

Neither the OT nor the NT makes any explicit statements as to the fall of the rebellious angels. The NT implies at most the notion

ranks

---

[95] Thus W. M. Swartley, "Intertextuality in Early Christian Literature," in R. P. Martin and P. H. Davids, eds., *DLNT*, 538.

[96] *1 Enoch* 6–9; 14:4; 20:5; 41–43; 46:2; 71:3; *Jub.* 15:31–32; *T. Dan* 6:2; cp. LXX Deut 32:8; Dan 10:13–21; and 12:1. In the book of Daniel, Michael is presented as "one of the chief rulers" (*'aḥad hassārîm hari'sonîm*, 10:13 and 12:1; LXX: *heis tōn archontōn tōn prōtōn*) and "the great angel" (*hassar haggādōl*; LXX: *ho aggelos ho megas*). In late Judaism, he achieves an incomparable stature, from which he mediates the prayers of the saints, offers the souls of the righteous, and accompanies the righteous into paradise.

that Satan, a fallen angel chief among many,[97] was cast down (cp. Luke 10:18; John 12:31; Rev 12:4,7,9–10), yet gives no clear time of the fall. Some, as did Origen, hold Jesus' words in Luke 10:18 as referring to an original fall.[98] Others believe the statement to be a dramatic way of expressing Satan's certain ruin.[99] Still others view the fall as coinciding with Jesus' ministry on earth.[100]

Corresponding typology to the fallen angels might well be drawn from several prophetic oracles in the OT—oracles that serve as graphic illustrations of fall or ruin: (1) Isa 14:5–23, a taunt (*māšāl*, v. 4) against the king of Babylon; (2) Isa 24:21–22, a symbolic representation of Yahweh's judgment; and (3) Ezek 28:1–19, a prophetic funeral dirge (*qînāh*, v. 12) against the king of Tyre. Both Isaiah 14 and Ezekiel 28 appear to be shaped similar to ancient Canaanite creation myths,[101] and both enunciate the same principal reason for the king's demise: pride, self-exaltation, and corruption. The object of condemnation in the Isaiah oracle is characterized by wickedness and oppression (vv. 2,6). In light of the great rejoicing (vv. 7–8), this must have been an archenemy. Evidence of his pompous nature are the multiple "I will" assertions (vv. 13–14), whereby he presumes upon the glory of the Most High, resulting in being "brought down to Sheol" (vv. 9,15), where the spirits of the departed (the *rĕphāʾîm*) greet him.

The funeral dirge in Ezekiel 28 is directed against an arrogant ruler (*nāgîd*, v. 2). This figure is corrupted through his own perception

---

[97] In *Jub.* 10:8 Satan is "Prince of the spirits" (cp. Eph 2:2: *ton archonta tēs exousias tou aeros*). In *T. Dan* 5:6 and *T. Sim* 2:7, he is *ho archon* and *ho archon tēs planēs*.

[98] Origen, *Paed.* 3.2.

[99] E.g., G. Aulén, *Christus Victor* (New York: Macmillan, 1956), 111, and J. W. Boyd, *Satan and Māra* (SHR 27; Leiden: Brill, 1975), 39.

[100] E.g., G. B. Caird, *Principalities and Powers* (Oxford: Clarendon, 1956), 31. Several features differentiate the angelology of the intertestamental period from that of the OT. In the former, their depiction becomes far more elaborate and systematic, with a number of figures having their names and functions expressly stated. Jewish apocalyptic literature knows between four and nine echelons of angelic authorities. The chief angels in heaven's multitiered hierarchy develop strategies, superintend nations, reveal secrets, intercede for the saints, and filter prayers of the righteous. In the book of Daniel, Michael is presented as "one of the chief rulers" (*ʾahad hassārîm hariʾsonîm*, 10:13 and 12:1; LXX: *heis tōn archontōn tōn prōtōn*) and "the great angel" (*hassar haggādōl*; LXX: *ho aggelos ho megas*). In late Judaism, he achieves an incomparable stature, from which he mediates the prayers of the saints, offers the souls of the righteous, and accompanies the righteous into paradise.

[101] Note, for example, the reference in Isa 14:13 to Mount Zaphon, the seat of the Canaanite deity. The use in 14:14 of *ʾel ʾelyôn* would seem to confirm its Canaanite background. See T. H. Robinson, "Hebrew Myths," in S. H. Hooke, ed., *Myth and Ritual* (London: Oxford University Press, 1933), 183; B. S. Childs, *Myth and Reality in the Old Testament* (Naperville: Allenson, 1960), 68–69; and R. J. Clifford, *The Cosmic Mountain in Canaan and the Old Testament* (Cambridge: Harvard University Press, 1972), 160.

of exaltedness.[102] Allusion to "Eden, the garden of God" (v. 13), "the anointed cherub" (vv. 14,16) and fire (v. 16) are reminiscent of the Genesis narrative and suggestive of traditions familiar to the readers.

The oracles of Isaiah 14 and Ezekiel 28, like Jude 6 and 2 Pet 2:4, reflect a catastrophic disenfranchisement, an utter fall from glory. Several elements are common to both the OT and NT texts. In each we encounter an abrupt transition from an earthly to a heavenly plain. This occurs without any explanation or bridge, suggesting that the readers are familiar with backgrounds that are likely assumed by the writer. Second, there is a correlation between the earthly and heavenly in all four cases; that is, the heavenly serves as a paradigm for the earthly. Third, in all four texts the objects of condemnation experience a fall from glory and are consigned to prisoner status.[103]

Although both 2 Pet 2:4 and Jude 6 allude to the punishment of rebellious angels, neither states when or why these angels were disobedient, only that they were judged for having "sinned" (2 Peter) and having "left their own abode" (Jude). Without explanation or commentary, and without necessarily endorsing conceptions of cosmic warfare that have their roots in pagan mythology, Jude and 2 Peter assimilate imagery current to their day and exploit it for their own theological purposes. The motif of "rebellion in heaven," a notion vaguely hinted at in the OT, illustrates graphically the effects of choosing to fall away. Within apocalyptic mythology, a frequent pattern tends to emerge: (1) war erupts in heaven, not infrequently depicted in astral terms,[104] followed by (2) a spilling over of this rebellion to the earth, then culminating in (3) ultimate vindication and punishment by the king of heaven.[105]

---

[102] The man of lawlessness in 2 Thess 2:4 makes a similar claim: *apodeiknunta heauton hoti estin theos.*

[103] While the idea of imprisoned spirits in the OT is undefined, in Jewish apocalyptic literature it is pronounced (e.g., *1 Enoch* 10:4,12–14; 13:1; 18:14,16; 21:3,6,10; 67:4; 69:8; 88:1,3; 90:23; *2 Apoc. Bar.* 56:13; *Jub.* 5:10; Rev 18:2; and 20:3), along with the notion of a pit or "abyss" (*1 Enoch* 10:4; 18:11; 21:7; 22:1–2; 54:5; 56:3; 88:1,3; 90:24,26; and Rev 20:3). Apart from Jude 6 and 2 Pet 2:4, traces of this appear in the NT—e.g., in Jesus' deliverance of the demon-possessed man as recorded in Luke 8:31 (whereupon the demons cast out implore the Son of God not to be cast into the abyss); Rev 9:1–3, which describes the opening of the abyss, out of which ascend locusts that are granted the power of scorpions on the earth; Rev 20:1–3, which describes the imprisonment of Satan for a thousand years in the abyss; and finally, the fascinatingly cryptic and difficult text of 1 Pet 3:18–20.

[104] This depiction we find in Jude, where the apostate are portrayed as "wandering stars" (*asteres planētai*, v. 13), but not in 2 Peter, where we encounter a more Hellenistic version, reminiscent of the Titan mythology.

[105] P. D. Hanson, "Rebellion in Heaven, Azazel, and Euhemeristic Heroes in 1 Enoch 6–11," *JBL* 96 (1977): 208.

We see this pattern on display in the NT Apocalypse: (1) the tail of the dragon draws "a third of the stars" and casts them down to the earth (Rev 12:4); war breaks out in the heaven, with the dragon and his angels fighting Michael and his angels (12:7); and the "king of heaven" vanquishes the dragon, who is cast out (12:8–9).

In 2 Peter, Noah and Lot become types of the faithful who are to expect deliverance from God despite enormous social obstacles. Noah's generation is prototypical of a faithless generation (cp. Matt 24:37–39 and Luke 17:26–28).[106] The message of 2 Peter, in contrast to Jude, is not categorical judgment; it simultaneously assures those who persevere that they will be delivered from the cultural furnace. Norman Hillyer captures the sense of these verses:

> Peter thus maintains his pastoral purpose of encouraging his readers to keep faith with God in their own situation. Such a loyal stand will neither go unnoticed nor fail to attract a similar divine protection from the consequences of sin of the godless . . . Yet, as God kept Noah and his family from perishing in the Flood which carried off the wicked of those times, so the same God will protect believers who remain faithful to him in later generations.[107]

In the typology of 2 Peter, then, the flood performs two functions: it saves the faithful and judges the faithless.

While Noah is a herald of righteousness both in the OT and in intertestamental literature,[108] Lot is by no means a righteous model in the OT. By the Genesis 19 account, he appears to be fully acculturated in Sodom, and in the end he must be removed from the city by physical force (Gen 19:16). Lot's "righteousness," however, is developed in a different direction in Jewish intertestamental literature,[109] although it can be indirectly attributed to Abraham's pleading in Gen 18:16–33. Contrast, not essential nature, is the

---

[106] See J. P. Lewis, *A Study of the Interpretation of Noah and the Flood in Jewish and Christian Literature* (Leiden: Brill, 1968).

[107] Hillyer, *1 and 2 Peter, Jude*, 188–89.

[108] E.g., Sir 44:17–18; Wis 10:4; *1 Enoch* 106–107; *Jub.* 5:19; Josephus, *Ant.* 1.3.1; *Gen. Rab.* 30:7; cp. Heb 11:7. See J. C. VanderKam, "The Righteousness of Noah," in J. J. Collins and G. W. E. Nickelsburg, eds., *Ideal Figures in Ancient Judaism: Profiles and Paradigms* (Chico: Scholars Press, 1980), 13–32.

[109] E.g., Wis 10:6; 19:17; and Philo, *Vit. Mos.* 2.58.

point of the Lot typology.[110] The catastrophe that befell the cities of the plain is intended to be didactic. The visitation of divine judgment made Sodom and Gomorrah "an example" (or "pattern" [*hupodeigma*]) for succeeding generations. And what is the pattern? Moral lapse, when it is allowed to take root and be justified, leads to a moral departure and darkening of one's heart, which—sooner or later—incurs divine wrath. As with Noah and his generation, so it was with Lot and his contemporaries.

Taken together, the ungodly in 2 Peter are reminiscent of one notable OT character—Balaam. Whereas only a brief standardization of type is found in Jude, in 2 Peter Balaam is fully typologized. The apostates are consequently depicted as "having abandoned the upright way and gone astray," following the road of Balaam son of Bosor, "who loved the wages of wickedness" (2:15). Balaam is notorious in Jewish tradition. He reflects a Jewish mind-set that is fascinated—and repulsed—by the prophet who led Israel into idolatry.[111] In rabbinic literature, Balaam is the antithesis of Abraham, the paradigm of self-seeking greed.[112] And because of his treachery Balaam had no place in the life to come.[113] The downfall of a prophet of God is a tragedy of monumental proportions.

With Balaam as their spiritual mentor, the apostates are vividly depicted in 2 Peter by means of a double metaphor: a dog returning to its vomit and a pig returning to the mud. While the dog metaphor finds a parallel in the book of Proverbs (26:11), the pig metaphor finds its analogue in the Egyptian Story of Ahiqar: "My son, you were to me like a pig which had been in a hot bath . . . , and when it was out and saw a filthy pool went down and wallowed in it."[114]

Ethics and virtue, exhortation and moral typology abound in 2 Peter. Where concreteness is necessary for the reader's instruction, moral paradigms are a common feature in the paraenetic tradition and serve the purpose of graphic illustration. Examples

---

[110] This is clarified by the syntax of 2 Pet 2:4–9 (*ouk epheisato . . . ouk epheisato . . . errusato*).

[111] E.g., Philo, *Vit. Mos.* 1.295–99; Josephus, *Ant.* 4.6.6; cp. Num 31:16.

[112] See G. Vermes, "The Story of Balaam," in *Scripture and Tradition in Judaism: Haggadic Studies* (SPB 4; Leiden: Brill, 1973), 127–77, and J. T. Greene, *Balaam and His Interpreters: A Hermeneutical History of the Balaam Tradition* (Atlanta: Scholars Press, 1992).

[113] *'Abot* 5:19 and m.*Sanh.* 10:2.

[114] Cited in R. H. Charles, *The Apocrypha and Pseudepigrapha of the Old Testament* (2 vols.; Oxford: Clarendon, 1913), 2:772.

from the past—some notorious, all instructive—communicate the writer's burden. In 2 Peter, they serve two functions: they simultaneously reiterate judgment and salvation. To the apostate they underscore a day of moral reckoning for which the wicked are being "reserved"; for the faithful they offer encouragement, insofar as God continues to be "savior" amidst the community's overwhelming social and cultural challenges.[115]

Theology and Christology of 2 Peter

The theology of 2 Peter is a theology of divine lordship. The 14 references in the letter to *kurios* most refer both to God and to Christ. The expression of that lordship is the divine prerogative to judge as well as to save. At the same time that Christ is identified as "Savior" in the epistle (1:1,11; 2:20; 3:2,18), which has enormous implications for the faithful, he is also presented as "Master" (2:1) and "Lord" (1:8,14–16; 2:20; 3:2,8–10,15,18). At issue—and probably being called into question—is the fact and extent of Christ's dominion. For the writer, this dominion is utterly cosmic in its dimensions. The writer further distinguishes himself by his tendency to couple together "Savior" and "Lord" (e.g., 1:11; 2:20; 3:2,18).

The writer uses "Master" and "Lord" as honorific titles, but they are more. They are necessary in accenting Christ's sovereign authority, because some in the community have "denied" (*arneomai*, 2:1) that authority over them. Such affirmation is critical for a believing community that is surrounded by hostile cultural forces and constant temptations to compromise. Those who are denounced for their apostasy are those who have turned their backs on the truth and deny Christ's lordship over them (see esp. 2:1–3). Hence a strong eschatological component is found in the argument of 2 Peter. This element has two sides: the very act of divine judgment that will destroy the wicked will also bring salvation for the righteous. Thus, the one who cultivates a virtuous life and perseveres can expect to experience divine mercy and deliverance. That person is promised the hope of entrance "into the eternal kingdom of our Lord and Savior Jesus Christ" (1:11).

---

[115] Elsewhere I investigate more fully the role of the moral paradigm in 2 Peter. See J. D. Charles, "The Function of Moral Typology in 2 Peter," in W. P. Brown, ed., *Character and Scripture: Moral Formation, Community, and Biblical Interpretation* (Grand Rapids: Eerdmans, 2002), 331–43.

The Day of the Lord is an important theological component of 2 Peter. It is important because of the moral skepticism and apostasy that are being condemned in the letter. Those being denounced are depicted in rather severe terms; they are likened to "false prophets" who secretly introduced "destructive heresies" (2:1). These are further said to deny the Master "who bought them" (2:1). The fate that awaits them is destruction (*apōleia*, used twice, in 2:1 and 3, underscoring both severity and certainty).

A catalog of descriptions paints a rather unsavory picture of these individuals: they are scoffers (3:3–4), indulging in lusts and despising authority (2:10). They are bold and blasphemous (2:11), irrational and reviling (2:12), pleasure-seeking (2:13) and adulterous (2:14), having gone astray (2:15). They are utterly "lawless" (3:17). What's more, these "accursed" individuals (2:14) are enticing the unstable with appetites that have been exercised in greediness (2:14). The combined moral typology of 2 Peter 2 serves to depict these individuals as apostate, and therefore, awaiting divine judgment—a judgment that though delayed[116] is nonetheless certain and catastrophic (3:3–10).[117]

The closing part of 2 Peter's argument is that the cosmos is to be dissolved in an eschatological conflagration. The arguments by Neyrey and others (see "Introduction") that 2 Peter 3 mirrors background pagan philosophical conceptions of cosmic transformation are certainly persuasive and provide helpful insight into the writer's rhetorical strategy. The writer may well be employing Day of the Lord imagery, drawn from Jewish and Christian apocalyptic, in response to standard views of the universe that absolve humans from ultimate moral accountability. In contrast to the apostates' bold denial of moral accountability, 2 Peter affirms the reality of moral accountability on the great day. That day will come unexpectedly, as a thief (3:10), in accordance with the OT prophetic and Christian apocalyptic tradition.[118] The promise of climactic and cataclysmic judgment both challenges the moral relativist's disregard for moral authority and undercuts contemporary philosophical notions of the cosmos.

---

[116] I have addressed the underlying assumptions of "early Catholicism" above (see "Authorship," "Date of Writing" and "Setting").

[117] The possible background to the eschatological argument in 2 Peter 3 is discussed above in the "Introduction."

[118] Cp., e.g., Matt 24:43–44; Luke 12:39–40; 1 Thess 5:2; Rev 3:3; 16:15.

Ethics in 2 Peter

Second Peter, as we have argued, is a call to moral progress. The writer has borrowed what is in Stoic moral philosophy a standard rhetorical and teaching device, the ethical catalog, in calling his audience to pursue a virtuous lifestyle (1:5–7). This catalog both presupposes the infusion and presence of divine grace and provision (1:1–4) and emphasizes the human factor in the acquisition of moral excellence:

> For this very reason [i.e., given the received righteousness and divine provision available to the Christian believer] make every effort to add to your faith virtue, and to your virtue knowledge, and to your knowledge self-control, and to your self-control perseverance, and to your perseverance godliness, and to your godliness brotherly kindness, and to your brotherly kindness love.[119]

This catalog assumes that there is a unity in the virtues, which is to say, the individual qualities may not be divorced from one another, and that faith is the foundation upon which the virtuous life is built, with the goal being *agapē*— a uniquely "Christian" virtue not found in pagan ethical lists.[120] While faith is present in 2 Peter, it is depicted as something initially received from God (1:1) and on which the believer is to *build* (1:5). The emphasis of 2 Peter is ethical and not doctrinal or theological. That is, it lies in what the

---

[119] My translation.

[120] For a more extensive discussion of the ethical catalog in Stoic thought, and its incorporation into Christian ethical teaching, see Charles, *Virtue Amidst Vice*, chapters 3–5. Unfortunately, the most extensive investigations of ethical lists in classical literature, and their transposition in Christian ethical teaching, remain untranslated from the German— among these: J. Stelzenberger, *Die Beziehungen der frühchristlichen Sittenlehre zur Ethik der Stoa* (Munich: Beck, 1933); A. Vögtle, *Die Tugend-und Lasterkataloge im Neuen Testament* (NTAbh 16/4–5; Münster: Aschendorff, 1936), and S. Wibbing, *Die Tugend-und Lasterkataloge im Neuen Testament und ihre Traditionsgeschichte unter besonderer Berücksichtigung der Qumrantexte* (BZNW 25; Berlin: Töepelmann, 1959). For the English-speaking audience, see G. Kidd, "Moral Actions and Rules in Stoic Ethics," in J. M. Rist, ed., *The Stoics* (Berkeley: University of California Press, 1978), 247–58, and T. Engberg-Pederson, *The Stoic Theory of Oikeiosis: Moral Development and Social Interaction in Early Stoic Philosophy* (SHC 2; Aarhus: Aarhus University Press, 1990); and more recently, Charles, *Virtue Amidst Vice*. On ethical lists as they appear in the NT, see B. S. Easton, "New Testament Ethical Lists," *JBL* 51 (1932): 1–12; N. J. McEleney, "The Vice Lists of the Pastoral Epistles," *CBQ* 36 (1974): 203–19; J. D. Charles, "The Language and Logic of Virtue in 2 Peter 1:5–7," 53–73; idem, *Virtue Amidst Vice*, chapters 6 and 7; idem, "On Angels and Asses" 1–12; and idem, "Vice and Virtue Lists," C. A. Evans and S. E. Porter, eds., *DNTB* (Downers Grove, IL: InterVarsity, 2000), 1252–57.

Christian must do, through works and the building of character, to validate authentic faith. To compromise the moral truth that is known is worse than never to have known it in the first place.

The forceful ethical call of 2 Peter is made clear by the strong paraenetic language (i.e., moral exhortation) used throughout 2 Peter 1: "for this very reason" (v. 5); "if you possess these qualities" (v. 8); "if anyone does not have them" (v. 9); "if you do these things" (v. 10); "for this reason I intend to remind you, even though you know them already and are established in the truth that has come to you" (v. 12); "I think it is right to refresh your memory" (v. 13); "remember these things" (v. 15). The rhetorical effect of this language, though easily lost on the modern reader, would have been unmistakable to its intended audience. Theirs is not a faith that is void of the moral life; rather, the distinctly Christian ethic is to shine forth in bold contrast to surrounding culture.

The adversaries in 2 Peter, described above (see "Themes," "Literary Features," and "Theology"), are said to "promise freedom" (2:19) and thereby "deny the sovereign Lord who bought them" (2:1), "follow their shameful ways" (2:2), and "bring the way of truth into disrepute" (2:2). In the end, they themselves are "slaves of depravity" (2:19). The language used to depict—and denounce—these individuals is clearly ethical. The root problem affecting the community is not in their doctrine; it is their morality—a hedonism that is unwilling to acknowledge any limits or moral authority over us. Second Peter, thus, constitutes a moral apologetic aimed at simultaneously pronouncing judgment upon the reprobate and promising deliverance and salvation to those who are faithful. The epistle closes with the admonition to live "holy and godly lives" (3:11), to be "found spotless" (3:14).

Attestation, Early Sources

Of the seven canonical documents designated "catholic" or General Epistles, only 1 Peter and 1 John were not considered to be "disputed writings" by the early church. At the same time, Eusebius informed the reader that even when the other five were disputed, they were not unknown: "Among the disputed writings [ta antilegomena], which are nevertheless recognized by many, are extant the so-called epistle of James and that of Jude, also the second epistle of Peter, and those that are called the second and third of John, whether they belong to the evangelist or to another person of the same name."[121]

And among the seven General Epistles, 2 Peter would seem to have had the greatest difficulty being accepted, for reasons explained by Eusebius and which are understandable, given the circulation in the second century of Petrine pseudepigrapha. He writes that although many had thought it valuable and had honored it alongside the other Scriptures, much of the church had been taught to regard it as uncanonical. In the case of other writings attributed to the apostle (e.g., *Acts of Peter*, *Apocalypse of Peter*, as well as the gospel carrying his name), we have no reason whatsoever, according to Eusebius, to include them among the traditional, and nowhere in the church are they cited.[122] And Eusebius further informs us that Clement of Alexandria (late second century) offered commentary on all the "catholic" epistles.[123]

Other early witnesses, however, paint an incomplete picture. Origen mentions one "acknowledged" letter of Peter and a second that was "doubted,"[124] even though he himself accepted it as one of Peter's "twin epistles."[125] Didymus the Blind commented on all seven General Epistles but considered 2 Peter to be a forged document (*esse falsatum*).[126] Didymus of Alexandria, by contrast, several centuries later cited 2 Peter as authentic, and thus, authoritative.[127] The authors of the spurious, second-century *Apocalypse of Peter* and *Acts of Peter* give evidence of having known of 2 Peter's existence. Complicating matters is the question of geography, since resistance to an acceptance of 2 Peter was greater in some areas—among Syrian churches, for example—may be related to the fact that the spurious pseudepigraphal works bearing the apostle's name were in circulation in those parts. This, at the very least, would reasonably explain why early patristic evidence supporting 2 Peter is scant. Nevertheless, by the late fourth century 2 Peter was acknowledged as canonical.[128]

---

[121] Eusebius, *Hist. eccl.* 3.25.

[122] Ibid., 3.3.

[123] Ibid., 6.14. Eusebius categorizes 2 Peter with James, Jude, 2 and 3 John as "disputed."

[124] Eusebius, *Comm. Jo.* 5.3.

[125] Eusebius, *Hom. Josh.* 7.1.

[126] PL 39.1742, 1811–18.

[127] See the textual evidence in B. M. Metzger, *The Canon of the New Testament* (Oxford: Clarendon, 1987), 213. An extensive summary of early patristic awareness of 2 Peter can be found in Bigg, ICC, 204–10.

[128] Thus Augustine, *Doct. Christ.* 2.12. Cyril of Jerusalem and Athanasius include 2 Peter in their catalogs of "catholic" epistles. Significantly, the fourth-century councils of Hippo,

One of the arguments against the authenticity of 2 Peter is that, linguistically and stylistically, it differs markedly from 1 Peter. Given the acknowledgment that in 1 Peter the apostle is using a secretary (5:12), one possible solution is to presuppose a different secretary or amanuensis being used, as Jerome suggested.[129] In his overview of the early Fathers' attitudes toward the epistle, Gerald Bray offers these very useful remarks:

> The Fathers all recognized that there are great differences between the first and second letters attributed to Peter, but they explained these variations in different ways. Some of them rejected the authenticity of the second letter and refused to accept it as part of the canon, but the majority were unwilling to go that far. They recognized that although there were many differences between the two letters, they were not as great as the differences between the letters, on the one hand, and other writings attributed to Peter that were known to be spurious, on the other.[130]

We do well to remember that 2 Peter is worlds removed from the fantasy and cumbersome devices found in the Petrine pseudepigrapha of the second century. Thus, even though 2 Peter had the greatest difficulty achieving canonical acceptance, its attestation far exceeds that of any of the noncanonical books.

In his extensive study of possible allusions to 2 Peter in early patristic literature, Robert Picirelli has maintained that the epistle is *probably* being alluded to 22 possible sources, including *1 Clement*, *Barnabas*, and *Hermas*.[131] The upshot of this is that, at the very least, NT critical scholarship *cannot* dogmatically contend that there are *unquestionably no references* to 2 Peter in the apostolic fathers. For this reason, authenticity will need to be debated on grounds other than whether the church fathers knew and used the epistle.

While contemporary biblical scholarship is not the first generation to entertain questions about 2 Peter's authenticity, it is instructive to

Laodicea, and Carthage, while accepting 2 Peter, rejected the letters of Clement of Rome and Barnabas, both of which previously had been held in high esteem. Mayor, *Second Epistle*, cxv–cxxiii, painstakingly examines possible allusions to 2 Peter in the writings of the early Fathers.

[129] Jerome, *Epist.* 120.11.

[130] Bray, *1–2 Peter*, 129.

[131] Robert Picirelli, "Allusions to 2 Peter in the Apostolic Fathers," *JSNT* 33 (1987): 57–83.

note how the church at other times handled the matter. Consider, for
example, the Protestant Reformers. Erasmus rejected the epistle, and
Calvin and Luther both had misgivings about it, though for reasons
that differed from those of modern scholarship. Luther's concern
about 2 Peter extended to James and Jude as well: the epistle was
not sufficiently Christological. Unhappily, Luther's judgment served
as a precursor to the unfortunate distinction in modern historical-
critical inquiry of a "canon within a canon." The core of the canon,
thereby, is thought to accord with what is "purely Pauline." Calvin,
in his assessment of authorship, was not entirely uncritical either. If
2 Peter is consensually received as canonical, he reasoned, we must
then permit Peter to be the author, based on the presence in the text
of his name in the greeting and his testimony of personal experience
with Christ. Significantly, Calvin did allow for a disciple of Peter to
do the writing, *though not one removed from the apostle himself.*[132]

Purpose

Historical-critical scholarship, as we have noted, has assumed
that doctrine—and specifically, false doctrine—is the chief burden
of the writer, based on the assumptions of an "early Catholic" reading of the letter that locate it, at the earliest, near the turn of the
century, or, at the latest, in the mid-second century. And because
the letter is likely a second-century document, it must do battle
with the forces of emergent, if not mature, Gnosticism.[133]

Does this interpretation, however, stand up to close scrutiny?
Why the amount of paraenetic language and examples of moral debauchery that form the heart of 2 Peter? The burden of the writer
is that his readers cultivate an ethos that "offers proof" (1:11) of a
virtuous lifestyle—proof, that is, both to the one who has provided
abundant resources for life and godliness (1:3–4) and to the moral
skeptic (3:3–7). "What kind of people ought you to be?" (3:11) is
the ringing question that the leaders are left to ponder.

Given the dominance of the "early Catholic" thesis and the presumption that Gnosticism is being combated, traditional commentary broadly assumes a doctrinal-eschatological argument in 2 Peter
3 that purports to counter a "Parousia delay." Closer attention to

---

[132] John Calvin, *Commentaries on the Catholic Epistles* trans. (J. Owen) Grand Rapids:
Eerdmans, 1959), 363.

[133] So Kelly, *A Commentary*, 231.

literary strategy, however, suggests that the material belongs to a foremost ethical argument, qualifying as a type of "moral apologetic." Structurally, the epistle develops in the following manner.

- The author initially admonishes his readers to virtuous living, in accordance with what they already know and have been taught (chap. 1).
- There are those who threaten the Christian community, whose lifestyle and moral obstinacy call to mind proverbial types of debauchery from Jewish tradition. These individuals are roundly condemned in no uncertain terms. What utterly condemns them is that they have a knowledge of the truth that is being denied. The language and logic being used are aimed at countering *apostasy* (chap. 2).
- Logically, apostasy breeds the necessity of returning to cosmological "first things." Carried to its end, apostasy manifests itself in wholesale denial of all authority—local as well as universal. It is the latter, the more fundamental denial, that would appear to lie behind the caricature of the moral skeptic in 3:3–6. This process entails an eventual—and calculated—denial of divine intervention in history (3:5–6). Such moral reasoning is catastrophic, ensuring that as in the past, divine judgment will visit the wicked. The faithful are to be exhorted toward moral excellence in light of this fact (chap. 3).

The effects of moral compromise—the influence of the moral skeptic—on the believing community are by no means benign. In truth they act as a cancer, undermining one's faith and expectation in the Lord, one's ability to live righteously, and one's capacity to discern properly divine judgment. While cosmic catastrophe in the past serves as a foreshadow of moral reckoning to come, it also teaches that there are divine limits as to what the Creator and Judge of the whole earth, morally speaking, will permit.

Much of the material in 2 Peter serves an apologetic and ethical rather than a strictly doctrinal purpose. But it also serves to rebut the assumption of the moral skeptic that there is no judgment, no moral accountability in the temporal order. Finally, and most fundamentally, it serves to remind believers of what they know, and it does so in creative, when at times forceful, ways. Having been reminded that God indeed does judge the unrighteous, the readers are admonished to live a life that is worthy of their calling as they await the final day of moral reckoning. While their social setting may be morally quite challenging, indeed to the point of severe vexation of the soul, living a virtuous life is not *impossible*.

Outline and Structure of 2 Peter

   I. Epistolary Introduction and Greeting (1:1–2)
  II. Exhortation toward Recall and Virtuous Living (1:3–16)
     A. Reminder of the Divine Resources Standing at the Believer's Disposal (1:3–4)
     B. Catalog of Virtues Underscoring the Need for Moral Progress (1:5–7)
     C. Reminder of the Need to "Confirm" Authentic Faith through One's Lifestyle (1:8–11)
     D. Reaffirmation of Apostolic Authority (1:12–16)
 III. Reminder of Judgment for the Wicked and Salvation for the Righteous (2:1–22)
     A. Exposure of Those Denying the Lordship of Christ through Moral Corruption (2:1–3)
     B. Moral Paradigms Underscoring the Certainty of Divine Judgment (2:4–9)
     C. Clarification of the Nature of Apostasy (2:10–22)
 IV. Declaration of the Divine Purpose Expressed through Judgment (3:1–18)
     A. Reminder of Apostolic Teaching and Authority (3:1–2)
     B. Past Judgment Being Put in Perspective (3:3–9)
     C. Concluding Exhortation (3:10–18)

Selected Bibliography

Commentaries Based on the Greek Text

Bauckham, R. J. *Jude, 2 Peter*. WBC 50. Waco: Word, 1983.
Bigg, C. *A Critical and Exegetical Commentary on the Epistles of St. Peter and St. Jude*. ICC. Edinburgh: T. & T. Clark, 1902.

Commentaries Based on the English Text

Beasley-Murray, G. R. *The General Epistles: James, 1 Peter, Jude, 2 Peter*. London/Nashville: Lutterworth/Abingdon, 1965.

Boring, M. E., et al., eds. *Hellenistic Commentary to the New Testament*. Nashville: Abingdon, 1995.

Bray, G., ed. *James, 1–2 Peter, 1–3 John, Jude*. ACCS 11. Downers Grove: InterVarsity, 2000.

Calvin, J. *Commentaries on the Catholic Epistles*. Translated by J. Owen. Grand Rapids: Eerdmans, 1959.

Charles, J. D., and E. Waltner. *1–2 Peter, Jude*. BCBC. Scottdale/Waterloo: Herald, 1999.

_____. "2 Peter," EBC 13. Rev ed. Grand Rapids: Zondervan, 2006.

Craddock, F. B. *First and Second Peter and Jude*. WBC. Louisville: Westminster John Knox, 1995.

Cranfield, C. E. B. *1 and 2 Peter and Jude*. TBC. London: SCM, 1960.

Green, M. (E. M. B.). *2 Peter and Jude*. TNTC 18. 3rd ed. Leicester/Grand Rapids: InterVarsity/Eerdmans, 1989.

Hillyer, N. *1 and 2 Peter, Jude*. NIBC. Peabody: Hendrickson, 1992.

James, M. R. *The Second Epistle General of St. Peter and the General Epistle of Jude*. Cambridge: Cambridge University Press, 1912.

Kelly, J. N. D. *A Commentary on the Epistles of Peter and Jude*. BNTC. London: Adam & Charles Black, 1969.

Kistemaker, S. J. *Peter and Jude*. NTC. Grand Rapids: Baker, 1987.

Knight, J. *2 Peter and Jude*. NTG. Sheffield: Sheffield Academic Press, 1995.

Kraftchick, S. J. *Jude, 2 Peter*. ANTC. Nashville: Abingdon, 2002.

Leaney, A. R. C. *The Letters of Peter and Jude*. Cambridge: Cambridge University Press, 1967.

Lucas, D., and C. Green. *The Message of 2 Peter & Jude*. BST. Leicester/Downers Grove: InterVarsity, 1995.

Mayor, J. B. *The Epistle of St. Jude and the Second Epistle of St. Peter*. New York/London: Macmillan, 1907.

Moffatt, J. *The General Epistles: James, Peter and Judas*. MNTC. London: Hodder & Stoughton, 1928.

Moo, D. J. *2 Peter, Jude*. NIVAC. Grand Rapids: Zondervan, 1996.

Mounce, R. H. *A Living Hope: A Commentary on 1 and 2 Peter*. Grand Rapids: Eerdmans, 1982.

Neyrey, J. H. *2 Peter, Jude: A New Translation with Introduction and Commentary.* AB 37C. Garden City: Doubleday, 1993.

Perkins, P. *First and Second Peter, James, and Jude.* IBC. Louisville: John Knox, 1995.

Plumptre, E. H. *The General Epistles of St. Peter and St. Jude.* Cambridge: Cambridge University Press, 1926.

Reicke, B. *The Epistles of James, Peter, and Jude.* AB 37. New York: Doubleday, 1964.

Richard, E. J. *Reading 1 Peter, Jude and 2 Peter: A Literary and Theological Commentary.* Macon: Smyth & Helwys, 2000.

Schreiner, T. R. *1, 2 Peter, Jude.* NAC. Nashville: Broadman & Holman, 2003.

Senior, D. *1 & 2 Peter.* NTM 20. 2nd ed. Wilmington: Michael Glazier, 1987.

_____, and D. J. Harrington. *1 Peter, Jude and 2 Peter.* Sacra Pagina. Wilmington: Michael Glazier, 2002.

Sidebottom, E. M. *James, Jude and 2 Peter.* NCB. London: Thomas Nelson, 1967.

Vaughan, C., and T. D. Lea. *1, 2 Peter, Jude.* BSC. Grand Rapids: Zondervan, 1988.

Wand, J. W. C. *The General Epistles of St. Peter and St. Jude.* WC. London: Methuen, 1934.

Foreign Language Commentaries

Balz, H., and W. Schrage. *Die katholischen Brief: Die Briefe des Jakobus, Petrus, Johannes und Judas.* NTD 10. Göttingen: Vandenhoeck & Ruprecht, 1973.

Brox, N. *Der erste Petrusbrief.* EKK 21.

Chain, J. *Les Épitres catholiques: La seconde épître de saint Pièrre, les épîtres de saint Jean, l'épître de saint Jude.* 2nd ed. EBib. Paris: Gabalda, 1939.

Fuchs, E., and P. Reymond. *A Deuxième Épître de Saint Pièrre. L'Épitre de Saint Jude.* CNT 13b. Neuchâtel: Delachaux & Niestlé, 1980.

Grundmann, W. *Der Brief des Judas und der zweite Brief des Petrus.* THKNT 15. Berlin: Evangelische Verlagsanstalt, 1974.

Knoch, O. *Der erste und zweite Petrusbrief. Der Judasbrief.* RNT. Regensburg 1990.

Michl, J. *Die katholischen Briefe.* RNT 8. 2nd ed. Regensburg: Pustet, 1968.

Schelkle, K.-H. *Die Petrusbriefe. Der Judasbrief.* HTKNT 13/2. 5th ed. Freiburg/Basel/Wien: Herder, 1980.

Spicq, C. *Les Épîtres de Saint Pièrre.* SB. Paris: Gabalda, 1966.

Vögtle, A. *Der Judasbrief, Der zweite Petrusbrief.* EKKNT. Neukirchen: Neukirchener Verlag, 1994.

Windisch, H. *Die katholischen Briefe.* 2nd ed. Tübingen: Mohr, 1930.

Wohlenberg, G. *Der erste und zweite Petrusbrief und der Judasbrief.* KNT 15. Leipzig: Deichert, 1915.

Studies

Bauckham, R. J. "2 Peter." In *DLNT*, 923–27.

_____. "2 Peter: An Account of Research." *ANRW*. II.25.22, 3713–52.

_____. "James, 1 and 2 Peter, Jude." In D. A. Carson and H. G. M. Williamson, eds., *It Is Written: Scripture Citing Scripture. Essays in Honour of B. Lindars.* Cambridge: Cambridge University Press, 1988, 303–17.

Charles, J. D. *Vice Amidst Virtue: The Catalog of Virtues in 2 Peter 1.* JSNTSS 150. Sheffield: Sheffield Academic Press, 1997.

Chester, A., and R. P. Martin. *The Theology of the Letters of James, Peter, and Jude.* NTT. Cambridge: Cambridge University Press, 1994.

Fornberg, T. *An Early Church in a Pluralistic Society: A Study of 2 Peter.* ConBNT 9. Lund: C. W. K. Gleerup, 1977.

Green, M. (E.M.B.) *2 Peter Reconsidered.* London: Tyndale, 1961.

Michaels, J. R. "Peter, Second Epistle of." *ISBE*, 815–19.

Pearson, B. A. "James, 1–2 Peter, Jude." In E. J. Epp and G. W. MacRae, eds., *The New Testament and Its Modern Interpreters.* Philadelphia: Fortress, 1987, 371–406.

Smith, T. V. *Petrine Controversies in Early Christianity: Attitudes Towards Peter in Christian Writings of the First Two Centuries.* Tübingen: Mohr, 1985.

Starr, J.M. *Sharers in Divine Nature: 2 Peter 1:4 in Its Hellenistic Context.* ConBNT 33. Stockholm: Almquist & Wiksell, 2000.

Watson, D.F. "The Second Letter of Peter." *NIB.* Vol. XII, 323–61.

Five

THE LETTERS OF JOHN

1 John: Assurance of Salvation

How do you know whether a person is really a Christian or rather an apostate, i.e., a professing but not a genuine Christian? John answers this question in his letter, which has a great application in our day.[1] Most people living today in the United States profess to be believers in Jesus. But we know from experience that there are not that many Christians. You may know people living down the street from you, or who work in the same office that you do, who say that, yes, they are believers in Christ; they may even be members of some church, but they have not the slightest clue as to what Christianity is all about. Nothing about their lifestyle or their basic thrust gives you any indication of Christian reality.

We have people in our churches who profess to be followers of Christ but who really are not. We even have people standing in some of the pulpits across our land who profess to know Christ but who really do not. So it is vital that we have some method of knowing how to tell the real from the false. John offers such a "reality check" in his letter. First-century Christians needed guidance to distinguish between truth and falsehood and orthodoxy and heresy. John sets forth several criteria for his readers to determine the reality of Christian faith. His letter is simple to read, and yet it is profound in its teaching. Its content convicts those who do not measure up to the criteria

Unless otherwise indicated, all Scripture quotations in this chapter are from the New King James Version (NKJV).

[1] I am indebted to my former professor, William E. Bell Jr., now retired, but formerly senior professor of religion at Dallas Baptist University, who instilled in me a deeper love of Scripture. Much of this article reflects and is based on his excellent teaching and notes I gathered from him on the letters of John. Any errors, however, should be counted as mine.

and is painful to read for those who are sometimes too sure of themselves when it comes to matters of Christian faith and practice.

And yet the epistle can also provide great comfort and assurance when understood and when its teachings are followed. Who was John? When did he write? To whom was he writing and why? The answers to these kinds of questions in a study which highlights this letter which is loved and memorized by many will help us appreciate it even more.

Author

External evidence for the authorship of 1 John points to John the apostle. Clement of Rome,[2] the *Didache*,[3] the *Epistle of Barnabas*,[4] and Polycarp[5] quoted or alluded to 1 John, without designating John as its author. Papias of Hierapolis was the first one to refer expressly to a letter of John as being the work of the apostle.[6] Irenaeus credited John with writing 1 and 2 John.[7] Origen designated the apostle as the author of all three letters.[8]

Internal evidence cannot point to a specific author without ambiguity because 1 John is strictly anonymous. Arguments put forth here ultimately center on 1 John's relationship with the Gospel of John. First John bears important similarities with the Fourth Gospel. For example, both writings use contrasts like light/darkness, truth/falsehood, life/death, and love/hate; both books share a similar Greek style and syntax; both documents have comparable prologues. Further, the use of eyewitness language in 1 John 1:1–4 to authenticate the incarnation supports the author as someone who actually saw and heard Jesus during His earthly ministry. The apostle John fits the bill.

Scholars who reject the apostolic authorship of 1 John point to significant differences between John's Gospel and 1 John. For example, they contend that *logos* is not used in 1 John (as it is

---

[2] *1 Clem.* 49:5; c. AD 96.

[3] *Did.* 10:5–6; c. AD 90–120.

[4] *Epistle of Barnabas* 5:9–11; 12:10; c. AD 130.

[5] Polycarp, *Phil* 7:1; c. AD 135.

[6] See Eusebius, *Hist. eccl.* 3.39.17.

[7] In *Haer.* 3.16.8, Irenaeus quoted verses from 1 and 2 John and identified John the apostle as the author; however, he did not refer to them as coming from two different Johannine letters but rather from "the Epistle."

[8] As reported by Eusebius in *Hist. eccl.* 6.25.10. Origen added, however, that not everyone considered them genuine.

in John's Gospel, 1:1,14) to refer personally to Jesus, but that it refers instead to a "message" or a "word" which produces life. But John's Gospel also uses *logos* with the meaning of "message" (see, e.g., John 8:31). Further, some scholars point out that *logos* in 1 John 1:1 ("word of life") is more of a personal reference than some are willing to admit. When all of the evidence is considered, we should accept the traditional view that John the apostle wrote 1 John.

Canonical Recognition

First John was considered obviously the work of the apostle John and was accepted and recognized as canonical from about the time of Irenaeus, c. AD 180.[9] The Muratorian Canon (late second century AD) refers to two epistles written by John—probably 1 and 2 John. Origen (c. AD 231) mentioned 1 John as being written by John, though he doubted 2 and 3 John when he said that John "left an epistle of a very few lines and, it may be, a second or third, for not all say these are genuine."[10] Eusebius (c. AD 325) placed 1 John among the "acknowledged books" (*homologoumena*)[11] in his *Ecclesiastical History*. Origen,[12] Dionysius,[13] and others counted 1 John as a "catholic" epistle, which in essence means "canonical."[14] Athnasius's list of 27 New Testament books (AD 367) included 1, 2, and 3 John, as did also the list of books approved by the councils of Hippo (AD 393) and Carthage (AD 397).

Literary Form and Structure

The Epistle of 1 John lacks the usual elements found in most first-century letters. The letter names no author, designates no recipients, expresses no personal greetings, and has no conclusion.[15] The absence of the usual epistolary form indicates that 1 John

---

[9] For fuller discussions of NT canonicity and the books therein, see Bruce M. Metzger, *The Canon of the New Testament* (Oxford: Clarendon, 1987), and F. F. Bruce, *The Canon of Scripture* (Downer's Grove, IL: InterVarsity, 1988).

[10] Cited in Eusebius, *Hist. eccl.* 6.25.10.

[11] Eusebius, *Hist. eccl.* 3.25.2–3.

[12] Origen, *Comm. on Matt.* 17.19.

[13] Eusebius, *Hist. eccl.* 7.25.7, 10.

[14] Eusebius, *Hist. eccl.* 2.23.25.

[15] B. F. Westcott (*The Epistles of St. John: The Greek Text, with Notes and Essays* [London: Macmillan, 1883], xxix) wrote that the letter has "no address, no subscription, no name is

was probably a general letter written with a wide circulation (see "Destination and Recipients").

Concerning the letter's structure, Burge maintains, "Discovering a recognizable pattern or structure of thought in 1 John has proven impossible."[16] Indeed, to discern a clear and logical structure to the contents of 1 John is extremely difficult. Akin rightly divides approaches to outlining the letter into three groups:

> (1) traditional scholars who seek to discern basic topic or subject divisions (even sources) and an overarching outline through inductive analysis; (2) discourse analysis—linguist scholars who apply principles of semantic structural studies or "discourse linguistics" to discover the semantic relations that weave the epistle together as a unified whole; (3) rhetorical criticism—students of ancient rhetoric who seek to discover what, if any, rhetorical strategies common to the author's world were used to set forth and further his argument.[17]

While trying not to neglect John's flow of argument, the method used in this study of 1 John is along the lines of the first approach. The letter seems to contain a general unity by means of thematic links among subsections.

Place of Writing and Date

First John does not identify a place of origin, so it is impossible to be certain about the letter's provenance. Early church tradition, however, suggests that John lived in Ephesus near the end of his life.[18] This city is as likely a place of origin as any for the letter, and especially so since Ephesus is consistent with church tradition.

---

contained in it of a person or place; no direct trace of the author, no indication of any special destination."

[16] Gary Burge, "Letters of John," in *DLNT* [Ed. R. P. Martin and P. H. Davids] Downers Grove, IL: InterVarsity, 1997), 597.

[17] Daniel L. Akin, *1, 2, 3 John* (NAC 38; Nashville: Broadman & Holman, 2001), 37. See also the helpful section in which Akin provides and analyzes the various types of outlines of each approach (37–47).

[18] Eusebius, *Hist. eccl.* 3.31.3; 5.24.3. Eusebius mentioned John's burial in Ephesus when quoting Polycrates of Ephesus in a letter written to Victor of Rome.

We think that the author of 1 John is also the one who wrote John's Gospel.[19] The date of writing for 1 John has become closely associated with that of the Gospel of John. We tentatively hold that John's Gospel was written c. AD 80–85.[20] The relationship of the date of 1 John to that of the Gospel of John is ultimately decided by what one sees as the purposes for each book. We hold that 1 John was written to confirm the faith of Christians facing the challenges of an incipient gnostic heresy. The framework for this heresy was present and growing in the latter part of the first century, and it became fully developed in the second century. As is well-known, some of the later gnostics used John's Gospel for their purposes, even though the Gospel's teachings (esp. Christ's incarnation in 1:14) confounded their speculations.

The development of this proto- or incipient Gnosticism in the late first century indicates that 1 John may have been written within that period. The use of John's Gospel by the gnostics suggests that some time had passed after the writing of John and before 1 John was written. The apostle was dealing with some of these false teachers in 1 John.

The traditional date for the writing of 1 John is about AD 95/96. Tradition tells us that after the apostle John was exiled to the island of Patmos (cp. Rev 1:9) during the reign of Domitian, he eventually was allowed to return to Ephesus. Most who have not studied this issue closely have the idea that John actually died on the island of Patmos and was buried there, but church tradition is against that idea. And the tradition found today in Ephesus and on Patmos is consistent with that which comes down to us through the church. The apostle left the island of Patmos after the death of Domitian (c. AD 96), returned to Ephesus, spent perhaps a few more years there and then died and was buried in the city of Ephesus. It is believed that he did most of his writing during this final period of his life in Ephesus.

As a matter of fact, it is entirely possible that he also wrote the book of Revelation there rather than on the island of Patmos. Undoubtedly John received the revelation on Patmos, but whether he put the book of Revelation in final form there is open to doubt.

---

[19] See D. A. Carson and Douglas J. Moo, *An Introduction to the NT* (2d ed.; Grand Rapids: Zondervan, 2005), 229–46 on the authorship of the Gospel of John for a full explanation.

[20] See Carson and Moo (*An Introduction to the NT*, 264–67) on the dating of the Gospel of John for a full explanation.

He could have, but it is also possible that he finished the book when he got back to Ephesus. At any rate, it seems possible that he wrote 1 John as well as 2 and 3 John after he returned from Patmos to Ephesus. So the date of writing for 1 John is arguably somewhere around AD 95/96, approximately the same time as 2 and 3 John, with a date in the early to mid-90s not being out of the question. The place of writing was probably Ephesus.

Destination and Recipients

First John does not tell us precisely who the recipients are. John simply refers to the readers as "my little children" (*teknia mou*, 2:1 HCSB). This designation means that they were Christians, with possibly many of them being converts of John, but he does not tell us precisely where they were or what group they made up. If Ephesus, however, is the correct place of writing, then John probably addressed Christians in the vicinity of that city. Since Ephesus was the chief city of Asia Minor in the Roman province of Asia, John probably wrote believers in the churches of Asia Minor. Thus, 1 John is a general letter written with a wide circulation.

Occasion and Purpose

The occasion of the epistle is twofold. First, put positively, John's purpose was to promote assurance of salvation (1 John 5:13)[21] for those who were Christologically sound, i.e., those who believed the "right things" concerning the person and work of Jesus Christ and for those who demonstrated a genuine love for God and for other believers in Christ, i.e., those whose lifestyle reflected a correct and orthodox theology.

Second, put negatively, John wanted to refute some interrelated heresies.[22] The growing movement of Gnosticism, which proved

[21] First John 5:13 ("These things I have written to you who believe in the name of the Son of God, so that you may know that you have eternal life" NKJV) is often and appropriately referred to as the letter's main purpose statement, but 1 John does contain other statements of purpose that should also be considered. For example, John writes: to promote Christian fellowship and joy in his life and in the lives of his readers (1:3–4); to keep these believers from committing sin (2:1); and to protect them from false teachers (2:26; 4:1–3). Citing D. Hiebert, Akin (*1, 2, 3 John*, 32) rightly notes, "The contents of the epistle . . . are most advantageously studied in the light of the writer's purpose as stated in 5:13."

[22] Scholars have found it difficult to determine with certainty the nature of the false teachers in 1 John. The best approach here is to study the text of the letter itself and to consider

troublesome to Christianity, was fully developed in the second century. But the framework which led to that fully developed heresy was already in place in the first century. John combated three different false teachings which seem to be part of an incipient or proto-Gnosticism. He refuted (1) an antinomian heresy, which many believe to be that of the Nicolaitans;[23] this antinomianism had to do with lawlessness, debauchery, licentiousness, and every kind of immorality. The antinomian heresy was closely related to early Gnosticism in that its advocates saw "the body as a mere envelope covering the human spirit, which . . . was inviolable"; others, according to Irenaeus, thought it possible to become truly "spiritual," where one progressed beyond the possibility of any defilement.[24] Accordingly, they thought that one could be righteous without practicing righteousness.

But in his letter John emphasized that God must be seen as holy and righteous, and thus he can require the same kind of holiness and righteousness from his creatures that would have fellowship with Him. And this teaching would knock out the heresy which says that you can live an unholy, immoral, licentious, debauched life and still have fellowship with God.

John also combated (2) a docetic Gnosticism which rejected the incarnation of Christ. Gnosticism gets its name from the Greek word *gnōsis* which means "knowledge," and it was an early heresy, the adherents of which claimed to have exclusive knowledge concerning spiritual things, a knowledge far beyond that which the average person had, a knowledge available only to those who submitted themselves to the rigors of and initiation into the gnostic order. They believed that matter is evil and spirit is good, an idea largely derived from ancient Greek philosophy. The outworking of this belief was that the material body, since it is a part of matter, is essentially evil. The soul, or the spirit, was good. Therefore, applying this idea to Jesus Christ—and remember, these people claimed to be Christians, and yet they were caught up in this heresy—if matter is evil and spirit is good, then obviously it is impossible for

---

statements found in the tradition of the early church. On the theological struggle and opponents in 1 John, see G. Burge, "Letters of John," in *DLNT*, 590–93.

[23] Irenaeus connected such moral laxity with the Nicolaitans who originated from Nicolas (Acts 6:5; cp. Rev 2:14–15); cited by Robert G. Gromacki, *New Testament Survey* (Des Plaines, IL: Regular Baptist Press, 1974), 370.

[24] John R. W. Stott, *The Letters of John* (TNTC; Grand Rapids: Eerdmans, 2002), 79.

the divine Christ to have had a material body because that would engage him in some way with evil.

This doctrine today is called Docetism, or "*docetic*" Gnosticism. The word *docetic* is related to the Greek word *dokeō*, which means "to seem" or "to appear." And this doctrine taught that Christ had no material body; he just "seemed" to have it; it "appeared" that way. In other words, he was a spiritual phantom, not a real, genuine human being. Therefore, as John refuted this heresy, he emphasized the reality of Jesus Christ as both God and man. The latter emphasis is prominent in this epistle. Passages like the affirmation of Christ's incarnation in 1 John 4:1–3 could well have been directed against docetic Gnosticism.

Another gnostic falsehood that John refuted came from the teachings of Cerinthus,[25] who made a distinction between a divine Christ-spirit and the man Jesus, who had a physical body. Cerinthus claimed that this divine Christ-spirit came upon the human Jesus at His baptism, then left Him just before His crucifixion. Consequently, Jesus the man, not the Son of God, died on the cross. First John 5:6 might have been marshaled against Cerinthian Gnosticism. John denied this heresy and affirmed that the Jesus Christ who died was the same Jesus Christ who was baptized.

John instructed his readers that because God is holy, He requires that those who are in fellowship with Him be holy also. He emphasized the holiness and righteousness of God. If God is holy and righteous, light rather than darkness, and love rather than hate, then upright living should be reflected in those who are a part of His family, i.e., those who are genuinely related to Him. Believers will not be infinitely holy as God is but will insofar as it is possible for human beings to measure up in those areas. Thus, any person who is consistently unrighteous, unholy, or has a belligerent and adversarial relationship toward his fellow Christians will automatically categorize himself as an unbeliever. Of course, those who do not have the proper view of the person and work of Christ will also be categorized as unbelievers. The epistle of 1 John essentially has to do with the criteria which determine the reality of Christian profession (5:13).

---

[25] Irenaeus said that John proclaimed his Gospel in order to refute the errors of Cerinthus (*Haer.* 3.3.4; 3.11.1).

Practical Teaching

In the light of all of the above, and as we shall see below in the letter itself, for John a genuine believer is one who

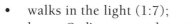

- confesses that he is a sinner (1:8,10);
- believes that Jesus is the Christ (2:22; 5:1);
- believes on the name of Jesus Christ (3:23; 5:10–13);
- confesses that Jesus Christ has come in the flesh (4:2);
- believes that Jesus Christ is the Savior of the world (4:14); and
- believes that Jesus is the Son of God (4:15; 5:5).

A genuine believer also acts in the following ways:

- walks in the light (1:7);
- keeps God's commandments (word) (2:3–5,17; 5:2);
- lives as Jesus did (2:6);
- loves (not hates) fellow Christians (2:9–11; 3:10,14–19,23–24; 4:7,12,16; 5:1);
- does not love the world (2:15–17);
- practices righteousness (2:29; 3:7,10);
- purifies himself (3:3);
- does not habitually sin (3:4–9; 5:18); and
- loves God (5:2).

According to 1 John, a genuine believer also has the Holy Spirit (3:24; 4:13).

Highlights of 1 John

John uses three criteria in his letter to determine the reality of Christian profession: righteousness, love, and belief:[26]

1. The criterion of *righteousness* requires obedient living (e.g., 2:29; 3:6,9; etc.).
2. The criterion of *love* insists on love for other believers (e.g., 3:11; 4:7–12, etc.).

---

[26] The most famous advocate of this approach was R. Law, *The Tests of Life: A Study in the First Epistle of St. John* (Edinburgh: T & T Clark, 1909). Stott (*The Letters of John*) later popularized this approach even further.

3. The criterion of *belief* (orthodox doctrine) demands that persons believe that Jesus Christ has come in the flesh (e.g., 4:1–6).

John repeatedly uses these criteria to help provide assurance of salvation for those readers who measure up to them. To show the reality of their Christian profession, individuals must meet the criteria in all three areas.

Prologue: Eyewitness Authentication for the Incarnation of Christ, Which Provides the Basis for Fellowship between God and Man (1:1–4)

God manifested his Word historically in the person of Jesus Christ (1:2). He is the basis for having fellowship with God. John maintained that Jesus Christ had existed in the beginning (1:1). He proclaimed the message of this "word of life" (NRSV) so that his readers might enjoy fellowship with him, God the Father, and Christ (1:3). This proclamation made John's joy complete (1:4).

Many of the words in 1:1–4—e.g., "we have heard . . . seen . . . looked at and touched" (NRSV)—clearly reflect eyewitness language. The protognostic heretics were saying that Christ was not a real man; he was a spiritual phantom. John said that idea was ridiculous, and he provided eyewitness apostolic testimony to both the humanity and the deity of Jesus Christ. He used the perfect tense in Greek several times: "have heard" (1:1,3,5), "have seen" (1:1,2,3), and "may be full" (1:4). The significance of the Greek perfect tense is that it describes an action which has been completed in the past, but the results of that action continue up to the present time.

The Criteria Which Determine the Reality of Christian Profession (1:5–5:13)

1. *God is light, and those in fellowship with him walk in purity also (1:5–2:2).* For the first criterion John emphasizes the moral implications of the Christian message (1:5–2:2). The basic content of the Christian message that John proclaimed is "God is light" (1:5 KJV); in other words, God is supremely good, pure, true, holy, etc. John contrasts this statement with the words, "And in him" (God) "is no darkness" (evil, error, impurity, etc.) whatsoever—not in any way, shape, or form (1:5 KJV).

In 1:6–10 John contradicts three false claims of the heretics. Each of these wrong assertions begins with the statement, "If we say that" (*ean eipōmen hoti*, 1:6,8,10 KJV). First, John fought the false teachers' claim that one could have fellowship with God while living in sin and darkness (1:6). No one can say that he knows God and is related to Him through Jesus Christ and practice a libertine lifestyle like that of the false teachers. John points out that the two are inconsistent with each other because fellowship with God requires a lifestyle of righteousness and obedience. He emphasizes that if we believe such a claim, then we are lying and are not practicing the truth (1:6). He goes on to say, however, that if we live obediently in the same sphere where God Himself is to be found, then we have fellowship with one another (1:7), i.e., with other Christians (cp. 1:3). Obedient believers have fellowship with God, but that fellowship leads in turn to fellowship with others.

Put another way, people cannot have fellowship with God if they do not have fellowship with other believers.[27] Further, when believers walk in the light, they become conscious of sin; that is to say, the very thing that separates them from God shows up in the light.[28] They may retreat into the darkness, or they can continue in the light and find that the blood of Jesus Christ keeps on cleansing them from every sin (1:7).

Second, John combats the heretics' claim that they possessed no inherent sin nature (1:8).[29] If we believe this, John maintains, then we are self-deceived and void of the truth. Rather than deny sin in our lives, John holds that "if we confess our sins,"[30] i.e., acknowledge that we are sinners by nature and by practice, then God is "faithful and just" to remit (forgive) our debt due to sin and removes (cleanses) the stain of sin (1:9 KJV). Verse 9 is crucial for every Christian to understand; this is how believers in Jesus handle sin after being saved. The verse instructs them how to get sins forgiven on a temporal basis after salvation so they may enjoy continual fellowship with God. Sin breaks fellowship with God, but the Father promises forgiveness and purification to those who confess their sin.

---

[27] I. Howard Marshall, *The Epistles of John* (NICNT; Grand Rapids: Eerdmans, 1978), 111.

[28] Ibid., 112.

[29] "Sin" here is in the singular and may refer to the inherited sin principle in man. Alternately, the aspect of the present tense *echomen* may indicate that they believed they were not currently sinning.

[30] To "confess" (present tense, continuous aspect) is regular confession of sin.

Third, John fights the false teachers' claim that they had never committed any sins (1:10); i.e., they were incapable of sinning. If you believe such a claim, John says, you accuse God of being a liar and show that His Word has no place in your lives (1:10). This is the case because God has said in His Word that mankind is sinful (e.g., Ps 14:3; Isa 53:6; 64:6; Rom 3:23; etc.).

Verses 8–10 constitute a classic and eloquent refutation of the doctrine of "perfectionism," held in those days by many of the protognostic heretics. The doctrine of perfectionism says when Christians get to a certain point (either at salvation or a later point) you cease to sin; you no longer sin.

John has vigorously denounced the false doctrine of sinless perfection (1:8,10) held by some of the protognostic heretics. Now, lest he be misunderstood as not being concerned that people should avoid sin, he explicitly states in 2:1a that his desire is that his "little children" (children in the faith)[31] do not commit even a single act of sin.[32] He knew that the ideal is not possible of perfect realization at this time. Until believers get their glorified bodies, they will sin. But if one does commit an act of sin (2:1b)[33]—and the *if* here assumes that one will at some point—all is not lost. Believers have an "advocate" (*paraklētos*, in secular Greek "a defense attorney in a hostile court"), Jesus Christ, who is perfectly righteous and can thus represent their case in the presence of a holy God.[34] He is their defense attorney in the court of a holy God who is totally opposed to sin.

What does this "advocate," this *paraklētos*, this defense attorney, do for believers? He represents them at court. The following story should not be taken literally; it is simply a helpful illustration and not a literal scenario. When a believer commits a sin, Satan says to God, "Did you see what he just did? He claims to be a Christian. He claims to be born again. He claims to be saved. He is the member of a Christian church. Did you see what

[31] This term is one of endearment. Remember that by this time John was an aged man and may have been in his nineties, and therefore in a fatherly fashion he referred to these Christians in Asia Minor as "my little children."

[32] This seems to be the force of the aorist tense verb.

[33] The verb is again the aorist tense.

[34] The word "advocate" (*paraklētos*) is the same word that is translated "comforter" several times in the Gospel of John, and there it refers to the Holy Spirit. Here, however, the term refers to Jesus Himself, not the Holy Spirit. One of the meanings of *paraklētos* in secular Greek was "a defense attorney in a hostile court," and that is obviously the sense in which John uses the term here.

he just did? Now if you are a holy and righteous God, then you have no other choice but to cast that person out of your sight forever; otherwise you are not just and holy." And then Jesus steps forward and presents his nail-pierced hands to the Father and says, "But wait, it is true that he has sinned, and it is true that is an awful thing he did, but I died for that sin, and therefore, it is already taken care of." And the Father says, "Case dismissed."

Though we should not take this story literally and no Scripture teaches that this actually goes on in that form, there is truth in that story. The presence of Jesus Christ, our substitute, our representative, in the holy presence of God, makes it possible for us to have access to God and for us to be related to Him. Incidentally, that is the basis of assurance for the Christian who fears he will lose his salvation. The only way a believer can ever lose his salvation is if Jesus Christ quits interceding for him. If Jesus Christ ever quits His work as intercessor, then believers are in trouble. But if He will not quit—and Scripture teaches that He will not—then we can be confident that He is our advocate, our defense attorney, the one who represents our interests in the courtroom of heaven.

Jesus is "the propitiation for our sins" (2:2 KJV). "Propitiation" is translated from the Greek word *hilasmos*, which literally means "satisfaction."[35] Propitiation means that the death of Jesus Christ "satisfies" the righteous demands of God concerning holiness. In other words, the death of Christ enabled God to forgive believers' sins without wreaking justice and vengeance upon them individually. God looks upon the penal, substitutionary atonement of Christ as the satisfactory payment for their sins—no other is required—and thus they are free from divine wrath (2:2). Jesus took their place; He died in their stead; He took the judgment for their sins upon Himself. But, John will say, Jesus is not only the propitiation, the satisfaction for "our" sins, i.e., for those of us who are Christians but also for the sins of the whole world (2:2).

Theologically speaking, the latter verse offers substantial support for what is known as the doctrine of "unlimited atonement"

---

[35] A great debate exists about whether to translate *hilasmos* in 2:2 as "propitiation" (the removal of God's wrath toward sin), or "expiation" (God removes the sin). The NIV tries to capture both ideas with the phrase "atoning sacrifice." "Propitiation" best captures the idea of "satisfaction." For a helpful discussion of this issue, see Akin, *1, 2, 3 John*, 82–86. See also Leon Morris (*Apostolic Preaching of the Cross* [rev. ed.; Grand Rapids: Eerdmans, 1965], 144–213), who wrote the classic defense showing that the biblical evidence overwhelmingly favors the propitiation view.

(cp. also John 3:16; 2 Cor 5:19; 1 Tim 2:6; 4:10; Titus 2:11; Heb 2:9; 2 Pet 2:1; 3:9). In other words, the death of Jesus Christ paid for the sins of *all people*.[36] This does not mean that all people will be saved, but it does mean that all people are rendered "save-able" by the death of Christ. The plain reading of this verse counters what is called the doctrine of "limited atonement," i.e., the doctrine of particular redemption which says that Christ died *only for the elect*, i.e., only for those whom God had chosen in eternity past. But it is difficult here to make the "whole world" mean the "whole world of the elect."[37]

---

[36] Stephen Smalley (*1, 2, 3 John* [WBC; Waco, TX: Word, 1984], 40) is right when he says that repeating the preposition *peri* before *holou tou kosmou* ("the whole world") indicates that it is the sins of the world rather than the world in general that is the concern of Jesus' propitiation.

[37] The decision between these two points of view is neither a matter of orthodoxy versus heterodoxy nor a matter of great concern. Even from the standpoint of unlimited atonement, it is obvious that those who do not believe in Jesus Christ will not be saved. And therefore, ultimately, in eternity, it will make little difference whether Christ died for them or not because they did not appropriate His death, even if it was available to them. So the end result is the same either way. Nonetheless, the Bible, arguably, does seem to teach unlimited atonement (1 John 2:2; John 3:16; 2 Cor 5:19; 1 Tim 2:6; 4:10; Titus 2:11; Heb 2:9; 2 Pet 2:1; 3:9).

The basis for the "limited atonement" view rests in two things, essentially. First, there is the logical argument concerning "double jeopardy." Double jeopardy is trying a person twice for the same crime, or bringing the same charges against two different people, even though one or the other would obviously be innocent. And in our laws today (and this has been true in Western jurisprudence for centuries), a person is not to be brought into double jeopardy. In other words, if he has once been acquitted of a crime, he is never to be tried again for that same crime. So the argument goes like this: If Jesus Christ died for the sins of all people, then the sins of all people are paid for, and one has already been judged for those sins, and therefore, if God would bring an unbeliever into judgment because of his sins, even though Christ has already died for those sins, God would, in effect, be putting that unbeliever in a position of double jeopardy. He would be charging him with crimes already judged upon another man, Christ Jesus. Therefore, the argument goes, since in our own laws we forbid this, surely we would not expect that God would do something which even we in our own laws would not permit. Surely God would not be so unjust, so unrighteous, as to try a person for a crime if he had already reaped judgment for that crime by the death of Jesus Christ. The argument of double jeopardy says that if the unbeliever's sins are already paid for in the death of Christ, then God would be unjust if he would visit judgment upon the unbeliever himself because he would then in effect be exacting double punishment for a single crime (sin).

Second, the position of limited atonement, or particular redemption, fits into the overall concept of "divine election" as understood by the Calvinist: total depravity, unconditional election, limited atonement, irresistible grace, perseverance of the saints. An essential, rational, and consistent part of the Calvinistic system is to say that if God chose in eternity past only certain people to be saved, then He would cause His Son to die for those people. And therefore, there would be no point, apparently, in His dying for the nonelect because God never intended to save them in the first place. And therefore, why extend the benefits of the death of Christ to the nonelect when, as a matter of fact, God has no intention of saving the nonelect? So therefore, as a part of the Calvinistic system, limited atonement is a consistent and absolutely reasonable assumption as part of the overall system. This reason, essentially,

2. *True Christians obey God (2:3–11).* John sets forth one (the moral test of obedience) of the several criteria in this epistle of the reality and genuineness of Christian profession (2:3–6). A genuine Christian is an obedient Christian. Notice verse 3: "And by this we may be sure that we know him." How? "*If* we keep his commandments" (KJV). One of the basic ways you can know whether a person is a Christian is whether he is obedient to the Word of God. Though no one is totally obedient to the Word of God all the time, a saved person cannot disobey it with impunity. He will feel guilty; he will feel convicted; the hand of God will be upon him in chastening, and he will be miserable until he gets it straightened out. But an unbeliever can live continually and habitually in disobedience and apparently think nothing of it. That is the difference between a Christian and a non-Christian.

Verses 4–5 read: "He who says, 'I know Him'" (meaning salvation), "and does not keep His commandments, is a liar, and the truth is not in him. But whoever keeps His word, truly the love of God is perfected in him. By this we know that we are in Him" (NKJV). The "love of God" in 2:5 is the love that believers have for

together with the idea of double jeopardy, is why the thoroughgoing Calvinist believes in the idea of particular redemption or limited atonement. Even the staunchest Calvinist would likely admit that there is no specific Scripture which says, in so many words, that Christ died only for the elect, but rather, Calvinists think that this is the overall theological inference from the whole system of the sovereignty of God and the divine, unconditional election of man.

Some might ask in response to the view that Christ died for *all* people (even though all people will not be saved), "How could God allow Christ to die for people who would never be saved?" We are not given a specific answer in Scripture, but those who hold to unlimited atonement might reason that perhaps it is in order that when a person stands before the great white throne judgment of God he could never say, "Of course I was not saved because Christ did not die for me." Now that scenario is hypothetical of course, but one might bring up that argument.

How would the unlimited atonement school of thought answer the double jeopardy argument of particular redemption or limited atonement? The answer would be something like this: Just because a reasonable analogy can be found does not mean that you can establish a biblical doctrine on it. As a matter of fact, you can bring up a reasonable analogy for unlimited atonement also. For example, take the polio vaccine which is available in this country. The vaccine is nearly 100 percent effective, and it is also available to every man, woman, and child in this country. If you cannot afford it, you can go to a public health clinic and get it for nothing. And yet we have not totally stamped out polio in this country because there are still people who do not get the vaccine. The fact that the vaccine is available, and is effective, and is available without charge does not automatically stamp out the disease. You still have to take the vaccine. So this side would say, even so with the death of Christ. The death of Christ is available to all people; it potentially covers all people, but it does not automatically save all people. It must be appropriated by faith. As one theologian has said, "The death of Christ renders all men *savable*, but it does not automatically forgive them; it does not automatically save them."

God—not God's love for them. Those who claim to know Christ ought to live like He did: in obedience to God. Jesus is the supreme example of one who demonstrated His love for God by obedience (2:6).

The "new" (yet old) commandment is to love other Christians. John sets forth a second test (social) to determine whether Christian profession is genuine. Put another way, one of the primary tests of obedience lies in the commandment that believers are to love one another (2:7–11; cp. 3:11–24; 4:7–12). John was probably aiming his remarks at the protognostic false teachers who held the simple Christians of Asia Minor in contempt because they did not possess their exalted knowledge and "liberty" of life. Such an attitude, according to John, identified them as unbelievers (2:9–11).

The command for Christians to love one another is, in one sense, an old and long-standing commandment (2:7), deeply rooted in Old Testament revelation (cp. Deut 6:5; Lev 19:18), but in another sense, it is a new commandment (2:8) in that Jesus gave it new life, depth, meaning, and application (cp. John 13:34). This commandment is new in the sense that it has been vividly demonstrated and illustrated by Jesus Himself. Christ's disciples were able to see the depth of Jesus' love for them and thus the depth of God's love for them. And now they were to reflect that same love for one another. Loving one another is the prime demonstration to the world that believers are Jesus' disciples (cp. John 13:35).

3. *The life of fellowship is available to all age groups (2:12–14).* John balances here his exposure of the protognostics with a note of commendation for the faithful, who are divided into three groups: (1) the little children, (2) the young men, and (3) the fathers (2:12–14). These references are not to their physical ages but to the various stages of their spiritual development. The "little children" (new Christians) are described in terms of their new assurance of forgiveness of sin and their relationship to God.[38] The "young men" (intermediate or more mature Christians) are portrayed in terms of their spiritual vitality and victory in spiritual conflict. They are more mature than the little children, but they are not yet as mature as the fathers. The "fathers" (most mature Christians) are described

---

[38] It is possible that John's use of *teknia* in 2:12 may be a reference to all of John's Christian readers, like what is found in 2:1. If so, John would be addressing two groups rather than three. The distinct content, however, of the messages for each group strongly suggests that these references are to three stages of spiritual development. So also Stott, *Letters of John,* 100.

in terms of their assured, stabilized, often-tested relationship to God. John encourages his readers and writes[39] to say that although false teachers abound in their midst, he knows they are sound, stable, and going on with the Lord.

4. *True Christians avoid worldliness (2:15–17)*. Genuine believers practice loving one another, but they also reject love for the world (2:15–17). These well-known verses become less confusing if we first discuss terminology. The word "world" (*kosmos*) is used in three different senses in the New Testament: (1) the physical, created universe (cp. Matt 13:35; 24:21); (2) the world of humanity (cp. John 3:16); and (3) the evil, Satanic world system (cp. John 8:23; 12:31, etc.). The third meaning is in view here, and this evil world system is described under three headings: (1) the lust of the flesh, (2) the lust of the eyes, and (3) the pride of life (2:16). The "lust of the flesh" is that which is inward, i.e., the basic drives or outworking of the Adamic sin principle in each person. The "lust of the eyes" is that which is outward. As C. H. Dodd has said, "The lust of the eyes is the tendency to be captivated by the outward show of things without inquiring into their real values." The "pride of life" is arrogance related to a person's earthly circumstances.

A biblical illustration of this description can be found in Gen 3:6 with the story of Eve and her contact with the serpent in the garden: "When the woman saw that the tree [of the knowledge of good and evil] was good for food, and that it was a delight to the eyes, and that the tree was to be desired to make one wise, she took of its fruit and ate" (NRSV). The tree was good for food (the lust of the flesh); it was a delight to the eyes (the lust of the eyes); it was going to make her wise (the pride of life). All three characteristics of the evil satanic world system were used by the serpent to entice Eve, and eventually Adam, into the transgression.

Christians are not to love the evil world system with its various characteristics. If they do, they are separated from God (2:15). If love for the world marks professing believers' lives, they are ungodly and have turned away from God to the enemy of God and His system. The world and the things that are in the world are

---

[39] John mentions six times that he "writes" to each group. The first three references are in the present tense while the second three are in the aorist tense. The aorist tense has caused some scholars to say that John is referring to a previous letter in which he wrote to each group. In all probability, however, the use of the aorist tense is just an epistolary aorist and refers to the present letter. See the discussion in Stott, *The Letters of John*, 100–101.

transitory; believers who do the will of God, on the other hand, will live forever (2:17).

5. *The threat of false teaching (2:18–27). Unbelievers deny that Jesus is the Christ.* The genuineness of Christian profession is demonstrated not only by one's conduct but also by one's theological beliefs. Despite disclaimers, theology is of paramount importance. Conduct arises from one's concept of and commitment to truth (cp. Prov 23:7). Central to Christian theology is the doctrine of the Trinity, which involves the full deity, humanity, and equality of Jesus Christ, the Son of God. Virtually every heresy denies the Trinity in some way. Protognosticism was no exception. The false teachers had a faulty view of Christ; they denied that He was actually God manifest in the flesh. Such denial, John says, is anti-Christian (2:18), and even though the heretics were identified with the Christian community (2:19), their faulty view of Christ marked them as infidels (2:22–23).

In 2:18 John did not deny the ultimate appearance of "Antichrist," that final satanic world ruler known elsewhere as "the man of sin" (2 Thess 2:3), "the beast out of the sea" (Rev 13:1–10), "the little horn" (Dan 7:8–27), etc. He meant that the current protognostic heretics were forerunners and precursors of the final, ultimate infidel.

Further, John says that these heretics "went out from us, but they were not of us" (2:19). In other words, these false teachers had been a part of the progressing, visible, Christian church; they were not atheists, agnostics, or people who openly and overtly denied the faith. These persons apparently were progressive Christians and part of the local church. They had identified themselves with the church of Jesus Christ and claimed to be Christians, i.e., members of the body of Christ. John maintains that though they went out from us, they did not really stem from the believing community as a source. If they had been of us—and they were not[40]—they would have no doubt continued with us. But, John insists, they went out that it might become evident that they were not of the church.

In 2:20,27 John does not, of course, teach that Christians are omniscient. He means that his readers had received Spirit-directed apostolic teaching and thus had no need for the supposed "super-knowledge" of the protognostics (cp. 2:26). Verse 27 is sometimes

---

[40] John writes this clause in such a way as to assume what he has said to be untrue—i.e., they were not of us.

erroneously used to deny the need for Christian instruction today, but compare Ephesians 4:11–13. The spiritual gift of teaching is one of God's gifts to His church, and believers ignore it to their own peril.

Verses 22–23 are crucial. John says that those who deny that Jesus is the Christ are liars; moreover, those persons are anti-Christians who deny the Father and the Son (2:22). He goes on to say that whoever denies the Son does not have the Father either; conversely, he who acknowledges the Son has the Father also (2:23). The God whom we worship is the God and Father of our Lord Jesus Christ. And if a person does not believe that Jesus is the Son of God and does not believe that he is in the godhead, then that person is not worshipping the same God. It is impossible for a person to be rightly related to God apart from Jesus Christ (cp. John 14:6). This means that all of those who practice some other religion outside of biblical, orthodox Christian faith, regardless of devotion and sincerity, are lost. Believers in Jesus are frequently accused of being narrow (all truth is narrow), bigoted, anti-Semitic, etc., but the fact remains: biblical Christianity identifies Jesus Christ as the only means of access to God (1 Tim 2:5). Any other view is anti-Christian.

6. *True Christians abide in Christ or keep His word (2:28–3:3).* John had exhorted his readers earlier to remain in Christ by acknowledging that He is the incarnate Son of God. Now he urges them to do so by reminding them of Christ's future return (2:28). If they continue in Christ, they can have boldness and confidence before Him so as not to shrink from Him on the last day (2:28). If they know factually (*oida*) that God is righteous, they will also "perceive as a logical consequence" (*ginōskō*) that those who practice righteousness have been born of Him (2:29).[41] Verse 29 was likely written with the protognostic heretics in mind; their initiation into *gnōsis* may have been viewed as regeneration. But John argues that righteousness, not knowledge, is the evidence of the new birth and the chief characteristic of regenerate persons.[42]

John begins chapter 3 by marveling at God's grace in making believers His children. Modern translations correctly insert "and such we are" (or something similar, which is omitted by the King James Version). What John is saying, in effect, is, "Imagine that frail, finite, sinful, rebellious creatures such as we are now actu-

---

[41] Stott, *Letters of John,* 122.
[42] Ibid.

ally a part of the intimate family of the sovereign, infinite, holy God! But we really are!"

Verse 1 moves from the wonder of being God's child to the problem which such a relationship creates: The "world" (*kosmos,* i.e., the satanic world system) does not understand what makes Christians tick and thus opposes them both in worldview and life-style (cp. John 15:18). The Christian, however, is sustained by his knowledge of the glory that awaits him ultimately in Christ's presence (3:2). The thing that sustains the children of God in the midst of a hostile world is the hope that they will one day be with Christ and be like Him. And those who fix their hope on Christ will purify themselves morally as He is pure (3:3).

7. *True Christians do not live in sin (3:4–10).* Verses 4–10 are crucial but frequently misunderstood because of the many unfortunate translations available. A cursory look makes it appear that John was teaching that a genuine Christian, one born of God, does not sin anymore; but this notion of perfectionism cannot be the case because of his previous remarks in 1 John 1:8,10. The key to understanding this passage is to recognize the present tenses of the Greek verbs with regard to sin and righteousness. The person who is genuinely born of God does not live perpetually and habitually in sin (3:6a,7,9). The one who does live perpetually and habitually in sin is of the devil (3:8,10a). Christians do sin (cp. 2:1–2), but they do not live perpetually and habitually in sin. The believer is a changed person (cp. 2 Cor 5:17). He cannot practice a lifestyle of sin because he has been born of God. God's "seed," i.e., something of the divine nature (perhaps a reference to the Holy Spirit), was implanted in him at the new birth (3:9).

The clear criterion in this passage identifies the false teachers of John's day as infidels (3:4,6b,10b,c) despite their Christian professions and associations. It does the same today for many professing Christians whose lives show no evidence of regeneration. There is such a thing as a carnal Christian (cp. 1 Cor 3:1–3), but there is no such thing as a *perpetually* carnal Christian.

Verse 4 is also poorly translated in some versions in that it is interpreted by some to define sin as the transgression of the Mosaic law. Yet the New Testament clearly teaches that Christians today are not under the Mosaic law (cp. Rom 7:6; Gal 3:17–4:7). The statement in 3:4 should be translated as "sin is lawlessness." That is to say, "sin" and "lawlessness" are interchangeable terms;[43] "lawlessness" is a definition of "sin." "Lawlessness" is an attitude of rebellion against God and all that God has ordained. It characterized the original sin of the devil who "sinned from the beginning" (3:8b HCSB) and also the original sin of man (cp. Gen 3). And it has characterized every sin since. Every act of disobedience to the revealed Word of God is an act of open rebellion and a "declaration of independence" from God. This rebellion is the essence and nature of sin.

But Christ appeared (a reference to Jesus' incarnation and all that He did while in that state) to take away sins (3:5a; cp. 2:2) and to destroy the devil's works (3:8c). The fact that there is no sin in Christ gives efficacy to His redemptive work (3:5b).

John summarizes this passage by saying that the children of God and those of the devil are easily distinguished. Anyone who does not practice righteousness as a lifestyle and who does not love his brother in Christ is not of God (3:10). The latter statement on loving fellow Christians also marks a clear transition to the next passage.

8. *True Christians love one another, while unbelievers hate, kill, etc. (3:11–24).* In the immediately preceding passage, John establishes that a genuine Christian is an obedient Christian. In this passage, he emphasizes a specific area of obedience, returning to the subject of a Christian's love for fellow Christians as a mark of genuineness. That believers should love one another is an essential part of the apostolic message which they had heard from the beginning (3:11).

The "love" spoken of in this passage (and the others) is *agapē* love, which refers to a volitional choice to meet the deepest needs of another, whether or not there is any reciprocation. It is an unconditional attitude which is not necessarily related to pleasure, excitement, thrill, or ecstasy. Thus, it can be commanded ("feelings," on the other hand, cannot be commanded). This fact explains, then, how believers can love (in an *agapē* sense) the unlovely. They may not feel any immediate emotional attraction. Indeed, in some cases they may feel just the opposite, but they can "will" to meet their needs and to treat them as those for whom Christ died, as precious in His sight. Surprisingly, a "feeling" of fondness and affection often develops also, but this aspect is not indigenous to the word.

John presents the murder of Abel by Cain as the classic opposite of *agapē* love (3:12). "Murder" is the Greek word *sphadzō,*

---

[43] Both words occur with the definite article in Greek.

which means "to cut the throat," and probably describes the method which Cain used to kill Abel (drawn from the method used in making animal sacrifices). Cain killed his brother because Abel's deeds were righteous while his own were evil. And John instructed his readers that the spirit of Cain was still active in the world— righteousness provokes the world's hatred toward those who are righteous (3:13). Love for fellow Christians is proof that believers have indeed been saved, i.e., have passed from death to life; to the contrary, hatred toward believers is evidence that one is not saved, i.e., he still abides in death (3:14).

Verse 15 enlarges upon 3:14. Anyone who hates fellow Christians is a murderer and does not have eternal life. Someone may ask, "Then how might we know love?" Verse 16 provides the answer: *Jesus is the pattern or prototype for Christians to love others*. He laid down His life for believers, and because He did so, they also should lay down their lives in love for their fellow Christians (3:16).

Love of this kind is more than an attitude. *Agapē* must work itself out in actual deeds (3:17–18) if it is authentic (cp. Jas 2:15–16). John says that genuinely unselfish acts of this kind not only minister significantly to the needs of others, but also the presence of such love in believers' lives gives them assurance of their relationship with God (3:19–24).[44] This assurance of a believer's standing with God results in further benefits: boldness and confidence before God (3:21) and effectiveness in prayer (3:22). Christians experience effectiveness in prayer because they obey God. They keep His commandments and please Him (3:22b). John then defines the commandment which is to be obeyed—believe in Jesus Christ and love fellow Christians (3:23). These two commands are so closely linked that John speaks of them as one commandment. Obedience is the proof that believers are abiding in God and He in them, and the presence of the Spirit in them further confirms God's indwelling (3:24). Verse 24b is transitional and looks forward to John's words in 4:1–6.

9. *True Christians affirm that Jesus Christ has come in the flesh (4:1–6)*. John continues the emphasis on sound doctrine and the

---

[44] The import and meaning of verse 20 has been much debated as to whether it refers to God's consolation or condemnation. Those who interpret this verse in accordance with the former viewpoint understand John to be saying that if our hearts condemn us, then we may appeal to God for reassurance because He is greater and knows everything (cp. John 21:17). Those who interpret this verse in accordance with the latter viewpoint understand John to be saying that if our hearts condemn us, then God will do so all the more. In other words, they see it as a warning to those who do not practice love.

need to recognize and identify false teachers (4:1–6). Verse 1 teaches that a person may masquerade as a Christian teacher (or prophet) and yet be anti-Christian and satanic. Scripture repeatedly warns of such people (cp. 2 John 7–11; Matt 7:15–23; Jude 3–4; 1 Tim 4:1–3; 2 Tim. 4:3–4; etc.). John commands that believers are not to accept every prophetic utterance as genuine just because the person giving it is speaking in God's name. The reason for this command is that many false prophets have gone out into the world. John explains that the crux of this specific criterion is doctrinal. Believers will declare and affirm Jesus as the incarnate Lord, but those who do not are anti-Christian because they mirror the spirit of the coming Antichrist (4:2–3). John provides his readers an assurance by instructing them on the character of false teachers. Those who follow God will heed godly, apostolic teaching, but those who follow the world will heed its teaching composed of falsehood and error (4:4–6).

Believers in Jesus should be particularly wary of those who would attempt to conceal their heresies. How did one "test" these supposed prophets (4:1)? In John's day, the spiritual gift of "discerning spirits" (cp. 1 Cor 12:10) was available, but then and now the principal means to compare a person's teaching and character with the Word of God.

10. *True Christians love God and one another (4:7–12).* John again emphasizes the criterion of loving fellow believers as a necessary mark of genuine Christian profession (4:7). He commands his readers to "love one another" because "love is from God" (NRSV). That is to say, *agapē* love comes from God; He is the source of all true love.

John maintains that believers must love one another because this is God's nature (4:8). Anyone who does not display this nature of love does not know God. The Greek construction of "God is love" (4:8b) makes love a *description* of God—not a definition (contrast 3:4—"sin is lawlessness").[45] That is to say, "love" is not all that God is; He is also holy, righteous, sovereign, etc.

Moreover, John urges his readers to love others because God has demonstrated His love for them in the death of Christ (4:9–11). Believers can know that God loves them because He sent His Son to be the propitiation for their sins (cp. 2:2). Because of that act of love, they ought also to love others.

---

[45] In Greek, the word *love* does not occur with the article.

Furthermore, John instructs his readers that if they love each other they make the presence of God, whom no one can see, a reality (4:12).[46] In other words, when believers in Jesus love one another, this indicates that God has indeed come to dwell in them and that is how God's love is brought to its end or goal (4:12).

11. *Summary of grounds for Christian assurance (4:13–5:3).* After emphasizing the importance of love toward one another, John now intersperses some of the criteria so that his readers might have assurance of genuine Christian profession. He emphasizes that the indwelling presence of the Holy Spirit (4:13; cp. Rom 8:14–16) in the lives of believers (for contrast, cp. Jude 19) enables them to acknowledge that Jesus Christ is the God-man[47] and to love others (4:13–16). Put another way, the gift of the Spirit (4:13), the acknowledgment of Jesus as the Son of God (4:14–15), and abiding in love (4:16) are evidences and assurances of God's indwelling.

John revisits the subject of love, though now he speaks of the completion of believers' love for God rather than His love in them (4:17–21). "Perfect love," a mature and developed love for God, will show itself in unashamed boldness and confidence before Him in the day of judgment (4:17–18) and display a rich love for other Christians (4:20–21).

John also teaches that whoever believes that Jesus is the Messiah was born of God and that those who genuinely love God will love God's children also (5:1). He insists that the reverse is true as well. If one genuinely loves fellow Christians, he will also love God and obey His commands (5:2–3). The two loves are inextricably linked. Believers should not find it difficult to obey God because His commands do not have a crushing, oppressive character and because (looking forward to the next section) they have been given power to keep them (5:3–4).

12. *Reiteration of the absolute necessity for belief in God's record of Christ's person and work (5:4–12).* In 5:4–12 John reiterates the absolute necessity for belief in God's record of Christ's person and work. He first relates why the commandments of God are not burdensome for believers: "For whatever is born of God overcomes the world" (5:4a). John uses the neuter participle *to gegennēmenon* to

---

[46] This clause is a third-class conditional clause in Greek, which indicates the possibility of not fulfilling the condition.

[47] That is, full, undiminished deity plus genuine humanity (cp. Col 2:9).

"emphasize not 'the victorious *person*' but 'the victorious *power*.'"[48] He attributes the Christian's victory to his faith (5:4b). He elaborates on the latter truth with the immediately answered question: "Who is the one who overcomes the world but the one who believes that Jesus is the Son of God" (5:5)?

John's thinking in 5:4–5 is consistent with what he wrote elsewhere. For example, in each of the seven letters to the churches of Asia (cp. Rev 2–3), Christ promises some special blessing to "those who overcome." What did He mean? The answer is similar to what is presented in this passage in 1 John. The "overcomers" are those who have been genuinely saved, and thus nothing can shake them from continuing allegiance to Christ.

If you compare versions which follow the Textus Receptus, i.e., the Received Text (KJV, NKJV), with modern translations (NASB, RSV, NIV, HCSB, etc.), you will find that the modern versions omit an additional part of verse 7 together with the words "on earth" in verse 8a. This extra section is known as the *Comma Johanneum*, or Johannine Comma. The omission reflects the fact that these portions occur only in a small number of rather insignificant manuscripts and should have never been included in the first place.

The meaning of 5:6–8 derives from the protognostic vocabulary of John's day. Some were teaching that the heavenly Christ came down upon the man Jesus at the time of His baptism (the water)— but departed from Him just prior to His passion (the blood). John denies this heresy and affirms that the Jesus Christ who died was the same Jesus Christ who was baptized. Jewish tradition required two or three witnesses to establish the veracity of any testimony. In 5:8 John cites three "witnesses" to the veracity of Jesus Christ: (1) the Holy Spirit; (2) the event of Christ's baptism (the water); and (3) the sacrificial death of Christ (the blood).

John says that since we receive the testimony of men, how much more should we accept God's testimony (the Spirit, the water, and the blood) because it is greater than that of men. His testimony ought to be received because it is the divine witness. The substance of this witness is that God the Father Himself has testified in history to His Son, Jesus Christ (5:9).

The witness of God to Christ evokes faith, and the inward witness of the Holy Spirit in the believer's life assures him of his com-

---

[48] Stott (citing Plummer), *Letters of John*, 176.

mitment to Jesus. However, the person who rejects God's testimony to Jesus makes God out to be a liar because he has not believed (5:10).

Verses 11–12 constitute a classic summary of the gospel (cp. John 3:16). The content of the divine witness is that God gave eternal life to believers, and it is found nowhere else but in Jesus Christ His Son (5:11); that is to say, He is the sole medium of this life. Verse 12 draws a conclusion from the previous verse: "He who has the Son has life; he who does not have the Son of God does not have life." In other words, those who respond to the testimony of God receive eternal life, while those who reject it do not.

13. *Statement of John's purpose for writing (5:13): assurance of salvation for those who measure up to the criteria.* John writes to provide assurance of salvation for those who measure up to the criteria put forth in his letter: (1) obedience to Christ's commands; (2) orthodox doctrine, particularly belief in Jesus as the incarnate Lord; and (3) love for fellow believers. Put another way from the more immediate context, those who have responded to the divine witness receive assurance that they have eternal life.

Conclusion (5:14–21)

1. *The power of prayer and the sin to death (5:14–17).* Those who have responded to the testimony about God also experience a second assurance: answered prayer (5:14–15). John speaks not so much of confidence in prayer as he does boldness (*parrēsia*) in approaching God, the outcome of which is answered prayer (5:14–15; cp. Heb 4:16). The sole qualification for answered prayer is that the requests be made in accordance with God's will (5:14). To be sure, God hears the petitions of believers if they are prayed in this way. As Stott has put it, "Prayer is not a convenient device for imposing our will upon God, or for bending his will to ours, but the prescribed way of subordinating our will to his."[49] Indeed, verses 14–15 constitute an integral part of the theology of prayer, the emphasis being on praying according to God's will (for a broader look at prayer, cp. also Mark 11:24; John 14:13–15; 15:7; 16:24; Rom 8:26–27; Eph 6:18; 1 Thess 5:17; Jas 1:6; 4:2–3; 1 John 3:22).

In the previous two verses John wrote about answered prayer in general (5:14–15). He turns next to the matter of intercessory

---

[49] Ibid., 188.

prayer (5:16–17). On the one hand, verse 16a is a specific example of prayer that is in accordance with God's will: if a Christian sees his brother committing a sin that does not lead to death, he is to pray for him. As a result God will grant (eternal) life to the sinning brother. On the other hand, John discourages intercessory prayer for those whose sin is the sort that leads to death (5:16b). Prayers of the latter type are not in accordance with God's will. Akin rightly notes that "although most of the scholarly debate is devoted to understanding the 'sin that leads to death,' John's real concern is to encourage believers to pray for those whose sin 'is not to death.'"[50]

The "sin to death" phrase (5:16) is difficult. There are two major explanations: (1) the physical death of a Christian is in view, as the ultimate phase of divine discipline (cp. 1 Cor 11:30); (2) the spiritual death of an unbeliever is in view, as the result of a final rejection of Christ (cp. Matt 12:31–32, the "unpardonable sin"). The context of 1 John seems to favor the second explanation. The heretics may apostatize from apostolic doctrine and practice to the extent that they have finally and irrevocably rejected Christ and are thus beyond the reach of intercessory prayer. Those who hear the gospel, profess some interest, but eventually harden themselves against it may find themselves in the same category.

John declares in 5:17 that "all unrighteousness is sin" because he does not want to be misunderstood. He indicates that no sin is trivial, including the sort which does not lead to death. He earlier defined sin as "lawlessness" (*anomia*, 3:4); now he states that it is unrighteousness (*adikia*, 5:17). In other words, sin is not only rebellion against God but also violation of God's standards of what is right.

2. *The Christian's assurance in Christ versus the satanic world (5:18–20).* John speaks in 5:18–20 of three certainties of assurance for the Christian. Each statement of certainty begins with the words "we know" (*oidamen*). First, John reiterates that believers born of God do not habitually commit sin; rather, Christ, the one born of God, keeps and protects them from the evil one, the devil (5:18). Second, he indicates that believers are of God while the rest of the world is in the power of the devil; no middle ground exists (5:19). Third, he teaches that the incarnate Christ has enabled believers to understand God. This God who is revealed and made known

[50] Akin, *1, 2, 3 John*, 211.

through Jesus Christ is the true God. Further, believers are united with the Father by being united with the Son; Jesus Christ is the source of eternal life (5:20).

3. *Final warning against idolatry (5:21)*. In closing, John issues a warning against idolatry, most likely against false conceptions of God like those the protognostic heretics were promoting. He instructs his readers to shun God substitutes. An admonition of this nature was fitting in Asia Minor because a place like Ephesus was not only full of idols carved in stone but also false ideas of God.

Study Outline of 1 John

I. Prologue: Eyewitness Authentication for the Incarnation of Christ, Which Provides the Basis for Fellowship between God and Man (1:1–4)

II. The Criteria Which Determine the Reality of Christian Profession (1:5–5:13)

    A God Is Light. Those in Fellowship with Him Walk in Purity Also (1:5–2:2)

    B. True Christians Obey God (2:3–11). The "New" [yet Old] Commandment Is to Love Other Christians

    C. The Life of Fellowship Is Available to All Age Groups (2:12–14)

    D. True Christians Avoid "Worldliness" (2:15–17)

    E. The Threat of False Teaching (2:18–27). Unbelievers Deny That Jesus Is the Christ

    F. True Christians Abide in Christ, i.e., Keep His Word (2:28–3:3)

    G. True Christians Do Not "Live in Sin" (3:4–10)

    H. True Christians Love One Another, While Unbelievers Hate, Kill, etc. (3:11–24)

    I. True Christians Affirm That Jesus Christ Has Come in the Flesh (4:1–6)

    J. True Christians Love God and One Another (4:7–12) Because God Himself Is Love

    K. Summary of Grounds for Christian Assurance (4:13–5:3)

        1. Possession of Holy Spirit

        2. Confession of Jesus as Son of God

        3. Obedience to God, i.e., Love for Christians

    L. Reiteration of Absolute Necessity for Belief in God's Record of Christ's Person and Work (5:4–12)

    M. Statement of John's Purpose in Writing (5:13) Assurance of Salvation for Those Who Measure Up to the Criteria ✍

III. Conclusion (5:14–21)

    A. The Power of Prayer and the Sin to Death (5:14–17)

    B. The Christian's Assurance in Christ versus the Satanic World (5:18–20)

    C. Final Warning against Idolatry (5:21)

2 John: Do Not Support False Teachers

3 John: Show Hospitality to Itinerant Christian Preachers

Showing Christian hospitality to people is an important virtue. Believers should show hospitality not only to people in general but especially to Christian missionaries who depend on the Lord and others for their support. But when Christians give they need to exercise discernment when doing so because not everyone may be what they claim to be. They need to be acquainted fully with the beliefs of those to whom they give. No one unwittingly wants to support a false teacher! Some of us may encounter people who do not want us to lend any support to genuine Christian missionaries unless *they say so.* They like being the authority and having the last words on such matters. They love to be first and want you to follow their agenda. Such issues as these are the type that John deals with in 2 and 3 John. Even though these NT letters have been neglected by Christian scholars, they contain important lessons for us.

Author

External evidence for the authorship of 2 and 3 John is not as substantial as that for 1 John. The letters' brevity, lack of quotable material, and personal character were likely factors in their neglect by the early church. Eusebius, the early church historian, classified both epistles as disputed but also pointed out that many accepted them.[51] Earlier we noted that Irenaeus credited John with writing 1 and 2 John and that Origen designated the apostle as the author of all three letters (see 1 John: "Author"). Strikingly, the authorship of 2 and 3 John is never attributed by any writer in the early church to anyone other than John the apostle.

As for internal evidence, the opening, closing, style, and outlook of 2 and 3 John are similar so the same author probably wrote both letters. Moreover, these two writings also share similarities in vocabulary and theme with the letter of 1 John. This indicates a shared authorship. For example, well-known is the fact that 1 and 2 John both say that Jesus "has come in the flesh" (1 John 4:2 // 2 John 7 NRSV), and both 1 and 3 John point out that those who practice doing good demonstrate that they are God's children (1 John 3:10 // 3 John 11).

The author of 2 and 3 John identifies himself as "the Elder." This detail, however, does not necessarily mean—as some have argued—that these letters were written by another John who is called the Elder. We know that another apostle, Peter, called himself an elder (cp. 1 Pet 5:1), so the practice must have been a common one. And the term is certainly an appropriate one for John to use to describe himself at this point in his life because he was an old man, the last of the apostles still alive! In the final analysis external and internal evidence both point to John the apostle as the author of 2 and 3 John.

Canonical Recognition

The epistles of 2 and 3 John were unknown by much of the church until rather late. These letters are short, and decades passed before some in the church realized that these letters were even in existence; communication in those days was not like today. Nonetheless, these epistles were eventually accepted and recognized as canonical. The Muratorian Canon (late second century AD) refers to two epistles

---

[51] Eusebius, *Hist. eccl.* 3.25.3.

written by John—likely 1 and 2 John but 3 John is not mentioned.
Origen (c. AD 231), the first person to mention all three epistles, had
considerable doubts about 2 and 3 John when he said that John "left
an epistle of a very few lines and, it may be, a second or third, for not
all say these are genuine."[52]

As we saw earlier, Eusebius (c. AD 325) included 1 John among
his "acknowledged books" (*homologoumena*), but he placed 2 and
3 John into his category of "disputed books" (*antilegomena*).[53] He
said that 2 and 3 John were "well known and acknowledged by
most," whether John the apostle wrote them or "another of the same
name" (speaking of the "John the elder" hypothesis). Eusebius was
convinced that 1, 2, and 3 John were each genuine.[54] Eventually,
2 and 3 John, along with 1 John, were counted among the "catholic" epistles. This term is practically synonymous for "canonical."[55]
Athnasius's list of 27 New Testament books (AD 367) included 2 and
3 John as did the canonical lists of accepted books compiled by the
councils of Hippo (AD 393) and Carthage (AD 397).

Destination and Recipients

Second John is addressed to the "chosen lady and her children"
(v. 1 NIV). Who is this "chosen lady and her children"? Some have
argued that this designation refers to a respected Christian matron
and her family. This conclusion is possible, but it is unlikely that
a family would be so well-known among Christians in Roman Asia
like, say, a church might be.[56] Some have maintained that the designation refers to the universal church, or the church as a whole.
This is not likely because verse 13 reports greetings from "your
chosen sister." In other words, the universal church is the church
as a whole and has no sister.[57] The words in verse 13 are best understood when referring to another congregation. Thus, the "chosen lady and her children" is likely a local congregation, perhaps a
house church; this conclusion makes the best sense.[58]

---

[52] Cited in Eusebius, *Hist. eccl.* 6.25.10.

[53] Eusebius, *Hist. eccl.* 3.25.2–3.

[54] Eusebius *Hist. eccl.* 6.25.10.

[55] Eusebius, *Hist. eccl.* 2.23.25.

[56] This rebuttal was offered by Lea, *The NT*, 570.

[57] This counterpoint was put forth by D. A. Carson, Douglas Moo, and Leon Morris,
Introduction to the NT (1st ed.; Grand Rapids: Zondervan, 1992), 451.

[58] Judith Lieu (*The Second and Third Epistles of John* [Edinburgh: T & T Clark, 1986],
64–68) suggests that John perhaps chose this form of address for its symbolic connections

Third John is addressed to Gaius (v. 1). This man was apparently a well-known Christian (vv. 1,3,5–6). At least three men named Gaius are mentioned elsewhere in the NT: (1) Gaius of Macedonia (Acts 19:29); (2) Gaius of Derbe (Acts 20:4); and (3) Gaius of Corinth (1 Cor 1:14). All three were probably converts of the apostle Paul,[59] but "the beloved Gaius" (NIV) seems to have been John's convert.[60] Consequently we know nothing of this Gaius except what we find in 3 John. He evidently was a commendable and hospitable member of some church in the Ephesus area over which John exercised spiritual charge.

Date and Place of Writing

Second and 3 John are best viewed as having been written after the Gospel of John. However, the dating of 2 and 3 John in relation to 1 John is difficult. For example, some argue that 2 John was written just prior to 1 John because in 2 John the heretics are still relying on the hospitality of Christians, whereas in 1 John they have separated from the Christian community. Still others maintain that certain ideas in 2 John seem to require an explanation from 1 John to clarify them (e.g., consider the reference to "Antichrist" in 2 John 7 in the light of 1 John 2:18–21); thus, 1 John would have been written first. If the date suggested earlier for the writing of 1 John is correct, then the epistles of 2 and 3 John were probably written near or within the same time period, c. AD 95 or 96. A date in the early to mid-nineties is not unreasonable.

Purpose

In light of the recent danger from false teachers, John wrote 2 John to urge the Christians in this congregation to continue loving fellow believers and to refuse any support to false teachers who denied Jesus as the incarnate Christ.

In 3 John the apostle urged Gaius to continue his generous hospitality toward the apostle's traveling preachers, despite the refusal

---

and its flexibility so that it might be used with respect to several congregations.

[59] This criticism was given by Gromacki, *NT Survey*, 382.

[60] John uses the term "my children" (*ta ema tekna*) in verse 4, which would include Gaius as one of his converts, i.e., children in the faith.

of such support by Diotrephes, a controlling and autocratic leader "who loves to be first" (v. 9).

Study Outline of 2 John

I. Greeting (vv. 1–3)
II. Love Fellow Believers (vv. 4–6)
III. Refuse Support to False Teachers Who Reject Apostolic Doctrine (vv. 7–11)
IV. Closing (vv. 12–13)

Highlights of 2 John

Greeting (vv. 1–3)

John identifies himself as "the Elder" (*ho presbuteros*) in his salutation. The term is one of dignity and could refer either to his position of spiritual oversight in the region of Ephesus or to his advanced age. The phrase "chosen lady and her children" (NIV) best represents a local congregation or house church (cp. v. 13), and not a Christian woman and her family. John wrote to the church for the sake of the indwelling truth and assured them of favor from the Father and Son in truth and love (vv. 1–3).

Love Fellow Believers (vv. 4–6)

John rejoices that some of the church members are living according to orthodox doctrine, and he asks them to continue loving fellow believers, which is Christ's foremost command (vv. 4–6). He rejoices that the church members he has met are walking in the truth as commanded (v. 4). He asks them to love fellow believers, as originally commanded (v. 5). Love is walking according to the commandments because the chief command, as originally given, is to walk in love (v. 6).

Refuse Support to False Teachers Who Reject Apostolic Doctrine (vv. 7–11)

John commands the church to guard against and to refuse support to the false teachers who rejected apostolic doctrine by denying that Jesus is the incarnate Christ (vv. 7–11). The background

to this command is that deceivers have gone out who do not acknowledge Jesus as the incarnate Lord (v. 7). The readers should
guard against these men so as not to lose their reward (v. 8). The
one to guard against was the false teacher who had not kept to apostolic doctrine but advocated an advanced teaching which denied
to him any relationship with the Father (v. 9). The readers should
refuse to support or encourage such a false teacher because to do
so would be to share in his evil (vv. 10–11).

Closing (vv. 12–13)

In closing, John wishes to visit them personally to fulfill his joy,
and he passes on the greetings of their sister church (vv. 12–13).

Study Outline of 3 John

   I. Greeting (vv. 1–4)
  II. Commendation of Gaius (vv. 5–8)
 III. Condemnation of Diotrephes (vv. 9–10)
 IV. Commendation of Demetrius (vv. 11–12)
  V. Closing (vv. 13–14)

Highlights of 3 John

Greeting (vv. 1–4)

The elder addresses his letter to Gaius, beloved in the truth,
wishing him prosperity and rejoicing to learn that he is living according to the truth (vv. 1–4).

Commendation of Gaius (vv. 5–8)

Gaius is commended for his hospitality toward traveling preachers of the gospel because they are God's workers (vv. 5–8). John
commends Gaius for his faithful support of traveling missionaries
and exhorts him to continue to support them (vv. 5–6). Gaius
should support these preachers because by helping them he will
become a fellow worker for the truth, since they are God's workers
depending on believers for support (vv. 7–8).

Condemnation of Diotrephes (vv. 9–10)

John condemns Diotrephes for his autocratic rejection of these traveling preachers (vv. 9–10). Because Diotrephes was domineering, he rejected John's request for hospitality from the church for these traveling preachers associated with John (v. 9). Diotrephes had slandered the apostle and his preachers, had refused aid to them, and had excommunicated everyone in the assembly who wanted to aid them. John determined to deal with him if he must visit the church (v. 10).

Commendation of Demetrius (vv. 11–12)

Demetrius is commended to Gaius as a model of a well-reputed minister of the gospel in contrast to the evil example of Diotrephes (vv. 11–12). Gaius is urged to imitate that which is good and godly rather than the opposite (v. 11). Demetrius is presented as a believer fully attested as an example that Gaius can imitate (v. 12).

Closing (vv. 13–14)

John concludes with greetings and a desire to speak with them personally about other important matters (vv. 13–15).

Selected Bibliography

Commentaries Based on the Greek Text

Brooke, Alan England. *A Critical and Exegetical Commentary on the Johannine Epistles.* ICC. New York: Scribner's, 1912; repr. 1994.

Culy, Martin M. *1, 2, 3 John: A Handbook on the Greek Text.* Waco, TX: Baylor University Press, 2004.

Smalley, Stephen S. *1, 2, 3 John.* WBC. Waco, TX: Word, 1984.

Westcott, Brooke Foss. *The Epistles of St. John: The Greek Text, with Notes and Essays.* London: Macmillan, 1883.

Commentaries Based on the English Text

Akin, Daniel. *1, 2, 3 John.* NAC 38. Nashville: Broadman & Holman, 2002.

Bray, Gerald Lewis, and Thomas C. Oden, eds. *James, 1–2 Peter, 1–3 John, Jude*. ACCS. Downers Grove, IL: InterVarsity, 2000.

Brown, Raymond E. *The Epistles of John*. AB 30. Garden City, NY: Doubleday, 1982.

Bruce, F. F. *The Epistles of John: Introduction, Exposition, and Notes*. Grand Rapids: Eerdmans, 1979.

Bultmann, Rudolf Karl. *The Johannine Epistles: A Commentary on the Johannine Epistles*. ET Hermeneia. Edited by Robert Funk. Translated by R. Philip O'Hara et al. Philadelphia: Fortress, 1973.

Burge, Gary M. *The Letters of John: From Biblical Text to Contemporary Life*. NIVAC. Grand Rapids: Zondervan, 1996.

Dodd, C. H. *The Johannine Epistles*. MNTC 19. London: Hodder & Stoughton; New York: Harper, 1946.

Edwards, Ruth B. *The Johannine Epistles*. NTG. Sheffield: Sheffield Academic Press, 1996.

Houlden, J. L. *A Commentary on the Johannine Epistles*. BNTC. Rev. 2nd ed. London: A & C Black, 1994.

Kruse, Colin G. *The Letters of John*. PNTC. Grand Rapids: Eerdmans; Leicester, England: Apollos, 2000.

Law, Robert. *The Tests of Life: A Study of the First Epistle of John*. Edinburgh: T. & T. Clark, 1909.

Marshall, I. Howard. *The Epistles of John*. NICNT. Grand Rapids: Eerdmans, 1978.

Rensberger, David K. *1 John, 2 John, 3 John*. ANTC. Nashville: Abingdon, 1997.

Schnackenburg, Rudolf. *The Johannine Epistles: A Commentary*. 3 vols. New York: Crossroad, 1992.

Smith, D. Moody. *First, Second, and Third John*. IBC. Louisville: John Knox, 1991.

Stott, John R. W. *The Letters of John: An Introduction and Commentary*. 2d ed. TNTC 19. Grand Rapids: Eerdmans; Leicester, England: InterVarsity, 1988.

Strecker, Georg. *The Johannine Letters: A Commentary on 1, 2, and 3 John*. Hermeneia. Translated by Linda M. Maloney. Edited by Harold W. Attridge. Minneapolis: Fortress, 1996.

Talbert, Charles H. *Reading John: A Literary and Theological Commentary on the Fourth Gospel and the Johannine Epistles*. RNT. New York: Crossroad, 1992.

Thompson, Marianne Meye. *1–3 John*. Downers Grove, Ill: InterVarsity, 1992.

Foreign Language Commentaries

Klauck, Hans-Josef. *Der erste Johannesbrief*. EKKNT 23/1. Zürich: Benziger/Neukirchen-Vluyn: Neukirchen Verlag, 1992.

_____. *Der zwitte und dritte Johannesbrief*. EKKNT 23/2. Zürich: Benziger/Neukirchen-Vluyn: Neukirchen Verlag, 1992.

Studies

Burge, Gary M. *The Anointed Community: The Holy Spirit in the Johannine Tradition*. Grand Rapids: Eerdmans, 1987.

_____. "Letters of John." In *DLNT*, 587–99.

Griffith, Terry. *Keep Yourselves from Id ols: A New Look at 1 John*. JSNTSup 233. Sheffield: Sheffield Academic Press, 2002.

Lieu, Judith M. *The Theology of the Johannine Epistles*. NTT. Cambridge; New York: Cambridge University Press, 1991.

Six

JUDE

Contend for the Faith

In the third century the letter of Jude was described by Origen as "a short epistle, yet filled with flowing words of heavenly grace."[1] This description is certainly high praise coming from a theologian and writer who represented the literary-philosophical spirit of Alexandria. And yet despite the uniqueness of this New Testament document, the message and world of Jude remain strangely unfamiliar—and unappreciated—to the modern reader. With good reason Jude has been labeled "the most neglected book in the New Testament."[2]

Traditionally, most discussion and study of Jude understandably has centered upon its relation to 2 Peter. For this reason much commentary, until fairly recently, has been highly derivative in nature. This work has been in debt for the most part to reigning "early Catholic" presuppositions about the epistle (see "Authorship" and "Setting"), by which Jude is presumed to be a pseudonymous work.

Given the challenges that both the text of Jude and the history of Jude's interpretation present, it is not surprising that the epistle has languished in the backwaters of NT interpretation. Comprehensive neglect of Jude extends from serious students of the NT to the casual reader. Biblical scholarship, in the main, has bypassed a thorough treatment of the letter. Where it is studied, Jude is usually lumped together with the other "catholic" epistles or subsumed

---

Unless otherwise indicated, all Scripture quotations in this chapter are from the New Revised Standard Version (NRSV).

[1] Origen, *Comm. in Ev. sec. Matt* 17.30 (PG 13: 1571).

[2] D. J. Rowston, "The Most Neglected Book in the New Testament," *NTS* 21 (1974/75): 554. Whether this neglect is "benign," as J. H. Elliott, *I–II Peter/Jude* (ACNT; Augsburg: Fortress, 1982), 161, suggests, is debatable. Indeed, the Christian community should hold it to be most unfortunate.

under the study of 2 Peter, given the parallel material in the two letters. The operating assumption is that Jude and 2 Peter reflect nearly identical historical occasions, with the later writing—normally held to be 2 Peter (see "Literary Features," 2 Peter)—presumably exhibiting either a considerable lack of literary originality or the need to "smooth out" particular features in Jude.

Happily, it can be said that in the last decade of the twentieth century NT scholarship began to rectify what D. J. Rowston lamented in 1975—that Jude was "the most neglected" among documents of the New Testament. Much of the impetus for the beginnings of this reversal can be attributed to an important 1978 essay by Earle Ellis, "Prophecy and Hermeneutic in Jude,"[3] and Richard Bauckham's masterful commentary on Jude and 2 Peter, part of the Word Biblical Commentary series, that appeared in 1983.[4] Although a significant number of works relating to Jude were published by German NT scholars in the 1970s, virtually all fell into two categories—arguments for pseudepigraphy in the NT[5] and one-volume commentaries that lumped together all of the General Epistles.[6] Hence, the quality of much commentary on Jude, with some exceptions, was fairly unoriginal, furthering the standard "early Catholic" interpretation of Jude that has been regnant for the last century and a half.

---

[3] Earle Ellis, *Prophecy and Hermeneutic in Early Christianity* (Tübingen: Mohr, 1978), 221–36. Earlier scholarly work that sought to identify the outworking of "midrash" in the NT serves as something of a precursor to more recent scholarship in the General Epistles that broadly assumes the presence of "pesher" and "midrashic" interpretation. See, e.g., W. H. Brownlee, "Biblical Interpretation Among the Sectaries of the Dead Sea Scrolls," *BA* 145 (1951): 54–76; idem, "The Background of Biblical Interpretation at Qumran," in M. Delcor, ed., *Qumran: sa piété, sa théologie et son milieu* (Paris: Duculot, 1978), 183–93; A. Robert, "Les Genres litteraires," in A. Robert and A. Tricot, eds., *Initiation biblique* (3rd ed.; Paris: Duculot, 1954), 305–9; R. Bloch, "Midrash," in L. Pirot et al., eds., *DBSup* (Paris: Libraire Letouzey, 1957), 5.1263–81; J. Doeve, *Jewish Hermeneutics in the Synoptic Gospels and Acts* (Assen: Van Gorcum, 1954); J. A. Fitzmyer, "The Use of Explicit Old Testament Quotations in Qumran Literature and in the New Testament," *NTS* 7 (1960/61): 297–333; idem, *Essays on the Semitic Background of the New Testament* (London: Chapman, 1971); M. Gertner, "Midrashim in the New Testament," *JSS* 7 (1962): 267–92; and A. G. Wright, "The Literary Genre Midrash," *CBQ* 28 (1966): 105–38, 417–57.

[4] Also deserving mention are two important essays by Bauckham that appeared in 1988: "James, 1 and 2 Peter, and Jude," in *It Is Written: Scripture Citing Scripture. Essays in Honour of B. Lindars*, eds. D. A. Carson and H. G. M. Williamson (Cambridge: Cambridge University Press, 1988), 303–17, which analyzed literary tendencies in these four epistles and built upon the interpretive insights of Ellis and his "The Letter of Jude: An Account of Research," in W. Haase, ed., *ANRW* 2.25.5: 3791–826.

[5] Representative is the work of J. A. Sint, W. Speyer, N. Brox, A. M. Denis, K. M. Fischer, J. M. Grintz, M. Hengel, M. Rist, and more recently, D. G. Meade.

[6] Among these authors are J. Michl, K.-H. Schelkle, W. Schrage, and H. Balz.

Several trends in Jude scholarship spanning the last two decades can be detected. One is the sheer volume of commentaries that have been published. Since 1990, commentaries on the epistle have been written by Hubert Frankmöelle (1990), Jerome Neyrey (1993), Anton Vögtle (1994), Pheme Perkins (1995), Jonathan Knight (1995), Fred Craddock (1995), J. David Turner et al. (1996), Douglas Moo (1996), J. Daryl Charles (1999), E. J. Richard (2000), and Steven Kraftchick (2002), Daniel J. Harrington (2002), and Thomas Schreiner (2003).[7] Second, a number of monographs on Jude—a remarkable development in and of itself, since one is hard-pressed to identify a single monograph before 1990 devoted solely to the interpretation of Jude—have appeared, indicating an interest among some in rediscovering "the most neglected" document of the New Testament. Among those who have authored such monographs are J. Daryl Charles (1993), Charles Landon (1996), Kenneth Ryle (1998), Ruth Ann Reese (2000), and Peter Jones (2001). Significantly, each of these works concerns itself with a particular aspect of the literary-rhetorical character of Jude (see "Literary Features"), which suggests that literature is incarnational in character.

A work of literature does not merely impart information to the reader; rather, it embodies meaning, combining precept with paradigm, with the aim of creating in sufficient detail a scenario in a way that allows the reader to *experience* it. Good writers exploit imagination and the sensory dimensions of discourse. Perhaps the much maligned and neglected Jude is beginning to get its due. Happily, this development appears to be the case. Along the way we discover that using an arsenal of elocutionary, structural, and inventive subtleties, the author of this brief epistle shows remarkable dexterity in the way he incarnates theological truth.

Authorship and Date of Writing

An "early catholic" interpretation of Jude, following 2 Peter, has been broadly assumed by New Testament scholars. "Early Catholicism" (see also "Setting") presupposes the existence of an ecclesiastical hierarchy several generations removed from the

---

[7] To this list should be added the volume edited by G. Bray, *James, 1–2 Peter, 1–3 John, Jude*, that is part of the Ancient Christian Commentary on Scripture series (vol. 11), published in 2000 by InterVarsity Press.

apostles. The chief rationale for an "early Catholic" reading is that a "creedal" faith had emerged guarded by the growing prominence of church leaders to counter heresy and a fading hope in Christ's return.[8] This development, it is argued, was necessary in order to bridge the gap between the apostolic and postapostolic eras.

Consequently, historical-critical scholarship has traditionally considered Jude to be of pseudonymous authorship,[9] a reflection of the subapostolic era, and thus has assigned a relatively late date to its composition. Several specific factors have contributed to this consensus: Jude's literary relationship to 2 Peter (typically viewed as second century as well), the lack of historical indicators in the epistle, the strident nature of Jude's warnings against antinomians mirroring problems that are advanced, and the assumption that Jude is rebutting a second century form of gnostic heresy, given the amount of the epistle that is devoted to denouncing the unfaithful (vv. 5–19), and the opening charge to 'contend for the faith' (v. 3). The view of Mayor earlier this century is representative: "The communications of the Apostles had now ceased, either by their death or by their removal from Jerusalem."[10]

Yet, as one NT commentator has astutely noted, "early Catholicism" wrongly assumes what it seeks to prove.[11] Nothing in Jude requires an "early catholic" reading of the epistle. The seeds of Gnosticism (which in the second and third centuries developed into sophisticated schools of thought) were already evident by the mid-

---

[8] So, e.g., E. Käsemann, "Eine Apologia für die urchristliche Eschatologie," *ZTK* 49 (1952): 272–96.

[9] While the matter of pseudonymity in the NT has been dealt with at length elsewhere (see "2 Peter" in this volume), see D. Guthrie, "The Development of the Idea of Canonical Pseudepigrapha in New Testament Criticism," in R. P. Martin, ed., *Vox Evangelica I* (London: Tyndale, 1962), 43–59; idem, "Acts and Epistles in Apocryphal Writings," in W. W. Gasque and R. P. Martin, eds., *Apostolic History and the Gospel* (Grand Rapids: Eerdmans, 1970), 328–45; idem, "Epistolary Pseudepigraphy," in *New Testament Introduction* (4th ed.; Leicester/Downers Grove, IL: InterVarsity, 1990), 1011–28; E. E. Ellis, "Pseudonymity and Canonicity of New Testament Documents," in M. J. Wilkins and T. Paige, eds., *Worship, Theology and Ministry in the Early Church: Essays in Honor of Ralph P. Martin* (Sheffield: Sheffield Academic Press, 1993), 212–24; T. D. Lea, "Pseudonymity and the New Testament," in D. A. Black and D. S. Dockery, eds., *New Testament Criticism and Interpretation* (Grand Rapids: Zondervan, 1991), 535–59; T. L. Wilder, "Pseudonymity and the New Testament," in D. A. Black and D. S. Dockery, eds., *Interpreting the New Testament: Essays on Methods and Issues* (Nashville: Broadman & Holman, 2001), 296–335; and idem, *Pseudonymity, the New Testament, and Deception* (Lanham, Md.: University Press of America, 2004).

[10] J. B. Mayor, *The Epistle of St. Jude and the Second Epistle of St. Peter* (New York: Macmillan, 1907), cxlv.

[11] M. Green, *The Second Epistle of Peter and the General Epistle of Jude* (TNTC; rev. ed.; Leicester/Grand Rapids: Inter-Varsity/Eerdmans, 1989), 53.

first century. Ample evidence for this, to illustrate, can be found in Paul's first letter to the Corinthians.[12] Furthermore, Jude alludes to what the apostles had *said* (*legō*) and not to what they had *written* (*graphō*). Nothing in Jude requires a considerable chronological gap between the apostolic and subapostolic era.

Moreover, the character of Jude's dispute with the opponents, based on the vocabulary and moral paradigms used, is more one of *moral* obligation than doctrinal heterodoxy.[13] In addition, the allusion to OT characters and intertestamental Jewish sources would be relatively insignificant in the second century, considering the church's expansion in the Gentile world. In a first-century Palestinian environment, on the other hand, moral typology drawing on Jewish tradition material would be pregnant with meaning. It is a notable tendency of the NT writers—especially in Matthew, James, Hebrews, Jude, and 1 and 2 Peter—to quote or allude to the OT.

But what of the imperative to "remember the words foretold by the apostles" (v. 17), adduced by many critical scholars as evidence that the writer is generations removed from the apostolic period? A plausible understanding of this admonition is simply that Jude's audience was familiar with apostolic teaching.[14] When these "predictions" were made is not indicated. As such, the statement neither provides a basis for dating nor proves, specifically, that the apostolic era is past.

A further significant feature in Jude is the absence of ecclesiastical terminology. Nothing in the text implies the need for ecclesiastical officials to intervene, as one would expect in the post-apostolic period. All of the letter's imperatives are directed at the readers themselves. *They* are to deal with the problem at hand; *they* are to keep *themselves* in the love and mercy of God. An "early catholic" reading of Jude, then, is not required.

The writer identifies himself as "Jude . . . a brother of James" (v. 1). Two of Jesus' disciples bore the name *Ioudas*, while multiple

[12] See in this regard P. Perkins, *Gnosticism and the New Testament* (Minneapolis: Fortress, 1990), and D. M. Scholer, ed., *Gnosticism in the Early Church* (SEC 5; New York/London: Garland, 1993).

[13] This view runs counter to the broader consensus of Jude scholarship. See R. J. Bauckham, *Jude, 2 Peter* (WBC 50; Waco: Word, 1983), 9; and J. D. Charles, *Literary Strategy in the Epistle of Jude* (Scranton/London/Toronto: University of Scranton Press/Associated University Presses, 1993), 48–52.

[14] So S. J. Kraftchick, *Jude, 2 Peter* (ANTC; Nashville: Abingdon, 2002) 21; contra J. N. D. Kelly, *A Commentary on the Epistles of Peter and Jude* (BNTC; London: Adam and Charles Black, 1969) 281; Gerhard Krodel, "Jude," in idem, ed., *The General Letters: Hebrews, James, 1–2 Peter, Jude, 1–2–3 John* (rev. ed.; Minneapolis: Fortress Press, 1995) 108; and others.

people of the same name surface in the Gospels and Acts (Matt 13:55; Mark 6:3; Acts 5:37; 9:11; 15:22). For this reason it should not seem inappropriate that this Jude is identified with "James." Which James is being signified is not clear. In the Gospels and Acts we encounter James the son of Zebedee (Matt. 10:2), James the son of Alphaeus and one of the Twelve (Matt 10:3), James the brother of Jesus (Matt 13:55), James the younger and son of Mary (Mark 15:40), James the father of Judas the apostle (Matt 10:3; Luke 6:16; Acts 1:13), and James the author of the NT epistle (James 1:1). Given the linkage between a James and Jude in Matt 13:55 (*his brothers James and Joseph and Simon and Judas*), the James of Jude 1 is more than likely the brother of Jesus, who, according to tradition (cf. also Acts 12:17; 15:13–21; Gal 2:9; and 1 Cor 15:7), became a leader in the Jerusalem Church and was stoned by the Sanhedrin in the year 62.[15] If Jude was younger than James—and this is suggested by the listing in Matt 13:55—a date of composition for the epistle of Jude that is situated in the 60s or 70s is quite plausible.

Important patristic witnesses inform us that the author of this epistle is Jude, the brother of James, the Lord's brother. They include Clement of Alexandria, Origen, Athanasius, Jerome and Augustine. Paul's reference in Gal 1:19 to "James the Lord's brother" makes it reasonable to assume that, particularly in Palestine, the Lord's brothers were widely known.

Standard commentary on Jude relates a story narrated by Hegesippus (second century) of two grandsons of "Jude the brother of the Lord" who had been accused by the emperor Domitian (AD 81–96) of being revolutionaries, although they were only simple farmers.[16] According to Hegesippus, the grandsons eventually became bishops in the church. Although some who favor placing Jude in the second century argue that Jude the Lord's brother would not have lived long enough to be the author, this tradition can be reconciled with the chronology of the NT. Earlier this century, J. B. Mayor sought to demonstrate that Jude could have been in his early 70's at the beginning of Domitian's reign.[17]

---

[15] Josephus, *Ant.* 20.200.

[16] Eusebius, *Hist. eccl.* 3.19–20.

[17] J. B. Mayor, *The Epistle of St. Jude and the Second Epistle of St. Peter* (New York: Macmillan and Co., 1907), chap. 8.

An extraordinarily wide range of dates for Jude exists within modern NT scholarship, although most commentators opt for a later date. The range extends from the late second century[18] to the early second century[19] to the late first century[20] to the 60s.[21] The matter of dating is inextricably linked to one's assessment of the "early Catholic" rubric. Those rejecting the interpretive constraints of "early Catholicism," which requires that Jude is pseudepigraphal, will opt for an earlier dating of the epistle.[22]

Setting, Audience Situation, Destination

In contrast to the writer's impressive use of Hellenistic literary and rhetorical conventions (see "Literary Features"), the content of Jude's polemic is best understood against the backdrop of Palestinian-Jewish Christianity. Chief evidence of this factor is the midrashic use of Jewish traditional material in verses 5–19 as well as the reliance on apocalyptic works such as *1 Enoch* and the *Testament (Assumption) of Moses*. Jewish Christians, by no means a homogenous group, were not conscious of a decisive rupture with their Jewish past. To the contrary, early apostolic preaching found in the book of Acts, not to mention the Gospels of Matthew and John, take great pains to establish the Christian community's link with its Jewish matrix. Moreover, James, Hebrews, and the NT book of Revelation join Jude in their indebtedness to the OT and Jewish tradition material. On the distinctly Jewish character of the components of Jude, S. Segert writes, "They go back to Jewish traditions; nevertheless the tools of Hellenistic rhetoric, known in Palestinian Judaism long before, were effectively used for conveying a non-Hellenistic message."[23]

The Epistle of Jude is an impassioned exhortation to a church that finds itself living in the midst of ethical lapse and doctrinal compromise. The writer's burden, however, while it has doctrinal implications, is

---

[18] E.g., T. Barns, "The Epistle of Jude: A Study in Marcosian Heresy," *JTS* 6 (1905): 391–93.

[19] E.g., E. M. Sidebottom, *James, Jude, and 2 Peter* (NCB; London: Thomas Nelson, 1967), 77.

[20] E.g., E. Fuchs and P. Reymond, *La Deuxième Épître de Saint Pièrre. L'Épître de Saint Jude* (CNT 13b; Neuchâtel: Delachaux & Niestle, 1980), 152.

[21] Green, *The Second Epistle of Peter and the General Epistle of Jude*, 56.

[22] On the authorship and dating of Jude, see also Charles, "Jude," *EBC*, 541–43.

[23] S. Segert, "Semitic Poetic Structures in the New Testament," in W. Haase, ed., *ANRW* 2.25.2: 1458.

foremost *ethical* in nature. Posing a threat to the Christian community is a self-indulgent group that spurns spiritual authority and at the same time arrogantly appropriates its own authority. The consensus among commentators of the past century has been that the adversaries of Jude are gnostic (and thus located in the second century) or protognostic in nature, in keeping with the "early Catholic" line of interpretation. Walter Grundmann, in his commentary on Jude and 2 Peter, is representative: "In the ancient church up through modern exegesis, there have not been enough attempts to correlate the false teachers of the epistle of Jude with a particular Gnostic system. . . . It is with precursors . . . that we have to do in Jude, yet the fundamental nature of this conflict is already apparent."[24]

Ferdinand Hahn is similarly convinced of a second-century dating for Jude because heresy *requires* a "fixed confession of faith": "Even though the implications might not yet be clearly seen, there is a practical awareness that the apostolic era is surely closed and that the immediate postapostolic period is soon ending. Hence, now the present tradition material must be preserved in its basic meaning and form."[25]

We have already challenged the prevailing early Catholic presumption in traditional Jude scholarship (see "Authorship").[26] Those markers in Jude that are thought to indicate a second-century setting—viz., gnostic or protognostic developments—may well mirror conditions in the mid-to-late first century. Indeed, a cursory examination of 1 Corinthians (mid-first century) reveals multiple features that might be described as "gnostic" or "protognostic"—e.g., sexual license, division, arrogance due to a distorted view of knowledge and spiritual mysteries, a disdain for the bodily or material, abuse of personal freedom, and questioning of apostolic authority. Central to identifying Jude's opponents, who have "smuggled themselves in"[27] among the members of the community is that they are schismatics (v. 19).[28] Jude's description of these individuals provides us with some sense of the danger that

---

[24] W. Grundmann, *Der Brief des Judas und der zweite Brief des Petrus* (THKNT 15; Berlin: Evangelische Verlagsanstalt, 1967), 31 (my translation).

[25] F. Hahn, "Randbemerkungen zum Judasbrief," *TZ* 37 (1981): 209–10 (my translation).

[26] An extended critique of "early Catholicism" is found in my treatment of 2 Peter.

[27] J. N. D. Kelly, *A Commentary on the Epistles of Peter and Jude* (BNTC; London: Adam & Charles Black, 1969), 248.

[28] A general consensus exists among most commentators that Jude's opponents are a certain variety of traveling, charismatic teachers who are sowing division, while encouraging moral laxness.

they pose. They retain a religious guise while supporting a lifestyle of licentiousness, and their fate is depicted in conspicuously
Jewish apocalyptic terms, which suggests a familiarity among his
readers with the Jewish apocalyptic tradition, and thus, their belonging to a Palestinian Jewish milieu. And to this end the writer
employs themes rooted squarely in the OT—election, predestination and divine foreknowledge, apostasy, theophany, judgment by
fire, and the Day of the Lord.

The general markings of the letter would indicate that Jude is
addressed to a particular situation with pressing needs. The writer
had intended to communicate earlier but evidently was prevented.
Consequently, he now writes with a double urgency (v. 3). The
need to use "reminder" terminology (v. 5) suggests that either the
writer and the audience had a prior relationship, or the audience
had prior theological instruction—or both. The recurring emphatic pronoun "these" (vv. 8,10–12,14,16,19) is further evidence that
certain individuals, particularly located, are being singled out for
censure and categorical condemnation.

Important Themes and Subthemes

The Ungodly-Faithful Antithesis

Two sets of triplets (vv. 5–7,11) are used by the writer as paradigms of ungodliness (*asebeia* or a cognate form occurs five times
in the letter's 25 verses). Unbelieving Israel, the disenfranchised
angels, Sodom and Gomorrah, as well as Cain, Balaam, and Korah
are united by their departure and subsequent judgment. The second triplet is marked by an ascending gravity: first they "walk,"
next they "abandon," and finally they "perish."

The fundamental dichotomy expressed in the epistle is the
tension between the ungodly and the faithful, between *houtoi* (vv.
8,10,11 [*autois*], 12,14,16, and 19) and *humeis* (vv. 5,17,18, and
20). Those threatening the community are depicted in terms of
ungodliness (vv. 4,15,18), licentiousness (v. 4), lust (vv. 16,18),
and divisiveness (v. 19). They "deny" the only Sovereign and
Lord himself (v. 4). The faithful, on the other hand, are portrayed in Jude as holy (v. 14), unblemished (v. 23), blameless
(v. 24), and persevering (vv. 20–23). This juxtaposing of oppo-
sites is a notable feature of OT wisdom literature (notably, the
book of Proverbs) as well as Jewish apocalyptic literature. In

Jude, fundamental contrast is a central literary-rhetorical device. Indeed, it permeates the entire letter.[29]

Election, Predestination, and Divine Foreknowledge

A feature not uncommon in the OT and apocalyptic litera-ture in particular is the notion of names recorded in heavenly books (e.g., Exod 32:32–33; Pss 40:4; 56:8; 69:29; 139:16; Isa 4:3; Jer 22:30; Dan 7:10; 12:1; Mal 3:16; *1 Enoch* 81:1–2; 89:62; 90:14,17,20,22; 104:7; 108:3,7; *T. Ass.* 7:5; *2 Apoc. Bar* 24:1; Rev 3:5; 5:1,7–8; 10:8–11; 20:12). These "heavenly books" reflect a religious self-understanding fundamental to Hebrew thought, namely, that the divine purpose, though hidden from human view, is predetermined and revealed in history. The "scroll" in Revelation, for example, is a view of that history from the divine standpoint. The heavenly books point to the divine foreknowl-edge by which "the chosen" of Israel were called to be Yahweh's own possession and, hence, instruments (note, in this regard, Ps 139:16 and Jer 1:5).

Reminiscent of Psalm 69(68):29—"May they be blotted out of the book of life and not be listed with the righteous"—Jude 4 re-fers to the ungodly as *hoi palai progegrammenoi eis touto to krima*, "those whose judgment was written down long ago." The essence of *prographō* is juridical, as reflected in Mal 3:16 and Jer 22:30: "This is what the LORD says: 'Record this man'" (NIV). It carries a specific penal sense, namely, that of a public accusation against criminals.[30]

The verb *prographō* also corresponds to *proephēteusen* in verse 14 and *tōn hrēmatōn tōn proeirēmenōn hupo tōn apostolōn* in verse 17. The past speaks prophetically to the present, and in the argument of the writer it finds fulfillment in "these" ungodly. Not insigni-ficantly, the audience is addressed as *klētois*, the "chosen," and *tetērēmenois*, "those who have been kept" (v. 1).

Keeping

A theme ancillary to election in Jude is that of "keeping." This "keeping" or "preserving" has multiple sides: it is both past and

---

[29] I develop the notion of contrast in Jude more fully in "'Those' and 'These': The Use of the Old Testament in the Epistle of Jude," *JSNT* 38 (1990): 109–24.

[30] Fuchs and Reymond, *La deuxième Épître de Saint Pièrre. L'Épître de Saint Jude*, 159.

present, and it applies to both the ungodly and the faithful. The same destiny that applies to ancient paradigms of wickedness, which have been "kept" for judgment of the great day (e.g., the disenfranchised angels), awaits their contemporary counterparts. But more importantly, the sovereign Lord also "keeps" the faithful. In fact, "safe keeping" forms something of an inclusio in the letter's opening and closing. Those to whom greetings are extended in the introduction are described as "called," "sanctified" as well as "kept" (*tēreō*) by God himself (v. 1). And the writer concludes with doxological praise for the glory and majesty of this God "who is able to keep [*phulassō*, a strengthened form of keeping, i.e., to safeguard]" the saints (v. 24). All told, "keeping" as a verb occurs six times in 25 verses of text, confirming the centrality of preservation in the writer's theological outlook.

Subordinate themes in Jude that support the writer's argument for "keeping" in addressing the adversaries all are owing to Old Testament motifs and a Palestinian-Jewish matrix. To be noted in Jude are the conspicuous juxtaposing of the ungodly and the faithful, theophany and the Day of the Lord, judgment by fire, divine foreknowledge and "safe keeping," and divine glory.[31] The contrast of doom and glory is accentuated in Jude. While the fate of the apostate is clearly and graphically illustrated through types from the past, Jude's readers, in remaining established in the faith, can be assured of future glorious presentation before the Lord.[32]

Apostasy

Jude issues a strong warning against and denunciation of certain "ungodly persons" who have "slipped in from the side" and "pervert the grace of our God into licentiousness and deny our only Master and Lord, Jesus Christ" (v. 4). Their influence is reminiscent of three notorious paradigms from Jewish tradition— unbelieving Israel, the fallen angels, and Sodom and Gomorrah (vv. 5–7). Their path is compared to the "way of Cain" and the "error of Balaam" (HCSB). Balaam is prototypical of apostasy (cp. 2 Pet 2:14–15). That these individuals "deny" (*arneomai*) Christ is significant. Whereas heresy is doctrinal at its core, apostasy is

---

[31] These motifs, as they interact throughout the letter, are discussed at greater length in Charles, *Literary Strategy*, 91–127.

[32] See also Charles, *Literary Strategy*, 99–101, and idem, *EBC* 13, 546–47.

ethical. The departure in Jude is foremost ethical (as the moral paradigms suggest), even when it seeks a form of "theological" justification for its departure from the truth. The faithful, by contrast, are admonished to "keep" themselves in the love of God (v. 21), whereby God in the end is able to "keep" them from falling (v. 24). See also "Important Themes," 2 Peter.[33]

Theophany, Judgment, and the Day of the Lord

Perhaps one of the most important themes of the OT is that of Yahweh's "coming." What is striking concerning Yahweh's appearance, however, is not so much the description given to his *form* as the *manner* in which He manifests Himself—through fire, a flood, a storm, etc.[34]

In searching for the relevance of Jewish apocalyptic literature, L. Hartman has noted the extent to which the OT furnishes the source of many details and motifs found in these works.[35] Specifically, the Enoch prophecy used in Jude 14–15 is explicitly derived (cp. *1 Enoch* 1:9) from the Sinai theophany and blessing of Moses in Deut 33:1–3.[36] "The LORD came from Sinai and dawned over them from Seir, he shone forth from Mount Paran. He came with myriads of holy ones from the south, from his mountain slopes. Surely it is you who love the people; all the holy ones are in your hand" (33:2–3 NIV).

The actual text of Jude 14–15 and *1 Enoch* 1:9, upon closer analysis, indeed would seem to be drawing from the pattern of theophany statements of the OT:

---

[33] On the problem of apostasy as it surfaces in Jude and 2 Peter, see the Appendix "Predestination, Perseverance and the Problem of Apostasy" in Charles, *Virtue Amidst Vice*, 159—74.

[34] C. Westermann, *Das Leben Gottes in den Psalmen* (Berlin: Töpelmann, 1963), 74, distinguishes between "theophany," revelation with the purpose of bringing a message, and "epiphany," revelation which brings help or salvation. J. Jeremias, *Theophanie. Die Geschichte einer alttestamentlichen Gattung* (WMANT 10; Neukirchen-Vluyn: Neukirchener Verlag, 1964), 123, cites four categories of theophany in the OT: hymns to Yahweh, prophetic announcements of judgment, prophetic announcements of deliverance, and narrative prose.

[35] L. Hartman, *Prophecy Interpreted. The Formation of Some Apocalyptic Texts and of the Eschatological Discourse* (ConBNT 1; Lund: Gleerup, 1966) and *Asking for a Meaning: A Study of 1 Enoch 1–5* (ConBNT 12; Lund: Gleerup, 1979).

[36] Apocalyptic writers, however, do not explicitly cite the OT. This stands in contrast to the prophets who are continually calling back with explicit reference to the Torah or wisdom tradition.

Behold he comes . . .	Deut 33:2; Judg 5:4; Ps 18:9; Isa 19:1; 26:21; 31:4,27; 40:10; Dan 7:10; Amos 1:2; Mic 1:3; Hab 3:3; Zeph 1:7; Zech 9:14; 14:1,3; Mal 3:1–3
With the myriads of his holy ones . . .	Deut 33:2; Ps 68:17; Isa 40:10; 66:15; Dan 7:10
To execute judgment . . .	Deut 10:18; Pss 76:9; 96:13; Isa 33:5; Jer 25:31; Dan 7:10,13,26; Joel 3:2; Zeph 3:8; Hab 1:12; Mal 2:17; 3:5
And he will destroy all the wicked . . .	Pss 46:8–9; 76:3–6; Isa 19:3; 27:1; 66:15–16; Jer 25:31; Zeph 3:8–18; Hag 2:22; Zech 14:2–3,12
And he will reprove all flesh . . .	Isa 66:15–24; Jer 25:31; Zeph 1:8,9, 12; Mal 3:3–5

The theophanic motif common to Jude and *1 Enoch* is worth noting.[37] In both works, the Lord appears for the purpose of judgment. It is, however, the catchword *asebeia*, ungodliness, appearing three times in Jude 15, which links both sources. The statement from *1 Enoch*, rooted in antecedents from the OT, rings prophetically true with regard to Jude's opponents. Theophany and judgment merge in the writer's response to the distortions of the ungodly (*asebeis*).

Apocalyptic eschatology—and specifically, the Day of the Lord imagery—is coupled with the OT theophanic tradition as part of a rhetorical strategy in Jude to counter those who threaten the Christian community. Instances of cataclysmic judgment from the past (vv. 5–7,11) are marshaled and coupled with the promise of judgment in the future (vv. 14–15) to serve as evidence that Jude's opponents are reserved for utter destruction. In contrast to 2 Peter, which accents

---

[37] Hartman *Prophecy Interpreted* (n. 28) and C. D. Osburn, "The Christological Use of 1 Enoch 1:9 in Jude 14, 15," *NTS* 23 (1976/77): 334–41, have explored this relationship.

both judgment and deliverance, in Jude this judgment is categorical. His list of paradigms does not allude to any being saved. Judgment is "coming,"[38] and it will be unmitigated and final.[39]

Divine Glory

A central biblical concept, that of divine glory,[40] is prominent in Jude (vv. 8,24–25). The glory of the divine presence that awaits the faithful stands in sharp contrast to "darkness" (*skotos*) and "gloom" (*zophos*), which await the apostate. Although the reference in Jude 8 to "glories" (*doxas*) is apocalyptic in mode (cp. *T. Jud.* 25:2; *T. Lev.* 18:5; *2 Enoch* 21:1,3; cp. Rev 18:1), the notion is rooted in the OT, where the cherub is the bearer of the divine glory (e.g., Ezek 9:3; 10:4,18,22). As vehicles for transmitting the divine glory, the angels thus became an extension of that glory; hence, they are *doxai*, "rays of glory" emanating from the throne of God.[41] Those commentators who understand *doxai* as a counter to gnostic theology essentially miss the mark and the Jewish flavor of the reference.[42] By reading into Jude 8 a second-century scenario, one overlooks the OT and apocalyptic sense in which the term is used.

Both the *doxas* and the *kuriotēs* of verse 8 stem from apocalyptic literature, which knows between four and nine levels of angelic hierarchy in the heavenly realm. The pseudepigraphal *Ascension of Isaiah* illustrates such usage: "Worship neither throne (*kuriotēs*) nor angel which belongs to the six heavens—for this reason I was sent to lead you—until I tell you in the seventh heaven."[43] The link in Jude between angels and the rebellious can be seen in the pseudepigraphal *Testaments of the Twelve Patriarchs*: "Do not become like Sodom, which did not recognize the Lord's angels and perished forever."[44]

---

[38] C. D. Osburn ("Christological Use of 1 Enoch 1:9") prefers to view Jude's promise as "Christophany" rather than "theophany."

[39] See Charles, "'Those' and 'These,'" 111–12, and idem, *Literary Strategy*, 94–99.

[40] In the LXX *doxa* appears 445 times (E. Hatch and R. A. Redpath, *A Concordance to the Septuagint and Other Greek Versions of the Old Testament* [2 vols.: Oxford: Clarendon, 1897], 1.341–43).

[41] Philo, *Spec.* 1.45, and Clement of Alexandria, *Adumb.* 1008 (PG 3.2080–81) also refer to the angels as *doxai*.

[42] So, e.g., Kelly, *A Commentary*, 262, and J. Cantinat, *Les Épîtres de Saint Jacques et de Saint Jude* (Paris: Librairie Lecoffre, 1973), 281.

[43] The text is reproduced in R. H. Charles, ed., *The Ascension of Isaiah* (London: SPCK, 1917), 47.

[44] *T. Ass.* 7:1.

Literary Features

The message and world of Jude are strangely unfamiliar to the modern reader. Whether among lay people, pastors, teachers, or seminarians, this unfamiliarity is conspicuous. With good reason the letter of Jude has "most neglected" status.[45] Most readers of the Bible, if they do approach the epistle, find themselves puzzled by cryptic references to Enoch, Michael the archangel, the devil, and a slate of OT characters, yet remain without clues as to the historical situation and pastoral needs lying behind their writing. After we have attempted to discern the author's intention, the recipients' setting, and controlling theological ideas, all of which challenge us considerably, Jude would seem to call for a different type of reading.[46]

Jude is a rather remarkable piece of literature,[47] causing us to concur with Origen that this short letter, rich and original in style and vocabulary, is indeed "filled with flowing words of heavenly grace."[48] Not only does Jude display astounding economy of thought, it also demonstrates a thorough acquaintance with and calculated use of Jewish literary sources. And unlike 2 Peter, the literary milieu of Jude is very much Palestinian Jewish-Christian, as the writer's use of sources and paradigms demonstrates. Extracanonical source-material—notably, the *Book of Enoch* (mid-second century BC–AD first century) and the *Assumption of Moses* (first or second century)—as well as OT figures are marshaled in a concise, well-conceived polemic that simultaneously exhorts the faithful and warns the unfaithful, and even though not a single explicit citation from the OT is to be found in Jude, the letter is nonetheless replete with prophetic typology. Densely packed prophetic typology, which draws on both OT and extrabiblical traditions, is marshaled against ungodly "antitypes." No fewer than nine subjects—unbelieving Israel, the fallen angels, Sodom and Gomorrah, Michael the archangel, Moses, Cain, Balaam, Korah and Enoch—are enlisted to decry the unfaithful who pose a danger to the believing community. It is

---

[45] Thus D. J. Rowston, "The Most Neglected Book in the New Testament," *NTS* 21 (1974/75): 554.

[46] So L. R. Donelson, *From Hebrews to Revelation: A Theological Introduction* (Louisville: Westminster John Knox, 2001), 87.

[47] Contra Kelly, *A Commentary*, 225, who remarks that, with 2 Peter, Jude is "lacking in quality."

[48] Origen, *Commentariorum in Evangelium secundum Matthaeum* 17.70 (*PG* 13.1571).

these unfaithful (vv. 4, 8, 10, 12, 14, 16, 19) who are the focus of Jude's invective.

Characterizing Jude's use of moral paradigms is a "midrashic" method of interpretation—what has been called "creative historiography"[49]—that bears some similarities to that of contemporary Jewish exegesis. Not unlike commentary on the OT found in the "pesharim" or commentaries of the Qumran community,[50] the epistle of Jude links types from the past with corollaries in the present in order to confront need prophetically and pastorally. Logistically, this is achieved by the use of catchwords—e.g., *these, keep, ungodly, judgment, error, blaspheme*—which form the links in Jude's polemical argument. As such, midrash might be viewed as an interpretive "activity" that allows its practitioner to address new problems and situations using past traditions.

Literature has been said to be incarnational in character. That is, rather than simply offering abstract propositions, an effective literary work combines precept and example, incorporating the whole range of imagination. In this sense Jude is effective literature, in which form is equally as important as the message. With passion yet exceeding brevity, and by exploiting sensory dimensions of language, Jude engages his audience in a manner that is graphic, intense, vivid, and, of course, morally serious. The tenor of the writer is that of a prophet more than an intimate friend, projecting a sense of urgency and authority. Historical lessons that are embodied in moral typology are applied haggadically to the present. The modern reader becomes witness to a literary-rhetorical artist at work,[51] as graphic symbolism, word-play, frequent alliteration, parallelism, the use of triplets, typology, midrash and woe-cry in a tightly-packed "word of exhortation"[52]—all this within the remarkably brief span of only twenty-five verses of text!

[49] A.G. Wright, "The Literary Genre Midrash," *CBQ* 28 (1966): 129–30.

[50] Thus E. E. Ellis, "Prophecy and Hermeneutic in Jude," in *Prophecy and Hermeneutic in Early Christianity* (Tübingen: Mohr, 1978), 226; Bauckham, *Jude, 2 Peter*, 4–5, 46–47; and idem, "James, 1 and 2 Peter, Jude," in D. A. Carson and H. G. M. Williamson, eds., *It Is Written: Scripture Citing Scripture. Essays in Honour of B. Lindars* (Cambridge: Cambridge University Press, 1988), 303–5.

[51] On literary compostion, see also Charles, "Jude," *EBC* 13, 543–45. D.F. Watson, *Invention, Arrangement, and Style: Rhetorical Criticism of Jude and 2 Peter* (SBLDS 104; Atlanta: Scholars Press, 1988), 32–76; T. R. Wolthuis, "Jude and the Rhetorician," *CTJ* 24 (1989) 126–34; J. D. Charles, "Literary Artifice," 106–24; and idem, *Literary Strategy*, 25–48.

[52] Thus v. 3: *anagkēn eschon grapsai humin parakalōn epagōnizesthai*. Compare in this regard the features of Paul's sermon in the synagogue at Pisidian Antioch (Acts 13) with those of Jude. On the *logos parainetikos*, see K. Berger, "Hellenistische Gattungen im Neuen

Many, though by no means all, of the NT letters were a means by which the writer could publicly address a congregation without being physically present. In the event that a personal visit was precluded, the epistle was in essence the apostle's or the writer's preaching. Hence, we would expect to find those documents possessing a distinctly homiletical character, and such is the case with Jude. The body of Jude (vv. 5–23) is strongly hortatory, as if prepared as a sermon. Yet with the initial identification of the sender, addressee, greetings, and stated purpose, Jude conforms broadly to the ancient epistolary genre, even when it does not include some of the standard Pauline features such as salutation, prayer, or thanksgiving.

Unlike more modernist schools of literary criticism in which formal literary devices are often separated from and opposed to content, the form-content dichotomy is absent among the ancients. In order to appreciate Jude's competence as a practitioner of the epistolary genre, consider several ancient definitions of what *epistolē* was thought to represent:

- The letter is, in effect, speech in written medium (Cicero).[53]
- A letter reflects the personality of its writer (Cicero).[54]
- It may be said that everybody reveals his own soul in his letters (Demetrius).[55]

Skill in the epistolary art was measured by the ancients according to numerous qualities—among these: plainness and clarity, use of metaphor and picturesque language, poetic diction, rhythm, grace of style in the arrangement of material, suitability for the occasion, skill and artistry, use of repetition to enhance vividness, euphony, harshness of sound when appropriate for effect, suitable embellishment, and brevity for maximum force.[56] If these features constitute artistry, then Jude is a master craftsman in the construction of his argument.

Testament," in *ANRW* 2.25.2: 1049–1148; L. Wills, "The Form of the Sermon in Hellenistic Judaism and Early Christianity," *HTR* 77 (1984): 277–99; and C. C. Black, "The Rhetorical Form of the Hellenistic-Jewish and Early Christian Sermon," *HTR* 81 (1988): 155–79.

[53] Cicero, *Att.* 8.14.1 (LCL; trans. E. O. Winstedt; Cambridge: Harvard University Press, 1913).

[54] Cicero, *Fam.* (LCL; trans. W. G. Williams; Cambridge: Harvard University Press, 1928).

[55] Demetrius, *Eloc.* 227 (LCL; trans. W. R. Roberts; Cambridge: Harvard University Press, 1932).

[56] Ibid., 81–276.

Three kinds of speech are to be found in Greco-Roman rhetoric: forensic (normally accusatory or defensive in character), deliberative (often political or persuasive in character), and epideictic (emotive and stylistic in character).[57] It was the view of Cicero (expressed in 55 BC) that "the listener will never be set on fire unless there is fire in the words that reach him." Thus, speech is to be persuasive, regardless of its specific purpose; it is to win over the audience. As practiced by the ancients, *how* one communicates is indivisible from *what* is being communicated. This author has argued elsewhere that Jude represents a mixture of all three rhetorical types. It is at times defensive and accusatory (forensic), at times seeking to persuade (deliberative) and certainly emotive and highly stylized (epideictic). This seeming disparity is seen in the conclusions of other commentators. For example, Duane Watson prefers a deliberative classification, even when acknowledging other elements as well. By contrast, Jerome Neyrey believes Jude is best understood forensically,[58] while S. J. Joubert holds the letter to be epideictic in character.[59]

As taught from the textbook, Greco-Roman rhetoric emphasized two stylistic elements—diction and composition.[60] The style of the writer was to be commensurate with the occasion and the needs of the audience. Cicero described three levels or degrees of style employed: grand, middle, and plain. Each is practiced according to the amount of ornamentation and force demanded by the rhetorical situation. It is unfortunate that the Greek used by the NT writers is widely viewed as the language of the street, lacking any sophistication. This stereotype, however, is patently false. N. Turner has noted, for example, that with regard to refinement of diction, Luke-Acts, Hebrews, and Jude approach the Atticists in comparison.[61]

---

[57] These basic classifications are used by Aristotle, *Rhet.* 1.3.15 and Cicero, *Inv.* 1.5.7; idem, *De or.* 1.31.141; and Quintilian, *Inst.* 2.4.6–8.

[58] Jerome Neyrey, *2 Peter, Jude: A New Translation with Introduction and Commentary* (AB 37C; Garden City: Doubleday, 1993), 27.

[59] S. J. Joubert, "Persuasion in the Letter of Jude," *JSNT* 58 (1995): 75–87.

[60] Cicero, *De or.* 5.16–17; idem, *Inv.* 1.7.9; and (author unknown) *Rhet. Her.* 1.2.3.

[61] N. Turner, "The Literary Character of New Testament Greek," *NTS* 20 (1974): 107. Augustine expressed his own admiration of NT writers' rhetorical skill when he commented that "these divinely-inspired men are not defective in any of those points which he has been taught in the schools of the grammarians and rhetoricians to consider of importance." In them is to be found "many kinds of speech of great beauty—beautiful even in our language, but especially beautiful in the original" (*On Christian Doctrine*, ed. P. Schaff [Buffalo: Christian Literature Company, 1887], 579).

The Epistle of Jude exhibits a sophisticated diction, vocabulary, and compository skill. Figures of speech, symbolism, ornamentation, and unusual brevity combine to strengthen the writer's polemic. Poetic force is marshaled for the urgency of the particular situation. Duane Watson has classified Jude as having a "middle" style of rhetoric.[62] If, according to Watson, the "middle" lacks intellectual force or appeal of the "grand," it is then difficult to account for the degree of literary-rhetorical artifice that is on display. If Jude does not belong to the grand category, then as a literary work it deserves high ground in the middle, particularly if, along with Hebrews, Jude has been placed by scholars of the Greek language in a category approaching Atticism.

Let us consider several aspects of Jude's literary style that are unique:

Grammatical-Lexical Distinctives

Jude shows a normal use of the Greek idiom with bits of artistic flare. He uses the article skillfully with participles and his generous use of participles—all told, participial forms occur 34 times in the 25-verse letter—would indicate a command of the Greek. Jude's fluid use of Christian technical terms such as *klētoi* (v. 1), *pistis* (vv. 3,20), *pneuma* (v. 19), *psuchikos* (v. 19), and *hagios* (v. 20) is similar to that of Paul. The use of the superlative *hagiōtatē* (v. 20), common to both secular and eccliastic usage, is a mark of the writer's skill.[63]

In light of the epistle's brevity, the richness of vocabulary and the abundance of *hapax legomena* are noteworthy. E. Fuchs and P. Reymond have called attention to at least 22 rare terms found in the epistle.[64] Such diversity within brevity magnifies the originality of the writer. Economy within such conciseness is indeed remarkable.

Paronomasia

Paronomasia may be defined according to recurrence of the same word or word stem, recurrence of like-sounding words, or simply a play on words. Each of these is done for the sake of literary effect. Specific forms of paronomasia include alliteration, assonance, rhyme, and word or name play. Technically speaking, imaginative and impas-

---

[62] Watson, *Invention, Arrangement, and Style*, 25.

[63] See A. T. Robertson, *A Grammar of the Greek New Testament in the Light of Historical Research* (Nashville: Broadman, 1934), 124–25.

[64] Fuchs and Reymond, *La deuxième Épître de Saint Pièrre. L'Épître de Saint Jude*, 138.

sioned literary works would generally call for a literary style more varied than simple narrative since the aim of the work is to persuade or convict. Jude's short but lively polemic is not lacking in colorful "sound structure" which achieves a notable literary effect.[65] For example,

v. 7	*ekporneusasai . . . apelthousai . . . prokeintai . . . hupechousai*
v. 8	*mentoi . . . houtoi enupniazomenoi*
v. 8	*miainousin . . . athetousin . . . blasphēmousin*
v. 9	*hote tō diabolō diakrinomenos dielegeto*
v. 10	*oidasin blasphēmousin . . . epistantai . . . phtheirontai*
v. 11	*eporeuthēsan . . . exechuthēsan*
v. 12	*aphobōs . . . anudroi . . . akarpa*
v. 15	*pasan psuchēn peri pantōn tōn ergōn asebeias autōn hōn*
v. 16	*Houtoi . . . mempsimoiroi . . . poreuomenoi*
v. 19	*Houtoi . . . hoi apodiorizontes, psuchikoi . . . echontes*
vv. 22–23	*hous . . . hous . . . hous*
vv. 22–23	*eleate . . . sōzete . . . eleate*

Parallelism and the Use of Catchwords

A notable feature of the epistle is the writer's use of catchwords. This practice serves several functions. It lends stylistic effect, it aids in clarifying the epistle's structure, it clarifies a particular emphasis, and it reveals a strategy in the writer's use of sources. Repetition or synonymous parallelism and contrast or antithetical parallelism achieve a similar effect.[66] Examples of the former include:

v. 3	making haste and having necessity
v. 4	Master and Lord
v. 5	reminding and knowing
v. 6	rule and habitation, judgment and gloom
v. 7	punishment and fire
v. 8	defiling, despising, and blaspheming

[65] On paronomasia in Jude, see also Charles, *Literary Strategy*, 39–40.
[66] On synonymous and antithetical parallelism in Jude, see ibid., 38–40.

vv. 8,25	authorities and glories/glory
v. 9	contending and arguing
v. 10	not knowing and being irrational
v. 10	knowing (*oidasin*) and knowing (*epistantai*)
v. 12	waterless and fruitless
v. 13	gloom and darkness
v. 14	prophesying and saying
v. 15	executing judgment and convicting
v. 16	grumblers and malcontents
v. 20	building up and praying
v. 20	most holy and holy
v. 21	love and mercy
vv. 22–23	having mercy, saving, having mercy
v. 23	saving and seizing
v. 24	preserving and presenting
v. 25	all the ages and all the ages

Examples of the latter are the following:

vv. 1,4	servant versus Master and Lord
vv. 3–24	these versus you
vv. 3,4,14,15,18,20,24	ungodly versus holy
vv. 2,4,6,9,15,21–23	mercy versus judgment
v. 4	grace versus licentiousness
v. 5	saving once versus destroying twice
vv. 6,8,25	gloom versus glory
vv. 7,23–25	fire versus glory
vv. 8–10	these versus Michael
v. 10	understanding versus irrational
vv. 12,23	fearless versus with fear
vv. 7,16,18,23–24	lust versus without blemish
vv. 16–17	their mouth versus prophets' words
vv. 19–20	dividing versus building up

The varieties of parallelism in the letter deepen, strengthen, and enrich the writer's overall argument and the broader contrast between the ungodly and the faithful. In its function parallelism does not merely repeat; rather, it amplifies.[67]

Triadic Illustration

Repetition is one of the most fundamental tools of literary or oral presentation. A matter, thesis, or description is repeated in order to fix the matter firmly in the mind of the hearer or listener. One cannot help but be struck by the abundance of triple descriptions in Jude. Not one or two illustrations suffice but three. The writer exploits the method of threefold "witness" to condemn his opponents while exhorting the faithful. The validity of testimony in the OT was affirmed by the mouth of two or three witnesses (Deut 17:6; 19:15). This principle finds continuity in the NT as well (Matt 18:16; John 5:31–33; 8:17–18; 2 Cor 13:1; 1 Tim 5:19; Heb 10:28). In essence the three represent one: a threefold concurrence validates and yields fullness.

All told, twenty sets of triplets appear within the letter's twenty-five verses.[68] A like phenomenon, demonstrating such a high degree of density, is unparalleled anywhere else in Scripture:

v. 1	the writer's self-designations (Jude, servant, brother)
v. 1	attributes ascribed to the audience (called, beloved, kept)
v. 2	elements in the greeting (mercy, peace, love)
v. 4	participles modifying the main verb (having been designated, making a pretext, denying)
vv. 5–7	paradigms of judgment (Israel, the fallen angels, Sodom and Gomorrah)
v. 8	actions of the opponents (defile, despise, blaspheme)

---

[67] See also Charles, *Literary Strategy*, 36–42, as well as my discussion of literary dependence between Jude and 2 Peter in my commentary on Jude in the revised edition of the EBC 13 (Grand Rapids: Zondervan, 2006), 545.

[68] Mayor (*The Epistle of St. Jude and the Second Epistle of St. Peter* lvi) has noted Jude's fondness for triplets. I would concur with Mayor but detect a greater "fondness" than he concedes; see Charles, *Literary Strategy*, 40–41, 125–25, and Charles, "Literary Artifice," 122–23.

v. 9	actions of Michael (disputed, did not presume, said)
v. 11	examples of woe (Cain, Balaam, Korah)
v. 11	escalating rebellious actions (walk, abandon, perish)
v. 12	traits of those at the love feasts (blemishes, feasting together, fearless)
v. 12	characteristics of the trees (autumn, fruitless, uprooted)
v. 13	characteristics of the waves (fierce, foaming, shameful)
vv. 14–15	actions of the Lord (came, performing judgment, rebuking)
v. 16	traits of the opponents (grumblers, malcontents, following their lusts)
v. 19	further traits of the opponents (dividing, fleshly, devoid of the Spirit)
vv. 20–21	participles modifying the main verb (edifying, praying, awaiting)
vv. 22–23	imperatives for the faithful (have mercy, save, have mercy)
v. 25	divine designations (God, Savior, Lord)
v. 25	view of time (before all time, now, forever)

Old Testament and Extrabiblical Tradition Material in Jude

Although Jude does not quote any OT texts per se, the reader encounters in this brief epistle a pervasive use of OT imagery and themes (see "Important Themes") as well as extracanonical Jewish traditions. Jude's primary method is the use of typology, by which he draws important parallels between the past and present.[69]

---

[69] Elsewhere I discuss Jude's use of typological exegesis at some length in *Literary Strategy*, 103–66; see also Charles, "'Those and 'Them,'" 109–24; idem, "Jude's Use of Pseudepigraphal Source-Material as Part of a Literary Strategy," *NTS* 37 (1991): 130–45; idem, "Old Testament in General Epistles," in *DLNT*, 834–41; idem, "Noncanonical Writings, Citations in General

Typology is integral to the question of the use of the OT in the NT. Typological exegesis reflects a definite awareness of continuity between covenants. The element of continuity is demonstrated by the scheme of promise and fulfillment. For Jude, a whole battery of OT types speaks prophetically to the ungodly who pose a threat to the faithful. Requisite for the application of this exegetical method is a historical connection or correspondence between the notorious ungodly types from the past and those of the present.[70]

Jude 5–7 contains a triplet of examples of unfaithfulness that belong to popular tradition. Similar paraenetic sayings are found in Ben Sira, Jubilees, Maccabees, the *Testaments of the Twelve Patriarchs*, the Damascus Document, and the Mishnah, all of which speak to hard-heartedness, apostasy, or disregard for God's commandments.[71] Several examples from apocryphal and pseudepigraphal writings are sufficient to illustrate. In Sirach 16:5–15 the writer gives a catalog of historical paradigms including Korah, Assyria, giants, Sodomites, Canaanites, and Israel's falling away. Similarly, 3 *Maccabees* 2:3–7 is a prayer for Israel that includes in its list Pharoah, Sodomites, and giants, and a warning against hard-heartedness.

Allusions to paradigms of unfaithfulness, then, are not unique to Jude (or 2 Peter). The most frequently occurring models of unfaithfulness or hard-heartedness in Jewish literature are Sodom and Gomorrah, the fallen angels or "watchers," the generation of the flood, and unbelieving Israel. In Jude, they are linked prophetically to those who have apostatized yet who threaten the community of faith (v. 4). Verses 5,6, and 7 in Jude represent evidence—exhibits A, B, and C—compounded against the guilty, the *houtoi* (vv. 8,10,11,12,14,16,19).

Unbelieving Israel (v. 5)

Jude's initial case illustration is Israel, the chosen (cp. v. 1, wherein the recipients of the letter are addressed as *hoi klētoi*, those "called"). Allusion to Israel would suggest that the apos-

---

Epistles," in *DLNT*, 814–19; idem, "Pagan Sources in the New Testament," in *DNTB*, 738–44; and idem, "On Angels and Asses: The Moral Paradigm in 2 Peter 2," in *Proceedings of the Eastern Great Lakes and Midwest Biblical Society* 21 (2001): 1–12.

[70] The most helpful resources on typology remain G. W. H. Lampe and K. J. Woollcombe, *Essays on Typology* (Naperville: Allenson, 1957), and L. Goppelt, *Typos: The Typological Interpretation of the Old Testament in the New,* trans. D. H. Madvig (Grand Rapids: Eerdmans, 1982).

[71] Sir 16:5–15; *Jub.* 20:2–7; 3 *Macc.* 2:3–7; *T. Naph.* 2:8–4:3; CD 2:14–3:12; and *m. Sanh.* 10:3.

tate are former orthodox, having formerly experienced divine redemption. The language here is noteworthy and emphatic: the readers already know "all things"; therefore they are to recall Israel of old. The writer is most likely drawing from material found in Numbers 11,14,26, and 32. Throughout the OT there is a constant calling back prophetically to Egypt. In Leviticus, Egypt is mentioned 11 times. In Numbers and Deuteronomy, Egypt is recalled 28 and 46 times respectively. Joshua and Samuel-Kings speak of Egypt a total of 67 times. Isaiah, Jeremiah, and Ezekiel each allude to Egypt over 30 times. And the latter prophets, with the exception of Obadiah, Zephaniah, and Malachi, make reference to Egypt. The past, for Jude, is therefore prophetic.

By implication, Jude is saying that the same applies of *Kurios-Iēsous*[72] to the *houtoi*. Because the effects of Jesus' redemptive work have perpetual validity and His saving act precludes the possibility of or need for repetition, those who have formerly experienced redemption and are fallen away will be judged at Jesus' coming the second time. The present need is for a reminder: *eidotas [humas] panta*. There is no excuse for not believing. God delivered Israel once-for-all (*hapax*) in the OT. The second time (*to deuteron*) God did not deliver; rather He judged.[73]

The Rebellious Angels (v. 6)

Aside from "the angel of the Lord," angels generally receive less prominence in the OT before the exile. Several features differentiate the angelology of the intertestamental period from that of the OT. In the intertestamental literature their depiction becomes far more systematic,[74] while a particular number have their names and functions expressly—and at times, elaborately—stated.[75] Michael the archangel, notably, achieves in intertestamental Jewish literature incomparable stature. Further, and of particular interest regarding

---

[72] B. M. Metzger, *A Textual Commentary on the New Testament* (Stuttgart: UBS, rev. 1975), 723–24, notes the substantial manuscript evidence supporting *Iēsous* over *theos* or *kurios* in verse 5.

[73] Note in this regard Num 14:11,22–23.

[74] See W. O. E. Oesterley, "The Belief in Angels and Demons," in *Judaism and Christianity—Vol. 1: The Age of Transition* (London: Sheldon, 1937), 195–206.

[75] For example, in *1 Enoch* the chief angels in heaven's multitiered hierarchy—apocalyptic literature knows from four to nine echelons—develop strategies (*1 Enoch* 6–9), superintend nations (20:5), reveal secrets (41–43; 46:2; 71:3) and filter prayers of the righteous (14:4). In *T. Dan* 6:2, Michael intercedes for the saints, and in *1 Enoch* 40:6, the archangel prays on behalf of those on the earth, "supplicating in the name of the Lord of the Spirits."

Jude 6, the intertestamental period exhibits a proliferation in speculative explanations as to Gen 6:1–4 and the "sons of God."

By the time of the Christian advent, most of Judaism—mainstream and sectarian—had embraced the notion, based on Gen 6:1–4, that the "sons of God" had introduced sexual promiscuity among the "daughters of men." Most commentary, past and present, tends to relate Gen 6:1–4 in some way to Jude 6 and 2 Pet 2:4. However, whereas in Jewish apocalyptic literature the angels' fall is ascribed explicitly to fleshly lust, in Jude it is a fall from *authority and position*. The picture is one of contrast (note the connective *alla*). As with unbelieving Israel (v. 5), the issue at hand is one of *privilege*. Having deserted their position, the angels were *cast down*.

While the idea of imprisonment of spirits in the OT is undefined, in Jewish apocalyptic literature it is pronounced (e.g., *1 Enoch* 10:4; 13:1; 18:14; 21:3; 67:4; 69:8; 88:1; 90:23; *2 Apoc. Bar.* 56:13; *Jub.* 5:1; cp. also Rev 18:2; 20:7), along with the notion of a "pit" or "abyss" (e.g., *1 Enoch* 10:4; 18:11; 21:7; 22:1–2; 54:4; 56:3; 88:1; 90:24; cp. also Rev 20:3). Jude combines typological treatment of the OT with conventions and imagery contemporary to sectarian Judaism which would have been readily understood by his readership. The apocalyptic surrounding the angels of verse 6 is strengthened in verse 13, where the *houtoi* of Jude's polemic are compared to "wandering stars," a description that would have readily triggered association with *1 Enoch* (e.g., 18:14–16; 21:6; 86:1–3; 90:24). In addition, within apocalyptic mythology, a frequent pattern tends to merge. War erupts in heaven, often depicted in astral terms, followed by a spilling over of this rebellion to the earth, then culminating in ultimate vindication and punishment by the king of heaven.[76]

Using a wordplay on the catchword "keep" (*tēreō*), Jude unites typologically in verse 6 the events of the fall with the theme of judgment. Without necessarily endorsing conceptions of cosmic warfare that have their roots in pagan mythology or Jewish apocalyptic imagination, Jude assimilates imagery current to his day, in order to illustrate the effects of "rebellion in heaven," a notion which at best is vaguely hinted at in the OT.

---

[76] See P. D. Hanson, "Rebellion in Heaven, Azazel, and Euhemeristic Heroes in 1 Enoch 6–11," *JBL* 96 (1977): 208. See also related commentary on the disenfranchised angels in "Old Testament in 2 Peter." I explore the OT and Jewish apocalyptic background to the fall of the angels more extensively in Charles, *Literary Strategy*, 108–16,145–49, and in the essay Charles, "Jude's Use of Pseudepigraphal Source–Material as Part of a Literary Strategy," *NTS* 37 (1991): 130–45.

Sodom and Gomorrah (v. 7)

Consistently throughout the OT and Jewish literature the example of Sodom and Gomorrah (Gen 19:1–29) stands out. Sodom's overthrow is reiterated again and again (e.g., Deut 29:23; 32:32; Isa 1:9–10; 3:9; Jer 23:14; 49:18; 50:40; Lam 4:16; Ezek 16:46–59; Amos 4:11; Hos 11:8; Zeph 2:9; *Jub.* 16:5,6,9; 20:5; 22:22; 36:10; Wis 10:6–7; Sir 16:8; *T. Ass.* 7:1; *T. Naph.* 3:4; 3 *Macc.* 2:5; *Gen. Rab.* 27:3; *m. Sanh.* 10:3; *Avot* 5:10; Philo, *QG* 4.51; Josephus, *J.W.* 5.566). Most striking about OT depiction of Sodom is its flaunting of sin (Gen 19:4–5,12; Isa 1:9) and the permanent nature of its judgment. The prophet enunciated that no man would henceforth live there (Jer 49:18; 50:40). In intertestamental Jewish literature, Sodom remained a classic example of immorality and a paradigm for the certain and consuming nature of divine judgment:[77]

> In the same way God will bring judgment on places where the people live by Sodom's uncleanness, in accordance with the judgment of Sodom (*Jub.* 16:5). But you, my children, shall not be like that . . . discern the Lord who made all things, so that you do not become like Sodom, which departed from the order of nature (*T. Naph.* 3:4).

According to the rabbis, later generations are to learn from the cities of the plain. Rabbinic teaching held that there were seven groups which had no portion in the coming world: the generation of the flood, the generation of the diaspora, the spies who brought back an evil report of the land, the wilderness generation, the congregation of Korah, the ten tribes, and the men of Sodom.[78]

The emphasis in Jude 7, it should be emphasized, is not the precise nature of the sin for which Sodom and Gomorrah were proverbial. Mention is made of the fact that their sin was sexual in nature; however, this aspect is secondary to the writer's main focus. Even though the sin of Sodom is linked to the angels in Jewish apocalyptic literature (e.g., 3 *Macc.* 2:4–5 and *T. Naph.* 3:4–5) Jude's intention is to link Sodom with the angels and with Israel; all three share *departure* in common.[79]

---

[77] Similar to the language used by Jude—*prokeintai deigma puros aiōniou dikēn hupechousai*—is that of 3 *Macc.* 2:5—[*Sodomitas*] *genomenous puri kai theiō katephlexas paradeigma*.

[78] *Gen. Rab.* 27:3 and *m. Sanh.* 10:3.

[79] Most commentators focus solely on the link between verses 6 and 7 and not on the thread uniting 5,6, and 7.

For Jude, Sodom and Gomorrah are the type par excellence for the finality of divine judgment. Their fate is continually on display.

Michael and the Devil (v. 9)

Jude appears to assume the readers' acquaintance with an apocryphal tradition concerning angelic dispute over Moses' body—a transaction that is not recorded in Deuteronomy 34. We learn first from Origen that this tradition was contained in the apocryphal *Assumption of Moses*.[80] The Moses tradition—with his burial—proliferated, as one might expect, within mainstream as well as sectarian Judaism.[81] Imagery from Zechariah 3, in which Satan rises up to accuse, and perhaps Daniel 10, combines with that of Deuteronomy 34 in the apocalyptic Jewish tradition. In Zechariah's vision, twice the command "The LORD rebuke you" is pronounced on behalf of Joshua. While the primary theme in Zechariah 3 is Joshua's unclean garments, a secondary theme is the authority of the angel Satan. The allusion functions in Jude as a forensic representation of conflict. The context is antithesis: the arrogance of the *houtoi*, who blaspheme, is juxtaposed to the humility of Michael the archangel. Further, the argument in Jude, verse 9, set forth in the language of legal disputation, preserves the link to verse 7; the men of Sodom affronted the angels sent by God.

Michael the archangel, in verse 9, is meant to stand in stark contrast to the *houtoi* of verse 8. They deride holy angels in a manner Michael would not even use against the prince of darkness himself. Although he who was superior could have railed at the prince of demons, he declined. Contrarily, the ungodly of verse 8, though considering themselves superior, are actually inferior.[82]

Cain, Balaam and Korah (v. 11)

A second triplet of OT paradigms follows; it belongs to the contextual flow that began in verse 8 ("Likewise these . . . But these . . . Woe to them"). The three are objects of a woe-cry, i.e., a prophetic denunciation, issued by the writer. Having blasphemed

---

[80] *Princ.* 3.2. Only part of the text is extant, and these fragments do not contain the allusion to Moses' burial. See R. H. Charles, *APOT*, 2:414.

[81] E.g., Josephus, *Ant.* 4.8.48; Philo, *Mos.* 2.291.

[82] Jude is essentially restating this with a possible hint of sarcasm in verse 19: "These are the ones who divide; they are natural, void of the Spirit."

(v. 8), much in contrast to Michael (v. 9), the opponents of Jude have brought themselves under divine curse.[83]

In Gen 4:3 we read that Cain brought as an offering to the Lord the "fruits" of the earth, while his brother Abel is said to have brought "firstfruits" (4:4). The Lord subsequently looked upon Abel with favor but not Cain (4:5; cp. Heb 11:4). To the Jewish mind, Cain represents the epitome of wickedness, the ungodly man par excellence.[84] He is the first man in the Hebrew Scriptures to defy God and despise God's unique creation. Interestingly, the rabbis, taking note of the wording of Gen 4:10 ("your brother's blood cries out," NKJV), charge Cain with destroying a whole world.[85] He is "type and teacher" of ungodliness.[86] Hebrews 11:4 presents Cain as the antithesis of faith, while 1 John 3:12 portrays him as the antithesis of love, set within the context of a comparison between the children of God and children of the devil.

The story of Balaam is a look at the growth of Jewish haggadah.[87] Numbers 22–24 is devoted to the account of Balaam, son of Beor. This material offers a mixed review of the Midianite prophet. Elsewhere in the OT, Balaam is portrayed in a strictly negative light; he hires himself out to curse Israel.[88] While being self-seeking and greedy, Balaam more importantly led Israel into idolatry and immorality at Baal-Peor (see Num 31:16). To the rabbis, Balaam served as the antithesis of Abraham. The three qualities associated with the latter were thought to be a good eye, a lowly mind, and a humble soul. Balaam, by contrast, had an evil eye, a haughty mind, and a proud soul.[89] The "deception [*planē*][90] of Balaam" is the deception of selfish profit. Balaam typically "loved the wages of wickedness."[91]

---

[83] Cp. Matt 23 and the seven woes pronounced by Jesus. In the view of the Lord, the Pharisaical distortionists were past the point of change.

[84] E.g., Wis 10:3. Cp. 1 John 3:12.

[85] See *m. Sanh.* 4.5.

[86] So Philo, *Post.* 38 and *Sacr.* 1.2–3 and 13.52.

[87] See G. Vermes, "The Story of Balaam," in *Scripture and Tradition in Judaism: Haggadic Studies* (SPB 6; Leiden: Brill, 1961), 127–77; M. S. Moore, *The Balaam Traditions: Their Character and Development* (SBLDS 113; Atlanta: Scholars, 1990); and J. T. Greene, *Balaam and His Interpreters: A Hermeneutical History of the Balaam Tradition* (Atlanta: Scholars Press, 1992).

[88] Numbers 31:16; Deut 23:4–5; Josh 13:22; 24:9; Neh 13:2; Mic 6:5.

[89] *Avot* 5.19.

[90] With Jude's allusion in verse 13 to *asteres planētai*, this may be another word play.

[91] 2 Peter 2:15.

The third exhibit in this prophetic triad, Korah, is perhaps the most arresting illustration of insubordination in all the OT. It is he who challenged the authority of the man who talked with God (Num 16). Moreover, siding with him were 250 men among Israel's leaders (Num 16:17,35). The term used in Jude 11 to describe Korah's rebellion, *antilogia*, is the same term used by the LXX in Num 20:13; Deut 32:51; Pss 80:8; 105:32 that is rendered "Meribah." Meribah is a symbol of the strife and contention of the wilderness. Along with the men of Sodom, Korah and his following, according to the rabbis, would find no place in the world to come.[92] In effect, Korah's fate is commensurate with his deed.

Cain, Balaam, and Korah are united in Jude by means of a woe-oracle or woe-cry. The woe-cry in the OT is found in several contexts—a call to attention, mourning for the dead, a cry of excitement, a cry of revenge, and the announcement of doom. Most of the incidents fall under the latter heading.[93] In the mind of the prophets, to whom the primary use of *hou* is restricted, the promise of judgment was synonymous with judgment itself. Presumed to have derived initially from a funeral setting, the woe-cry came to incorporate a vengeance pattern, and hence, a reversal image. For Jude's purposes, the trio of verse 11 foreshadows the fate of the *houtoi* who blaspheme (vv. 8,10). With the cry of condemnation and the threat of divine vengeance hanging over their heads, Jude's opponents await the execution of irrevocable judgment.

Enoch (vv. 14–15)

One of the reasons the Epistle of Jude struggled for acceptance into the canon of the NT was its citation of *1 Enoch*. Bede expressed the view that has been consensual in the church throughout most of its history:

> The book of Enoch . . . belongs to the Apocrypha, not because the sayings . . . are of no value or because they are false but because the book which circulates under his name was not really written by him. . . . For

---

[92] *m. Sanh.* 10.3.

[93] See E. Gerstenberger, "The Woe-Oracles of the Prophets," *JBL* 81 (1962): 249–63; R. J. Clifford, "The Use of HÔY in the Prophets," *CBQ* 28 (1966): 458–64; and W. Janzen, *Mourning Cry and Woe Oracle* (BZAW 125; Berlin/New York: de Gruyter, 1972), for discussion of possible settings of the woe cry.

if it were genuine, it would not contain anything contrary to sound doctrine. But as a matter of fact it contains any number of incredible things . . . this passage
which Jude takes from Enoch is not in itself apocryphal or dubious but is rather notable for the clarity
with which it testifies to the true light.[94]

The phrase "the seventh from Adam" would appear to be a postbiblical development in Jewish literature. It occurs twice in *1 Enoch*
(60:8; 93:3) and is also found in Jewish apocrypha,[95] in Philo,[96]
and in rabbinic literature.[97] Although in other verses of Jude traces of Enochic language and imagery can be detected,[98] the text of
Jude 14–15 is particularly significant in that it confronts the reader
with an explicit citation from *1 Enoch* 1:9.[99] What purpose do these
words, drawn from a pseudepigraphal work, serve in Jude's literary-
rhetorical strategy? Jude and *1 Enoch* share in common numerous
touch points—for example: theophany, the disenfranchised angels,
the recurring antithesis between the faithless and the faithful, cosmic disorder linked to spiritual causes, apostasy, and the certainty
of final cataclysmic judgment.

In Jewish tradition the roles of Enoch are many and diverse.
The brevity and mystery surrounding the biblical allusion to
Enoch spawned countless traditions and legends which ascribed
multitudes of functions to the patron saint of apocalyptic preachers. The biblical account of Enoch's translation (Gen 5:24) provided much grist for the haggadist mill.[100] The most important
touch points between Jude and *1 Enoch* would appear to be the

---

[94] Bede, *On Jude*, in *PL* 93:129. The English translation of Bede is reproduced in G. Bray,
ed., *James, 1–2 Peter, 1–3 John, Jude* (ACCS 11; Downers Grove: InterVarsity, 2000), 255.

[95] *Jub.* 7:39.

[96] Philo, *Post.* 173.

[97] *Lev. Rab.* 29:11.

[98] On the similarities between Jude and *1 Enoch*, see B. Dehandschütter, "Pseudo-Cyprian,
Jude and Enoch. Some Notes on 1 Enoch 1:9," in *Tradition and Re-Interpretation in Jewish and
Early Christian Literature. Essays in Honour of J. C. H. Lebram* (Leiden: Brill, 1986), 114–20.

[99] A surface reading of Jude 14–15 might lead one, like Tertullian, to conclude that the
writer is alluding to the ancient antediluvian. However, several obstacles attend Tertullian's
view. While the prophets of the OT are frequently cited by writers of the NT for ethical reasons, the patriarchs typically appear in the context of promise and fulfillment. Prepatriarchal
figures, with two exceptions (Heb 11:4–7 and 1 John 3:12), are not cited as ethical paradigms
in the NT. Furthermore, the OT does not call Enoch "the seventh from Adam"; rather, this
appears to be a postbiblical development.

[100] While the patriarch enjoyed unparalleled status in the Pseudepigrapha, the rabbis accorded him a lesser station. *First Enoch* is cited with some frequency in patristic literature, giving

catchwords *asebeia* (ungodliness) and *arneomai* (denial). An intriguing parallel to Jude 4c—"denying our only Master and our Lord" (NKJV)—occurs multiple times in *1 Enoch* (38:2; 41:2; 45:2; 46:7; 48:10)—"denying the name of the Lord of the Spirits." *Asebeia* not only furnishes a parallel between the two works, it also forms the structure of the prediction in *1 Enoch* 1:9: "Behold he comes with myriads of his holy ones in order to execute judgment upon all, and he will destroy all the ungodly which they have done (*hōn ēsebēsan*) and for the harsh things which ungodly sinners (*hamartōloi asebeis*) have spoken against him."

Significantly, *asebeia* (ungodliness) and cognate forms appear three times in Jude's pronouncement, a reworking of *1 Enoch* 1:9. "Behold, the Lord comes with myriads of his holy ones to execute judgment upon all, and to reprove every person on account of all their ungodly works (*ergon asebeis autōn*) which they have done (*hōn ēsebēsan*) and for all the harsh things which ungodly sinners (*hamartōloi asebeis*) have spoken against him." Thus, the statement from *1 Enoch*, shaped by conditions that helped birth a pre-Christian apocalyptic Jewish repentance movement,[101] rings prophetically true with regard to Jude's opponents. As in OT antecedents,[102] and as in the Enoch prediction of 1:9, the Lord "comes" for the purpose of dealing with the ungodly.

Applying the specific Enochic prediction, Jude writes, "And also of these individuals the seventh from Adam, Enoch, prophesied" (v. 14a).[103] This statement allows itself to be rendered in several ways. It could mean: (1) Enoch joins *other persons*, for example, OT prophets, who also predict the same; (2) Enoch also predicted, *among other things*, the apostasy of these men; (3) Enoch's prediction also applies to *these men, among others*. Standard commentary on Jude assumes that the writer held the work *1 Enoch* as inspired, given the near-verbatim citation by Jude.[104] If, on the other hand, to Paul a Cretan is a "prophet"

the impression of apparent authority in the early church. The majority of the patristic allusions, however, seems to be found in the context of Jude's authenticity, not *1 Enoch's* authority.

[101] The writer(s) of *1 Enoch* and similar apocalypses and testaments appear to be influenced by second-century BC reactions to Hellenism. It is commonly thought that both the Pharisees and the Essenes stem from this reaction.

[102] See "Theophany and Judgment" above.

[103] One might translate the words *Proephēteusen de kai toutois hebdomos apo Adam Henōch* in the following manner: "For even (your own) Enoch, the seventh from Adam, prophesied of these."

[104] Representative is J. H. Charlesworth, for whom the distinction between canonical and noncanoncial is not helpful. See his *The Old Testament Pseudepigrapha and the New Testament*

(Titus 1:12), and Jannes and Jambres (2 Tim 3:8), court magicians of Pharaoh according to Jewish lore, can serve the purposes of illustration, then Enoch can "prophesy."

Thus, Jude 14–15 need not be construed as a citation of *1 Enoch* predicated on Jude's elevation of the work so much as Jude's adaptation of *1 Enoch* for his own particular literary-rhetorical purposes. Such might be all the more effective if we presuppose behind Jude a Palestinian literary milieu.[105]

Theology and Christology in Jude

The dominance of the "early Catholic" reading of Jude, already examined, has had significant implications for understanding the letter's setting, its authorship, and its theology. Because the "early Catholic" epistles of the NT are purported to reflect the institutionalization of the church several generations removed from the apostles, Jude is believed to mirror the codification of beliefs into creedal confessions, a normative "rule of faith," a fading of the parousia hope, and a general pervasive postapostolic mentality. K.-H. Schelkle sees numerous markers in Jude that reflect a second-century setting:

- v. 3: the faith once delivered as pertaining to apostolic teaching several generations removed;
- v. 4: reference to the ungodly who were "formerly recorded for judgment" as pertaining to statements made earlier by the apostles;
- v. 12: allusion to love feasts as a reflection of a later defilement of the sacraments;
- v. 17: remembrance of the words of the apostles as pertaining to an earlier era; and
- vv. 4,8,12,18,22,23: indications that a full-fledged heresy is growing.[106]

Schelkle's verdict is unequivocal: "The letters [Jude and 2 Peter] say themselves that the generations of the church are past. . . . The

---

(SNTSMS 54; Cambridge: Cambridge University Press, 1985), 74.

[105] I have discussed Jude's relationship to *1 Enoch* and *1 Enoch's* relationship to the canon more extensively in Charles, *Literary Strategy*, 153–66.

[106] K.-H. Schelkle, *Die Petrusbriefe. Der Judasbrief* (HTKNT 13/2; Freiburg/Basel/Wien: Herder, 1970), 145–68.

apostolic era is closed and lies behind."[107] E. M. Sidebottom similarly concludes that Jude emits definite traces of second-century influence.[108] And H. Windisch is convinced the epistle is "catholic" inasmuch as the opponents of Jude are threatening the *entire* church, which is a decidedly second-century phenomenon.[109] According to Ferdinand Hahn, the main anchor for a second-century dating of Jude is heresy: Jude, it is universally believed, is denouncing heresy, and heresy requires a "fixed confession of faith."[110]

But is the reference to "the faith" in Jude 3 and 20 the creedal form of second-century confessionalism? Based on the text, what is the evidence? Nothing in the text itself requires that we understand *pistis* to be confined to the second century. And the imperative of Jude "to remember the words already spoken by the apostles" (v. 17) need not be interpreted as a statement of *distance* between the writer and the apostles. Rather, it fits naturally as an exhortation by a brother of Jesus and James who was not one of the twelve apostles yet who in humility considers himself a "servant" (v. 1) of Jesus. "Remembering" the apostles' words, furthermore, points to the danger in forgetting, not a particular time lapse.

Given the broad-based verdict on Jude by proponents of the "early Catholic" thesis, it is no wonder that Jude is cited for its theological contribution to the NT. And yet, for its notable brevity, Jude is rich in Christology—particularly its lordship Christology (vv. 4,9,14,17,21,25). *Kurios* occurs roughly once every five verses—i.e., with remarkable frequency. Further, Christ's lordship is strengthened by several elements: the lord-servant analogy implicit in verse 1, the "only God our Savior" epithet of verse 25, and the description of Jesus in verse 4 as both *kurios* and *despotēs*, which conveys the notions of "legitimate authority" as well as arbitrariness.[111] Relatedly, as J. Fossum has argued, the text of verse 5[112] can support

[107] K.-H. Schelkle, "Spätapostolische Briefe als frühkatholisches Zeugnis," in J. Blinzer et al., eds., *Neutestamentliche Aufsätze für J. Schmid* (Regensburg: Pustet, 1963), 225 (my translation).

[108] E. M. Sidebottom, *James, Jude, and 2 Peter* (NCB; London: Thomas Nelson, 1967), 79.

[109] H. Windisch, *Die katholischen Briefe* (2d ed.; Tübingen: Mohr, 1950), 38.

[110] Ferdinand Hahn, "Randbermergungen," 209–10.

[111] In the *koinē*, *kurios* and *despotēs* are frequently used interchangeably, although the former carries the inflection of one who disposes while the latter denotes one who possesses. See W. Bousset, *Kyrios Christos* (2d ed.; Göettingen: Vandenhoeck & Ruprecht, 1921); W. Foerster and G. Quell, *Lord* (London: Adam & Charles Black, 1958), 5–9; and O. Cullmann, *The Christology of the New Testament* (Philadelphia: Westminster, 1959), 195–237. Cullmann rectifies some of the imbalances in Bousset's work from earlier in the century.

[112] An *Iēsous* reading for verse 5 is found in Alexandrinus, Vaticanus, a few old Latin manuscripts, a Coptic version, and in Origen.

the notion that *kurios*-Jesus is the one who "saved a people out of the land of Egypt."[113]

Not only is Christ pronounced as Lord in Jude, He is also Judge, in line with our interpretation of verse 5. The train of thought is clearly one of sober warning and doom since those who threaten the community are already condemned (v. 4). Whether one understands Jesus' judgeship as that of the "angel of the Lord" or as the mediator of eschatological judgment is a secondary matter. The point to be made is the connection between verse 4 and verse 5. Sovereignty is being emphasized—a sovereignty that has been "denied" by Jude's opponents. Christology reaches its apex in the letter's conclusion. Jesus' sovereignty is confirmed in the closing doxology, whereby Jesus receives the attributes of God. To Him are ascribed "glory, majesty, power, and authority, before all time and now and forever" (cp. Rev 5:12–13).

The readers are admonished eagerly to await the appearance of Christ's mercy and eternal life (v. 21). Thus, the hope of the Lord's return (the Parousia), as it turns out, is very much alive in Jude, contrary to the supposition of most scholars who read Jude through an "early Catholic" lens. It would appear that the language of lordship and the focus on the Lord's return place Jude squarely within a first-century NT environment, alongside writings such as the Corinthian and Thessalonian correspondence.

Ethics in Jude

The Epistle of Jude is a call to guard faithfully the historic Christian faith, to resist the forces of apostasy, and to pursue ethical living. As with 2 Peter, the emphasis in Jude is primarily ethical, even when the presence of heretical components suggests that apostasy seeks a theological or doctrinal justification. The character of those who threaten the community is established foremost in ethical terms. They "pervert" divine grace into "licentiousness" and "deny" the Lord as Master. They resist, indeed rail against, any authority and are compared to animals in terms of their irrationalism and their appetites. They walk, depart, and, in the end, perish. The saints, by contrast, are to be morally unstained, not corrupted by the flesh. In this way they can expect to be presented spotless before the Lord of glory.

---

[113] J. Fossum, "Kyrios Jesus as the Angel of the Lord in Jude 5–7," *NTS* 33 (1987): 226–43.

Attestation, Early Sources

"Jude's eventual recognition in the fourth century as part of the NT canon,[114] not surprisingly, followed a path not unlike that of 2 Peter, another of the "disputed" documents. This occurred even when 2 Peter seemed to encounter stiffer resistance, doubtless due to the circulation of Petrine pseudepigrapha. The epistle of Jude is cited by writers as early as Tertullian, Clement of Alexandria, and Origen, with possible traces in Clement of Rome, Polycarp, Athenagoras, Barnabas, and the *Didache*. As indicated by its inclusion in the Muratorian Canon (c. AD 170), evidence strongly suggests that Jude was viewed as sacred Scripture in the early church. Given the fact that apocryphal and pseudepigraphal writings were in relatively wide circulation, it is not surprising that Eusebius includes Jude among the so-called "disputed" books (*antilegomena*).[115] This, however, is less an argument against its authenticity than it is a reflection of concerns, in the eastern churches, that issued from Jude's near-verbatim citation of *1 Enoch*[116] (vv. 14–15) and his allusion to the *Assumption of Moses* (v. 9). Thus, according to Jerome, Jude is a *plerisque reiicitur*.[117]

Nonetheless, Eusebius, acknowledging its "disputed" status, also concedes that Jude, along with the other "catholic epistles," is well known and publicly used by most of the churches, implying that some consensus is already present by his own day. Jude's status is perhaps best, and most succinctly, summarized by Michael Green: "By AD 200 it was accepted in the main areas of the ancient church, in Alexandria (Clement and Origen), in Rome (Muratorian Canon), and in Africa (Tertullian). Only in Syria were there objections, and even there these could hardly have been in unison . . ."[118] In the end, we find little to prevent us from affirming, with the early church, that Jude the brother of James as well as our Lord, wrote the epistle."[119]

[114] So, for example, in Athanasius', listing in the year 367 (*PG* 26.1437).
[115] Eusebius, *Hist. Eccl.* 3.25.3.
[116] *1 Enoch* 1:9.
[117] Cp. also the defense of Jude by Didymus (*PG* 39.1811ff).
[119] On patristic witnesses to Jude, see C. Bigg, *A Critical and Exegetical Commentary on the Epistles of St. Peter and St. Jude* (ICC; Edinburgh: T. & T. Clark, 1901), 305–8, and D. Guthrie, *New Testament Introduction* (4th ed.; Leicester: InterVarsity, 1990), 901–2.
[118] Green, *2 Peter and Jude*, 49.

Purpose

The epistle of Jude mirrors a sharp and calculated polemic against certain opponents (*tines anthrōpoi, houtoi:* vv.
4,8,10,12,14,16,19) who were posing a threat to the community
(*humeis*, vv. 3,5,12,17,18,20). By means of unusual verbal economy, apocalyptic force, strategic use of catchwords and wordplay,
the ungodly-faithful antithesis, and triadic illustration, the writer
associates past paradigms of ungodliness with his opponents of the
present. There exists throughout the short epistle a fundamental
tension between the ungodly and the faithful. Both poles of this
contrast are said to be "reserved" for their appointed end—the *houtoi* for divine retribution and the *humeis* for divine inheritance.

Both triads of moral types highlighted in Jude (vv. 5–7,11) share
a common feature. In both, there is a movement from privilege to
dispossession. As a group, Israel of old, the angels who fell and the
cities of the plain were utterly disenfranchised, while the second
threesome, united by means of a woe-cry, moves from deception
(Cain) to error (Balaam) to destruction (Korah). This is the movement, both past and present, of apostasy. Jude's literary-rhetorical
strategy, therefore, in this "word of exhortation" is to rebuke in unconditional terms those "certain individuals" who threatened the
community by denying Christ's sovereign lordship and perverting
divine grace into licentiousness (v. 4).

Outline and Structure of Jude

Elsewhere I have attempted to show how the unfolding of the
structure of Jude's epistle can be seen through the repetition of
particular catchwords, which are not arbitrary but rather rhetorically significant.[120] What is remarkable is that in a mere twenty-five
verses, *nine* terms occur five times or more, with five of these appearing seven or more times.[121]

- ungodly/ungodliness vv. 4,15[3x],18
- you vv. 3[3x],5[2x],12,17,18,20[2x],24
- keep/guard vv. 1,6[2x],13,21,24
- these vv. 4[some],8,10,11,12,14,16,19

---

[120] See Bauckham, *Jude, 2 Peter*, 3–6; Charles, *Literary Strategy*, 30–32; and idem, *EBC*,
547.

[121] Charles, *Literary Strategy*, 30.

- Lord vv. 4,5,9,14,17,21,25
- holy vv. 3,14,20[2x],24[blameless]
- love/beloved vv. 1,2,3,12,17,20,21
- mercy/show mercy vv. 2,21,22,23
- judgment/condemnation vv. 4,6,9,15

Not only the deliberate and rhetorically strategic use of catchwords but the writer's syntax, as seen through his use of connectives, amplifies the logical progression of Jude's argument:

vv. 1–2, greeting	
vv. 3–4, occasion/purpose	[for] certain individuals have slipped in
vv. 5–19, illustrative paradigms, reminder	[Now] I wish to remind you [for] the Lord destroyed [and] the angels who did not keep [rather] abandoned [just as] Sodom and Gomorrah . . . gave themselves over [Yet] in the very same manner these dreamers also defile [But] Michael did not dare [rather] he said [yet] these blaspheme [for] they walk [Indeed] Enoch . . . prophesied [but] you, beloved, remember [for] they said
vv. 20–23, exhortation	[But] you, beloved, build [and] be merciful [and] save [and] save[122]

Selected Bibliography

Commentaries Based on the Greek Text

Bauckham, R. J. *Jude, 2 Peter*. WBC 50. Waco: Word, 1983.

---

[122] See also Charles, "Jude," *EBC* 13, 547–48.

Bigg, C. *A Critical and Exegetical Commentary on the Epistles of St. Peter and St. Jude*. ICC. Edinburgh: T. & T. Clark, 1901.

Commentaries Based on the English Text

Charles, J. D. "Jude," in EBC 13. Rev ed. Grand Rapids: Zondervan, 2006.

_____ with Erland Waltner. *1–2 Peter, Jude*. BCBC. Scottdale/Waterloo: Herald Press, 1999.

Craddock, F. B. *First and Second Peter and Jude*. WBC. Louisville: Westminster/John Knox, 1995.

Cranfield, C. E. B. *1 & 2 Peter and Jude*. London: SCM, 1960.

Elliott, J. H. *I–II Peter/Jude*. ACNT. Augsburg: Fortress, 1982.

Green, Michael. *The Second Epistle of Peter and the Epistle of Jude*. TCNT. Leicester/Grand Rapids: InterVarsity/Eerdmans, 1989.

Hillyer, N. *1 and 2 Peter, Jude*. NIBC. Peabody: Hendrickson Publishers, 1992.

Kelly, J. N. D. *A Commentary on the Epistles of Peter and Jude*. BNTC. London: Adam & Charles Black, 1969.

Kistemaker, S. J. *Peter and Jude*. NTC. Grand Rapids: Baker, 1987.

Knight, J. *2 Peter and Jude*. NTG. Sheffield: Sheffield Academic Press, 1995.

Kraftchick, S. J. *Jude, 2 Peter*. ANTC. Nashville: Abingdon, 2002

Krodel, G., ed. *The General Letters: Hebrews, James, 1–2 Peter, Jude, 1–2–3 John*. Rev. ed. Minneapolis: Fortress, 1995.

Lawlor, G. L. *The Epistle of Jude*. Phillipsburg: Presbyterian & Reformed, 1972.

Leaney, A. R. C. *The Letters of Peter and Jude*. Cambridge: Cambridge University Press, 1967.

Lucas, D., and C. Green. *The Message of 2 Peter and Jude*. BST. Leicester/Downers Grove: InterVarsity, 1995.

Mayor, J. B. *The Epistle of St. Jude and the Second Epistle of St. Peter*. New York: Macmillan, 1907.

Moffatt, J. *The General Epistles: James, Peter and Judas*. MNTC. London: Hodder & Stoughton, 1928.

Moo, D. J. *2 Peter and Jude*. NIVAC. Grand Rapids: Zondervan, 1996.

Neyrey, J. H. *2 Peter, Jude: A New Translation with Introduction and Commentary*. AB 37C. Garden City: Doubleday, 1993.

Perkins, P. *First and Second Peter, James, and Jude*. IBC. Louisville: Westminster/John Knox, 1995.

Plummer, A. *The General Epistles of St. James and St. Jude.* New York: Ármstrong and Son, 1893.

Plumptre, E. H. *The General Epistles of St. Peter and St. Jude.* Cambridge: Cambridge University Press, 1892.

Reicke, B. *The Epistles of James, Peter, and Jude.* AB. New York: Doubleday, 1964.

Richard, E. J. *Reading 1 Peter, Jude and 2 Peter: A Literary and Theological Commentary.* Macon, GA: Smyth & Helwys, 2000.

Schreiner, Thomas R. *1, 2 Peter, Jude.* NAC. Nashville: B&H, 2003.

Senior, D., and D. J. Harrington, *1 Peter, Jude and 2 Peter.* Sacra Pagina. Wilmington: Michael Glazier, 2002.

Sidebottom, E. M. *James, Jude, and 2 Peter.* NCB. London: Nelson, 1967.

Turner, J. D., et al. *Jude—A Structural Commentary.* Jamestown: Mellon Biblical Press, 1996.

Wand, J. W. C. *The General Epistles of St. Peter and St. Jude.* WC. London: Methuen, 1934.

Foreign Language Commentaries

Frankmölle, H. *1. Petrusbrief, 2. Petrusbrief, Judasbrief.* NECHTB 2d ed. Würzburg: Echter Verlag, 1990.

Fuchs, E., and Reymond, P. *La Deuxième Épître de Saint Pièrre. L'Épître de Saint Jude.* CNT 13b. Neuchatel: Delachaux & Niestle, 1980.

Schelkle, K.-H. *Der Petrusbriefe—Der Judasbrief.* HTKNT 13/2. 3rd ed. Freiburg/ Basel/Vienna: Herder, 1970.

Schneider, J. *Die Briefe des Jakobus, Petrus, Judas und Johannes: Die katholischen Briefe.* NDT 10. 9th ed. Göttingen: Vandenhoeck & Ruprecht, 1961.

Vögtle, A. *Der Judasbrief, Der zweite Petrusbrief.* EKKNT. Neukirchen: Neukirchener Verlag, 1994.

Studies

Bauckham, Richard J. "Jude, the Epistle of." *ABD.* Pages 1098–1103.

_____. "James, 1 and 2 Peter, Jude." In D. A. Carson and H. G. M. Williamson, eds. *It Is Written: Scripture Citing Scripture. Essays in Honour of B. Lindars.* Cambridge: Cambridge University Press, 1988. Pages 303–17.

_____. *Jude and the Relatives of Jesus in the Early Church.* Edinburgh: T. & T. Clark, 1990.

_____. "The Letter of Jude: An Account of Research." W. Haase, ed. *ANRW* II.25.5. Pages 3791–3826

Charles, J. Daryl. *Literary Strategy in the Epistle of Jude.* Scranton/London/Toronto: University of Scranton Press/Associated University Presses, 1993.

Chester, A., and R. P. Martin. *The Theology of the Letters of James, Peter, and Jude.* NTT. Cambridge: Cambridge University Press, 1994.

Landon, C. *A Text-Critical Study of the Epistle of Jude.* JSNTSS 135. Sheffield: Sheffield Academic Press, 1996.

Seven

REVELATION

Christ Will Return in Triumph

Revelation is the only New Testament book that is essentially prophetic. In the Greek New Testament the first word is *apokalupsis*, meaning "unveiling" or "revelation." Although some English Bibles title it "The Revelation of John," the work self-consciously claims to be a revelation *by* Jesus Christ *to* John. As the final work in the New Testament canon, it deliberately calls itself a prophecy at both its beginning and its end (1:3; 22:18–19).

Arguments about the precise message of Revelation have been endless. Yet almost all interpreters agree that the book originally intended to teach that Jesus is to return to earth as King and Lamb-Bridegroom and that faithfulness to Jesus ultimately triumphs over all the evils of this world. Thus, the essential truth that Revelation teaches can be stated in the following terms: "Jesus the Lord of history will return to earth, destroy all evil and all opposition to Him, and bring the kingdom of God to its glorious culmination" (see 1:7).[1]

Why was Revelation originally written? The debates continue to swirl. Yet a consensus about the author's overall *practical* purpose for his readers (past and present) is not uncertain. "The sovereignty of God and Christ in redeeming and judging brings them glory, which is intended to motivate saints to worship God and reflect his glorious attributes through obedience to his word"[2] (see 22:9).

Unless otherwise indicated, all Scripture quotations in this chapter are from the Holman Christian Standard Bible (HCSB).

[1] Kendell Easley, *Holman QuickSource Guide to Understanding the Bible* (Nashville: Broadman & Holman, 2002), 399.

[2] Gregory K. Beale, *The Book of Revelation: A Commentary on the Greek Text* (Grand Rapids: Eerdmans, 1999), 151.

Authorship

"John" wrote the book (1:1,4,9; 22:8). He had great authority, even from his place of banishment, the tiny island of Patmos many miles out in the Aegean Sea. There are only three possibilities about who he was. They are discussed in order from the least likely to the most likely.

"John" Is a Pseudonym for the Unknown Author of Revelation

A few critical scholars have suggested that an unrecognized Christian prophet borrowed the name John in an attempt to bolster the authority of his work as if the apostle John wrote it. If this were so, however, the author missed the opportunity to claim to be the *apostle* John; further, there is no evidence that early Christians ever knowingly accepted pseudonymous works.[3] A variation of this view is that an anonymous member of a hypothetical "Johannine community" or "school" produced Revelation. Proof that such a school ever existed is sorely lacking, and Revelation contains no material that is better understood by such a theory of its composition.[4]

"John the Prophet" Wrote Revelation

As early as the AD 200s, Dionysius, the bishop of Alexandria (and Origen's pupil), was arguing that a John other than the apostle wrote Revelation. According to the early Christian historian Eusebius, Dionysius's objections were based on internal evidence. First, Revelation did not claim to be written by the *apostle* John. Second, the content and arrangement of Revelation is inconsistent with the content and arrangement of the Gospel according to John and the First Epistle of John. Third, the Greek of Revelation is incompatible with the Greek of the other Johannine books.[5] Most critical scholars have accepted Dionysius's conclusions as their own. An otherwise unknown "John the Prophet" is said to be the writer. The same three kinds of objections Dionysius raised have dominated recent academic discussion concerning the authorship of Revelation.

---

[3] Donald A. Carson, Douglas J. Moo, and Leon Morris, *An Introduction to the New Testament* (Grand Rapids: Zondervan, 1992), 472; R. H. Charles, *A Critical and Exegetical Commentary on the Revelation of St. John* (Edinburgh: T. & T. Clark, 1920), 1:xxxviii–xxxix.

[4] Adela Yarbro Collins, *Crisis and Catharsis: The Power of Apocalypse* (Philadelphia: Westminster, 1984), 33.

[5] Eusebius, *Hist. eccl.* 7.25–27.

1. The author did not name himself as the apostle John. In addition to this, the author never mentioned events from the life of Jesus, nor did he claim to have known Jesus personally. The writer did not connect himself directly with "the Lamb's twelve apostles" (21:14).[6]

2. The theology is unlike the theology of the Gospel or the First Epistle. A number of contrasts have been noted. For example in John, Jesus is the Redeemer; in Revelation He is the Ruler. In John God's love is the focus; in Revelation His wrath. In John the focus is on what Jesus has already accomplished for His people; Revelation emphasizes what has not yet happened.[7]

3. The Greek of Revelation is incompatible with the Greek of the Gospel or the First Epistle. Revelation in fact is full of grammatical irregularities. Correct noun cases, for example, are sometimes ignored, and the author seems to follow his own rules of Greek syntax. R. H. Charles concluded that the style of Revelation is "unlike any Greek that was ever penned."[8]

Of these three arguments against apostolic authorship for Revelation, the third is the strongest. The combined weight of them has caused most scholars either to hesitate about affirming the traditional ascription of Revelation to the apostle John or to reject it altogether. For example, G. K. Beale concluded, "While the Apostle may well have written the book, another John also could have written it. The issue is not important to settle."[9]

John the Apostle Wrote Revelation

With the exception of Dionysius, all orthodox Christian testimony[10] mentioning authorship of Revelation—from the period before the New Testament canon was established until the modern period of critical inquiry—affirmed John the apostle as the author. Early external testimony includes the following:[11]

- Justin Martyr (c. AD 100–165) attributed it to the apostle (*Dial.* 81).

---

[6] Charles, *Revelation*, 1:xliii–xliv.

[7] Carson, Moo, and Morris, *Introduction*, 479.

[8] Charles, *Revelation*, 1:xliv.

[9] Beale, *Revelation*, 35.

[10] The heretic Marcion rejected Revelation as did a sect called the Alogoi, who rejected John's doctrine of Christ as the Logos. See Donald Guthrie, *New Testament Introduction*, 4th ed. (Downers Grove: InterVarsity, 1990), 931.

[11] Ibid., 930–31, helpfully organizes the early evidence.

- Irenaeus (c. AD 140–203) cited Revelation as being written by John, a disciple of the Lord (*Haer.* 4.20.11; 5.26.1).
- The Muratorian Canon (c. AD 170) accepted Revelation as authentic.
- Tertullian (150–222) affirmed that John the apostle was the author (*Marc.* 3.14).
- Clement of Alexandria (c. AD 155–215) cited Revelation as Scripture and as apostolic (*Quis div.* 42).
- Origen (c. 185–253) quoted Revelation as Scripture and as apostolic (see Eusebius, *Hist. eccl.* 6.25.9).

Much evidence from within Revelation favors apostolic origin. The author was well acquainted with the seven churches of Asia and expected his message to be received without hesitation. This accords with the early tradition from Irenaeus (apparently received from Polycarp, a disciple of John) about John's ministry in Ephesus (*Haer.* 2.1.2; see also Eusebius, *Hist. eccl.* 5.20.5–6). The author was self-consciously aware of his inspiration and claimed to have written a book that could be ignored only with peril (22:18–19).

Comparison of the Revelation with the Gospel according to John and the First Epistle of John indicates many common ideas, a shared theology, and many shared terms.[12] Consider the following common features between the Gospel and Revelation.

- The only NT references to Christ as the *Logos* or Word (John 1:1; Rev 19:13)
- The only NT references to *eating* manna (John 6:49,58; Rev 2:17 [Heb 9:4, the only other NT reference simply mentions the jar of manna]).
- References to Christ as the Lamb (*amnos*, John 1:29,36; *arnion*, Rev 5:6,28 other instances).
- References to Christ as shepherd or pastor (John 10:11,14; Rev 7:17).
- References to Christ's provision of eternal life as like drinking water (John 10:14; Rev 21:6).
- References to the impending obsolescence of an earthly temple (John 4:21; Rev 21:22).

---

[12] Many scholars, of course reject apostolic authorship of these books. If shared authorship for the Gospel, the First Epistle, and Revelation appears likely, however, it makes the case for otherwise unknown men named John less likely.

Additionally, the Gospel, the First Epistle, and Revelation make great use of contrasting pairs, such as light versus dark (John 1:5; 8:12; 1 John 2:8–10; Rev 21:23); true/truth versus false/falsehood (John 14:6,19,35; 1 John 5:20; Rev 19:11); life versus death (John 5:21; 1 John 5:11–13; Rev 21:27; 22:1–2).

Finally, it should be noted that John and Revelation are the only two New Testament books that make much use of series of sevens. The overwhelming use of seven in Revelation is obvious. John's Gospel famously includes seven preresurrection signs (miracles) of Jesus and seven "I am" affirmations.[13]

If these elements point toward apostolic authorship, what shall be said of the arguments that Dionysius and his recent followers have made? These opinions are a matter of internal observation rather than external evidence, for which sufficient answer can be made.

First argument. The author did not name himself as the apostle John. But why should he, given the nature of his book? If he were well-known to his readers, the name John would have been sufficient. The book is about Jesus' future coming, not his first appearance, so the author's historical knowledge of Jesus would have been out of place. Further, his distancing himself from the apostles is only apparent and is similar to the reference in Eph 2:20.[14]

Second argument. The theology of Revelation is different from the theology of the Gospel or the First Epistle. This fact, in itself, proves little. The same author is free to emphasize different aspects of the same theological perspective whenever his purpose changes. There is nothing impossible about the same author viewing Jesus as both Redeemer and Ruler, seeing God as both loving and wrathful, knowing that the first coming accomplished much that is still to be consummated in the second coming.

Third argument. The Greek of Revelation is incompatible with the Greek of the Gospel or the First Epistle. A number of suggestions have been made to account for the unusual Greek of Revelation; the net result of all of them is that Revelation's Greek is different but not incompatible with the other Johannine Greek in the New Testament.

---

[13] The seven preresurrection signs: water to wine (chap. 2); official's son (chap. 4); man by pool (chap. 5); 5,000 fed (chap. 6); walking on water (chap. 6); man born blind (chap. 9); Lazarus (chap. 11). The seven "I ams": bread of life (6:35,38); light of the world (8:12; 9:5); gate/door (10:9); good shepherd (10:11, 14); resurrection and life (11:25); way, truth, and life (14:6); true vine (15:1). Not as obvious is that John seems to structure both the beginning and end of Jesus' public ministry around seven days.

[14] Pauline authorship of Ephesians is here assumed without argumentation.

F. J. A. Hort thought that Revelation was written several decades before John's Gospel and that his Greek improved over time.[15] George Ladd and Leon Morris suggested that Revelation might have been written without the aid of a professional scribe (amanuensis).[16] Another idea is that because of the ecstatic nature of John's visions, he was in haste to write without grammatical niceties.[17] On the other hand, it is equally possible that John wrote with a deliberate set of grammar rules to achieve a certain effect (now lost in an age in which *koinē* Greek is no longer a spoken tongue).[18] In fact, the Greek style of Revelation is more like the style of John and 1 John than like other parts of the New Testament.

In conclusion, there is no good reason to deny that the author was indeed the apostle, also the composer of the Fourth Gospel and three epistles. What is known from the New Testament about him? He was the son of Zebedee and brother of James the apostle, who was killed by Herod Agrippa I about AD 44 (Matt 4:21; Acts 12:1–2). Salome was probably his mother (compare Matt 27:56 with Mark 15:40). The family lived in Galilee, probably Bethsaida. John fished professionally on the Sea of Galilee with his father and brother (Mark 1:19–20).

Jesus called John to fish for men (Matt 4:18–22; Mark 1:16–20; Luke 5:1–11). Later John was chosen to become an apostle (Matt 10:2–4; Mark 3:13–19; Luke 6:12–19). Jesus named John and James "Boanerges," sons of thunder, because of their unrestrained temperament (Mark 3:17). John was one of the three apostles closest to Jesus. According to Acts, John was the leader of Christianity in Jerusalem (along with Peter). In the rest of the New Testament, John's name is mentioned in Paul's letters once (Gal 2:9) and in Rev 1:1,4,9; 22:8. Reference has already been made to the information of Irenaeus and Eusebius about John's last years in Ephesus.

Date of Writing

Revelation originated during a time of Roman persecution of Christians. Discussions about the date of Revelation center on

---

[15] F. J. A. Hort, *The Apocalypse of St. John I-III* (London: Macmillan, 1908), xii.

[16] George Eldon Ladd, *A Commentary on the Revelation of St. John* (Grand Rapids: Eerdmans, 1972), 7–8; Leon Morris, *Revelation*, rev. ed. (Grand Rapids: Eerdmans, 1987), 39.

[17] Ibson T. Beckwith, *The Apocalypse of John* (New York: Macmillan, 1919), 39.

[18] Charles, *Revelation*, 1:xliv.

answering the question, "Who was the Roman emperor when Revelation was written?" Two major possibilities exist—Nero (ruled AD 54–68) and Domitian (ruled AD 81–96).[19] As in the discussion of authorship, these are presented in order from the less likely to the more likely.

Revelation Was Written During the Last Years of Nero's Rule

This understanding is based on three elements.

Nero is the sixth king of Rev 17:10. The most obvious way of reading this text is that the sixth Roman emperor was in power when Revelation was written. If Julius Caesar (the first to claim the rights of emperor) was the first, then Nero was the sixth.[20]

Nero best fits the interpretation of 666 in Revelation 13:18. On the basis of transcribing the name "Nero(n) Caesar" into Hebrew and then summing up the Hebrew number value of each letter, the total 666 is reached.[21]

Jerusalem was still standing when Rev 11:1–2 was written. The measurements of the temple in Revelation 11 suggest a pre-70 date (the year Jerusalem and the temple were demolished by Roman legions under Titus).

These arguments all have merit, but each can be sufficiently answered.

It is by no means certain that Nero was the sixth king. Augustus was the first actually to reign as emperor, and by the reckoning of most historians imperial Rome began with his rule. This makes Nero the fifth emperor and raises the question of how (or whether) to include in the numbering the three minor figures—Galba, Otho, and Vitellus—who claimed the throne during the civil unrest after Nero's death. Further, it is possible that the reference in Revelation 17:10 is not to first-century rulers at all.[22]

That Nero fits the mystery of 666 is highly speculative. This suggestion is recent, and it flies in the face of what seems evident. The calculation of the number of the name should be done in Greek,

---

[19] Minor views argued for the date include the reign of Claudius (ruled AD 41–54); the reign of Vespasian (ruled AD 70–80); and the reign of Trajan (ruled AD 98–117).

[20] The six are Julius, Augustus, Tiberius, Gaius (= Caligula), Claudius, and Nero.

[21] Fritzsche first proposed this view in 1831. See Guthrie, *NT Introduction*, 959, fn. 4.

[22] For example, see Kendell Easley, *Revelation* (Nashville: Broadman & Holman, 1998), 310–11.

the language in which Revelation was composed. This suggestion can hardly be a guide to dating the composition of the book.

There is no need to presume Jerusalem was still standing when 11:1–2 was written. As biblical parallel, one should consider the many precise dimensions of the temple measured in Ezekiel 40–42. The temple measured there was not standing in Ezekiel's day.[23]

Revelation Was Written During the Last Years of Domitian's Rule

The earliest reference to the date of Revelation is found in Irenaeus, *Against Heresies* 4.30.3, asserting that Revelation came originally from the end of Domitian's rule. Most other early traditions followed Irenaeus's lead. Internal evidence from Revelation suggests the following reasons to concur with this conclusion.

The severity of persecution better fits what is known of the reign of Domitian. John had been exiled to Patmos because of his commitment to Christ (1:9). Antipas, a Christian from Pergamum, had been killed for his faith before Revelation was written (2:13). Christians of Smyrna were about to be imprisoned (2:10). Many passages suggest that widespread persecution was imminent (17:6). Although Nero persecuted Christians in and around Rome after the fire of AD 64, there is no documentation that official Roman persecution of Christians extended as far as the province of Asia in Nero's day. On the other hand, the evidence of Christian tradition, particularly Eusebius, is that persecution during the time of Domitian was severe. Ancient secular historical confirmation of such persecution is admittedly scarce, but there is no good reason to dismiss the evidence of Christian writers.

The decline of the seven churches better fits the reign of Domitian. The churches of Ephesus, Sardis, and Laodicea were in a woeful spiritual condition when Revelation was written (2:4–5; 3:1–2,15–17). At least two of these cities, Ephesus and Laodicea, were home to thriving churches as late as the writing of Colossians and Ephesians (Col 2:1; 4:13–16; Ephesians throughout), probably composed not earlier than AD 60. It is hard to suppose that these churches deteriorated in less than a decade to the condition indicated in Revelation. Further, the Nicolaitans, whoever they were,

---

[23] No biblical expert can claim to have the final word on precisely which temple is referenced in these chapters.

were present in the Ephesian church (as well as in the church in Pergamum) in a way that suggests a long-term identity (2:6,15).

This all can be much more satisfactorily accounted for by a Domitianic date for Revelation, some thirty years after the Neronic date. All the churches of Revelation 2–3 seem to have a history of several decades rather than of simply a few years. This is especially true in light of Christ's reprimand of the insipid Laodiceans (3:16).

The implied emperor worship better fits the reign of Domitian. Emperor worship became a greater and greater factor as the first century progressed. Although Caligula desired to be worshipped, his rule was too short and his sanity too impaired for this to have been taken seriously. Nero was the first emperor seriously to be accorded divine honors during his lifetime, yet this was evidently limited to the area around the city of Rome. From Nero's time to Domitian's, however, the political and religious climate supported the rapid growth of emperor worship.

Domitian ordered that others acknowledge him as *Dominus et Deus* ("Lord and God"; Suetonius *Domitian* 13). Sooner or later such a claim clashed with the Christians' supreme loyalty to Jesus, although secular Roman proof that this occurred during Domitian's reign is lacking. Most scholars support the conclusion that the kind of emperor worship conceived of in Revelation is better supported by what is known of the period of Domitian's rule, rather than any earlier period. (In fact, the earliest surviving official Roman document concerning emperor worship belongs to the reign of Trajan early in the second century.)

The Jewish hostility against the churches better fits the reign of Domitian. The Christians both of Smyrna and of Philadelphia had endured attacks from "the synagogue of Satan" (2:9; 3:9). While surely enmity between Jew and Christian arose from the earliest time the gospel came to Asia, during Paul's lifetime, at least, there was the hope that many Jews would turn to Christ in faith (Rom 10:1–2). The line between synagogue and church was still permeable to a degree. Sometime after the fall of Jerusalem in AD 70, the Jewish synagogues and the Christian congregations permanently separated. By the time Revelation was written, members of synagogues who persecuted Christians could be referred to as undeserving of the name Jew. This fits more clearly during the time of Domitian than during the time of Nero, who died before the destruction of Jerusalem.

The possibility of a "return of Nero" myth better fits the reign of Domitian. Revelation 13 and 17 speak of the beast's recovery from a mortal wound. Some scholars have thought that this alludes to a first-century belief that arose only after Nero's death: he was to return to life and come back to Rome leading a Parthian army. Because Revelation does not mention the Parthians and because Revelation 13 and 17 can be interpreted without reference to any "return of Nero" myth, it is best not to base any judgment on this factor one way or the other.

In conclusion, the weight of the evidence, both internal and external, supports the last years of Domitian, perhaps AD 90–96, as the likely date for the origin of this book. If this is so, Revelation was the last book of the New Testament to be composed. John was writing as the last living apostle of Jesus. On one hand it was a time characterized by governmental persecution of Christians that was growing in intensity; on the other hand the churches had declined miserably. The persecution of Christians may have been exacerbated by the growing insistence by Domitian to be reverenced as "Lord and God" and by the steadfast insistence of Jesus' followers to worship only Him as Lord and God.

Place of Origin

Revelation was written from the island of Patmos (1:9). According to the (secular) historian Pliny, Roman authorities used it as a place of exile (*Natural History* 4.23). Lying about 40 miles out in the Aegean Sea from Ephesus, the place was notably rocky and barren. As a small island (four miles by six miles), it had few places where someone could get away entirely from the sound of the crashing waves. This may be the inspiration for the description of some of the sounds and voices in Revelation (1:15; 14:2).[24]

Destination

The original cities targeted in Revelation were not John's choice. The One who initiated the visions of the book dictated these destinations

---

[24] Carson, Moo, and Morris, *Introduction*, 473.

to him. Good roads connected these seven cities, and it was easily possible for a letter carrier, arriving at the port of Ephesus from Patmos, to travel north to Smyrna and on around to all the seven cities in the order listed in Revelation 2–3, concluding with Laodicea.

More than a century ago, Sir William Ramsay published a monograph that included a definitive archaeology of these cities.[25] More recent studies, such as John Stott's commentary on Revelation 1–5, contribute a vivid sense of these places as they existed during John's day.[26] The following paragraphs are cited verbatim from the present author's commentary on Revelation.

Ephesus had been an important seaport city for over a thousand years by the time John wrote Revelation.[27] It had been ruled by both the Persians and the Greeks before coming under Roman rule in 133 BC. In the first century Ephesus was the most important commercial center of the Roman province of Asia, the de facto capital with perhaps 300,000 residents. By the AD 300s, its harbor on the eastern shore of the Aegean Sea had been silted up from the flow of the Cayster River so that today the site is an uninhabited ruin several miles inland.

During the time of the apostle John, Ephesus was truly splendid. A broad street lined with columns (the Arcadian Road) led east from the harbor to the city amphitheater, which seated 25,000 (Acts 19:23–41). Like most ancient cities, it featured finely sculptured temples to rival deities. The most magnificent of all was the temple to Artemis, the local fertility goddess. Archaeologists have uncovered its ruins. About 400 feet long by about 200 feet wide, the marble building took up more space than a football field. It was supported by 127 columns some 60 feet tall and was one of the largest buildings in the world, deserving its reputation as one of the seven wonders of the ancient world.

Smyrna[28] was an important and prosperous seaport city on the eastern Aegean Sea about 35 miles north of Ephesus. In 290 BC it was reestablished as a Greek city after a period of destruction. It had grown to become a lavish and beautiful city with a population of about 200,000. In AD 178 a severe earthquake destroyed much

---

[25] William Ramsay, *The Letters to the Seven Churches of Asia* (London: Hodder & Stoughton, 1904).

[26] John R. W. Stott, *What Christ Thinks of the Church* (Wheaton, IL: Harold Shaw, 1990).

[27] Easley, *Revelation*, 45.

[28] Ibid., 46–47.

of the city, but it was rebuilt and remains today as the Turkish city of Izmir.

During the time of the apostle John, Smyrna had typical urban features such as broad avenues, public marketplaces, temples, a library, gymnasium, stadium, and theater. The people of Smyrna had long been known for their extreme loyalty to Rome. Early Christians there were familiar both with the temple in honor of the emperor Tiberius as well as one to the "Mother Goddess." The early Christians also faced a large and hostile Jewish population that became a source of persecution ("synagogue of Satan," 2:9).

Pergamum,[29] 55 miles north of Smyrna, but 15 miles inland from the Aegean, had a long and splendid history. It was built on the south slope of a hill rising almost one thousand feet from the surrounding plain, providing both breathtaking scenery and military security. (The word *pergamum* meant "citadel" in Greek.) A cultural and religious center, Pergamum had been ruled by Persians, Greeks, and Romans. The golden age of Pergamum was a 150-year period (283–133 BC) when the king of Pergamum ruled a substantial independent kingdom. Pergamum served as the official capital of the Roman province of Asia from 133 BC. Today the Turkish town of Bergama lies at the foot of the hill.

Pergamum practiced careful city zoning. The poor lived at the foot of the mountain; at the next level up was the business district; above that the rich lived in their villas; finally, at the top were the important public buildings and temples. Four such buildings are especially noteworthy.

The huge and highly decorated altar to Zeus, some 120 by 112 feet, stood at the top of the hill. The ruins of this altar are still impressive, and it could easily be called "Satan's throne" overlooking the city.

The temple in honor of Augustus was the first one built for a Roman emperor in Asia (around 29 BC), and the people of Pergamum proved to be extremely loyal to Rome. This temple might also be called "Satan's throne" in the days when it was dangerous not to confess, "Caesar is lord."

In the lower part of the city was the famous Asclepion, a complex of several buildings serving as a combination hospital-temple. Patients came from all over the world expecting to be healed by the

[29] Ibid., 47–48.

god Asclepius, although current medical technology was also practiced. The symbol of Asclepius was two snakes twined around a
pole, a still-familiar medical icon. Because the Bible calls Satan "the
serpent," some have suggested that the Asclepion was the "Satan's
throne" of Revelation 2.

Finally, Pergamum's world-renowned public library stood on
the upper level. Built by one of the kings of Pergamum early in
the second century BC, it contained over 200,000 handwritten
scrolls. Only the great library of Alexandria rivaled it. The people
of Pergamum loved books so much they invented parchment, a way
of using animal skins as paper. (The Greek word translated "parchment" is *pergamēnos*, derived from *Pergamos*, "Pergamum.")

Thyatira[30] was a minor town on the Circular Road of Asia,
20 miles southeast of Pergamum and halfway between Pergamum
and Sardis. It had served as a military outpost for the kingdom of
Pergamum in 133 BC. Today the large Turkish town of Akhisar is
on the same location.

The most famous early Christian of Thyatira was Lydia, a seller
of purple fabric who was converted to Christ during Paul's ministry
in Philippi (Acts 16:14). Thyatira was known for its many trade
guilds, particularly among the coppersmiths and the fabric weavers
and dyers. (Highly colored fabric was rare, desirable, and expen-
sive. Purple dye was derived from the murex shellfish; a red dye
came from certain roots.)

Little is known of the physical layout of Thyatira. Participation
in the popular and successful trade guilds, something like modern
labor unions, was important for business success in the town. This
association probably included eating fellowship meals together at
a pagan temple ("food sacrificed to idols") and other unbridled
excesses.

Sardis[31] had been the splendid and wealthy capital of the kingdom of Lydia in the days before the rise of the Persian Empire.
About 50 miles inland from the Aegean Sea and 30 miles south of
Thyatira, it lay at the foot of Mount Tmolus that rose 1,500 feet
above the valley of the Hermus River. The acropolis was a natural citadel on the northern spur of Mount Tmolus. Under King
Croesus, it became fabled for its wealth.

---

[30] Ibid., 48.
[31] Ibid., 64–65.

Sardis had fallen to the advancing Persian army of King Cyrus in 546 BC, when the citadel had been breached in a surprise night-time attack. Alexander the Great had also captured Sardis. More than three centuries after Cyrus, the Seleucid army of Antiochus III (the Great) used the same tactic to conquer the city (214 BC). (This Antiochus III was the father of Antiochus IV [Epiphanes], of infamy because of his desecration of the temple in Jerusalem and the ensuing Maccabean Revolt of the Jews.)

Sardis never regained its splendor, although its population in the first century has been estimated at 120,000. After a devastating earthquake in AD 17, Sardis was rebuilt with the colonnaded marble road, 50 feet wide and 4,600 feet long, dividing the northern and southern sections of the city. Rome later rejected Sardis's bid to build an imperial temple, choosing rival Smyrna instead. Recent excavations have unveiled much information about the city, including the ruins of a splendid synagogue. The Turkish town of Sart now occupies the site.

Philadelphia[32] was the "city of brotherly love" as its name implies. Eumenes II, a king of Pergamum in the second century BC, apparently founded the city. His brother Attalus II was so loyal and devoted to the king that Attalus was known as "Philadelphus." The city was named to commemorate this affection.

About 30 miles inland from Sardis, it lay at the head of a fertile plateau. From this position it had become commercially important. Unfortunately, the area around Philadelphia was an earthquake zone. In AD 17 a severe quake devastated the city, causing many citizens to leave for a safer place. (Incidentally, an earthquake occurred there in 1969.) After it was rebuilt with imperial aid, it took the name "Neocaesarea" in gratitude. In Vespasian's day (a few years before Revelation was written) it was renamed "Flavia." Because no detailed archaeological work has been done on the site, little is known of the exact size or layout of the city. The Turkish town of Alashehir now occupies the site.

Laodicea[33] was one of three sister cities in the valley of the Lycus River. Colossae (with famous cold springs), Hierapolis (with hot medicinal springs), and Laodicea were in the region of Phrygia, some 40 miles southeast of Philadelphia. If this was the last stop on the original postal carrier's route for dispatching Revelation, he

[32] Ibid., 65.
[33] Ibid., 66–67.

could return to Ephesus, his starting point, by traveling a hundred miles due west.

Laodicea was founded in the third century BC by Antiochus II, the Seleucid king. (He named the city for his wife, Laodice. Their grandson, Antiochus III, would later conquer Sardis.) It lay at the juncture of both east-west (Pisidian Antioch to Ephesus) and north-south (Pergamum to Attalia) highways. Being a vital cross-roads city made it a major commercial success.

In New Testament times Laodicea had a great reputation as a banking center. Laodicea's famous textile industry specialized in black woolen fabric. The most serious problem with Laodicea was its lack of reliable water. The stone Roman aqueduct that piped water into the city from springs south of town had to be designed to clear the stones of mineral deposits. Even then the water was barely drinkable.

Like other cities of the region, Laodicea was subject to earth-quakes. Several occurred throughout its history. When Nero offered imperial aid to help the people recover from the disastrous quake of AD 60, the city was wealthy enough to decline his offer. The site was eventually abandoned, but the modern town of Denizli is nearby.

First Audience

The original recipients of the book were "the seven churches" of the seven cities of Roman Asia (1:11). Direct information about the Christians in these churches is located in chapters 2 and 3. Both the predictions and exhortations of the rest of the book provide indirect information that has become the basis for a great deal of scholarly speculation about believers in these churches.[34] This introduction focuses on what is stated straightforwardly in Revelation 2–3.

The Past of the Churches

As noted in the discussion of date of composition, every indication is that these churches had an extensive history by the time Revelation was composed. The gospel came to the Roman province of Asia during Paul's great ministry in Ephesus, as reported in Acts 19. During the space of two to three years (around AD 54–56),

---

[34] See, for example, the excellent review in Beale, *Revelation*, 28–33.

people throughout the entire province of Asia heard about Christ (Acts 19:10; 20:31).

It seems probable that six of these churches (excluding Ephesus, of course) were established as daughter churches of Ephesus, as Paul's converts in Ephesus fanned throughout the province. Assuming a Domitianic date for the composition of Revelation, some of the recipients had been followers of Christ for four decades. Such long-term Christians were surely in view in Christ's rebuke to Christians in Ephesus and Sardis that they "remember" their past and return to their former spiritual fervor (2:5; 3:3).

As previously noted, early tradition (Irenaeus, *Haer.* 2.1.2, and Eusebius, *Hist. eccl.* 5.20.5–6) indicates that Ephesus was the center of the apostle John's later ministry, almost certainly some years after Paul's death. His Gospel and epistles may have been composed there, and verses 3 and 7 of 3 John suggest that John was involved in supervising an entire network of traveling preachers throughout the area.

Thus the churches addressed in Revelation had a rich history of association with Christ's apostles, in particular Paul and John. Yet no spiritual entity can presume upon past greatness, as a comparison of the Epistle to the Ephesians and Christ's rebuke of the Ephesians in Revelation makes clear.

The Present of the Churches

Three factors dominated the present circumstances of the seven churches of Asia. Some were facing pagan (Roman) hostility. Some were facing hostility from Jewish sources. Most had so spiritually compromised that they were challenged to repent of their sins.

Pagan hostility was a fact of life for believers in Pergamum. One church member, the otherwise unknown Antipas, had been martyred in the city. The believers there were warned that Satan's throne was in their city and that he lived there (2:13). Similarly, believers in Thyatira were being exposed to the sexual immorality taught by "Jezebel," along with the temptation to participate in pagan feasts (2:20). Whether this temptation had anything to do with emperor worship is unknown. It may be assumed, however, that throughout Roman Asia Christians were being cast under a cloud of suspicion by devotees of other religions and by those in charge of enforcing public veneration of the emperor as divine.

At least two of the seven churches faced hostility from Jewish sources. The Jewish population of Smyrna and of Philadelphia was strong enough to slander and harass the Christians of those cities (2:9; 3:9; see earlier discussion of what this implies for the date of composition of Revelation).

Harassment and tribulation often purify a church; other times they may dishearten believers. For five of the seven churches, spiritual stagnation—even heresy and immorality—had crept in. An otherwise unknown sect called the "Nicolaitans" had affected the churches in Ephesus and in Pergamum. Christ required all the churches except Smyrna and Philadelphia to repent (2:5,16,22; 3:3,19).

The Future of the Churches

The letters in Revelation 2–3 promise both suffering and glory to the believers in the seven churches. Those in Smyrna were told that a devilish trial lay ahead for them that would include imprisonment of some. On the other side of trial and death lay the crown of life (2:10). Believers in Thyatira were told to expect the Lord's temporal judgment on those who had compromised morally with "Jezebel," including the death of some members (2:22–23). The Philadelphians were warned about a worldwide trial about to come (3:10). The loss of spiritual love among the Ephesians threatened the existence of that congregation (2:5), and those in Pergamum who had fallen prey to Balaam's teaching or the Nicolaitans' teaching were threatened with divine judgment.

The letter to each church concluded with Christ's word about the ultimate future of its members, making a promise to those who overcame. In some instances it is possible to find a connection between the immediate negative circumstances of the believers in a particular city and the promise made. For example, overcoming Philadelphians—living in an earthquake zone—were promised to become unshakeable pillars in God's temple (3:12). Collectively, the promises made to overcomers in the seven churches anticipated the glorious future developed in more detail in Revelation 21–22:

- overcomers of Ephesus will eat from the tree of life in paradise (2:7; 22:14);
- overcomers of Smyrna will not be hurt by the second death (2:11; 21:8);

- overcomers of Pergamum will receive hidden manna and a white stone with a new name (2:17; 22:4);
- overcomers of Thyatira will rule the nations with an iron scepter and have the morning star (2:26–28; 22:16);
- overcomers of Sardis will be dressed in white and have their names in the book of life forever (3:5; 21:27);
- overcomers of Philadelphia will become pillars in God's temple and have names written on them (3:12; 22:4; contrast 21:22); and
- overcomers of Laodicea will sit on the throne with Christ (3:21; 22:3).

Whatever else we may say about the immediate circumstances of the churches addressed in Revelation, a glorious future lay ahead for those who were faithful and overcame the obstacles to faithfulness in their path. In the meantime, however, they would face the direst of circumstances.

Occasion

By "occasion" is meant what prompted the human author to compose his book. If it is accepted that John wrote from Patmos as the book claims, then the author stated explicitly what prompted him to write. While John was exiled on Patmos, the exalted Lord appeared to him and gave him visions that he was instructed to write down. The command to write is pervasive (1:11,19; 2:1,8,12,18; 3:1,7,14; 14:13; 19:9; 21:5). This book, more than any other in the New Testament, bears a sense of divine dictation.

If John did not write Revelation from Patmos as claimed, then one can only speculate as to the motives of the human writer. Whatever his motives, they were other than as stated plainly in the book, and one critic's guess is as valid as any other's.

Genre

Interest in the exact kind of literature that Revelation represents has consumed a great deal of scholarly inquiry. A number of special study groups and symposia, for instance, have focused on the matter of identifying "apocalyptic" and whether Revelation is, in fact, an "apocalypse" in the formal sense.[35] Most contemporary students have concluded that this work uniquely combines elements of three different genres: epistle, apocalypse, and prophecy. Assessments as to the relative weight to give each of these factors are varied.

Revelation as Epistle

The prologue (1:1–8) and the epilogue (22:6–21) show many of the marks of the New Testament epistles. They are letters sent by an apostle (or prophet) of Jesus Christ to specific readers for information and encouragement. The pattern of Revelation follows the fourfold pattern of most of the other New Testament letters:

- salutation, including an indication of the author, the recipient, and a formal word of greeting (1:1–5a);
- thanksgiving or doxology to God for the recipient (1:5b–8);
- main body of the letter (1:9–22:5); and
- final greetings (22:6–21).

Revelation, however, plainly does not fit the normal pattern of New Testament epistles. For one thing, within the "main body" of the book are found seven other short letters—letters within a letter (chaps. 2–3). Its essential genre is distinctively different, and the history of interpreting Revelation shows that it must be considered as belonging to another category of literature altogether.

Revelation as Apocalypse

Some students of Revelation have classed Revelation as apocalyptic literature. However, the first (and only) instance of the term "apocalypse" (*apokalupsis*) is as the first word of the book.[36] It seems to be used as a title rather than as a description of the kind of writing contained in the book.

---

[35] The Society of Biblical Literature's Apocalypse Group published findings in 1979 (J. J. Collins, "Introduction: Towards the Morphology of a Genre," *Semeia* 14 [1979]: 1–20). The Uppsala Colloquium on Apocalypticism published a monograph in 1983 (D. Hellholm, ed., *Apocalypticism in the Mediterranean World and the Near East* [Tübingen: Mohr, 1983]). The Society of Biblical Literature's Seminar on Early Christian Apocalypticism published findings as volume 36 of *Semeia* (1986).

[36] The term appears 17 other times in the New Testament, all of which bear the ordinary meaning "unveiling," rather than any suggestion of describing a kind of literature: Luke 2:32; Rom 2:5; 8:19; 16:25; 1 Cor 1:7; 14:6,26; 2 Cor 12:1,7; Gal 1:12; 2:2; Eph 1:17; 3:3; 2 Thess 1:7; 1 Pet 1:7,13; 4:13.

The kind of writing called apocalyptic, then popular among Jews,[37] had a number of features, including the following:

- the claim to originate from God through a mediating being,
- prediction of future events as "soon,"
- the use of symbolic creatures and actions,
- bitter conflict between this evil age and the coming age, and
- future events are not subject to change even if humans repent.[38]

On all these points, Revelation has a high degree of affinity. Yet there are certain other elements generally present in Jewish apocalypses that Revelation lacks. Among these are the following:

- a claim to be written by a famous Old Testament character,
- extensive interpretation by an angelic guide, and
- belief that the Messiah's coming was still future.

Thus, while the Jewish apocalypses may offer a helpful paradigm for understanding parts of Revelation, we should probably not identify Revelation as an example of apocalyptic literature.

Revelation as Prophecy

The Old Testament prophets were preeminently those who spoke the word of God to people of their own day and then wrote the message down for a wider audience. It is widely agreed that these prophets both "forth told" as well as "foretold" God's message for God's people. They included both calls to the faithful to stay true to God and calls for the wayward to repent. Sin against God was often denounced as spiritual adultery. The predictive elements of the Old Testament prophecies often foretold both near and remote events, with the first or second coming of Christ as the remote event.

Revelation is most clearly to be identified as a prophecy in this sense. It is self-consciously a prophecy (1:3; 22:7,10,18,19; cp. 11:3–6; 19:10).[39] Everything just noted about the Old Testament prophecies

---

[37] 1 (Ethiopic) Enoch, Jubilees, Assumption of Moses, 2 Esdras (= 4 Ezra), Apocalypse of Baruch, 2 (Slavonic) Enoch, Testaments of the Twelve Patriarchs, Psalms of Solomon, and Sybilline Oracles are the major Jewish apocalyptic works.

[38] George Eldon Ladd, "Why Not Prophetic-Apocalyptic?" JBL 76 (1957): 192–200.

[39] The other instances of "prophecy" (propheteia) in the New Testament are Matt 13:14; Rom 12:6; 1 Cor 12:10; 13:2,8; 14:6,22; 1 Thess 5:20; 1 Tim 1:18; 4:14; 2 Pet 1:20–21.

applies to Revelation (except that the Messiah's first coming has already been accomplished). Ways in which Revelation especially is to be distinguished from apocalyptic literature are as follows:

- call for God's own people to repent,
- author does not claim to be an Old Testament character,
- no narration of historical events as if they were prophecy,
- little interpretation by an angel, and
- belief that the Messiah and the end times have already come.

Some scholars understand prophecy and apocalypse as two separate literary genres with overlapping elements. It may be better, however, to see prophecy (at least in Scripture) as the larger category within which apocalyptic is a subcategory. The book of Revelation is best understood as a prophecy, a message exhorting God's people to remain faithful to Him and predicting both near and remote future events. The apocalyptic elements are important but secondary to the prophetic thrust of the book.[40] The genre of Revelation is "a prophecy cast into an apocalyptic mold and written down in a letter form."[41]

Greek Style

On one hand, the Greek style of Revelation is simple. It is composed in *koinē* (common, nonliterary) Greek just as is the rest of the New Testament. Those who have read the Greek Testament will readily attest that its style is more like the Greek of the Fourth Gospel and the three epistles of John than any other part of the New Testament.

On the other hand, the book has numerous grammatical peculiarities that make its Greek unusual in places. As noted in the earlier discussion of authorship, this was one of the concerns of Dionysius of Alexandria, a concern which caused him to reject apostolic authorship. He noted that the "use of the Greek language is not accurate, but he employs barbarous idioms, in some places committing downright solecisms [grammatical mistakes]" (Eusebius, *Hist. eccl.* 7.25.26–27).

---

[40] See Easley, *Revelation*, 24–25.
[41] Carson, Moo, and Morris, *Introduction*, 479.

For those who accept apostolic authorship, many suggestions have been made to account for these difficulties. On the one hand, some are satisfied with notions centering around the idea that these difficulties were *unintentional*. The following are examples of such ideas:

- John lost (or changed) his scribal assistant so that he wrote ungrammatically.
- John was so eager to write down his visions that he wrote hastily and ungrammatically.

The alternative is to suggest that John *intentionally* wrote these irregularities. A number of reasons for doing so have been suggested:

- John (a Jew) was writing in a deliberately Semitic or Hebrew style.
- John was writing idiosyncratically as a protest against standard *koinē* Greek.
- John used irregularities to draw attention to Old Testament allusions.[42]

Because no modern New Testament student speaks *koinē* Greek, it is impossible for anyone to be conclusive about whether the Greek style is deliberate and, if so, what its effect on original readers might have been. The following, however, seems to be a judicious conclusion: "The overall purpose of these Septuagintalisms, stylistic Semitisms, and awkward OT allusions was probably to create a 'biblical' effect in the hearer and, hence, to show the solidarity of the writing with that of the OT."[43]

Place in the Canon and Handwritten Manuscripts

As noted in the earlier discussion concerning the authorship of Revelation, attestation to its apostolic (and therefore implicitly scriptural) status was early: Justin Martyr, Irenaeus, Tertullian,

---

[42] This last suggestion has been innovated by Beale, *Revelation*, 101. He lists the following verses as containing such solecisms: 1:4,5,10–11,12,15; 2:13,20; 3:12; 4:1; 5:6,12; 7:4,8,9; 8:9; 9:14; 10:2,8; 11:4,15; 12:5,7; 14:7,19; 19:6,20; 20:2. See also Charles, *Revelation*, 1: cxvii–clix, "A Short Grammar of the Apocalypse."

[43] Beale, *Revelation*, 103.

Clement of Alexandria, and Origen. Among the Western churches, a general acceptance of Revelation as canonical prevailed.[44] For the Western churches, the Council of Carthage of AD 397 became the first occasion for publishing a full list of the New Testament canonical books—30 years later than Athanasius's list but identical to it (see below).

Among the Eastern churches, the objections to apostolic authorship raised by Dionysius of Alexandria (noted earlier under the discussion of authorship) had a decided impact. For example, the earliest Syriac version of the New Testament (Peshitta), probably to be dated in the early 400s, omitted Revelation, although the Syriac version of a century later (Philoxenian) included it. Nevertheless, the Paschal (Easter) Letter of Athanasius of AD 367 set out the canon of his day in detail, including Revelation (and indeed only the 27 books of the New Testament). There seems to have been little deviation among the Eastern churches after that time.

As the Greek-speaking churches developed lectionaries—books containing portions of Scripture appointed to be read in public worship on specific days of the year—Revelation alone of the New Testament books was excluded for reasons not entirely clear. Thus, the manuscript history for the text of Revelation is significantly different from that of any other New Testament book, although many relatively late medieval manuscripts survive.

Papyrus 47 is the earliest manuscript of Revelation (third century), but it is incomplete; the five other known papyri contain only a few verses each (18,24,43,85,98).[45] The oldest complete manuscript of Revelation is the famous Sinaiticus Codex ("Aleph")—a parchment uncial from the fourth century.[46] Two fifth-century parchment uncials, Alexandrinus ("A") and Ephraemi Rescriptus ("C") are considered by textual scholars to be particularly valuable witnesses to the original form of Revelation. There are only eight other known uncial manuscripts containing all or part of Revelation (025 [Porphyrianus], 046, 051, 052, 0163, 0169, 0207, and 0229).[47]

---

[44] Minor exceptions include Marcion (who favored Pauline works), the "Alogoi" (a small group who rejected the *logos* doctrine found in the Johannine writings), and possibly Jerome; see further in Guthrie, *Introduction*, 931.

[45] David Aune, *Revelation 1–5*, WBC 52a (Dallas: Word, 1996), cxxxvi–cxxxviii.

[46] Those acquainted with New Testament textual criticism are aware that the Sinaiticus manuscript usually goes hand in hand with the Vaticanus manuscript. Vaticanus, however, is missing Revelation.

[47] Aune, *Revelation 1–5*, cxxxviii.

There are 293 minuscule (cursive) medieval manuscripts of Revelation currently known, which means that the evidence for the Greek text of Revelation is found in barely more than 300 handwritten documents.[48] These can all be generally categorized as belonging to one of two traditions: first, those which follow readings found in Andreas of Caesarea's commentary on Revelation (late 500s or early 600s); second, those that are purely Byzantine.[49]

As is usual for the rest of the New Testament, the text of Revelation is also witnessed in a variety of other ancient sources. These include certain Greek and Latin fathers as well as early translations of Revelation (Old Latin, Vulgate, Armenian, Georgian, Coptic, Ethiopic, and Syriac). These are all appropriately referenced, of course, in the textual apparatus of the standard critical editions of the Greek New Testament.

The unusual textual history of Revelation has one more fascinating twist. Desiderius Erasmus, the great humanist scholar and later theological opponent of Martin Luther, determined to publish the Greek New Testament for the first time. In his haste he had access to only one twelfth-century Greek manuscript of Revelation, and it was missing the last six verses. Therefore, Erasmus translated the Vulgate of Revelation backward from Latin into Greek. In so doing he introduced several readings into the Greek text of Revelation that were unknown until his 1516 published Greek Testament. These errors made their way into the *Textus Receptus* and were not seriously challenged until the rise of textual criticism as a science in the nineteenth century.[50]

Despite these challenges to establishing the original wording of the text of Revelation, scholars have made significant progress. Modern critical editions of the Greek text (such as those of the United Bible Societies and the Nestle-Aland editions) have virtually recovered the original wording of the inspired text. Today's readers of the Greek (and English) text of Revelation may be confident of the wording of the original. With Revelation—as with the

---

[48] This standard work is H. C. Hoskier, *Concerning the Text of the Apocalypse* (London: Bernard Quartich, 1929). The minuscules are exhaustively listed and described in Aune, *Revelation 1–5*, cclx–clxvii.

[49] Uncial manuscript 025 ("P") is considered a representative of the "Andreas" stream; uncial 046 is a representative of the Byzantine type.

[50] Bruce M. Metzger, *The Text of the New Testament: Its Transmission, Corruption, and Restoration*, 2d ed. (New York: Oxford, 1968), 99–100. The major study of the Greek text of Revelation remains H. C. Hoskier, *Concerning the Text of the Apocalypse.*.

rest of the New Testament—it is wise to be aware of alternatives to the critical text as indicated in the critical apparatus (of the Greek Testament) or in translator's footnotes (in English versions).

Unity

Was Revelation originally composed and published in the form in which it now exists? For those who accept apostolic authorship, the answer must be yes. No Greek manuscripts know of any form of Revelation other than as the complete literary work now extant. Not surprisingly, however, with the rise of historical criticism of the Bible, some have argued that Revelation originally existed in several pieces that have been put together as an edited product. The bases of these arguments were observations of supposed internal contradictions within the book. In general three varieties of this view have been proposed:[51]

- Revelation originated as several short (Jewish apocalyptic) sources that have been Christianized and brought together by an editor.
- Revelation originated as a Jewish apocalypse that was reworked by a Christian editor.
- Revelation originated as a Christian work into which an editor incorporated fragments of Jewish apocalypses in several places.

The recent trend in New Testament scholarship has shifted from an interest in historical criticism. (What sources and processes lay *behind* the biblical texts as we now have them?) The newer emphasis is in what might be called literary criticism. (What can be understood about the shape of the biblical texts *as they now exist?*)[52] The same is true for Revelation. None of the historical-critical theories of composition ever really caught on with a majority of scholars, and all seem at present to be more or less arbitrary; the critics see lack of unity wherever they want to see it. To presuppose the original unity of the book is by far the best way to account for the appearance of unity evident within the book. The supposed

---

[51] See Guthrie, *Introduction*, 968–70 for a fuller discussion that lists critics associated with each of these varieties.

[52] See also the section below, "Revelation Studies in the Twentieth Century."

contradictions found between parts of the book may be accounted for as the "normal variations in literary productions of an apocalyptic kind."[53]

Old Testament Foundations

Revelation is filled with references to the Old Testament, but John rarely if ever quoted it directly. For example, the editors of the fourth edition of the United Bible Societies' *The Greek New Testament* have not acknowledged any direct citations from the Old Testament. The translators of the Holman Christian Standard Bible acknowledge only 1:7 (= Dan 7:13; Zech 12:10) and 2:27 (= Ps 2:9). On the other hand, there are hundreds of allusions to the Old Testament. The books of Ezekiel and Daniel are the most important background books for interpreting Revelation. Exodus, Psalms, Jeremiah, and Zechariah are also significant for understanding the book.[54]

Because Revelation does not quote the Old Testament, it is impossible to know which form of Scripture the author knew. The allusions depart both from the wording of the Septuagint (LXX) and from the Hebrew text. Three degrees of closeness to Old Testament passages may be noted:[55]

- *Clear allusions.* The wording is close to word-for-word like the Old Testament and could hardly have anything but a particular Old Testament passage in mind.
- *Probable allusions.* The wording is not close but contains ideas that are clearly based on a particular Old Testament passage.
- *Possible allusions.* The wording is reminiscent of an Old Testament text but cannot be shown to be based on a particular passage.

Readers of Revelation who know the Old Testament may find the following points of connection.

---

[53] Guthrie, *Introduction*, 970.

[54] Beale, *Revelation*, 77; Easley, *Revelation*, 2. Only Joshua, Ruth, 1 Chronicles, Ezra, Ecclesiastes, Song of Solomon, Jonah, Habakkuk, and Haggai are without any reference in Revelation.

[55] Beale, *Revelation*, 78.

- *Modeling.* An Old Testament event has served as a proto-type for an event in Revelation. For example, the plagues of Exodus 4–11 are evidently the models for understanding the trumpet plagues and the bowl plagues of Revelation 8 and 16. Ezekiel 37–48 provides a foundation for Revelation 20–22.
- *Thematic development.* The "Day of the Lord" is an example of an Old Testament motif that Revelation assumes and develops. Important ideas such as "judgment of evil" or "persecution of God's people" are Old Testament notions that find ultimate expression in Revelation.
- *Transposing Old Testament expectation.* Occasionally Revelation teaches something that seems to be the reverse of what the Old Testament anticipated. These may be thought of as biblical par-adoxes. The easiest example is Rev 3:9, that Jews will become subject to (Gentile) Christians—reversing such passages as Isa 45:14. In another example, Dan 7:21 (the "horn" that overpow-ers the "saints") is reversed so that Michael and his angels over-power the horned serpent (Rev 12:7 8).

Because Revelation is the capstone for the New Testament, it is not surprising that in many ways it recapitulates much of the Old Testament as well. Diligent students of Revelation do well to make generous use of the cross-references to Old Testament texts found in study editions of the Bible (or in the cross-reference apparatus of critical editions of the Greek New Testament). The United Bible Societies' *Greek New Testament* provides an outstanding "Index of Allusions and Verbal Parallels," another valuable resource for this kind of study.

Numbers, Colors, and Sounds

More than any other New Testament book, Revelation relies on numbers and colors to communicate its message. The large specific numbers in the book (666, 1,000, 12,000, and 144,000) challenge every interpreter. Are they to be understood literally, or do they have symbolic value? Entire theological systems have been built around interpretations of "1,000 years" in Revelation 20.

On the other hand, the use of smaller numbers—above all the number seven—seems to have symbolic value. The following may be suggested:

- Fractions: Incompleteness; partialness (6:8; 8:7; 9:15)
- Four: The earth or land (7:1–2; 20:8)[56]
- Five: Punishment (9:5)
- Seven: God or heaven (4:5; 5:1,6; 8:2; 10:4)
- Twelve: Completeness, entirety (12:1; 21:12; 22:2)

Colors are noticeably absent from most pages of the New Testament. The book of Revelation brims with color descriptions, as might be expected due to the visual nature of the book. The symbolic value of the colors may be as follows:

- White: Purity or holiness (1:14; 3:4; 6:11; 7:14; 19:11; 20:11)
- Green: Death (6:8)
- Gold: Value or worth (1:12; 3:18; 5:8; 14:14; 21:18)
- Red: Sin (6:4; 12:3)
- Black: Famine (6:5)

Sounds figure prominently in Revelation, although probably not in a symbolic way. They seek to gain attention, impress, and overwhelm the reader or listener. Examples include:

- Jesus' trumpet-like voice (1:10)
- A voice like many waters (1:15)
- Living creatures and elders chanting or singing (4:8–11)
- Martyrs calling (6:9–10)
- Seven trumpets sounding (8:7–12)
- Seven thunders speaking (10:3)
- A woman screaming in labor (12:1–2)
- Merchants lamenting (18:11)
- Hallelujahs (19:1–6)

Poetry

More than other New Testament books, Revelation contains poetry. Repetition of thought rather than rhyming or rhythm is the key element. Not all scholars agree on the extent or identification of

---

[56] The most prominent "four" is the four living creatures, prominently in chapters 4–5. They evidently represent an excellent example from each of the four categories of creatures on the earth (but not the seas): wild (lion), domestic (ox), human, flying (eagle).

certain passages as poetry. The 31 poems in the list are based on the fourth edition of the United Bible Societies' *Greek New Testament*.

The five kinds of poetry may be briefly described:

- Hymn (17 total): Praise for God's person and work
- Prophecy (7 total): Prediction of divine certainties
- Lament (4 total): Sorrow because of death
- Portrayal (3 total): Vivid description of a character

Passages set as prose rather than poetry in the twenty-seventh edition of the Nestle-Aland text are indicated in the following list by an asterisk following the reference in the list.

Reference	Speaker/Writer	Kind	Summary of Contents
1:7	John	Prophecy	Every eye will see Him
2:26b–27*	Jesus	Prophecy	One who overcomes will rule
3:7b*	Jesus	Portrayal	The One with the key
4:8b	Four living creatures	Hymn	Holy, holy, holy
4:11	24 elders	Hymn	God, you are worthy
5:9–10	Creatures and elders	Hymn	Lamb, you are worthy
5:12	Thousands of angels	Hymn	Worthy is the Lamb
5:13	All created beings	Hymn	Glory to God and the Lamb

Reference	Speaker/Writer	Kind	Summary of Contents
7:10	White-robed throng	Hymn	Salvation to our God
7:12	Angels, elders, creatures	Hymn	Amen, amen
7:15–17[+]	One of the elders	Prophecy	Promises to tribulation victims
10:5b–6*	John	Portrayal	The One who lives forever
11:15b	Loud heavenly voices	Hymn	Our Lord will rule forever
11:17–18	24 elders	Hymn	The time for judgment
12:10–12	Loud heavenly voice	Portrayal	The accuser of the brothers
13:9–10a	John	Prophecy	Destined for doom
15:3b–4	Victors over the beast	Hymn	Who will not fear You?
16:5–6	Angel of the waters	Hymn	You gave them blood to drink
16:7	Voice from the altar	Hymn	Your judgments are true
18:2–3*	Angel with authority	Prophecy	Fall of Babylon the Great
18:4–8*	Another heavenly voice	Prophecy	Come out of sinful Babylon

[+] Nestle-Aland begins with verse 14.

Reference	Speaker/Writer	Kind	Summary of Contents
18:10	Kings of the earth	Lament	Woe because of Babylon's doom
18:14	Merchants of the earth	Lament	Babylon's splendor gone
18:16	Merchants of the earth	Lament	Woe because wealth is gone
18:19–20	Mariners of the earth	Lament	Woe to Babylon but joy to heaven
18:21–24	Strong angel with a stone	Prophecy	Babylon will never rise again
19:1–2	Great heavenly throng	Hymn	First hallelujah chorus
19:3	Great heavenly throng	Hymn	Second hallelujah chorus
19:4	Creatures and elders	Hymn	Third hallelujah chorus
19:5	Voice from the throne	Hymn	Praise our God
19:6–8	Great throng	Hymn	Fourth hallelujah chorus

Structure and Outline

Although some continue to debate the point, the *literary* structure of Revelation is fairly straightforward. Three important markers show how the main body (not counting the epistolary introduction and conclusion, discussed earlier under "genre") is organized. First, each of the four series of "sevens" develops a particular concept (churches, seals, trumpets, and bowls). Second, there is clear indication of four great visions, of which the second is the longest.[57] The beginning of each vision is announced with the words "in the Spirit" (1:10; 4:2; 17:3; 21:10), which apparently means, "I had a new vision brought about by the Holy Spirit." Third, the phrase "great sign" (12:1; 15:1) marks the beginning of a new section. This results in the following organizational pattern for the book:

1:1–8	Epistolary prologue
1:9–3:22	**Vision 1: Jesus and the Seven Churches**
	1:9–20 — Opening vision (the exalted Jesus)
	2:1–3:22 — Seven (imperfect) earthly churches
4:1–16:21	**Vision 2: Seals, Trumpets, and Bowls**
	4:1–5:14 — Opening vision (the throne and the Lamb)
	6:1–8:6 — Seven seals opened
	8:7–11:19 — Seven trumpets blown
	12:1–14:20 — Visionary interlude
	15:1–16:21 — Seven bowls poured out
17:1–21:8	**Vision 3: Prostitute City and Bride City**
	17:1–19:5 — Babylon, the prostitute
	19:6–20:15 — Wedding (and victory) of the Lamb
	21:1–8 — New Jerusalem, the bride
21:9–22:5	**Vision 4: Heaven on Earth**
	21:9–27 — One (perfect) heavenly city
	22:1–5 — Closing vision (the exalted servants)
22:6–21	Epistolary epilogue

---

[57] Ladd, *Revelation*, 15–16.

Survey of Contents

The author's previous commentary on Revelation was organized around the main idea and supporting ideas for each of Revelation's 22 chapters.[58] These are here adapted as an expanded summary of the message of each chapter of the book.

Revelation 1. The exalted Lord Jesus, who walks spiritually among his churches, gave John a revelation of himself that focuses on his certain glorious return.

> **1:1–3.** This book is a prophecy that Jesus revealed to John for him to record. God blesses all those who obey its teachings.
>
> **1:4–8.** Jesus is worthy of all praise because of who He is and what He has done. His second coming will be glorious and public because the Lord God Almighty will make it happen.
>
> **1:9–20.** One Lord's day Jesus appeared to John in symbolic form that emphasized both His humanity and His deity, so John responded in worship.

Revelation 2. Jesus knows the strengths and weaknesses of each local congregation and gives them proper compliments and challenges.

> **2:1–7.** Christ compliments the Ephesian Christians for their many good deeds but criticizes them because they no longer love one another as they used to do.
>
> **2:8–11.** Christ commends the Smyrnan Christians for enduring persecution and pledges them eternal life, even though their troubles are about to intensify for a short time.
>
> **2:12–17.** Christ commends the congregation in Pergamum for maintaining their commitment to Him, even though some have perverted moral truths.
>
> **2:18–29.** A false teacher was leading many Christians of Thyatira to embrace open immorality, but an all-knowing, all-powerful Lord will punish her followers severely.

---

[58] Easley, *Revelation*, passim.

Revelation 3. Jesus continues to give the proper compliments and challenges to local congregations because He knows their strengths and weaknesses.

> **3:1–6.** Christ criticizes the majority of the Sardian Christians for being spiritually asleep, so they must repent and return to their earlier spiritual liveliness.
>
> **3:7–13.** Christ encourages the congregation of Philadelphia to take heart that the open door to heaven is theirs despite human and satanic hostility and to "hold on" as Christ promises to protect them in the face of a coming worldwide trial.
>
> **3:14–22.** The church of Laodicea is guilty of such self-sufficiency that they must repent and receive Christ's provision of righteousness in order again to experience intimate fellowship with him.

Revelation 4. God on His heavenly throne is praised without end by His court of throne-room guardians who shout and sing about their holy Creator.

> **4:1–2a.** The One who first spoke to John summons him to come through a heavenly door to see what will certainly take place.
>
> **4:2b–6a.** In heaven God dazzles like jewels on His throne, and there are crowned elder-angels and other wonderful sights.
>
> **4:6b–8.** The four ever-watching six-winged guardians of God's throne appear to be something like various earthly creatures. Their ceaseless praise celebrates God's holiness and power.
>
> **4:9–11.** The 24 elders worship God by falling down and offering their crowns and by singing in honor of God's creative power in making and sustaining all there is.

Revelation 5. Worthy to open the judgment scroll of destiny, Christ the slaughtered Lamb receives worship from all the heavenly court.

> **5:1–5.** Christ alone is worthy and able to break the seals and open the judgment scroll written and

sealed up by God, for only Christ can enact the coming judgments.

5:6–8. Christ is like a slaughtered lamb, and He takes the judgment scroll from God's hand as the heavenly court falls down in worship.

5:9–14. The elders, the angels, and the entire universe praise the Lamb.

Revelation 6. Between Christ's two comings military aggression will keep terrorizing humanity. Christians will continue to be martyred. Natural disasters will wreak havoc.

6:1–8. Since Christ's first coming conquest, warfare, famine, and death ravage humanity, but God limits their power.

6:9–11. Between the two comings of Christ, the number of martyrs will continue to grow, but Christ will bestow special honors on such martyrs.

6:12–17. God permits natural disasters that cause people to respond by seeking to preserve themselves and by blaming God.

Revelation 7. All those whom God marks as His own people will without fail one day enter His presence victorious forever.

7:1–8. A large and specific group of people (perhaps all Christians living on earth before the trumpet judgments) will be spared the experience of His wrath outpoured on earth.

7:9–17. Multitudes of the redeemed come out of great tribulation entering the presence of God and worshipping Him.

Revelation 8. A great period of tribulation unfolds with four plagues in which a third of earth, sea, rivers, and heavenly bodies are destroyed.

8:1–6. At the breaking of the seventh seal a new phase of God's judgment begins as the seven angels prepare to blow their trumpets.

8:7–12. With the blowing of the first four trumpets the world of nature is devastated as a warning for people to repent of their sins.

8:13. A great flying bird of prey announces that the coming three judgments will be especially horrible.

Revelation 9. God allows demonic forces to torture unbelievers with pain, and other demonic forces kill a third of humanity.

9:1–12. Fierce and terrifying demons unleash for a limited time a plague of painful misery.

9:13–21. A second multitude of demons slaughters a third of the human race, but even so the survivors refuse to repent of their wickedness.

Revelation 10. The sounding of the seventh trumpet will bring about the full completion of God's judgment plan, and His word is both sweet and bitter to those who receive it.

10:1–4. A glorious angel, probably Gabriel, descends. "The thunders" reply with a judgment message that John was not allowed to record.

10:5–7. The glorious angel swears a solemn oath that God's purposes will be brought to their climactic conclusion without delay with the sounding of the seventh trumpet.

10:8–11. John eats the glorious angel's small scroll, a message both sweet and sour, because the people of God must suffer further before the end comes.

Revelation 11. The ungodly world silences for a short time a prophetic witness, but then the angelic blowing of the seventh trumpet heralds the consummation of all things.

11:1–13. Powerful witnesses during the final days of great suffering are scorned by the world but vindicated by God in a way that terrifies their enemies.

11:14–19. The blowing of the seventh trumpet proclaims Christ's long-awaited public reign, beginning with the time of judgment both for God's saints and for those who are depraved.

Revelation 12. The great story that explains the consummation begins by highlighting the ongoing bitter spiritual warfare of the devil against Christ and His people.

> 12:1–6. God sees His people idealized as a resplendent woman. He sees Christ as the King of destiny and the devil as a powerful, hostile dragon. Much of human history is about the devil's hatred against Christ and God's people.
>
> 12:7–12. Before Christ's return the devil loses his status as accuser of the brothers. This advances the kingdom of God, bringing joy to heaven but grief to earth.
>
> 12:13–17. The devil will never be able to destroy the church as a whole, but he makes terrible war against those who obey God's commands.

Revelation 13. The great drama that explains the consummation continues by showing that corrupt political and religious powers will climax in two wicked and powerful persons—the Antichrist and the false prophet.

> 13:1–10. Throughout the ages God has seen political evil as a horrible water monster. This beast becomes a personal, powerful Antichrist that receives worship and wages war against God's people.
>
> 13:11–18. Throughout the ages God has seen religious evil as a horrible earth monster. This beast becomes a personal false prophet that brings about the loyalty of earth's people to Antichrist.

Revelation 14. The great drama concludes by previewing the victorious Lamb's perfected people, telling final angelic warnings of judgment, and picturing the return of Christ both as a harvest (of the righteous) and as a vintage (of the wicked).

> 14:1–5. All the people of God sealed in Revelation 7 are now seen in their glorified condition because God has powerfully protected every one of His servants.

14:6–13. Three angels proclaim the arrival of judgment and the fall of Babylon the Great. The Spirit promises everlasting rest to the Christian dead.

14:14–16. The return of Christ for His saints is pictured in terms of a grain harvest (as Jesus Himself did in the Gospels).

14:17–20. The return of Christ for the wicked is pictured in terms of a grape harvest in which the winepress of God's wrath overflows (as the prophets did in the Old Testament).

Revelation 15. The victorious people of Christ praise Him with a song. Then the seven last plagues of God's wrath are announced.

15:1–4. One way the victorious people of Christ praise Him is by singing "The Song of the Lamb."

15:5–8. The avenging angels who will pour out the last plagues come out of the heavenly temple, where the holiness of God is expressed with awesome power.

Revelation 16. God's final display of wrath unravels the forces of nature and the forces of Antichrist, pointing to one final battle on the great day of God Almighty.

16:1–9. The first four bowls of wrath intensify and conclude the devastation of nature that began with the first four trumpet judgments.

16:10–16. The fifth and sixth bowls of wrath cause Antichrist's political, economic, and religious control to disintegrate.

16:17–21. The seventh bowl completes both the devastation of nature with the ultimate earthquake and the final devastation of the beast.

Revelation 17. The final product of civilization is seen as a great wicked city, persecutor of God's people, destined for the wrath of God.

17:1–6. Civilization is portrayed as an extravagant, drunken prostitute, riding on the Antichrist monster.

17:7–18. Antichrist, an eighth and final head of the seven-headed sea monster, brings about the destruction of the great city and, in turn, will go to destruction.

Revelation 18. When God destroys godless civilization (a great wicked city), its commerce and culture will vanish forever because it enticed people away from true religion and holiness into false religion and impurity.

18:1–8. The angelic announcement of Babylon's doom includes a warning for God's people to come out of her.

18:9–19. Monarchs, merchants, and mariners lead the mourning at the death of Babylon because of their own losses.

18:20–24. Because she persecuted God's people, all activities in Babylon cease as quickly and totally as a boulder thrown into the sea sinks from view.

Revelation 19. With heavenly "hallelujahs" resounding, Christ returns to earth as conquering King of kings, with birds sent to gorge on the corpses while the Lamb's bride enjoys her wedding feast.

19:1–5. Just as three earthly groups lamented Babylon's fall, so three sets of heavenly voices shout hallelujah for Babylon's fall.

19:6–10. The consummation of the ages is compared to a great marriage and the wedding supper of the Lamb.

19:11–16. The return of Christ is pictured as a glorious King coming from heaven accompanied by his faithful armies.

19:17–21. At His return Christ conquers all his opponents, with the Antichrist and false prophet the first to be thrown into the fiery lake.

Revelation 20. After the martyrs have been gloriously rewarded for their sacrifice and the devil has been finally forever defeated, Christ judges all the dead at the last judgment.

20:1–6. After Satan is bound in the abyss, the martyrs live and rule with Christ, their special reward given at last.

20:7–10. After Satan has deceived the nations of the world into one last battle against God's people, he is thrown into his final place of eternal fiery torment.

20:11–15. At the last judgment only those whose names have been written in the book of life escape being sent into eternal torment by Christ the Judge.

Revelation 21. The bride city of the Lamb (New Jerusalem) descends to earth in the new creation. Christ is eternally present with His people.

21:1–8. The arrival of the New Jerusalem symbolizes God's everlasting presence among His resurrected, redeemed people.

21:9–21. The fourth vision of Revelation begins with an angelic tour that highlights the features of the New Jerusalem viewed from the outside.

21:22–27. The eternal presence of God and Christ among the redeemed is described in terms of never-ending light.

Revelation 22. The glories of the final state of the redeemed are assured because of the solemn truthfulness of this prophecy. The Lord Jesus will return soon.

22:1–5. In Jesus' eternal presence, the final state of redeemed humanity with the river of life and the tree of life greatly surpasses the garden of Eden in splendor.

22:6–16. Several persons confirm the truthfulness and certainty of the entire book.

22:17–21. Because Christ is coming soon, all people are invited to come and partake of His gift of eternal life.

Views of the Millennium

Every survey of the theological implications of Revelation must take into account the four major interpretive perspectives concerning the meaning of "the thousand years" in chapter 20. The following descriptions are included here with little elaboration for the sake of the historical discussion that follows. The views are listed in the order in which they developed among Christian interpreters.

Premillennialism

Premillennialists teach that after His visible, bodily return, Christ will rule literally and visibly on the earth for a thousand (or for an indefinite number of) years. Believers will enjoy prestige and power with Him as He rules the nations with an iron scepter. After this will come one last human rebellion, to be crushed by Christ, and then the new heavens and the new earth. Those who held this view before the medieval period called it "chiliasm," based on the Greek word *chilias*, "1,000."

Today's adherents who identify with this ancient view are apt to call themselves "historical premillennialists" to distinguish themselves from "dispensational premillennialists" (see below). Premillennialism—in both its historical and dispensational forms— is the most pessimistic of the views regarding the course of this age and the success of worldwide gospel proclamation.

Amillennialism

This view dominated throughout the entire medieval period. Many denominations and individuals still hold the view. Rather than deny the thousand-year reign (as the name may suggest), adherents hold that the millennium is the spiritual (but invisible to earthly eyes) rule of saints during the period between the first and second comings of Christ.

This reign has been variously understood as the saints' experience of victorious living during their earthly life or as the saints' enjoyment of victory in heaven with Christ after their bodies die as they wait for His return. Of all the views this is the simplest. It is neutral regarding the course of this age and the success of the spread of the gospel.

Postmillennialism

Adherents of this post-Reformation development of amillennialism hold that the spread of the gospel will become so globally successful that the world as a whole will become Christianized. The spiritual victory of believers will become visible and embraced by the world's peoples. A long worldwide era of peace and goodwill will ensue, and Christ will at length return to the adoring world like a king returning from a long voyage.

This view almost disappeared after the tragic events of World War I—in which both sides claimed to be Christian—shattered belief that world peace was at hand.[59] Postmillennialism is the most optimistic of the views regarding the course of this age and the worldwide success of gospel proclamation.

Dispensationalism

This nineteenth-century development of premillennialism, unlike the previous three views, maintains a rigorous distinction between "Israel" and "church." God's promises concerning ancient Israel's restoration as the head of the nations will be literally fulfilled. A restored national Israel will enjoy prestige and power with Christ.

Dispensationalists believe that Revelation tells about a future tribulation for Jews (from which the church is exempted by its secret rapture). The future millennium is for Jews in which Gentile Christians are more or less secondary figures. As Israelite culture flourished under Solomon the king, so it will flourish perfectly under Christ the King. After this will come one last rebellion, to be crushed by Christ, and then the new heavens and the new earth.

History of Interpretation

The First Four Centuries

The earliest Christian writers who referred to Revelation believed that its prophecies would be fulfilled literally, just as many Jewish scholars had believed that their apocalypses would be literally fulfilled. All taught a form of chiliasm. These figures include Justin Martyr and Irenaeus (see earlier discussion under "authorship"), who expected vicious persecution of Christians by the Roman beast or Antichrist and Christ's return very soon. Hippolytus (died 235) expected the millennium to begin in the year 500. Victorinus (martyred 303) believed

---

[59] Postmillennialism survives today through a number of nineteenth-century hymns that are still popular and sung enthusiastically, even by premillennialists. Among these are the carol, "It Came upon the Midnight Clear," and the missionary song, "We've a Story to Tell to the Nations."

he was living in the days of the sixth seal and that Nero would soon come back to life as the beast or Antichrist. He was apparently the first to teach the recapitulation theory of Revelation—that the events described do not follow a continuous chronological series but rather some passages recapitulate (restate from another perspective) previous passages, a view often suggested by today's interpreters.

An allegorical (spiritualizing) approach for interpreting all of Scripture grew in influence by the end of this period. Origen, the famous interpreter of Alexandria (died c. 254), opposed chiliasm. He believed the Lord's return would be invisible, in spirit, and that the visions of Revelation must be understood allegorically (e.g., the seven heads of the dragon were the seven deadly sins). When the Roman Empire became officially Christian after Constantine's conversion, it was no longer conceivable for Christian teachers to equate either emperor or empire with the beast or Antichrist.

The Donatist sect, through their interpreter Ticonius, believed that the millennial kingdom and the millennial reign of the saints occurred to the true church (i.e., themselves) during the period between the first and second comings of Christ. Augustine's interpretation of Revelation is found in *The City of God*, the most influential book of Christian theology for a thousand years. His approach was similar to that of Ticonius (avoiding the errors of the Donatists). After the triumph of the allegorical approach to Scripture, chiliasm ceased to be presented as an interpretation for Revelation.[60]

The Medieval Period (from AD 400 to AD 1500)

This period reflected the dominance of the allegorizing hermeneutic applied to all Scripture, not only to Revelation. Two sixth-century commentators essentially continued the influence of Ticonius's spiritualizing approach. Andreas (bishop of Caesarea) wrote the fullest and most influential Greek commentary. He believed the thousand-year kingdom began with Christ's earthly life and would continue until knowledge of Christ was complete and worldwide. On the other hand, he did believe in a future beast or Antichrist as a real human person. About the same time Primasius (bishop of Hadrumetum in Africa) wrote an influential Latin commentary in which he credited Ticonius and Augustine and adopted little that was new.

---

[60] This section is based on Ibson T. Beckwith, *The Apocalypse of John* (1919; repr., Grand Rapids: Baker, 1967), 318–25.

A great deal of interest in Christ's return was sparked by the year 1000. If the "1,000 years" of Revelation had begun with Christ's first appearance, then probably the end was not far away. By this time, moreover, it was evident that within Christendom corrupting forces had been at work. Joachim (abbot of Fiore, died 1201) wrote an influential work in which the events of his own time were seen as presaged in Revelation. He saw the beast or Antichrist as Islam, wounded by the Crusades yet now restored. The false prophet equaled the heretics of his day, from which the church must be purified. He anticipated a literal future millenium (to begin in 1260) in which monastic life would become the universal ideal, after which Christ would return.

A new approach appeared with Nicolas of Lyra (teacher of theology in Paris, died 1340). He argued that Revelation was a prophecy about all of Christian history throughout time. He was able to find many specific details—the rise of Islam, the Crusades, Charlemagne—all predicted, but he believed the millennium was already (spiritually) present.[61]

Reformation and Enlightenment Periods (from AD 1500 to AD 1900)

Nicolas's view that all of Christian history was previewed in Revelation became fairly standard as the view all interpreters held. As early as 1520, Luther branded the pope as the beast or Antichrist, soon to be brought down. John Calvin is noted in this regard because, of all the New Testament books, Revelation is the only one for which he did *not* produce a commentary. Protestant commentators characteristically interpreted Revelation based on the following three principles:

- Revelation forecasts the history of the church.
- Revelation condemns the corruption of Roman Catholicism.
- Revelation includes specific information about the commentator's own time.

Roman Catholic interpreters returned the favor: Luther and the other Reformers were Antichrist; Protestantism in its various forms was the false prophet. The Spanish Jesuit scholar Ribera's late-sixteenth-century commentary was noteworthy for a return to an approach of the earlier fathers: Up through the fifth seal, Revelation

---

[61] This section is based on Beckwith, *Apocalypse*, 325–29.

was concerned with events of the first and second centuries. Then there was a major break that lasted for centuries. Then, beginning with the sixth seal, literal events that were yet to occur were prophesied. L. Alcasar, another Spanish Jesuit, in 1614 creatively interpreted Revelation as follows. Chapters 5–11 referred to the conflict of Christianity against Judaism; chapters 12–19 dealt with the conflict of Christianity against Roman paganism; and chapters 20–22 depicted the victory of Christianity beginning with Constantine and lasting until the end of the world.

The Dutch theologian and statesman Hugo Grotius wrote an influential commentary (1644) in which he attempted to use the rules of grammar and historical setting in interpretation. He therefore denied that the pope was the beast and generally adopted the principles of Ribera and Alcasar. Henry Alford's distinguished 1884 commentary was the last great Protestant commentary based on the view that Revelation portrays church history.

Another development stemmed from the Puritan successes both in England and in New England. Many Protestants became optimistic that the Reformation marked the beginning of the time when true knowledge of Christ would soon spread around the world. The golden age prophesied in the OT was about to be fulfilled in the church. Christ would at length come back to a world eager to receive him. This postmillennialism also enjoyed support because of the growth of the modern missionary movement in the eighteenth and nineteenth centuries. The successful completion of Christ's Great Commission would result ultimately in a golden age of worldwide peace.

With the coming of the Enlightenment in Europe, it was only a matter of time until more scientific approaches to the Bible developed. For example, J. G. Eichhorn, a pioneer in historical criticism, developed in 1791 a theory that Revelation was a great historical poem, picturing dramatically and poetically the victory of Christianity over Judaism (Jerusalem) and paganism (Rome). Inevitably, from that point onward biblical interpretation in general (and Revelation interpretation in particular) began focusing on the context of the original author and readers, looking for the original practical purposes of the book.

Inquiries into the relationship of Revelation to Jewish apocalyptic literature and critical study of the unity of Revelation (i.e., sources used by John) became the new focus of attention. Because many historical-critical scholars rejected the notion that the Bible (including Revelation) contained genuine prophecy, they were no longer willing to seek in Revelation any reliable predictions at all. Theology was suppressed, and "scientific" interpretations of Revelation prevailed.[62]

In the English-speaking Protestant world, a theological shift began in some quarters because of the popular success of Irish Plymouth Brethren leader J. N. Darby (1800–1882), the acknowledged founder of dispensationalism. His thought marked a return to the chiliasm of the early fathers with an innovative twist: the thousand years of Revelation 20 would be the time that Christ ruled a glorified *Israel*.[63] This view was championed in the United States by C. I. Scofield (1843–1921), friend of Dwight L. Moody, who became a popular Bible conference speaker and editor of the highly influential *Scofield Reference Bible* (1909).

Schools of Interpretation

By common consent, interpretations of Revelation can be organized into four perspectives. A fifth view, which may be termed "eclectic," draws from the others.

Preterist Views

Most critical interpreters of Revelation see the book essentially in terms of its original readers. Its message was directed to the past (*preter* is Latin for "past"). Those who hold to a Neronian (early) date have argued that "Babylon" was corrupt Judaism (opposed to Christianity) and was judged by Jesus by the fall of Jerusalem in AD 70.[64] Those who date Revelation in Domitian's time see "Babylon" as Rome. The book predicts the fall of the Roman Empire, which occurred in the fifth century AD. A more radical form of this view is that the author was mistaken in his (devout but misguided) "prophecies."

---

[62] This section is based on Beckwith, *Apocalypse*, 330–34.

[63] Dispensationalism by definition distinguishes sharply between the dispensation of law (Moses to Christ), grace (the church age), and kingdom (the millennium for Israel). Dispensationalists think of the church as a kind of parenthesis between the two dispensations of God's dealing with Israel (law and kingdom). Thus, they necessarily hold to pretribulationism: that "the church" will be removed from the earth at "the rapture" before God resumes His direct dealings with Israel again during "the great tribulation" immediately before the return of Christ. The classic dispensational commentary is by John F. Walvoord, *The Revelation of Jesus Christ* (Chicago: Moody, 1966).

[64] Kenneth L. Gentry Jr., *Before Jerusalem Fell: Dating the Book of Revelation* (Tyler, TX: Institute for Christian Economics, 1989).

This view is sometimes called the contemporary-historical (*zeit-geschichtlich*) view. The strength of this approach is that it gives proper attention to the original setting of the book. The weakness is that those who hold to this view find only indirect value in studying Revelation today since no future element is left. R. H. Charles's commentary is well established as the (critical) preterist standard.

Historicist Views

Beginning in the late medieval period and going through the Reformation and post-Reformation periods, Revelation was largely seen as a forecast of history up to the time of the interpreter. All manner of events are there to behold: the conversion of the Roman Empire, the rise of Islam, the Crusades, the Reformation, Napoleon, Mussolini.

This perspective is sometimes called the church-historical (*kirchengeschichtlich*) view. The strength of this approach is that it made Revelation "come alive" for the people living in the interpreter's own time. The weakness is that no two persons who hold to this view can agree on the details; further, there would have been little value in studying Revelation by the original readers. Contemporary interpreters have largely abandoned this view.

Futurist Views

A variety of interpretations of Revelation hold that the book is mainly about specific events that will happen at the (still future) end of the age, beginning at 4:1 (or 6:1 or 8:1). In the twentieth century, the dispensational form of futurism gained growing influence, largely because of powerful pulpit ministries. According to dispensationalism, Revelation teaches the following sequence:[65]

- Jews restored to their promised land in a national identity;
- the rapture of Christians before the tribulation;
- seven years of tribulation against Jews, who at last turn to Christ;
- Antichrist's rule over a united world;
- Christ's second coming and defeat of Antichrist;
- Christ's 1,000-year rule over redeemed Israel;
- the final rebellion of Satan and last war;

[65] See Beale, *Revelation*, 47.

- the last judgment; and
- the final state: new heavens and new earth.

A more moderate form of futurism,[66] with roots going back to the early chiliast interpreters of Revelation (and often including recapitulation in its understanding of the events of Revelation), sees the following taught in Revelation:[67]

- Antichrist's rule over much of the world;
- a limited-duration tribulation against Christians;
- Christ's second coming and defeat of Antichrist;
- (Christ's 1,000-year rule as King of kings);
- (the final rebellion of Satan and last war);
- the last judgment; and
- the final state—new heavens and new earth.

This view is sometimes called the eschatological (*endgeschichtlich*) view. The strength of futurist interpretations is its great insistence on the final victory of Christ against all sin and evil. The weakness of the view is that it was of no direct benefit to the original recipients, and, in its dispensational form, it is hard to know why Christians should be interested in a book that is essentially about the future of ethnic Israel.

Idealist Views

Also known as the "symbolic" perspective, this interpretive approach denies that Revelation originally intended any specific events or persons. Instead, Revelation vividly portrays the ongoing conflict between good and evil, God and Satan, Christ and anti-Christian forces. More than a century ago, William Milligan proposed that "we are not to look in the Apocalypse for special events, but for an exhibition of the principles which govern the history both of the world and the Church."[68]

Such approaches may be seen as continuations of an allegorical method of interpreting Scripture that stretches back to Origen. The strengths of such interpretations are that (1) every generation of

---

[66] Historical premillennialism and some forms of amillennialism can be identified with this perspective.

[67] See Easley, *Revelation, passim.*

[68] William Milligan, *The Revelation of St. John,* 2d ed. (London: Macmillan, 1887), 154–55.

believers can apply the message of the book, and that (2) the book itself, full of symbols, begs to be interpreted in this way. The weakness is that it denies any specific consummation to human history. There is no literal second coming of Christ.

Eclectic Views

Realizing that all of the major perspectives have strengths and weaknesses, some interpreters have adopted parts of two or more of the above. On one hand, a moderate futurist view can easily incorporate elements of the preterist view. On the other hand, an essentially symbolic interpretation can incorporate a few futurist elements, in particular affirming a final consummation and judgment in the (future) visible return of Christ.[69]

Revelation Studies in the Twentieth Century

At the beginning of the twentieth century, New Testament scholarship was generally focusing on matters of sources and historical background of the books. (Easily the most well-known example of this focus is the postulation of "Q" as a source for Matthew and Luke.) By the last third of the century, scholarly attention was turning to other areas: genre, social background, and literary technique. This turn of attention held true for Revelation as well.[70] The following are examples of the kinds of questions that have been asked (and answered):

- Could a "Christian prophetic circle" have produced Revelation?[71]
- What can we know about the social background of Revelation?[72]
- Can we know more about "apocalyptic" as a genre?[73]

---

[69] Beale (*Revelation*) 48, prefers "eclecticism" as a convenient summary for his view, which he otherwise called "a redemptive-historical form of modified idealism."

[70] See Elizabeth Schüssler Fiorenza, *The Book of Revelation: Justice and Judgment* (Philadelphia: Fortress, 1985), 12–32.

[71] David E. Aune, "The Prophetic Circle of John of Patmos and the Exegesis of Revelation 22:16," *JSNT* 37 (1989): 103–16.

[72] Adela Yarbro Collins, *Crisis and Catharsis: The Power of the Apocalypse* (Philadelphia: Westminster, 1984).

[73] David Hellholm, ed., *Apocalypticism in the Mediterranean World and the Near East* (Tübingen: Mohr, 1983).

Dispensational	Purely Futurist	Preterist-Futurist	Preterist	Idealist
J. B. Smith, 1961	V. Eller, 1974	G. R. Beasley-Murray, 1970	W. Barclay, 1959	R. Calkins, 1920
M. C. Tenney, 1957	H. Lilje, 1955	I. T. Beckwith, 1922	G. B. Caird, 1966	P. Carrington, 1931
J. F. Walvoord, 1966		F. F. Bruce, 1969	R. H. Charles, 1920	W. Hendriksen, 1940
		G. E. Ladd, 1972	J. M. Ford, 1975	M. Kiddle, 1940
		L. Morris, 1969	T. F. Glasson, 1965	W. Milligan, 1909
		R. H. Mounce, 1977	W. J. Harrington, 1969	P. S. Minear, 1968
			W. H. Heidt, 1962	M. Rissi, 1966
			A. Pieters, 1954	
			R. Summers, 1951	
			J. P. M. Sweet, 1979	
			H. B. Swete, 1906	

- What historical enemies of the churches are implied in Revelation?[74]
- What accounts for John's unusual Greek?[75]
- What attitude has the church taken toward Revelation throughout the centuries?[76]

The twentieth century also saw a number of commentaries on Revelation. Alan Johnson helpfully categorized significant works. The chart on the preceding page is a summary of his conclusions.[77] There are as yet few indications about what new insights will be gained in Revelation research in the twenty-first century.

Purpose

The introductory paragraphs to this chapter suggest the present writer's understanding about the purpose of Revelation: *The book originally intended to teach that Jesus is to return to earth as King and Lamb-Bridegroom and that faithfulness to Jesus ultimately triumphs over all the evils of this world.* The main doctrinal teaching is the fact of Christ's return to destroy all opposition and to culminate His everlasting kingdom. The main practical purpose was (and is) to motivate saints to worship God and obey His word, even to the point of death.

Without doubt, however, the presuppositions one brings to Revelation about the millennial question are a major factor in shaping one's view of the book's purpose. Even more important is the matter of the interpretive school one adopts in approaching the book. As is true in many areas of biblical and theological understanding, where one begins (assumptions) often determines where one ends (conclusions). Thus, in the discussion that follows, matters are presented as broadly as possible, but

---

[74] Alan James Beagley, *The "Sitz im Leben" of the Apocalypse, with Particular Reference to the Role of the Church's Enemies*, BZNW (Berlin: de Gruyter, 1987).

[75] Gerard Mussies, *The Morphology of Koine Greek as Used in the Apocalypse of John*, NovTSup (Leiden: Brill, 1971).

[76] Gerhard Maier, *Die Johannesoffenbarung und die Kirche*, WUNT (Tübingen: Mohr, 1981).

[77] Alan F. Johnson, "Revelation," in *EBC* 13 (Grand Rapids: Zondervan, 1981), 412–13. Johnson named only nineteenth-century authors as "historicist": H. Alford, 1884, and E. B. Elliot, 1828. Of the two massive commentaries produced at the end of the twentieth century, the one by D. Aune is preterist while the one by G. Beale is idealist. G. Osborne's 2002 commentary is eclectic.

with awareness that true objectivity is neither possible nor desirable. It is intended that biblical students who identify with historical premillennialism or amillennialism, and some view of futurism or idealism, will find a measure of agreement with the following.

Doctrinal Themes

Doctrine, of course, deals with beliefs. John's initial readers surely recognized the following teachings contained in the prophecy. Modern readers are called on to affirm these truths as well.

The Second Coming of Christ

The central fact taught in Revelation is the personal visible return of Jesus Christ to earth. This begins as early as 1:7, the theme verse of the book, and continues on through Christ's solemn promises to return quickly at the end of the book (22:7,12,20), and to John's own final prayer (22:20). The longest description of the second coming in the Bible is Revelation 19. God—the One seated on heaven's throne—is seen as the primary mover who will bring about the return of Christ and the end of the world.

The Kingdom of God

During His public ministry, Jesus' first and principal message was the coming of the kingdom. In fact, God's kingdom-building plan is the best way for understanding the unity of the entire Bible.[78] The kingdom theme in Revelation can hardly be missed. Christ is the victorious King wearing many diadems. He comes and judges the world's peoples at the end. One of the great announcements in Revelation, near the center of the book, is that the kingdoms of this world have become Christ's, and that He will reign forever (11:15). Revelation shows that the divine plan to bless all nations through the covenant God began with Abraham (Gen 12) reaches final fulfillment. The kingdom of God inaugurated with Jesus' first coming will be consummated at his second coming.[79]

---

[78] See Kendell H. Easley, *Illustrated Guide to Biblical History* (Nashville: Broadman & Holman, 2003), *passim.*

[79] The twentieth-century American scholar who most helpfully uncovered the implications of the "kingdom of God" motif was George Eldon Ladd. See *Commentary on the Revelation of St. John* to see how he showed this theme in Revelation.

The Sovereignty of God in History

Revelation teaches the supremacy and glory of God in all things. No Bible book more fully teaches how God is moving time, history, and all creation to the goal He has determined. The scenes presented in the book were not meant to form a seamless story; rather Revelation zigzags through time. John recorded events from the very beginning (12:4; 17:8) to the first century AD (chaps. 2–3) to the new heavens and new earth (chaps. 21–22).[80] All is under the watchful plan of the Almighty, whose sovereignty is affirmed particularly in the throne room scene of Revelation 4.

The Holiness and Justice of God

The living creatures around heaven's throne constantly cry "holy" (4:8), and God's unique holiness is plainly affirmed (15:4). Because He is holy, He will bring justice to the world. His justice is declared by a victorious multitude (15:3) as well as by heavenly beings (16:5,7). The imagery of the great white throne in the final judgment scene overwhelmingly shows God's justice in judging the works of all the dead (20:11–15).

The Wrath of God against Evil

The righteous wrath of a holy God is fully displayed in Revelation. "Wrath" (*orgē* in Greek) occurs six times in the book (6:16,17; 11:18; 14:10; 16:19; 19:15), always with reference to divine wrath. The Father (the One on the throne) and the Son (the Lamb) equally pour out their wrath against evil. "Fury" (*thumos* in Greek) occurs 10 times in the book, but not always of divine wrath. Revelation 14:10,19; 15:1,7; 16:1,19; 19:15 are the seven instances in which the term applies to God's wrath. Revelation 16:19 and 19:15 are the two places in the book in which "wrath" and "fury" are combined in an extraordinary reference to the winepress of God's righteous anger.

The Vicious but Limited Power of Evil

Evil is painted in lurid detail throughout Revelation. Yet without fail, evil persons and forces cannot stretch their hand beyond what God's plan allows. The most vivid portraits include the following:

---

[80] For futurist interpreters, the events through chapter 3 (or 6) focus on the period up to the "great tribulation," while the things described beginning with chapter 4 (or 7) seem to belong to the end-time scenario.

- locusts from the pit, limited to five months of harm (9:1–12);
- 100,000,000 horses, who kill only a third of mankind (9:13–21);
- the seven-headed dragon, thrown into a prison and then into hell (12:3,17; 20:3,10);
- the sea beast, whose power is limited to 42 months, loses a great battle, and is then sent to hell (13:1–8; 19:19–20); and
- Babylon, the harlot city, destroyed never to rise (17:1–18:24).

Christ as Conquering King and Slaughtered Lamb

The four Gospels provide no clue about the physical appearance of Jesus during the time of His first coming. Strikingly, Revelation provides three highly symbolic descriptions of the exalted Christ.

First, He appears to John on Patmos as the glorious "Son of Man," to whom worship is the only possible response (1:12–20).

Second, He is portrayed as the rider on the white horse, the conquering King who will judge the entire world (19:11–16). Christ's return is portrayed in glorious but highly symbolic language. The shared element between the portrait of Christ as Son of Man and of Christ as conquering King is the sharp sword from His mouth with which He strikes down all opposition (1:16; 19:15).

Third is the strangest and most frequently occurring image of Christ in Revelation. He appears in heaven as the slaughtered Lamb (*arnion* in Greek), yet occupying heaven's throne (5:1–14). This imagery continues throughout the book, with *arnion* being used 29 times in all. Because of the Lamb's death, He is worthy to unroll the scroll (5:9). John heard about the wedding of the Lamb (19:7); the new Jerusalem is the wife of the Lamb (21:9); and in that city the Lamb's servants minister to him eternally (22:3).

Practical Themes

Sometimes in Scripture the practical themes—the "so what?" or the behavioral ramifications—are implicit. Sometimes interpreters have to work out the implications for readers of biblical texts. For other books the practical teachings are explicit in the text. Revelation belongs to this latter category.

Importance of Worship and Obedience for Believers

The opening paragraphs of this chapter argued that Revelation was written to motivate saints to worship God and obey His Word.[81] The great throne room scenes of chapters 4–5 invite believers to worship God on earth even as He is perfectly worshipped by the heavenly beings. John models worship of Christ (1:17). Exhortations to worship are scattered throughout the book (14:7; 15:4; 22:9). The new Jerusalem will be a place of perfect worship. The poems in Revelation (discussed above) were surely composed with an eye to the worship of God's people.[82]

The worship of God contrasts with the worship offered to those who follow the beast (13:8,12,15). In fact, in Revelation, at least, there are only two kinds of people—those who worship God and the Lamb and those who worship the beast.

Part of worship is obedience to the One who is worshipped. Thus, Revelation abounds with imperatives, commands for the people of God who read the book. Among these are the following:

- Be faithful unto death (2:10).
- Fear God and give Him glory (14:7).
- Come out of Babylon (18:4).
- Rejoice over God's judgments (18:20).
- Come [to the living water] (22:17).

Reality of Persecution for God's People

Already in the first century, martyrs were being made among the seven churches of Asia (2:13). When the fifth seal was broken, John saw the souls of martyrs in heaven and heard that there were a full number of martyrs yet to come (6:9–11). The beast kills God's two witnesses (11:7). The dragon (Satan) wars against those who keep God's commands and have the testimony of Jesus (12:17). Those who refuse to worship the beast are killed (13:15). The harlot is drunk on saints' blood (17:6).

Whatever one's interpretive or millennial perspective, it is impossible to deny that Revelation intends to teach Christians to be faithful even to death by persecution. Twenty centuries of Christian history have confirmed that tribulation caused by the world and

---

[81] Beale, *Revelation*, 151.

[82] One need think only of G. F. Handel's "Hallelujah Chorus" from *The Messiah* to consider the role that the poetry of Revelation has had in the church's worship.

the devil is often the lot of those who follow Jesus. It will continue to be so until the Lamb's final victory.

God's Salvation and Protection of His People

Salvation from sin in Revelation is presented in terms of something God purchased through the death of the Lamb (the first coming of Christ, 5:9). Those who are saved oppose evil by the blood of the Lamb and by the word of their testimony (12:11). Final salvation after the resurrection is presented mainly in terms of the holy city, new Jerusalem (21:2). The noun "salvation" (*sōtēria* in Greek) occurs only three times in Revelation (7:10; 12:10; 19:1), always as the prerogative of God alone. (The verb "save" does not appear in Revelation.)

There are two kinds of "sealed" human beings in Revelation— those who follow the Lamb (and bear his special mark, 7:4) and those who follow the beast (and bear his mark, 13:16). Those who follow the Lamb may be persecuted and killed, but in the end the Lamb raises and rewards them with a thousand-year reign (20:4). (The mark on the beast's people was a false promise of protection, for all these are painfully judged, 16:2.)

Need for Lukewarm Christians to Repent

Revelation is not sparing of the need for sinful Christians to repent. Five of the seven churches of Asia were charged by the risen Christ to repent of a variety of sins (Ephesus, 2:5; Pergamum, 2:16; Thyatira, 2:22; Sardis, 3:3; Laodicea, 3:19). In this way Revelation is shown to be like the prophecies of the Old Testament written against sinful Israelites. By way of contrast, evil people in Revelation are characterized by their refusal to repent of sins and so even curse God (9:20–21; 16:9–11).

Reality of Final Judgment for All Humanity

The various millennial interpreters of Revelation may disagree about the precise time of the judgment scene described at the end of chapter 20. There is no doubt, however, that Revelation warns all people of the coming time of divine judgment for the kind of life they have lived. The 24 elders announce the certainty of coming judgment for all (11:18). A flying angel announces impending judgment (14:7). The judgment of Babylon is certain and complete (18:8,20; 19:2). At the great white throne judgment, all the dead are rewarded for their good works or lack thereof (20:11–15), and only those whose names are in the Lamb's Book of Life are spared eternity in the lake of fire. Thus, this sobering warning is to all who read the book of Revelation: prepare to face judgment by coming to the Lamb before it is too late.

Blessings for God's People

In conclusion, one series of sevens easy to overlook in Revelation is the seven "blesseds" or beatitudes. (This is the same word [*makarios*] found repeatedly at the beginning of the Sermon on the Mount, Matt 5:3–11; Luke 6:20–22.) It is appropriate to conclude this study of Revelation with a reminder that God's favor is with the following people:

- those who read, hear, and keep the prophecy of Revelation (1:3);
- those who die in the Lord, for they have rest and their deeds will follow them (14:13);
- those who stay spiritually awake so that they are not caught unclothed (16:15);
- those who are invited to the marriage supper of the Lamb (19:9);
- those (martyrs) who have a part in the first resurrection (20:6);
- those who keep the prophecy of Revelation (22:7); and
- those who wash their robes (in the Lamb's blood) so that they may enter the heavenly city (22:14; cp. 7:14).

Selected Bibliography

Commentaries Based on the Greek Text

Aune, David E. *Revelation 1–5*. WBC 52a. Dallas: Word, 1997.
_____. *Revelation 6–16*. WBC 52b. Nashville: Nelson, 1998.
_____. *Revelation 17–22*. WBC 52c. Nashville: Nelson, 1998.
Beale, Gregory K. *The Book of Revelation: A Commentary on the Greek Text*. New IGNTC. Grand Rapids: Eerdmans, 1999.

Charles, R. H. *A Critical and Exegetical Commentary on the Revelation of St. John.* ICC. 2 vols. Edinburgh: T. & T. Clark, 1920.

Osborne, Grant R. *Revelation.* BECNT. Grand Rapids: Baker, 2002.

Commentaries Based on the English Text

Beasley-Murray, G. R. *The Book of Revelation.* NCB. Rev. ed. Grand Rapids: Eerdmans, 1981.

Caird, George B. *A Commentary on the Revelation of St. John the Divine.* HNTC. New York: Harper & Row, 1966.

Easley, Kendell. *Revelation.* HNTC. Nashville: Broadman & Holman, 1998.

Fiorenza, Elizabeth Schüssler. *The Book of Revelation: Justice and Judgment.* Philadelphia: Fortress, 1985.

Ford, J. Massingberde. *Revelation.* AB. Garden City, NY: Doubleday, 1975.

Hendricksen, William. *More than Conquerors: An Interpretation of the Book of Revelation.* 6th ed. Grand Rapids: Baker, 1952.

Johnson, Alan F. "Revelation," EBC. Grand Rapids: Zondervan, 1981.

Ladd, George Eldon. *A Commentary on the Revelation of St. John.* Grand Rapids: Eerdmans, 1972.

Milligan, William. *The Revelation of St. John.* 2d ed. London: Macmillan, 1887.

Morris, Leon. *Revelation.* TNTC. Rev. ed. Grand Rapids: Eerdmans, 1987.

Mounce, Robert H. *The Book of Revelation.* NICNT. Rev. ed. Grand Rapids: Eerdmans, 1997.

Smalley, Stephen S. *The Revelation to John* Downers Grove, IL: InterVarsity, 2005.

Summers, Ray. *Worthy Is the Lamb.* Nashville: Broadman, 1951.

Tenney, Merrill C. *Interpreting Revelation.* Grand Rapids: Eerdmans, 1957.

Wall, Robert W. *Revelation.* NIBC. Peabody, MA: Hendrickson, 1991.

Walvoord, John F. *The Revelation of Jesus Christ.* Chicago: Moody, 1966.

Wilcock, Michael. *The Message of Revelation.* BST. Downers Grove, IL: InterVarsity, 1975.

Studies

Bauckham, Richard. *The Climax of Prophecy: Studies on the Book of Revelation.* Edinburgh: T. & T. Clark, 1993.

_____. *The Theology of the Book of Revelation.* Cambridge: Cambridge University Press, 1993.

Beagley, Alan J. *The "Sitz im Leben" of the Apocalypse, with Particular Reference to the Role of the Church's Enemies.* BZNW 50. Berlin: de Gruyter, 1987.

_____. *John's Use of the Old Testament in Revelation.* JSNTSup 166. Sheffield: Sheffield Academic Press, 1998.

Beale, Gregory K. *The Use of Daniel in Jewish Apocalyptic Literature and in the Revelation of St. John.* Lanham, Md.: University Press of America, 1984.

Collins, Adela Yarbro. *Crisis and Catharsis: The Power of the Apocalypse.* Philadelphia: Westminster, 1984.

Hemer, Colin J. *The Letters to the Seven Churches of Asia in Their Local Setting.* JSNTSup 11. Sheffield: JSOT, 1986.

Maier, Gerhard. *Die Johannesoffenbarung und die Kirche.* WUNT 25. Tübingen: Mohr-Siebeck, 1981.

Michaels, J. Ramsey. *Interpreting the Book of Revelation.* Grand Rapids: Baker, 1992.

Ramsay, William. *The Letters to the Seven Churches of Asia.* London: Hodder & Stoughton, 1904.

Stott, John R. W. *What Christ Thinks of the Church.* Wheaton, IL: Harold Shaw, 1990.

ABBREVIATIONS

AB	Anchor Bible
ABD	*Anchor Bible Dictionary*. Edited by D. N. Freedman. 6 vols. New York. 1992.
Abr.	Philo, *De Abrahamo*
ACCS	Ancient Christian Commentary on Scripture
ACNT	Augsburg Commentaries on the New Testament
Adumb	Philo, *Adumbrations in the Epistle of Jude*
AJT	*Asia Journal of Theology*
ANRW	*Aufstieg und Niedergang der römischen Welt: Geschichte und Kultur Roms im Spiegel der neueren Forschung*. Edited by H. Temporini and W. Haase. Berlin, 1972–
Ant.	Josephus, *Antiquities of the Jews*
ANTC	Abingdon New Testament Commentaries
Apoc. Bar.	*Syriac Apocalypse of Baruch*
APOT	*The Apocrypha and Pseudepigrapha of the Old Testament*. Edited by R. H. Charles. 2 vols. Oxford, 1913.
ASNU	*Acta seminarii neotestamentici upsaliensis*
AThR	*Anglican Theological Review*
Att.	Cicero, *Epistolae ad Atticum*
AUSS	*Andrews University Seminary Studies*
Avot	*'Abot*
BA	*Biblical Archaeologist*
Bapt.	Tertullian, *De baptismo*
Barn.	*Barnabas*
BASORSup	Bulletin of the American Society of Papyrologists: Supplement
BBR	*Bulletin for Biblical Research*
BCBC	Believers Church Bible Commentary
BECNT	Baker Exegetical Commentary on the New Testament series
BG	Bible Guides
Bib	*Biblica*
BIBS	Biblische Studien (Neukirchen, 1951–)
BJRL	*Bulletin of the John Rylands Library of Manchester*
BNTC	Black's New Testament Commentaries
BSac	*Bibliotheca Sacra*
BSC	Bible Student's Commentary

BST	The Bible Speaks Today
BTB	*Biblical Theology Bulletin*
BZ	*Biblical Zeitschrift*
BZAW	Beihefte zur Zeitschrift für die alttestamentlische Wissenschaft
BZNW	Beihefte zur Zeitschrift für die neutestamentliche Wissenschaft
CBC	Cambridge Bible Commentary
CBQ	*Catholic Biblical Quarterly*
CBSC	Cambridge Bible for Schools and Colleges
CC	Communicator's Commentary
CD	Cairo Genizah copy of the *Damascus Document*
CEC	*Catena in Epistolas Catholicas*
Clem.	*1, 2 Clement*
CNT	Commentaire du Nouveau Testament
Comm. Jo.	Origen, *Commentarii in evangelium Joannis*
Comm. on Matt.	Origen, *Commentary on Matthew*
ConBOTNT	Coniectanea neotestamentica or Coniectanea biblica: New Testament Series
CTJ	*Calvin Theological Journal*
DBSup	*Dictionnaire de la Bible: Supplément.* Edited by L. Pirot and A. Robert. Paris. 1928–
De or.	Cicero, *De oratore*
Dial.	Justin Martyr, *Dialogue with Trypho*
Did.	*Didache*
DLNT	*Dictionary of the Later New Testament and Its Developments.* Edited by R. P. Martin and P. H. Davids. Downers Grove, 1997.
DNTB	*Dictionary of New Testament Background.* Edited by Craig A. Evans and Stanley E. Porter. Downers Grove and Leicester, 2000.
Doct. Christ.	Augustine, *De doctrina Christiana*
DSB	Daily Study Bible
EBC	Expositor's Bible Commentary
EBib	*Etudes bibliques*
EC	Epworth Commentary
EKKNT	Evangelisch-katholischer Kommentar zum Neuen Testament
Eloc.	Demetrius, *De elocutione*
Epist.	*Epistolae*
ER	*The Encyclopedia of Religion.* Edited by M. Eliade. 16 vols. New York, 1987.
ET	English translation

EvQ	*Evangelical Quarterly*
ExpTim	*Expository Times*
Fam.	Cicero, *Epistolae ad familiares*
FLBS	Faith and Life Bible Studies
Gen Rab	Genesis Rabbah
GNC	Good News Commentary
GNS	Good News Studies
Greg	*Gregorianum*
GTJ	*Grace Theological Journal*
Haer.	Irenaeus, *Adversus haereses*
Herm.	*Shepherd of Hermas*
Hist. eccl.	Eusebius, *Historia ecclesiastica*
HNT	Handbuch zum Neuen Testament
HNTC	Harper's New Testament Commentaries
HolNTC	Holman New Testament Commentary
Hom. Josh.	Origen, *Homilies on Joshua*
HTKNT	Herders theologischer Kommentar zum Neuen Testament
HTR	*Harvard Theological Review*
IB	Interpreter's Bible
IBC	Interpretation: A Bible Commentary for Teaching and Preaching
ICC	International Critical Commentary
IDB	*Interpreter's Dictionary of the Bible*
Inst.	Quintilian, *Institutio oratoria*
Int	*Interpretation*
Inv.	Cicero, *De inventione rhetorica*
ISBE	*International Standard Bible Encyclopedia.* Edited by D. L. Sills. New York. 1968–
IVPNTC	IVP New Testament Commentary
J.W.	Josephus, *Jewish War*
JBL	*Journal of Biblical Literature*
JBR	*Journal of Bible and Religion*
JETS	*Journal of the Evangelical Theological Society*
JSJ	*Journal of Jewish Studies*
JSNT	*Journal for the Study of the New Testament*
JSNTSS	Journal for the Study of the New Testament: Supplement Series
JSNTSup	Journal of for the Study of the New Testament: Supplement Series
JSS	*Journal of Semitic Studies*
JTS	*Journal of Theological Studies*
Jub.	*Jubilees*

KEK	Kritisch-exegetischer Kommentar über das Neue Testament (Meyer-Kommentar)
KKNT	Kritisch-exegetischer Kommentar über das Neue Testament
LCL	Loeb Classical Library
LEC	Library of Early Christianity
Lev. Rab.	*Leviticus Rabbah*
Macc.	*3, 4, 5 Maccabees*
Marc.	Tertullian, *Adversus Marcionem*
MelT	*Melita Theologica*
MJT	*Midwestern Journal of Theology*
MNTC	Moffatt New Testament Commentary
Mos.	Philo, *De vita Mosis*
NABPRSS	National Association of Baptist Professors of Religion Special Studies Series
NAC	New American Commentary
NBC	New Bible Commentary
NCB	New Century Bible
NCBC	New Cambridge Bible Commentary
Neot	*Neotestamentica*
NIB	New Interpreter's Bible
NIBC	New International Biblical Commentary
NICNT	New International Commentary on the New Testament
NIGTC	New International Greek Testament Commentary
NIVAC	NIV Application Commentary
NovT	*Novum Testamentum*
NovTSup	Novum Testamentum Supplements
NTAbh	Neutestamentliche Abhandlungen
NTC	New Testament Commentary
NTD	Das Neuen Testament Deutsch
NTG	New Testament Guides
NTM	New Testament Message
NTS	*New Testament Studies*
NTT	New Testament Theology
Paed.	Clement of Alexandria, *Paedagogus*
PEGLMBS	*Proceedings, Eastern Great Lakes and Midwest Biblical Societies*
PG	Patrologia graeca
PL	Patrologia latina
Phil	Polycarp, *To the Philippians*
PNTC	Pillar New Testament Commentary
Post.	Philo, *De posteritate Caini*

Princ.	Origen, *De principiis*
QH	*Hodayot,* or *Thanksgiving Hymns*
QR	*Quarterly Review*
QS	*Serek Hayahad,* or *Rule of the Community*
Quis div.	Clement of Alexandria, *Quis dives salvetur*
Rab.	*Rabbah*
RAC	*Reallexikon für Antike und Christentum.* Edited by K. Kluster et al. Stuttgart, 1950–
ResQ	*Restoration Quarterly*
Rhet.	Aristotle, *De rhetorica*
Rhet. Her.	*Rhetorica ad Herennium*
RNT	Reading the New Testament
RQ	*Römische Quartalschrift für christliche Altertumskunde und Kirchengeschichte*
Sacr.	Philo, *De sacrificiis Abelis et Caini*
m. Sanh.	*Mishnah Sanhedrin*
SB	Sources bibliques
SBB	Stuttgarter biblische Beiträge
SBEC	Studies in Bible and Early Christianity
SBLDS	Society of Biblical Literature Dissertation Series
SBLMS	Society of Biblical Literature Monograph Series
SBLSBS	Society of Biblical Literature Sources for Biblical Study
SBLSP	*Society of Biblical Literature Seminar Papers*
ScrHier	Scripta hierosolymitana
SE	*Studia evangelica*
SEC	Studies in Early Christianity
SHC	Studies in Hellenistic Civilization
SHR	Studies in the History of Religion
Sir	Sirach/Ecclesiasticus
SNT	Studien zum Neuen Testament
SNTSMS	Society of New Testament Studies Monograph Series
SPB	Studia Post Biblica
Spec.	Philo, *De specialibus legibus*
SPS	Studies in Peace and Scripture
SwJT	*Southwestern Journal of Theology*
T. Abr.	*Testament of Abraham*
T. Dan	*Testament of Dan*
T. Naph.	*Testament of Naphtali*
T. Sim.	*Testament of Simeon*
TBC	Torch Bible Commentaries

TDNT	*Theological Dictionary of the New Testament.* Edited by G. Kittel and G. Friedrich. Translated by G. W. Bromiley. 10 vols. Grand Rapids, 1964–1976
Tg. Ps.-J.	*Targum Pseudo-Jonathan*
ThEd	*Theological Educator*
THKNT	Theologischer Handkommentar zum Neuen Testament
T. Jud.	*Testament of Judah*
T. Lev.	*Testament of Levi*
TNTC	Tyndale New Testament Commentary
TQ	*Theologische Quartalschrift*
TS	*Theological Studies*
TynBul	*Tyndale Bulletin*
TZ	*Theologische Zeitschrift*
UBS	United Bible Societies
VE	*Vox evangelica*
Vit. Mos.	1, 2 *De vita Mosis*
WBC	Word Biblical Commentary
WC	Westminster Commentaries
WeBC	Westminster Bible Companion
Wis	Wisdom of Solomon
WMANT	Wissenschaftliche Monographien zum Alten und Neuen Testament
WUNT	Wissenschaftliche Untersuchen zum Alten und Neuen Testament
ZNW	*Zeitschrift für die neutestamentliche Wissenschaft*
ZTK	*Zeitscrift für Theologie und Kirche*

CONTRIBUTORS

J. Daryl Charles, who wrote the sections on Hebrews, 1 and 2 Peter, and Jude in the present volume, is associate professor of Christian Studies at Union University in Jackson, Tennessee. He previously taught at Taylor University and during 2003–2004 was a visiting fellow of the Institute for Faith and Learning at Baylor University. He holds the Ph.D. in hermeneutics from Westminster Theological Seminary. He has written extensively for several theological journals including *New Testament Studies*, *Zeitschrift für die neutestamentliche Wissenschaft*, *Journal for the Study of the New Testament*, *Bulletin of Biblical Research*, and others. He is the author of *Literary Strategy in the Epistle of Jude* (University of Scranton/ Associated University Presses, 1993), *Virtue Amidst Vice: The Catalog of Virtues in 2 Peter 1* (Sheffield Academic Press, 1999), *The Unformed Conscience of Evangelicalism: Renewing the Church's Moral Vision* (InterVarsity, 2002), and *Between Pacifism and Jihad: Just War and Christian Tradition* (InterVarsity, 2005).

Kendell Easley, who wrote the section on Revelation in the present volume, is professor of Christian Studies and Program director for the Master of Christian Studies at Union University (Germantown, Tennessee campus). He previously taught at Mid-America Baptist Theological Seminary and Toccoa Falls College. He holds the Ph.D. in New Testament from Southwestern Baptist Theological Seminary. He has published a number of books with Broadman & Holman including *Revelation* in the *Holman New Testament Commentary* (1998), *The Illustrated Guide to Biblical History* (2005), *52 Words Every Christian Should Know* (2006), and the *Holman CSB Harmony of the Gospels* (edited with Steven Cox, 2007).

Terry L. Wilder, who served as general editor and wrote the sections on James and 1, 2 and 3 John in the present volume, is Academic Acquisitions and Project Editor for B&H Academic in Nashville, Tennessee. He served 10 years as Associate Professor of New Testament and Greek at Midwestern Baptist Theological Seminary in Kansas City, Missouri. He earned the Ph.D. in New

Testament from the University of Aberdeen, Scotland. He has written for several other theological journals, contributed a chapter on pseudonymity and the New Testament to the book *Interpreting the New Testament* (Broadman & Holman, 2001), and is the author of *Pseudonymity, the New Testament, and Deception* (University Press of America, 2004).

NAME INDEX

SUBJECT INDEX

SCRIPTURE INDEX